Arnold Newman

CHAIRING
THE ACADEMIC
DEPARTMENT

CHAIRING THE ACADEMIC DEPARTMENT

Leadership among Peers

Second Edition

ALLAN TUCKER

AMERICAN COUNCIL ON EDUCATION • MACMILLAN PUBLISHING COMPANY

NEW YORK

Collier Macmillan Publishers

LONDON

Macmillan Publishing Company
A Division of Macmillan, Inc.
866 Third Avenue, New York, N. Y. 10022

Collier Macmillan Canada, Inc.

Library of Congress Catalog Card Number: 83–22208

Printed in the United States of America
printing number
        7 8 9 10

Library of Congress Cataloging in Publication Data

Tucker, Allan
  Chairing the academic department.

  (American Council on Education/Macmillan series on
higher education)
  Includes bibliographical references and index.
  1. Departmental chairmen (Universities)—United States.
2. Universities and colleges—United States—Administration. I. Title. II. Series.
LB2341.T78 1984   378'.111   83–22208
ISBN 0-02-933090-4

Contents

List of Figures and Tables

Figures

Tables

Foreword

An institution can run for a long time with an inept president but not for long with inept chairpersons. Given the importance of the chairperson's position, the lack of published material about it is surprising. Occasional studies and compendia of journal articles about the position have appeared but have usually been of little immediate help to those struggling to be good chairpersons. Practitioners have not been well served by this literature, since it is written for students of the position and directed to theoretical rather than practical dimensions. In an attempt to correct this situation, the American Council on Education published the first edition of this book in 1981.

As evidence of our continuing concern, ACE is pleased to be publishing this improved, revised, and expanded second edition. This work, coupled with ACE's continued sponsorship of the Departmental Leadership Workshop Institutes, which Dr. Tucker directs, and the publication of *Managing the Academic Department: Cases and Notes* by John B. Bennett, at long last places a more concrete and constructive emphasis on the critical role of the Departmental Chair within the college and university structure.

Three characteristics of the position of department chairperson have become increasingly clear in the last decade. First, as institutions have grown more complex, more decisions are being made by chairpersons. As the basic academic unit, the department is the place where colleges and universities actually conduct the majority of their activities. Decisions made here are very difficult to undo elsewhere. Effective leadership and competent administration of the department, therefore, are essential to the sound operation of the institution.

Second, the selection of chairpersons is often based more on academic considerations or the person's reputation as a scholar than on his or her management qualifications. Traditionally selected from faculty ranks, chairpersons are now called on to exercise a variety of administrative skills not usually acquired as faculty members. Fresh to the office, many chairpersons find themselves facing a bewildering array of issues with little to guide them.

Third, the position of department chairperson is frequently the first rung of the academic administrative ladder. While some chairpersons will return to their faculty positions, others will aspire to further administrative challenges. Solid grounding in administrative style and technique early in one's career can pay lasting dividends, allowing one to assume additional and more complicated responsibilities.

The second edition of *Chairing the Academic Department* focuses on precisely the kinds of concerns that new chairpersons have. Moreover, it is sufficiently comprehensive that even old hands can profit from reading it. The Council welcomes this opportunity to help chairpersons fulfill their responsibilities, for sound management at the department level can only further higher education's goals.

J. W. PELTASON, *President*
American Council on Education

Preface

A key position in the hierarchy of college and university administration is that of department chairperson, for it is the chairperson who must supervise the translation of institutional goals and policies into academic practice. Yet most chairpersons are drawn from faculty ranks and assume the position having had little administrative experience. Moreover, few opportunities for orientation and training are available to them.

This paradox became more and more apparent to me during the eleven years I served as academic vice chancellor of the State University System of Florida. Subsequently, after joining the faculty of Florida State University as professor of higher education, I submitted to the W. K. Kellogg Foundation a proposal requesting funds to design and test a model for enhancing the planning, management, and leadership competencies of department chairpersons. In 1977 the Kellogg Foundation awarded a major grant to Florida State University for this purpose.

To help define the primary issues confronting departments, chairpersons in the nine state universities of the Florida university system were questioned about their own experiences. In addition, information was gathered from their counterparts in many institutions of higher learning outside Florida. Materials were developed to address the topics suggested by the initial inquiry. These materials were presented and tested in a series of seminars and workshops for chairpersons in Florida's state universities and were eventually published in book form in 1981.

The reaction to the first edition was positive and many university and community college chairpersons made excellent suggestions for changes and additions to accommodate needs not addressed in the first set of materials. This second edition, therefore, is in response to the many thoughtful comments made by chairpersons who read the first edition and/or participated in one or more department leadership workshops where the book was used as the text and basis for discussion. In making changes, concerns expressed by community college chairpersons were taken into account and incorporated in some of the chapters, thus making them applicable to community colleges as well as to baccalaureate granting institutions.

The second edition contains two brand new chapters, new material in several of the existing chapters, and extensive revisions in several more.

Chapter 1, dealing with the chairperson's roles, powers, and responsibilities, has been reorganized with clearer definitions and more examples of the different types of "power" available to chairpersons.

Chapter 2, which originally dealt with types of departments and leadership styles, has been revised and now deals with types of departments, divisions, and institutions. A new section contains the historical development of departments, shows some of the differences between university departments and community college divisions, and compares perceptions of university chairpersons with those of community colleges in terms of what is most and least important at their respective institutions. The section dealing with size and maturity of departments remains the same.

Chapter 3, dealing with leadership styles, has been reorganized and expanded.

Chapter 5 is a new chapter dealing with recruitment and affirmative action and describes how to include these two important activities as part of short- and long-range plans for attaining departmental goals. It also suggests procedures for recruiting and selecting new faculty members within affirmative action guidelines.

Chapter 8, dealing with faculty evaluation, has been reorganized and expanded to include a new section stressing the importance and value of human judgment in the evaluation process.

Chapter 12 is a new chapter dealing with legal obligations and liabilities of department chairpersons and gives examples of types of actions and decisions that could lead to litigation. It advises that chairpersons can avoid legal pitfalls by being sensitive to faculty and student concerns.

Chapter 16 deals with managing curriculum and human resources. A new section dealing with the management of part-time faculty has been added.

Chapter 17, originally describing faculty views about management, has been expanded to include a section dealing with the joys of being a chairperson.

The remaining chapters have not been changed except for minor editing.

Besides the revisions and additions mentioned above, the lists of references for each chapter have been updated and the number of questions and exercises at the end of each chapter has been expanded.

These questions are especially designed to help the reader relate the contents of the chapter to his or her own institution and situation. The questions can also be used as a basis for discussion in department leadership seminars and workshops.

Departments vary considerably in size, age, and level of maturity. Modes of department governance also vary greatly, as do chairpersons' personalities and leadership styles. To develop a set of absolute prescriptions that would provide every chairperson with solutions to every problem would be an almost impossible task; no such attempt has been made here. The book does, however, present examples of common department problems and shows how some of these were solved. It suggests ways to recognize and approach these problems, but it is not intended to be a definitive document that must be slavishly followed if a department is to be effective. Rather, the book will, I hope, spur chairpersons to analyze their own departments and to compare them with those described here. The cases discussed may or may not be directly applicable to each department, but the process of comparison may help generate solutions to similar problems.

ALLAN TUCKER

Acknowledgments

I wish to thank the W. K. Kellogg Foundation for its generous support of the department leadership program, from which this book has evolved. I am particularly grateful to Dr. Arlon E. Elser, a program director of the Kellogg Foundation, for his valuable suggestions concerning the design and development of the project and for participating in many of the workshops. Dr. E. T. York, former chancellor of the State University System of Florida, Dr. Bernard F. Sliger, president of Florida State University, and Dr. Jack Gant, dean of the college of education, Florida State University, provided vital encouragement and moral support during the design and testing of the project materials. Many other persons—including presidents, vice-presidents, deans, and chairpersons within and outside Florida—also provided assistance in the form of suggestions and critiques. In addition, I wish to express my appreciation to Dr. Jerry Miller, vice-president for academic affairs and institutional relations, American Council on Education, for his continuing interest and support.

The responsibility for determining the order, content, and style of each chapter has been mine. At least four persons, including myself, were involved over a period of three years in the writing, revising, editing, and rewriting of each chapter. Following is a list of the contributors who, under my direction, participated in the preparation of the manuscript:

George F. Aker, professor of adult education, Florida State University

Joseph C. Beckham, attorney and associate professor of higher education, Florida State University

Neil Betten, professor of history, Florida State University

John R. Bolte, associate vice president for academic affairs, University of Central Florida

Robert A. Bryan, vice president for academic affairs, University of Florida

Gary W. Peterson, associate professor of educational technology, Florida State University

Emanuel I. Shargel, associate professor of educational research, development, and foundations, Florida State University

Ilona Turrisi, former director of budget and analysis, Florida State University

John S. Waggaman, associate professor of higher education, Florida State University

I accept full responsibility for any of the book's errors and inadequacies, and I share wth my colleagues any credit for its contribution to the well-being of academic department chairpersons.

1

The Chairperson's Roles, Powers, and Responsibilities

The present economic crisis in higher education raises a fundamental question concerning the ability of colleges and universities to fulfill their traditional functions. Specifically, can institutions of higher learning maintain flexibility and viability, preserve quality, remain accountable, and respond effectively to the changing needs of society within the context of continuing inflation and steady-state or even declining resources? Academic departments are the organizational units within an institution that are most severely affected by steady-state or declining resources, and those who chair these departments can have considerable influence in resolving this problem.

Paradoxically, most department chairpersons are drawn from faculty ranks and have had, at best, very little administrative experience. A 1977 survey of 400 department chairpersons in the State University System of Florida found that 68 percent had no prior administrative experience, the turnover rate was 15 to 20 percent per year, and the chairpersons' term of service was usually six years. Forty-one percent of these chairpersons were elected by their colleagues, and another 44 percent were appointed by their deans with faculty consultation.*

While specially designed national and regional workshops are conducted for new presidents, vice presidents, and deans to help prepare them for their new responsibilities, few such opportunities are available to department chairpersons, who outnumber all other types of university administrators combined. The increasing complexities of operating institutions of higher education, along with shrunken budgets, have led deans and other university administrators to delegate more and more tasks to department chairpersons. Thus, it is in the best interests of colleges and universities to ensure that department chair-

*Survey conducted by Allan Tucker, unpublished.

1

persons become as knowledgeable as possible about planning, management, and leadership techniques. The following list shows, by category, the astonishing variety of tasks and duties that face the department chairperson:

Department governance

Conduct department meetings

Establish department committees

Use committees effectively

Develop long-range department programs, plans, and goals

Determine what services the department should provide to the university, community, and state

Implement long-range department programs, plans, goals, and policies

Prepare the department for accreditation and evaluation

Serve as an advocate for the department

Monitor library acquisitions

Delegate some department administrative responsibilities to individuals and committees

Encourage faculty members to communicate ideas for improving the department

Instruction

Schedule classes

Supervise off-campus programs

Monitor dissertations, prospectuses, and programs of study for graduate students

Supervise, schedule, monitor, and grade department examinations

Update department curriculum, courses, and programs

Faculty affairs

Recruit and select faculty members

Assign faculty responsibilities, such as teaching, research, committee work, and so forth

Monitor faculty service contributions

Evaluate faculty performance

Initiate promotion and tenure recommendations

Participate in grievance hearings

Make merit recommendations

Deal with unsatisfactory faculty and staff performance

Initiate termination of a faculty member

Keep faculty members informed of department, college, and institutional plans, activities, and expectations

Maintain morale

Reduce, resolve, and prevent conflict among faculty members

Encourage faculty participation

Student affairs

Recruit and select students

Advise and counsel students

Work with student government

External communication

Communicate department needs to the dean and interact with upper-level administrators

Improve and maintain the department's image and reputation

Coordinate activities with outside groups

Process department correspondence and requests for information

Complete forms and surveys

Initiate and maintain liaison with external agencies and institutions

Budget and resources

Encourage faculty members to submit proposals for contracts and grants to government agencies and private foundations

Prepare and propose department budgets

Seek outside funding

Administer the department budget

Set priorities for use of travel funds

Prepare annual reports

Office management

Manage department facilities and equipment, including maintenance and control of inventory

Monitor building security and maintenance

Supervise and evaluate the clerical and technical staff in the department

Maintain essential department records, including student records

Professional development

Foster the development of each faculty member's special talents and interests

Foster good teaching in the department

Stimulate faculty research and publications

Promote affirmative action

Encourage faculty members to participate in regional and national professional meetings

Represent the department at meetings of learned and professional societies

As part of their responsibilities, chairpersons find it necessary to deal with various categories of people, within and outside the institution. Within the institution, chairpersons deal with presidents, vice-presidents, deans, registrars, personnel officers, maintenance personnel, faculty committees, students, other department chairpersons, department associates, staff personnel, and others. Individuals and agencies outside of the institution with whom chairpersons must relate include alumni, legislators, civic organizations, regional and national professional organizations, high school and junior college students, high school and junior college counselors, townspeople, and professional colleagues.

In dealing with various kinds of persons, the chairperson assumes those roles most appropriate to accomplish his or her objectives. The role indicates how or in what capacity the chairperson relates to an individual or a group in performing an activity. Following is a list of twenty-eight possible roles that chairpersons assume to some degree at one time or another:

teacher	representer	decision maker
mentor	communicator	problem solver
researcher	evaluator	recommender
leader	motivator	implementor
planner	supervisor	facilitator
manager	coordinator	entrepreneur
advisor-counselor	anticipator	recruiter
mediator-negotiator	innovator	peer-colleague
delegator	peacemaker	
advocator	organizer	

The chairperson's job, obviously, is difficult and complex. A brilliant university or college administration with inept chairpersons cannot survive; an inept administration, with the help of a group of brilliant chairpersons, usually can. The position of department chairperson, then, is an important one. The discussion that follows is an attempt to describe and, to some degree, define the role of the chairperson.

The Paradoxical Nature of the Role

One distinctive characteristic of the chairperson's role is its paradoxical nature. The chairperson is a leader, yet is seldom given the scepter of undisputed authority. He or she is first among equals, but any strong coalition of those equals can severely restrict the chairperson's ability to lead. Deans and vice-presidents look to chairpersons as those primarily responsible for shaping the department's future, yet faculty members regard themselves as the primary agents of change in department policies and procedures. The chairperson, then, is both a manager and a faculty colleague, an advisor and an advisee, a soldier and a captain, a drudge and a boss.

Chairpersons are the only academic managers who must live with their decisions every day. The dean and the vice president make many important administrative decisions, such as which colleges or departments will get the lion's share of the year's operating budget. The dean and the vice president, however, do not have to say good morning—every morning—to their colleagues in the department; they do not have to teach several times a week alongside their colleagues; they do not have to maintain a family relationship with their faculty members. The department chairperson, on the other hand, does. He or she must be acutely aware of the vital statistics of each family member—births, deaths, marriages, divorces, illnesses, and even private financial woes.

This intimate relationship is not duplicated anywhere else in the college or university because no other academic unit takes on the ambience of a family, with its personal interaction, its daily sharing of common goals and interests (with frequent contention over how those goals are to be pursued), and its concern for each member. No matter how large the department, no matter how deeply divided over pedagogical and philosophical issues it may be, its members are bound together in many ways: they have all had the same general preparation in graduate school; their fortunes generally rise or fall with the fortunes of the discipline to which they all belong; and they share the same general value system of their profession. Working alongside the members of this "family" is the chairperson, a manager who is sometimes managed, a leader who is sometimes led, a parent who continually strives to keep peace for the sake of mutual benefit and progress.

These conditions are not the only ones that make the department chairperson's role paradoxical. He or she must deal with the expectations and desires of the students in the department, the personal and professional hopes and fears of the department faculty members, the goals and priorities of the college dean, the often perplexing and—from the department's perspective—sometimes shadowy priorities of the central administration, the sometimes naïve and sometimes jaundiced views of the alumni, and the bureaucratic procedures of accrediting agencies. Few administrators can, by themselves, face these conflicting constituencies and find solutions to all problems. Yet the chairperson must induce these constituencies to work together to help solve the problems they themselves generate.

A department chairperson's constituencies, in addition to department faculty members, include students and alumni. Students often seem to want less work and more entertainment. Undergraduates generally want the department to reduce the number of required courses for the major or to abolish certain degree requirements, such as specific courses in foreign languages, statistics, mathematics, humanities, or laboratory science. Graduate students generally want the scope of the qualifying examinations reduced and the language requirement modified or abolished; graduate assistants often want their teaching and research duties reduced. Students, until they become alumni, want "interesting" lecturers who give "fair" tests and don't require much outside reading or problem solving. Alumni want almost the opposite. Faculty members often want to increase the requirements for the department major to equal the number of credits necessary for the baccalaureate degree; they also are inclined to double the duties of the teaching and research assistants.

An astute chairperson will strive to establish a creative tension among these three constituencies—students, alumni, and faculty members—to reach a rational compromise on these particular issues. The compromise should not revolutionize higher education, fragment the already delicately balanced undergraduate curriculum, or increase the cost of the graduate program to the point that it drives the department into bankruptcy.

College deans, the central administration, and professional accrediting agencies pose other problems. The first two groups are seldom at odds with each other over department priorities, and only a powerful and supremely confident department chairperson should attempt to generate creative tension between them. The professional accrediting agencies, with their seemingly narrow interests and excessive demands, are seldom concerned with the institution's general academic welfare. Occasionally the chairperson can persuade the college dean and the central administration to join with the department against the accrediting agency. He or she could also enlist the aid of the agency and the dean to educate the idealists in the central administration about the hard realities of life in the department trenches. Or, in a daring maneuver, the chairperson could, in a pincer movement, catch the college dean between the central administration and the accrediting agency and, for example, make the dean surrender more resources to the department. Whatever the alignment of forces and whatever the issues at hand, the department chairperson almost always becomes the fulcrum in the balancing act of allocating institutional resources.

Power and Authority

To be a leader, a person must start with some power and authority. Yet, many chairpersons believe they are not given sufficient power or authority to carry out the responsibilities of the position. Although the term "power" is acceptable in government, military, and business organizations, it is an intimidating word in the academic community. The discussion which follows is based primarily on the dictionary definition which states that power is the ability of an individual to effect a change in someone's behavior—a change that might not otherwise occur.

In many cases, power is acquired by having access to or actually possessing certain resources that others desire. These resources may be physical, personal, economic, or psychological. In a college or university setting, the ability to persuade or influence may be the most effective power available to individuals in positions of leadership. Generally speaking, the power of administrators, managers, and leaders can be categorized into three types depending on how and from where it is acquired, namely, power from formal authority, position power, and personal power.

Power from Formal Authority

Authority granted officially from a higher level in the bureaucracy of the institution is called "formal authority." It gives an individual the right to command resources or to enforce policies or regulations. The ultimate power from this source exists when a person to whom the authority is granted is able to make final decisions and firm commitments for his or her department without requiring additional signatures of approval. In the case of a state college or university system, the board of regents or board of trustees is empowered by the state legislature to operate and control the system. The board, in turn, delegates authority and responsibility to the college or university presidents for the operation of the individual institutions. The presidents delegate authority to vice-presidents and deans. Any official authority chairpersons may have has been delegated to them by their deans; deans cannot delegate more authority than has been delegated to them by their vice-presidents. Faculty members will permit their behavior to be influenced or affected by the chairperson if they believe that he or she has formal authority or is close to someone who has it. Generally speaking, chairpersons and deans are perceived by their faculties to have more formal authority than they really have. In any case, the ability to influence or effect a change in some people's behavior will depend to some extent on the amount of formal authority that a chairperson is perceived to have.

Position Power

Power that comes from having an appropriate title or being in an important position is called "position power." Recommendations made by people with certain types of "position power" are generally given more serious consideration than recommendations made by individuals who do not have it. Department chairpersons by virtue of holding the title may have influence, not only with faculty members of their own respective departments but with people in and outside of the college over whom they have no authority or jurisdiction. Those who have such influence are perceived by some as having power. Chairpersons not only have the authority and responsibility to recommend salary raises, promotion, tenure, and teaching assignments, but they can often provide certain types of assistance to faculty members that faculty members need but cannot provide for themselves, such as helping them develop professional acquaintances, recommending them for membership in select professional associations, nominating them for executive positions in these associations, helping them obtain sabbaticals or funds for travel to professional meetings, and helping them make contacts leading to paid consulting jobs. Moreover, chairpersons frequently are asked by their faculty members to write letters of reference to other institutions in support of applications for new positions, or to banks or mortgage companies in support of applications for loans.

Many of the preceding prerogatives of chairpersons are possible because of the misconception that the title "chairperson" carries with it considerable formal authority. Chairpersons who use the influence of their position or title are often able to obtain opportunities for individual faculty members or for the department as a whole. Position power, however, may not be enough. What may be needed to complement it is "personal power."

Personal Power

In providing leadership to their faculty members, chairpersons also use whatever personal power they may have. The definition of "power" used in this chapter is the ability of an individual to effect a change in someone's behavior. Faculty members will permit themselves to be influenced or affected in some way by the chairperson if they respect the particular individual holding the position. Personal power derives from peers' respect for and commitment to the chairperson. It is informally granted to the chairperson by the faculty members and depends on how they perceive him or her as an individual and as a professional. A chairperson with a great amount of personal power is usually perceived by the faculty as possessing some of the following characteristics: fairness and evenhandedness in dealing with people; good interpersonal skills; national or international reputation in the discipline; expertise in some area of knowledge; influence with the dean; respect in the academic community; ability and willingness to help faculty members develop professionally; ability to obtain resources for the department; highly regarded by upper level administration; knowledgeable about how the college operates; privy to the aspirations, plans, and hidden agendas of the institution's decision makers; and ability to manage the department efficiently.

Personal power is not a power that can be delegated: it is a power that a chairperson must earn—and not just from faculty members. The same characteristics which earn the respect of the faculty members can earn the respect of the dean and vice-president. A chairperson who has developed credibility with the dean and is respected for being knowledgeable, fair, and reasonable will influence the dean more frequently than will a chairperson who lacks these characteristics. Chairpersons who are successful in influencing the deans are perceived by their faculty members to have power.

Leadership

Leadership, especially in the collegial environment, has seldom been simply a function of personal charisma. Charisma can help one amass power and authority, but charisma alone will not get the job done. The department chairperson begins with a good deal of power and authority, most of which is not readily discernible to the casual observer. It is best for all concerned if he or she uses the levers of power and authority unobtrusively. In this way, he or she can become an invisible leader, which, most will agree, is the best kind, especially in an institution of higher education.

In most colleges and universities the chairperson's power is manifested by the exercise of certain roles. Following are examples of roles that can provide the chairperson with power and authority: the bearer of news—good and bad—to department faculty members; the defender of the department; the primary contact for the department faculty members with regard to external professional assignments and consulting; the appointer of committees and committee members; the sometime initiator and constant arbitrator of curriculum development and reform; the allocator of department resources; the maker, even if by proxy, of the schedule of course offerings; the final arbiter for assigning courses and teaching loads to individual faculty members; one of the most influential voices in tenure and promotion cases; in most institutions, the official evaluator of faculty members; and the person who usually sets or recommends salaries for the department faculty members.

Even some of the most onerous tasks that a department chairperson must undertake can bestow a power and authority that, if used consciously and carefully, help enhance his or her leadership role. Consider three relatively minor aspects of the chairperson's professional administrative life: bearing good and bad news; defending the department; and being the primary contact for outside organizations seeking to enlist department members for various professional activities and consulting.

We all know that knowledge is power, and the chairperson generally is the first department faculty member to know what the institution's budget for the next year will be or what programmatic priorities the board of trustees, the board of regents, the central administration, or the college dean have decreed for the future. It is the chairperson who must make this news, good or bad, known to the faculty members. If, in sharing bad news, the chairperson is quick to blame the dean, the central administration, the institution's control agency, or specific individuals among those groups, he or she is probably unhappy or insecure in the job. Sometimes, of course, specific persons are to be blamed for bad news, but within the complex social structure of a college or university, there is seldom one villain responsible for the setbacks suffered by a department faculty. The same can be said for good news: rarely is one person in an institution responsible for a department's good fortune. In imparting information, however, the chairperson can shape the faculty members' opinion about that news and, in the process, establish an ambience—a set of attitudes, a good psychology—that can last for a year or perhaps longer. It is important, then, that chairpersons learn how to share information with colleagues.

The first lesson for chairpersons is that knowledge must be shared. A department that is kept in relative ignorance about budget, programs, and personnel development is a department mismanaged and unable to defend itself against decisions made about its destiny by those outside it.

The chairperson generally is the first line of defense for the department and the spokesman for the department in budget fights with the dean's office and the central administration offices. The faculty members expect their leader to be a vigorous advocate of the department's programmatic and philosophical positions, and the proper exercise of this role confers a degree of authority. A wise chairperson, of course, makes sure that his or her advocacy of a certain issue reflects the department faculty's consensus or at least has the support of the senior faculty members, who are often responsible for the chairperson's appointment. If the chairperson's aspirations for the department are continuously inconsistent with the faculty's, one of two things can be safely assumed: the department will soon have a new leader, or the department has been in such serious trouble that the dean or the central administration has appointed the chairperson to act as a troubleshooter and to implement drastic change.

The chairperson is also responsible for the department's external communications. Outsiders flood the department chairperson's desk with requests for help and advice. An alumnus wants a speaker for a luncheon or a dinner; a high school principal wants a commencement speaker; a professional organization wants a consultant; a newspaper feature writer wants to write a story on what is going on in the department. Other requests come from the dean's office or the central administration. The president wants expert advice on an issue he or she is writing or talking about; the vice-president is establishing yet another university-wide committee, council, or task force and wants "some good people who will make constructive contributions"; a new visiting trustee or regent must be entertained or educated.

That the chairperson must respond to these requests is in itself a sign of authority and power. But more important, these requests generally represent golden opportunities for advancing the cause of the department and its members. These requests, in their innocent form, are also acid tests of the chairperson's judgment, for the wrong responses can turn the opportunities from gold to brass, damage the department's reputation, and ensure a brief term of office for the chairperson.

Yet another seemingly innocent duty, that of appointing committees and committee members, turns out, on close examination, to be a source of power and authority, especially in medium-sized and large departments. An academic department can be led—but not run—by one person. It is too familial in character to be organized along the lines of a military hierarchy. Authority must be dispersed so that the collegial nature of this important academic unit can flourish; hence, the necessity for committees.

The department chairperson has the power to establish new committees and, although not always without a fight, dispense with old ones. Through this influence on committee structure, the chairperson's strength of purpose is tested. At least three important functions are assigned to committees: tenure and promotion recommendations, salary matters, and curriculum development. In small departments the entire faculty may serve as the committee that deals with each of these tasks. In larger departments separate committees are formed for each function. Sometimes the department faculty elects committee members, sometimes not.

Generally, institutional policy limits membership on the tenure and promotion committee to senior faculty, although some institutions make a point of including junior faculty. The policy of including junior faculty seems democratic and laudable, but the junior members of tenure and promotion committees almost always suffer from the conflicts within these committees. If the members of the promotion and tenure committee are elected, the chairperson must act as a precinct captain and get out the vote—the right vote—or risk losing a large measure of control over the department's future. The salary committee is usually shunned by the wiser faculty members, for much unhappiness results from its deliberations. But a department should have such a committee, even though it, like all other committees, is advisory. With the advice and, indeed, the protection of such a committee, the chairperson is able to face the faculty each fall when classes begin. Prudent appointments to the curriculum committee can help maintain a delicate balance of firebrands and wary old conservatives. A department must avoid the extremes of a silly, faddish curriculum that earns the derision of faculty members outside the department and of an obsolescent curriculum that arouses the contempt of funding agencies, the profession itself, and the students.

A department may have other committees, including a search committee, a library committee, an equipment committee, and a social committee. The only one that possesses any real leverage is the faculty appointments or search committee, which recommends the hiring of new faculty members. This committee, like the tenure and promotion committee, makes recommendations to the chairperson (and sometimes to the department faculty) about scholars who may eventually become part of the family. It is of utmost importance, therefore, that the members of this committee be of one mind with the chairperson. The chairperson, moreover, must see to it that the committee conducts its business in a manner that ensures the future health of the department.

Although administrators may be the least likely agents of curriculum development and reform, the chairperson can—and should—have a strong influence on such activities within the department. Most faculties are exceedingly conservative about curriculum development and reform unless faced with such harsh realities as dramatically declining enrollments. The advent of such realities usually causes an unnatural burst of creativity among the faculty; new courses, programs, and proposals for reduced prerequisites bloom like flowers in May. In such cases it is the chairperson's responsibility to protect the discipline and the profession that the department represents and to see that the department's curriculum and degree programs maintain their integrity.

At the same time, the chairperson must be the conscience of the faculty members. He or she must continually prompt them on many matters: the dangers of a rigid curriculum; new developments in the profession; the dire consequences of sliding into obsolescence; new teaching techniques; the services available to them through the institution's office of instructional resources (or other similar agency); the condition of the department's library holdings, its laboratories, and its research and teaching equipment. This concern, visibly and continually expressed, automatically confers the power that goes with conscientious leadership. The performance of these duties, as routine as many of them may seem, gives the chairperson what he or she most needs—the trust and respect of the faculty.

In most departments, a key role of the chairperson is the allocation of resources within the department. Resources are always limited; there are never enough for everyone. And someone must be the final arbiter in the allocation of these resources. Rarely can a group of single-minded, aggressive individuals reach a rational compromise on the distribution of limited resources. Such things may happen in utopian novels but seldom in the real world. Hence the chairperson must preside over this important task. The authority to allocate resources is the most visible of the chairperson's levers of power; consequently, it must be used with great tact and courage. Decisions about resource allocation will never be enthusiastically received by all concerned, but such decisions must be made. Furthermore, the rationale for these decisions should be logical and openly stated.

One great temptation that any chairperson faces is the urge to spread the department resources as evenly as possible. Such a procedure gives everyone a little piece of the action and avoids arguments over that bête noir of all academic administrators—enforcing program or personnel priorities. The problem with spreading resources evenly is that this practice inevitably pleases no one and irritates everyone. Departments, like colleges and universities, must have priorities and must follow them. If a college or university has no priorities, department chairpersons are usually the first to argue that the institution lacks leadership, that it is rudderless, and that no one knows where it is going. The same observations apply to departments in which certain programs and certain faculty members get more resources than others.

One way to get the department faculty to agree on a priority system for resource allocation is to reach a consensus that strength must be built on strength. Nearly every department has its strengths, and the faculty is well aware of these strengths. For example, the senior professors in organic chemistry may be the best teachers and researchers and have the best laboratory in the department; the three young associate professors in European history may be the best teachers and researchers and may have the best library holdings; the microelectronics group may have the greatest national visibility and the most contract and grant work. Certain programs and faculty members are the obvious choices for receiving the biggest share of the department resources, and few in the department (and virtually no one outside the department) will long contest a decision to allocate these programs and professors a goodly share of the budgeted operating resources for the year.

The rub comes when the department chairperson must, with the support of at least part of the faculty, decide whether to let a weak program die, whether to keep a weak program alive at the expense of stronger programs, or whether to start a new program that, because of new developments in the field, will aid in attracting students and federal or private financial assistance. Sometimes department members cannot be persuaded to let a weak program die with dignity; sometimes such a program has a life of its own, usually because those involved in it are incapable of working on another program or because of tradition, sentiment, or nostalgia or any combination of these factors. Clearly, the chairperson has the duty to assess the program's weakness and then act on the assessment and cut the program's resources. If the chairperson keeps alive a weak program, he or she has a further duty to point out to department colleagues that the program survives at the expense of resources that could go to stronger programs.

Establishing and implementing a new program is almost always a risky business, and leadership plays a crucial role. Almost any chairperson, regardless of leadership style or personal authority, can impede and usually stifle the establishment and growth of a new program. Department faculty members generally recognize this fact; consequently, the chairperson is apt to be heavily lobbied in these affairs. There is no sure formula for success in such an undertaking, but certain caveats are relevant.

- Woe to the chairperson who tries to establish a new program without the support of an influential segment of the department faculty.
- Woe also to the chairperson who, at the behest of a starry-eyed dean or a zealot in the central administration, tries to start a program without the consent or advice of the department's best faculty members.
- Woe to the chairperson who starts a program, for whatever reason, without consulting others in the discipline outside the university, outside the state, and outside the region.
- Woe to the chairperson who does not inform the faculty that the financial consequences of starting a new program will affect the entire department.

Another somewhat obscure but real source of the chairperson's power is his or her jurisdiction over assigning courses and teaching loads to faculty members. Clearly this task is not as visible, glamorous, or influential an activity as resource allocation, but it affects the emotional and intellectual life of every faculty member.

The heart's and mind's desire of most faculty members is to teach the subject that is, to them, the most important thing in their life. A person does not become a professor to make money or to acquire power, although these latent yet thoroughly natural motivations can burst into bloom in a sometimes alarming manner after a few years of teaching and research. Most professors can lead a happy and useful life if they are allowed to teach courses they *want* to teach to those students who will profit most from that teaching. Nothing—except salary—so concerns a professor as much as what he or she is scheduled to teach. (Younger faculty members who are building a knowledge of their subjects and the platform for their professional careers are especially concerned with course assignments.) Nothing—again, except a low salary—so dispirits a faculty member as to be relegated to teach three sections of a Western civilization survey, three sections of trigonometry and algebra, or four sections of the principles of physics. Most faculty members live to teach their subject specialty to superior students. This happy state is the edenic vision, the academic Shangri-la, that lurks in every professor's mind and is often the prime motivation for his or her work. Consequently, the chairperson, by means of the authority to assign courses, can shape the careers and professional destinies of most of the department members and, in essence, make the majority of them basically happy or unhappy.

The responsibility for assigning courses plays such a crucial role in the life of the department that its power is generally shared by department committees that recommend who should teach what courses and when they should be taught. The task is delegated to a committee not because it is drudgery, but because the function itself is so important to all faculty members. Yet, as in resource allocation, there must be a final arbiter, and that arbiter is the department chairperson. Hence, like it or not, the authority to assign courses and teaching loads becomes a source of power that may be used to reward deserving faculty members.

Obviously, the department chairperson plays an extraordinarily influential role in matters of promotion and tenure. At many universities and colleges the chairperson can override the vote of the faculty in promotion and tenure decisions; at others, the vote of the faculty must be sent to the dean, whether or not the chairperson agrees with that vote. But at virtually all institutions, the chairperson must make his or her recommendation to the dean regarding every tenure and promotion case. This recommendation is almost always heavily weighed by the dean, the central administration, and whatever institution-wide review board or committee may exist. Last but not least, the institution's president or chancellor takes seriously the recommendation of the department chairperson; consequently, his or her views on a particular candidate for tenure or promotion are critical.

As in the case of resource allocation, the decisions on promotion and tenure are not going to please everyone. It is impossible for the chairperson to avoid facing at least one difficult promotion or tenure decision every two or three years. Those who try to avoid making a difficult decision are apt to find themselves in the same predicament that results when available resources are spread evenly across all programs. Such nonactions—which, in fact, *are* actions—please no one and irritate everyone. Chairpersons who stand before the department faculty or the dean and wash their hands of the matter fool no one; furthermore, they lose the respect of the faculty, the dean, and the central administration. Chairpersons who ask a higher level of review to make a hard tenure or promotion decision that they failed to make are evading responsibility. They may succeed in escaping the pain once—or maybe even twice in a very tolerant administration—but a third attempt usually leads to a request from the dean for a change in department leadership. The chairperson's role in promotion and tenure decisions, as in resource allocation decisions, is an important and highly visible one. Here again, power must be used with tact and prudence.

The act of evaluation—at most universities an annual occurrence —is clearly linked to promotion and tenure, and at almost all institutions the responsibility for this spring ritual falls to the chairperson. But woe to those who regard it *only* as a ritual, because each evaluation will become a plank in the platform upon which rests other crucial decisions regarding promotion and tenure. Furthermore, evaluation is another of the chairperson's highly visible levers of power, and a merely ritualistic observance of the evaluation process might erode its effectiveness. This particular function is very important and will be discussed later at greater length.

The final and most visible of all the chairperson's powers is the responsibility to set or recommend annual salaries for each faculty member in the department. At some institutions the chairperson has sole authority for setting salaries (within his or her budget, of course); at other institutions he or she merely makes recommendations about salaries to the college dean. Whatever the institution's procedure, the chairperson, through this power, establishes the value system by which the department lives and operates. As noted earlier, a faculty salary committee usually assists the chairperson in this responsibility. The chairperson's interaction with this committee is probably unique, for, having done the annual evaluation of all the faculty members, the chairperson can better judge the relative value of each of them. Of course, the committee members are in the awkward position of having to consult with the chairperson, at least in an indirect way, about their own salaries. Setting salaries and recommending the setting of salaries is a job no one wants, and the committee is usually less than zealous in its recommendations. Inevitably, the basic decisions turn out to be the chairperson's, and with this painful task comes the final and most important source of his or her power.

Special Responsibilities and Functions

In the discussion of the chairperson's general power, authority, and functions, a constant note has been sounded about his or her role in shaping the department's future. Many of the chairperson's standard functions, functions through which power and authority are derived, automatically make him or her the department's chief planner. This role is an almost imperceptible one, because seldom does any of these standard functions appear to be solely a planning function. The sum of these standard functions, pursued almost on a daily basis, makes the chairperson the chief architect of the department's future.

Consider once again how the chairperson's actions affect the department's future. The appointment of the curriculum committee members helps shape the department's enrollment patterns, its degree programs, its standing in the institution and in the profession. The appointment or selection of promotion and tenure committee members helps shape the character of the department, as well as its programmatic strengths and weaknesses and its standing in the institution and the profession. The allocation of department resources down to the smallest detail —who gets the new line item for a secretary, for example—has obvious implications for the department's future. Assigning courses and teaching loads profoundly affects the lives of the faculty members. The way in which the chairperson conducts the annual faculty evaluations and renders these judgments also affects the lives of individual faculty members. And, finally, recommending or setting salaries will stimulate a series of behavior patterns that, for better or worse, will deeply affect the department's future.

The chairperson is the department's chief planner, whether we choose to recognize this fact or not. Some departments may have a committee on the future that reports at reasonable intervals to the faculty at large, and this committee—and the department, as well—may believe that it controls the department's destiny. In the largest sense of the term *planning*, the committee may in fact effect some changes. For example, departments can consciously decide to deemphasize analytical chemistry and build up organic chemistry, junk the international program in political science and concentrate on public administration, or starve the power grid group in electrical engineering and fatten up the photovoltaic group. None of these planning decisions, however, can come to fruition if the day-to-day decisions of the chairperson and his or her committees run counter to such plans.

Some additional examples may illustrate how difficult it is for plans to be realized unless the chairperson is conscious of his or her role as planner. The chemistry department knows that all the agency funding will be concentrated in organic chemistry, yet the enrollment in analytical chemistry, particularly the graduate enrollment, keeps going up. In addition, the best candidate for the assistant professor position in the department, who was interviewed at the November national meetings, is an analytical chemist. Why did the department even interview an analytical chemist? Because the senior professor in the department—who is also an analytical chemist, a member of the promotion and tenure committee, and a member of the appointments committee—asked the chairperson to interview the young chemist as a courtesy because "some of the fellows in the Society thought we ought to have a look at him."

Another example: The political science department, during the October national meetings, couldn't find just the right person for its public administration position. Lo and behold, the appointments committee chairperson, a black, puts on the chairperson's desk the stunning resumé of a young black political scientist who states that she would like to begin her professional career in that department but whose specialty is international relations. The chairperson shifts uneasily in his seat as he reads the resumé, remembering last month's tongue-lashing from the dean and the provost about the department's lack of minorities and women.

And another example: Several members of the state's society of professional engineers, on their way home from lobbying the governor for a new building for the engineering college, stop off to talk to the chairperson of the electrical engineering department. They remind him that little work is being done on increasing the efficient transmission of electricity in power lines and that all this nonsense about photovoltaics is simply a way of avoiding thinking about real-life power grid problems. The chairperson, unable to enlighten this group and depressed about the recent editorial in the local newspaper about the eroded influence of the department's once-favored power grid group, stares out the window wondering, "Just where is photovoltaics going?"

The point of each example is this: There are two kinds of planning—both necessary. One is the abstract generalized planning that establishes goals and priorities without much regard for the realities of an ever-changing existence. The other is the kind of planning that is not perceived as planning at all but as a routine activity. The "routine" kind of planning, however, can have more effect on the department's future than all the position papers a committee on the future could write in any given year. The chairperson should establish or help establish a rational plan for the department's future, a plan that clearly includes a system of priorities yet that is realistic. At times the priorities must be reversed; at other times the system must be defended and upheld no matter how withering the opposition may be. In planning, perhaps more than in any other acitivity, the metaphor of the chairperson as hybrid is apt—he or she must be both a lion and a fox.

In any organization with the ambience of a family, someone must be the magister, the trainer of tyros; and in the academic department, this duty generally falls to the chairperson. The chairperson—initially, at least—is perceived by the new faculty members as the leader, for he or she knows about the local folkways, the institutional pitfalls, and the way in which a faculty member may succeed professionally. If graduate advisors had done their job properly, their students, upon becoming faculty members, would not need so much coaching from a department chairperson, and the chairperson's chore would be considerably lightened.

The majority of the nation's graduate schools successfully educate and train their doctoral candidates in the mastery of a subject, but few new Ph.D.s are well versed in how to conduct themselves as teachers and as department members. The chairperson must remember that although many new faculty members have had experience as teaching assistants, that experience may have been poorly monitored and generally unstructured. Often graduate teaching assistants, through the neglect of their superiors, have picked up bad teaching habits and have brought them along to their first full-time faculty job. One of the worst habits new teachers can bring to the classroom is an attitude that implies that students somehow hinder the faculty's serious work. Although this attitude is seldom ingrained, many new faculty members have assimilated it while working on their dissertation or preparing for doctoral qualifying examinations. Under those circumstances, they come to the mistaken opinion that teaching is only of secondary importance.

The chairperson, then, must see to it that the new faculty members learn how to conduct themselves in a classroom. The attitude that students are hindrances is easy to overcome, for it is not a natural attitude; otherwise faculty members would not be faculty members but would be pursuing other goals in industry or government. But someone must tell newcomers about the department's traditions, its goals, and its place in the college and in the institution. Someone has to tell them about the feuds within the department, the idiosyncracies of its members, the whole rhythm and flow of department life. In short, someone has to socialize the new members, else they are likely to have a bruising first year or two. In some quarters, this bruising experience may be viewed as a necessary rite of passage, but it is nonetheless an inefficient use of time and resources and can be of seriously damaging experience. The chairperson or a trusted faculty member must conscientiously train new members. The chairperson cannot ignore these matters; for the general welfare of the department, he or she must take a personal interest in new faculty members.

Earlier, the paradoxical nature of the chairperson's job was noted and the role of advocate briefly discussed. That role should be examined more closely, because it is no simple matter. Clearly, the chairperson must be an advocate for the department. He or she must be an advocate in budget negotiations with the college dean and the central administration. Success in these negotiations depends on how carefully data are prepared to support the needs of the department, how clearly and honestly the data are presented, and how relevant the data are to regional and national priorities of the profession or discipline represented by the department. For example, the chairperson of the English department should never march into the dean's office and invidiously compare the budget of the English department with that of the chemistry department. A dean who knows something about cost analysis and who has the priority system of the institution's departments firmly in mind can easily ignore internal comparisons. Most deans, provosts, and vice-presidents hate to be told that one department gets better budget treatment than another, and these administrators are generally well armed with elaborate defenses built around cost analyses and priority systems. In a budget fight, for example, the best way to be a successful advocate for the department is to shame the dean into concessions by comparing the department's budget and its professional standing with other departments of the same discipline in competitive institutions in the state, region, or nation. This tactic, however, can be successful only if the department has a good record of performance and, in the uncomfortable language of budgeteering, has been "productive."

The chairperson must at times be an advocate for one or more faculty members. These kinds of situations generally arise from salary allocations and promotion and tenure cases. Again, rhetoric seldom wins the day in salary allocation disputes. The presentation of simple, compelling, honest data is the chairperson's best instrument as advocate. Sometimes the dean, the institutional review board, or even the president will not agree with a department recommendation on tenure or promotion. Immediately, all concerned are treading on dangerous ground. If the department has insisted on sending forward a promotion or tenure recommendation with which the department chairperson disagrees, if the institution's policies and procedures allow the recommendation to go to the next highest level, and if, at that and subsequently higher levels, the recommendation is turned down, the chairperson should not fight the case. The chairperson, however, must tell the department at the outset what his or her recommendation is going to be and inform the department that he or she will not fight. In this difficult situation, to state one's intention is a more honest way to conduct oneself than to yield to the temptation to be a hero and "fight for the department."

Although fighting for the department has great possibilities for high drama—or comedy—it is not good for one's self-esteem or intellectual integrity. If the chairperson and the department are fully united in a promotion or tenure case, however, then they should fight for it all the way. If they lose, the loss is an honorable one, and at least they gain markers that can be called in at the next confrontation with the higher administration, whether it be over budget, curriculum, space, or personnel.

But turnabout, as college deans are fond of saying, is fair play, and sometimes the chairperson must be the advocate of the dean or the central administration. Just as departments must have priorities, so too must colleges and institutions. Not every department can always be designated a high-priority department. Indeed, some, because of the character of the institution, can never attain prominent status. (One such example might be a humanities department in a technological university.) When resources are allocated for each year's operating budget, the chairperson must report as fully and as honestly as possible not only on the resources allocated to the department, but also on the reasons for those allocations. When decisions that adversely affect the department are handed down, the chairperson must be able to share the institution's perspective and try to implement even an unfavorable decision with some grace and style. If the chairperson is strongly opposed to a decision and, consequently, his or her relationship with the faculty and the dean deteriorates, he or she should consider resigning. The matter is as simple and as cold as that. The chairperson who cannot accept the decisions of the higher administration in resource allocation or other institutional matters does no one a service by staying on; all that results is the embitterment of everyone concerned. The chairperson can always devote his or her energies to changing those institutional or collegiate priorities—and even have fun mounting such a challenge—but once the decisions are made for the year, the only thing to do is to put those decisions to work for the good of the institution and wait until next year.

Perhaps the most important of the chairperson's special responsibilities is that of faculty evaluator. Here he or she becomes the judge on the bench, the dispassionate, if possible, evaluator of each faculty member's performance. In an increasing number of institutions around the country, the process of evaluation has been formalized as a legal requirement that must be fulfilled each year. But even in those institutions in which the evaluation process is not formalized, chairpersons cannot escape the role of evaluator. Wittingly or unwittingly, they enact this role in all their functions: appointing committees, assigning courses, allocating resources, recommending promotion and tenure, and setting or recommending annual salaries. Hence, the annual evaluation meeting between chairperson and faculty member, even if not required, is a good way of fulfilling the evaluation responsibility. The meeting should have a specific agendum, or an external frame of reference, to give each participant a sense of purpose; otherwise, the meeting is likely to become a social visit or the discussion is apt to turn to more agreeable business than the awkward matter of how one has performed one's job during the past year.

The agendum should be related to department priorities, resource allocation, or the department's plans for itself. It is easier for the chairperson and the faculty member to discuss job performance if the department has established certain goals for itself and its members. How did the faculty member help fulfill the department's objectives during the past year? If there were problems, what were they and what caused them? Not all faculty members are team players, nor should they be. Some persons cannot be judged by what they contribute toward achieving the department's stated goals for the year or the next five years. Too much emphasis on team playing can inhibit or even stifle a faculty member's creativity.

If certain members of the department have not overtly contributed to the department's goals and are not likely to, however, then it becomes necessary for the chairperson to establish, year by year, a set of individual goals for these persons. The goals should not be too specific, or else both the chairperson and the faculty member may find themselves trapped by undue specificity. For example, to suggest that the faculty member should, in the next year, publish three articles in learned journals is probably too bureaucratic, but both chairperson and faculty member can comfortably agree that a reasonable goal for next year would be the publication of some research in a reputable journal. Sometimes, however, the chairperson must be specific, both for the good of the faculty and the reputation of the department. The associate professor who has spent three years writing a book may have to be told that for only one more year will he receive special resources (clerical help, graduate assistants, and so forth) to help bring the book to completion. Or the bright young assistant professor may have to be told that she has conducted enough experiments to validate a hypothesis; next year she must send off a research grant proposal to a funding agency and free up some department resources so that others in the department can begin to write research proposals. All these matters are relative and depend on the chairperson's good judgment and personal knowledge of each faculty member's capabilities.

The important point is that evaluation must be viewed as a constructive, not a destructive, act. For it to be constructive, the chairperson must establish goals against which yearly job performance can be measured. If no goals have been set, then the evaluation inevitably becomes either too personalized or so vague as to be worthless or insulting. The chairperson must realize that most faculty members *want* to be evaluated; they want their performance judged and, of course, praised. But no faculty member can walk into an annual evaluation conference expecting to be praised if he or she knows that the goals agreed upon last year have not been met. And even if they have not been met, the faculty member will usually welcome the opportunity to explain why not.

The annual evaluation conference, then, should not be viewed by the chairperson or the faculty as a painful or awkward ordeal. It can and should be a chance for colleagues to examine together what the year's work has produced, what went right, what went wrong, and why it went wrong. But this useful and constructive experience is possible only if chairpersons set goals for colleagues—with, of course, their help—and address those goals each year, no matter how painful it may be at times to keep the evaluation process focused on those goals.

As we have seen, the department chairperson assumes many roles, and some of these roles may, at times, conflict with others. The dean may have certain expectations about the chairperson's role, the faculty may have others, and the chairperson may have yet others that do not correspond to those of the dean or the faculty. Such a dilemma may have no easy or satisfactory solution. The chairperson must become accustomed to being in an atmosphere beset by contradiction.

The various kinds of power that chairpersons exercise daily have also been discussed. Few of these powers are based on formally delegated authority. Instead, these powers may depend, to a large degree, on precisely how they are perceived by the chairperson as well as by the faculty members. Chairpersons who perceive that they have no power usually have none; chairpersons who perceive that they have power usually do. In any event, the exercise of this power must be tempered with sound judgment.

Questions

1. What roles do you think your faculty expects you to assume as chairperson?
2. What roles do you think your dean expects you to assume as chairperson?
3. What roles would you like to assume most as chairperson?
4. Which of these roles seem to conflict? Why and how do they conflict? What problems do conflicting roles pose for the chairperson? How may chairpersons resolve these problems?

5. What are your personal visions or goals toward which you would like to move your department during your time as chairperson?

6. Some chairpersons are elected to the position by faculty members; others are appointed by the dean with or without faculty consultation. What are the similarities and differences between these two kinds of chairpersons in terms of (1) the tasks for which the chairperson is responsible; (2) how the chairperson relates to his or her faculty and dean; and (3) strategies used in getting the job done? What are the reasons for these similarities or differences?

7. In universities that have collective bargaining, some chairpersons are members of the bargaining unit whereas others are considered part of management. What are the similarities and differences between these two kinds of chairpersons in terms of (1) the tasks for which the chairperson is responsible; (2) how the chairperson relates to his or her faculty and dean; and (3) strategies used in getting the job done? What are the reasons for these similarities or differences?

8. Generally speaking, will a dean delegate more formal authority to one chairperson than to another with regard to the fulfillment of similar departmental responsibilities? Give reasons for your answer.

9. Is it conceivable that the dean may delegate more informal authority to one chairperson than to another? What factors determine the amount of informal authority that deans delegate to their chairpersons?

10. Many department chairpersons say they do not have enough formal authority to do all of the things they have to do—or if they had more authority, they could be a more effective chairperson. What authority or power does the dean currently have that you as a chairperson would be interested in acquiring through delegation? (Remember, the dean cannot delegate authority that he or she does not have.)

11. To what extent do you believe that most chairpersons use all the power available to them in carrying out their responsibilities?

12. What kind of power or influence does a chairperson use in getting faculty members promoted or tenured? Is it power from formal authority, position power, personal power, or a combination of two or more? With whom is the power used?

13. What kind of power or influence does a chairperson use (formal authority, position power, personal power) and with whom is it used in helping faculty members obtain opportunities to:
   a. travel to professional conferences
   b. be members of important committees in the institution

   c. be members of important committees in professional and scholarly societies
   d. engage in consulting activities.
14. Some chairpersons believe that each institution should have a written statement spelling out in detail the duties, responsibilities, and formal authority of its chairpersons. Other chairpersons strongly oppose the idea. To what extent, if any, might such a written statement be helpful to the chairperson? To what extent might it be a hindrance? If it were decided at an institution that such a statement should be developed, what sorts of things should be included— what might best be excluded? Why?
15. How might a chairperson deal with a situation in which the dean and the faculty members are on the opposite side of an issue? Give examples of such situations.
16. Suppose a chairperson came to you for advice. He claimed that at least one half of his recommendations to the dean were turned down. He knows for a fact however, that two of his fellow chairpersons had most of their recommendations accepted by the same dean. He wants to know why the dean seems to be more favorably disposed to his colleagues than to him and what he can do to improve his standing with the dean. What additional information do *you* need before you can make any suggestions? What possible kinds of suggestions could you make?
17. Other than being able to recommend dismissal, no promotion, or no merit increases, what powers are available to a chairperson for penalizing faculty members who continue to perform in an unsatisfactory manner?
18. Compare formal authority with personal power as they relate to the chairperson's effectiveness.

References

BOOTH, DAVID B. "Institutional and Disciplinary Ideas for Development." *Educational Record*, Winter 1977, pp. 85–90.

BRANN, JAMES, AND EMMET, THOMAS A., eds. *The Academic Department or Division Chairman: A Complex Role*. Detroit: Balamp, 1972.

BROWN, J. DOUGLAS. "Departmental and University Leadership." In *Academic Departments*, edited by Dean E. McHenry, pp. 188–94. San Francisco: Jossey-Bass, 1977.

DRESSEL, PAUL L.; JOHNSON, F. CRAIG; AND MARCUS, PHILIP M. *The Confidence Crisis*. San Francisco: Jossey-Bass, 1971.

EHRLE, ELWOOD B. "Selection and Evaluation of Department Chairmen." *Educational Record*, Winter 1975, pp. 29–38.

HEIMLER, CHARLES H. "The College Departmental Chairman." *Educational Record*, Spring 1967, pp. 158–63.

HERSEY, PAUL, AND BLANCHARD, KENNETH H. *Management of Organizational Behavior: Utilizing Human Resources.* 3rd ed. Englewood Cliffs, N.J.: Prentice-Hall, 1977.

HEYNS, ROGER W. "Leadership Lessons from Watergate." *Educational Record*, Summer 1973, pp. 172–74.

HEYWOOD, STANLEY J. "The Department Chairman—An Essential Leader." Paper presented at Western Interstate Commission on Higher Education Administrative Leadership Conference, 14 November 1969.

HILL, WINSTON W., AND FRENCH, WENDELL L. "Perceptions of the Power of Department Chairmen by Professors." *Administrative Science Quarterly*, March 1967, pp. 548–74.

LESLIE, DAVID W. "The Status of the Department Chairmanship in University Organization." *AAUP Bulletin*, December 1973, pp. 419–26.

McKEACHIE, WILBERT J. "Memo to New Department Chairmen." *Educational Record*, Spring 1968, pp. 221–27.

NEUMANN, YORAM. "The Perception of Power in University Departments: A Comparison Between Chairpersons and Faculty Members." *Research in Higher Education*, 1979, 11(4), pp. 283–93.

NEWMAN, FRANK. "Taking the Helm." In *The Third Century: Twenty-six Prominent Americans Speculate on the Educational Future.* New Rochelle, N.Y.: Change Magazine Press, 1976.

ROACH, JAMES H. L. "The Academic Department Chairperson: Functions and Responsibilities." *Educational Record*, Winter 1976, pp. 13–23.

SCHUTZ, MAX F. "Management of the Multi-Department." *ADE Bulletin*, May 1978, pp. 34–39.

SNYDER, ROBERT A.; HOWARD, ANN; AND HAMMAR, T. "Mid-Career Change in Academia: The Decision to Become an Administrator." *Journal of Vocational Behavior*, October 1978, pp. 229–241.

2

Types of Departments, Divisions, and Institutions

Historical Development

Before categorizing departments and divisions into their various types, it may be useful to reflect upon the ways in which their respective institutions evolved into present-day organizational patterns. Universities have not always been organized into discipline departments. In fact, if one looks back over the some six hundred years that universities have existed, departmentalization is a relatively recent idea. While scholars point to an exception here and there, equivalents of academic departments do not show up until the second half of the 1700s; even then such a pattern was an exception. Prior to and shortly after the Civil War, American colleges were administered by presidents who personally served as scholar, leader, teacher, chief disciplinarian, librarian, admissions officer, keeper of student records, business manager, secretary of the faculty, and secretary of the board of governors.

As enrollments began to grow, presidents found it necessary to appoint individuals with special expertise to assume some of these presidential functions. The first appointment was that of librarian and the second was that of registrar. The need to establish a registrar's office became apparent in the 1880s, according to some historians, when elective curricula began to appear at some of the colleges and the task of keeping academic records became more complicated. As enrollments and curricula continued to expand, increased numbers of disciplinary and academic problems could not be solved with routine answers. In the 1890s the first deans were appointed to whom curricular and disciplinary authority was gradually delegated. Academic deans became chief personnel officers for the faculties, and deans of men and deans of women assumed responsibilities for student services. The addition of new administrative positions such as director of admissions, business manager, and public relations officer continued well into the twentieth century.

The office of vice-president was first established in the late 1800s in a few of the larger universities. By the middle of the twentieth century, however, this office was in place at most institutions of higher learning in the United States. In the beginning, librarians, registrars, deans, and other appointed officials considered their administrative responsibilities as part-time jobs and continued to serve in faculty capacities as scholars, teachers, and student advisers. As the number of students increased, it was necessary for presidents to employ full-time tutors and professors. In the middle 1800s faculty members at both Harvard and the University of Virginia began to group themselves into separate departments of instruction.

The rise of departments grew out of a need to improve the organization and management of the academic process as knowledge expanded at an ever accelerating pace. The day of the "tired clergyman" teaching everything from rhetoric to natural philosophy was over. The influence of the German universities and their search for scientific truth led to the era of disciplinary specialization. Kerr* and others point to this influence, especially at the graduate level, as the driving force behind undergraduate departmentalization of American colleges and universities. In retrospect, it appears inevitable that the increase in specialization and departmentalization would change the perspective of the faculty. Critics charged, and still charge, that publishing, research, and concern for tenure have pushed teaching into a subordinate position. Allegiance to the discipline has become more important than loyalty to, and concern for, the college or university. Can students learn interdisciplinary approaches to living in a complex sophisticated world at universities divided into departments?

In the 1950s some of the larger American universities began to establish institutes, centers, and bureaus for specialized teaching and research. These new units frequently cut across departments and were intended to encourage interdisciplinary studies and activities. Although there are many such units in institutions of higher learning throughout the country, the discipline department remains the mainspring in the organization of academic work at our colleges and universities.

---

*Clark Kerr, "Administration in an Era of Change and Conflict." *Educational Record,* Winter 1973, p. 41.

Departments and Divisions

A pure discipline department is one in which all its faculty members are trained, have common backgrounds, and teach in the same discipline. Pure departments such as history, chemistry, English, and mathematics are more apt to occur in large colleges and universities. In smaller colleges, where a discipline has too few faculty members to justify departmental status, several discipline programs may be housed in one department for administrative and economic efficiency; for example, a department of sociology and anthropology, or a department of history, philosophy, and religion. An administrative unit containing several different academic or vocational disciplines is often called a division and has a division director or chairperson who reports to a dean or a vice-president depending on the size of the division and the institution.

Some institutions are organized such that several departments comprise a division and each department has a chairperson who is responsible to the division director or chairperson. It is often the case that at the same institution some divisions are composed of departments and some are not. Although the divisional structure is found at some small to medium sized baccalaureate granting colleges, it is the one most commonly found in community colleges.

Community Colleges and Divisions

Although public junior colleges first appeared in the early 1900s, the junior college movement grew slowly until the 1920s when it experienced a period of rapid growth. Its rate of growth accelerated again during the period following World War II and once again in the 1960s.

Today there are over 1200 community, junior, and technical colleges in the United States. Of this number approximately one-tenth have enrollments of more than 10,000; one-sixth have enrollments of between 5,000 and 10,000; half have enrollments of between 1,000 and 5,000 and about one-quarter have enrollments of less than one thousand.* Although they started out with the departmental structure, two-year institutions today are most often organized into divisions, with each division being responsible for several academic disciplines

---

*Based on data from the 1981 *Community, Junior and Technical College Directory,* published by the American Association of Community and Junior Colleges.

or vocational programs. In large community colleges, divisions are sometimes subdivided into departments according to discipline, depending on the size of the program offered in that discipline.

Some community colleges have only division chairpersons and some have both division and department chairpersons. The nomenclature varies from one college to another even though the functions of the chairpersons may be similar. In any case, the number of division and department chairpersons per community college ranges from seven to 75 with an average of about 21 per institution. The total number for all community colleges is approximately 27,000.

In baccalaureate granting institutions, department chairpersons perceive themselves primarily as faculty members with some administrative responsibilities. In community or junior colleges, division chairpersons generally perceive themselves as administrators with some faculty and teaching responsibilities. Even in instances when the amount of effort devoted to administration is the same in both cases, the difference in self-perception of these chairpersons still persists.

Since university departments are more likely to be pure in the sense that most faculty members have similar training and teach in the same discipline, faculty members of these departments are usually able to reach a consensus in matters of curriculum and department policy without too much difficulty. This may explain in part why department chairpersons who emerge from this type of faculty tend to think of themselves primarily as faculty members rather than as administrators. Community college divisions, on the other hand, usually contain several different and perhaps unrelated programs taught by faculty members with diverse backgrounds. Because of their diversity, division faculty members are likely to have more difficulty in reaching consensus on some issues than members of a pure university department. Community college chairpersons therefore may tend to conduct their division business in a somewhat less collegial fashion and to work more closely with central administrators than do chairpersons of departments in four-year institutions. The former seem to have greater opportunity to be involved in college-wide decisions and are expected to serve more as extensions of the administration than as advocates of the faculty. Many of them have been employed in a community college for several years prior to obtaining a doctorate and hence may be less discipline oriented than their university counterparts. Their loyalty therefore is generally stronger to their institution than to their discipline, and because of the nature of their responsibilities they perceive themselves more as administrators than as faculty members.

Although most institutions, regardless of type, will have similar lists of responsibilities for chairpersons (see Chapter 1), the real or perceived importance of any particular responsibility on the list may vary from one chairperson to another depending on the missions, goals, and functions of the institution. The discipline oriented research function obviously separates community colleges from universities but not from all four-year colleges. Some of their course offerings and types of curricula, especially in vocational areas, also set them apart from other types of institutions, resulting in a difference in the rank ordering of responsibilities according to importance.

Comparing the roles of chairpersons from different types of institutions is made more difficult because of the differences in personalities, goals, and abilities of the chairpersons themselves. Provided with a menu of possible tasks and activities, chairpersons tend both to select those items which better match their strengths and to shun, or at least put off, those items that fall into areas in which they are less comfortable. Such avoidance behavior may have a significant impact on shaping the role of an individual chairperson and the importance he or she attaches to specific responsibilities. Conversely, a dean may recognize certain abilities in a chairperson and by way of special assignments contribute a shift in the individual's actual role.

An interesting pattern emerges when comparing community college chairpersons with university chairpersons in terms of how they rate the importance of each of the responsibilities listed in Chapter 1. They were asked to select the ten responsibilities they considered most important. Both groups of chairpersons included the following five in their top ten although not necessarily in the same rank order.

- Fostering of good teaching
- Maintenance of faculty morale
- Recruitment and selection of faculty
- Communicating needs to the dean and interaction with upper level administration
- Updating curriculum courses and programs.

Three additional responsibilities included in the community college chairpersons' top ten were ranked considerably lower in importance by university chairpersons. These were:

- Providing for the flow of information to the faculty to inform them of plans, activities, and expectations at various organizational levels
- Dealing with unsatisfactory performance
- Preparation and presentation of proposed departmental budgets.

Three additional responsibilities included in the university chairpersons' top ten were ranked considerably lower in importance by community college chairpersons. These were:

- Recognition and rewarding of faculty in accordance with their contribution to academic programs
- Evaluation of faculty for tenure, raises, and promotions

- Encouragement of faculty to participate actively in professional meetings.

The data obtained from this survey showed that overall, university and community college chairpersons are fairly close in how they rank-ordered the importance of most of the responsibilities. Both groups agree on the top importance of five of the responsibilities. There was marked disagreement, however, in their rankings of six of the responsibilities, which may be a reflection of the differences between the two groups in how they perceived their roles as chairpersons. As can be seen from the data, community college chairpersons ranked the importance of administrative and bureaucratic tasks much higher than did their university colleagues. University chairpersons, on the other hand, placed greater importance on activities that are faculty related.*

With the exception of references to graduate instruction and research, most of the topics discussed in the remainder of this book will have as many implications for community college chairpersons as for chairpersons of other types of institutions. Community college chairpersons will find that from an administrative and leadership point of view, their institutions may have more in common with four-year institutions than they realized.

Size and Maturity of Departments

For the sake of analysis, departments may be divided into four categories: small, large, immature, and mature. Overlappings among these categories do occur, of course, but the categories can serve as benchmarks for our discussion of departments. We shall define a "small" department as one that has up to nine full-time faculty members, including the chairperson. Departments with four or fewer members are not really departments but programs that have achieved department status because of their excellence or because of tradition, sentiment, nostalgia, or tolerance on the part of the central administration. We shall define a "medium-sized" department as one that has between ten and nineteen full-time faculty members, and a "large" department as one that has twenty or more full-time faculty members.

Hersey and Blanchard define *maturity* as "the capacity to set high but attainable goals . . . , willingness and ability to take responsibility, and education and/or experience of an individual or group. *These vari-*

---

*Keith T. Samuels, "A Study of Community College Division Chairpersons With Comparisons to University Department Chairpersons in Florida's System of Public Higher Education." Unpublished doctoral dissertation, Florida State University, 1983, p. 130.

*ables of maturity should be considered only in relation to a specific task to be performed."** According to this definition, a mature academic department is one in which the faculty members have the experience and capacity *as a group* to work together, set high but attainable goals, reach group decisions, and readily accept responsibility for their decisions and assignments. Not only are some departments more mature than others, but a department may display more maturity in one situation than another, depending on the problem or task with which it is dealing. An immature department is one that has great difficulty in reaching consensus or in developing and implementing a plan of action; its members are either unable or unwilling to work together effectively. Generally, mature departments are those that have been in existence for a long time, say fifteen years or more. Of course, age does not guarantee maturity; in fact, a mature department can regress to immaturity. Generally, however, a young department, whether small or large, is an immature department, according to our definition, simply because the process of learning to work cooperatively takes time and effort.

Let us first discuss small departments, both immature and mature. The members of an immature small department are usually highly self-conscious and defensive about its existence in the college or the institution. Repeatedly, the department is called on to justify its own existence, to defend its intellectual premises and its place in the great chain of academic being, and to resist budget raids by older, more powerful departments. In the formation and development of its curriculum, such a department often tends toward polarization; it may become faddish or wildly eclectic in its course offerings and degree programs, or it may hunker down behind a stodgy, traditional program in an attempt to gain instant respectability and acceptance from the rest of the institution. Its value system for promotion and tenure is undeveloped, although guided by institutional policy. Often it either rebels against such policy by claiming the virtues of innovation and uniqueness, or it interprets institutional policy as rigidly and conservatively as possible in an attempt, once again, to gain acceptance and credibility within the institution.

These polarities of behavior tend to follow disciplinary lines. The new, small science department—particularly the chemistry department—is likely to be more traditional and conventional than its mature counterparts in other institutions. The new social science depart-

---

*Paul Hersey and Kenneth H. Blanchard, *Management of Organizational Behavior: Utilizing Human Resources*, 3rd ed. (Englewood Cliffs, N.J.: Prentice-Hall, 1977), p. 161.

ment—especially the sociology department, which is itself a newcomer to the pantheon of academic disciplines—is likely to be innovative, eclectic, and chaotic as it struggles to establish itself.

The extreme behavioral patterns exhibited by immature small departments often lead the dean or central administration to appoint as chairperson a faculty member with a dominant personality who will try to run the department like a platoon. This response is only a natural one and usually quite necessary.

Leaders of immature small departments must continually remind themselves and their faculty members that they are going through a necessary stage of development and that life will not always be so difficult. The curriculum established now will have an effect on the department's future, as will promotions, tenure awards, and resource allocations. This phase of a department's existence is the stormiest, and all department members should try to remember that since things will inevitably change, they should not commit themselves to decisions that will make change more difficult to realize.

In the mature small department, conditions are entirely different. This type of department has long since lived through the development stage and often takes on the relaxed air of a country club as it goes about its business. Since all its members know each other, they usually share a unity of purpose and a sense of group cooperation seldom found in any other kind of department. Of course, there may be personality clashes or grave philosophical differences among the members, but the strife is genteel, as it is in a country club. Seldom is the chairperson of such a department a hard-driving platoon leader. Usually he or she comes from the faculty ranks. Often the position in such a department becomes, intentionally or not, a rotating position, institutional policies to the contrary notwithstanding.

Yet beneath this serene surface, danger abounds. The department's very strength, its close-knit unity, and its lack of visible strife may be its undoing. Decisions tend to be made in town-hall fashion; the whole department may decide, with the chairperson as presiding officer, on resource allocations, curriculum development and reform, course assignments and teaching loads, and, if institutional policy permits, promotion and tenure.

The problem with this kind of democratic activity is that it makes establishing and implementing priority systems extremely difficult, although not impossible. Everyone defers to everyone else, and even the chairperson may follow the path of least resistance—spreading the resources evenly, giving each faculty member's courses and programs equal billing in the catalog and in the schedule of courses, promoting everyone's friend, tenuring all newcomers as soon as possible, and trying to give everyone the same salary (prorated, of course). In five years—at the most—such a department will be in serious trouble with its faculty members, the dean, and the central administration.

Chairpersons of mature small departments must be perhaps more strong-willed than those of other kinds of departments. Not only must they be strong-willed; they must also be the most graceful and patient diplomats of them all. The chairperson's position in the mature small department may offer a severe test, and anyone who takes the job should not be deceived by the surface calm, for he or she will have to work continually to keep the department from sliding into senility.

The preceding examples represent the extremes of maturity ranges of small departments. Real departments may lie anywhere between these extremes.

Immature large departments tend to have the same sorts of problems as their smaller counterparts. If anything, such departments more compellingly invite the implementation of the department-as-platoon concept than do smaller departments. To state it simply, a strong will and steel nerves are necessary requisites for leading an immature large department. Again, in every decision made with colleagues, the chairperson's best course of action is to remind them continually that present decisions affect the department's future. An immature large department should be almost wholly concerned with the future, not with the present. An immature large department is often the result of a merger of several more mature, smaller ones. The new organization makes it imperative that the members learn to work with their new colleagues to overcome the tribulations of immaturity.

Mature large departments have a tendency to organize themselves either into feudal territories or into assembly lines. In the last thirty years department organization has tended toward internal atomization or fragmentation. This tendency is a natural one, for as knowledge increases and becomes ever more specialized, units within academic disciplines begin growing apart from the parent discipline.

The classic example of this kind of fragmentation is found in the psychology department, typically a mature large department. It often has so many subunits that it can be considered a school. In psychology, the experimentalists are a breed apart, as are the clinical psychologists. Indeed, there appears to be a trend in some institutions to set up the clinical psychology subunit as a separate department. Add to these subunits such groups as the social psychologists, the school psychologists, and the consumer behavior psychologists—to name a few—and the problems of a psychology department chairperson are easy to understand. Chemistry departments also tend to become atomized. The larger and more mature the chemistry department, the greater the differences among the organic, inorganic, theoretical or quantum, and analytical groups. In such departments, the chairperson's major challenge lies, of course, in resource allocation. Each territorial group, powerful in itself, presents its case to the chairperson, and consensus-based decisions are extremely difficult to achieve.

In the mature large department, promotion and tenure issues are generally easier to resolve than resource allocation problems, for the competing units develop a sense of pride and *esprit de corps* and seldom recommend weak cases to the entire department. The best course of action for the chairperson is to encourage, not discourage, competition among subunits. Fostering open competition is better than stifling initiative and innovation or attempting to administer these warring units according to the principle of sharing the wealth. But competition means that in the resource allocation process there will be some winners and some losers, and departments that adopt this mode of operation should be prepared to make and to accept decisions that recognize firmly established priorities.

In addition to the tendency towards fragmentation, mature large departments also exhibit a tendency to adopt the assembly-line concept of operation. This approach is almost inevitable. Large numbers of freshmen must be run through the introductory courses in such departments as chemistry, English, mathematics, economics, and speech. At the same time, there are large numbers of graduate students who must be taught, whose theses and dissertations must be approved, and whose teaching assistantships must be supervised. Under these circumstances the chairperson and the faculty have a difficult time maintaining the necessary collegial mode of operation, and the family ambience of a small or medium-sized department begins to dissolve under these pressures. The administrative hierarchy begins to grow under the pressures of numbers: the chairperson has to appoint an associate or vice-chairperson, a director of freshman English, a director of the undergraduate chemistry labs, and a director of introductory speech courses. With its increasing variety of assistant and associate chairpersons, the department's internal structure begins to resemble the hierarchy of the institution's central administration.

These developments may be inevitable, but they tend to isolate the chairperson. To resist this isolation, the chairperson must continually seek ways to improve communication with faculty members; he or she must continually "get out among 'em" and not succumb, for example, to the tempting argument that because the department is so large, department faculty meetings are useless.

Department meetings in mature large departments are almost always stressful for the chairperson, and it is only natural to wish to avoid stress. Such meetings must be held regularly with agenda posted in advance.

The chairperson must spend time with heads of department divisions and, above all else, communicate to each division head the needs and goals of the other divisions. Only in this way can a spirit of teamwork and department unity be maintained. This approach is time-consuming and requires hard work, but if the chairperson of a mature large department is to avoid becoming just another academic bureaucrat, he or she must bend every effort to the goal of personal communication and interaction with faculty members.

Academic departments can be classified in other ways, of course. In fact, this kind of analysis could easily become an art. All chairpersons, however, no matter what category their department falls into, must remember that most faculty members still cling, consciously or subconsciously, to the Platonic ideal, even with regard to the academic department. This eternal absolute undergirds the premises of many an argument voiced in department faculty meetings when such issues as resource allocation, course assignments, course and program development or revision, and promotion and tenure cases arise. The ideal department is one in which every professor is a superstar and every course and program is vital to the welfare of the department, the college, the institution, the nation, and the whole human community. The ideal department is well funded, and its members' salaries are generous. The chairperson serves only as the clerk of the court, duly recording the faculty's judgments and seeking always to implement those judgments.

The Platonic ideal is, like all ideals, unattainable, but it nevertheless exists in the minds of the faculty members. Although most faculty members are hardheaded enough to recognize that the ideal is, after all, only an ideal, this perception of academic life led most of them to join the profession in the first place. A wise department chairperson never forgets the Platonic ideal; if resourceful, he or she can use it to help the department grow in unity and maturity.

Questions

1. Does your department or division contain only one discipline program or does it contain more than one? If only one, indicate how many full-time and part-time faculty.
2. If more than one, please name the number of different discipline programs contained in your department or division and indicate how many full-time and part-time faculty members there are in each program.
3. How many years has your department or division been in existence

in its present form? Was it originally established this way or has it undergone one or more changes in organization to reach its present administrative arrangement?

4. The following review of "group maturity" is provided as a basis for responding to questions about the maturity of your department or division.

Maturity is defined by Hersey and Blanchard in their Situational Leadership Theory as the capacity of a group of individuals to set high but attainable goals, the willingness and ability to take responsibility, and the education and/or experience of the group to accomplish those goals. A group is neither mature nor immature about everything. The variable of maturity should be considered only in relationship to specific tasks or activities. In considering maturity we can divide groups into four main categories:
- those who are neither willing nor able to take responsibility;
- those who are willing but not able to take responsibility;
- those who are able but not willing to take responsibility; and
- those who are willing and able to take responsibility.

The lowest level of maturity is the first category listed; the highest level is fourth.

a. On the basis of the preceding definition, how would you rate the maturity of your whole department or division on the majority of those issues requiring a department or division consensus—low, moderate, or high?

b. How would you rate the maturity of the group of faculty members in each program in your department or division on the majority of issues requiring a program consensus—low, moderate, or high?

References

AMERICAN ASSOCIATION OF COMMUNITY AND JUNIOR COLLEGES. *1981 Community, Junior and Technical College Directory.* Washington, D.C., 1981.

ANDERSON, G. LESTER. "Organizational Diversity." In *New Directions for Institutional Research: Examining Departmental Management,* no. 10, edited by John C. Smart and James R. Montgomery. San Francisco: Jossey-Bass, 1976.

BRUBACHER, JOHN S., AND RUDY, WILLIS. *Higher Education in Transition,* third edition. New York: Harper and Row, 1976.

COHEN A. M., AND BRAWER, F. B. *The American Community College.* San Francisco: Jossey-Bass, 1982.

CORSON, JOHN J. *The Governance of Colleges and Universities.* New York: McGraw-Hill, 1960.

CUMMINGS, L. L., AND DUNHAM, RANDALL B. *Introduction to Organizational Behavior: Text and Reading.* Homewood, Ill.: Richard D. Irwin, 1980.

DURNIN, RICHARD G. "The Role of the Presidents in the American Colleges of the Colonial Period." *History of Educational Quarterly,* 1, June 1961, pp. 23–30.

HERSEY, PAUL, AND BLANCHARD, KENNETH H. *Management of Organizational Behavior: Utilizing Human Resources.* 3rd ed. Englewood Cliffs, N.J.: Prentice-Hall, 1977.

JOHNSON, F. CRAIG. "Data Requirements for Academic Departments." In *New Directions for Institutional Research: Examining Departmental Management,* No. 10, edited by John C. Smart and James R. Montgomery. San Francisco: Jossey-Bass, 1976.

KERR, CLARK. "Administration in an Era of Change and Conflict," *Educational Record,* Winter 1973, pp. 38–46.

KOPECEK, R. I., AND CLARKE. R. G. "One Dimension of Organizational Structures of Middle-Sized Community Colleges," *Community College Review,* 1982, 10, pp. 33–40.

MILLETT, JOHN D. *Management, Governance and Leadership: A Guide for College and University Administrators.* New York: American Management Associations, 1980.

MILLETT, JOHN D. *New Structures of Campus Power: Success and Failures of Emerging Forms of Institutional Governance.* San Francisco: Jossey-Bass, 1978.

RYAN, DORIS W. "The Internal Organization of Academic Departments," *Journal of Higher Education,* June 1972, pp. 464–482.

SAMUELS, KEITH T. "A Study of Community College Division Chairpersons with Comparisons to University Department Chairpersons in Florida's System of Public Higher Education." Unpublished doctoral dissertation, Florida State University, 1983.

SMART, JOHN C., AND ELTON, CHARLES F. "Administrative Roles of Department Chairmen." In *New Directions for Institutional Research: Examining Departmental Management,* No. 10, edited by John C. Smart and James R. Montgomery. San Francisco: Jossey-Bass, 1976.

STEWART, W. G. "Selected Management Functions in the Role of Division Chairpersons in Multi-Campus Community Colleges." (Doctoral dissertation, North Texas State University, 1981). *Dissertation Abstracts International,* 1982, 42, 3034-A (University Microfilms No. 8128298).

3

Leadership Styles

Leadership may be defined as the ability to influence or motivate an individual or a group of individuals to work willingly toward a given goal or objective under a specific set of circumstances. The term "leadership" implies that where there is a leader, there must be one or more followers and a goal or objective toward which the followers are being led. This definition applies to any situation in which one person influences the behavior of another. An individual does not necessarily have to be in a position of authority to be a leader. The leader–follower relationship can occur between friends, colleagues, associates, students, relatives, and so on.

Just as there are many kinds of departments, so there are many kinds of department chairpersons; their variety is as infinite as the variety of human nature. It is possible, however, to generalize about human nature and to categorize the types of leadership styles. Several models will be described in this chapter. Some chairpersons will be able to identify completely or partly with one or more of the styles described below. Others may find no leadership style described here to which they can relate and may wish to search the literature or describe their own. In either case, what follows is found to be the situation to some degree in many academic departments.

The Directive-Supportive Behavior Model

Leadership styles may be categorized as directive or supportive. Some leaders are very directive. "Directive" behavior at its extreme consists primarily of one-way communication from the chairperson to faculty members in which he or she explains what is to be done, when, where, and how. In addition to providing detailed guidance, the leader carefully monitors the department's performance. Chairpersons who practice this type of leadership evidently believe that the task or assignment will not be accomplished properly without detailed direction and monitoring. In some cases, this chairperson may be correct in his or her belief. Conversely, there are chairpersons who are nondirective in their approach. After explaining what needs to be done, they give very little direction or guidance and provide practically no monitoring during the course of the activity. The expectation is that the faculty members are capable and willing to do what is necessary without much direction. Most chairpersons are neither 100 percent directive nor nondirective but fall somewhere between the two extremes.

Some leaders are very supportive. "Supportive" behavior consists of two-way communication between the chairperson and the faculty members. Here the chairperson provides personal or psychological support, including encouragement, praise, and general concern for the personal and professional welfare of each faculty member. On the other hand, there are chairpersons who are nonsupportive. They communicate very little with their faculty members and do not encourage faculty members to communicate with them. Here again, most chairpersons are neither 100 percent supportive nor nonsupportive but fall somewhere in between the two extremes. Some chairpersons are capable of moving from one extreme to another in terms of how supportive they are and try to provide the amount of support that faculty seem to need. The extent to which a chairperson is supportive may also be related to his or her ability to communicate and encourage communication in return.

A chairperson's behavior is neither exclusively directive nor supportive; leadership style consists of a mix of both. Leadership behavior varies, however, according to the particular mix of these behavior patterns. The proportion of directive behavior to supportive behavior indicates the chairperson's leadership style. We can visualize four different mixes of behavior patterns by plotting directive behavior on a horizontal axis and supportive behavior on an intersecting vertical axis. The result is a graph with four quadrants, with each quadrant representing a different mix of directive and supportive behavior (see Fig. 3.1):

Quadrant 1—High directive and low supportive (a great deal of direction to the faculty members, not much personal and psychological support)

Quadrant 2—High directive and high supportive (a great deal of direction to the faculty members, a great deal of personal and psychological support)

Quadrant 3—Low directive and high supportive (not much direction to the faculty members, a great deal of personal and psychological support)

FIGURE 3.1.   Leadership style graph

Quadrant 4—Low directive and low supportive (not much direction
  to the faculty members, not much personal or psychological support)
Each quadrant in the preceding figure represents a different leadership style in terms of directive and supportive behavior. The most effective leadership style, according to some authors, is one that takes
into account the maturity level of the group and provides the appropriate amount of direction and support needed to achieve a specific goal
or objective. Academic departments, like other groups, vary in their
levels of maturity. As described in the preceding chapter, a mature academic department is one in which the faculty members have the experience, capacity, and willingness to work effectively as a group, to set
high but attainable goals, and to reach group decisions, and they readily accept responsibility for their decisions and assignments. The maturity of a group should not be confused with the maturity of the individual members who comprise the group. Each member of the department
may be mature on an individual basis, but the members may not be able
to work together effectively as a group. Since a group may perform ma-
turely in achieving one objective and immaturely in trying to achieve
another, it is neither mature nor immature all the time.

Immature groups or departments generally need more direction than mature groups. The need for direction decreases as a department becomes more mature and its members learn to work together effectively. Mature departments need very little direction most of the time and often resent receiving too much. Although most faculty members enjoy receiving personal and psychological support from the chairperson, mature departments, as a whole, do not need as much psychological support as do less mature departments. The notion of the directive-supportive behavior model assumes that an effective chairperson will be able to adjust his or her leadership style to meet different situations. If the department is immature, the chairperson spends a lot of time being directive, assigning tasks, and monitoring them. As the department matures, the chairperson gives proportionately less direction but becomes more supportive. A department's progression toward maturity can be viewed as a continuum, and the chairperson must be able to estimate the level of maturity with which he or she is dealing at any given time. When the department approaches the highest level of maturity, the chairperson according to this model must be able to change styles to one of nondirection.

Each of the four quadrants in the figure represents not only an identifiable leadership style but also a stage in a continuum of changing leadership styles, which can accommodate the appropriate maturity level in the continuum of changing maturity levels of a group. It can be argued that Quadrant 1 exemplifies the best approach for dealing with an immature department, while Quadrants 2, 3, and 4, in that order, exemplify styles appropriate to a department as it progresses to a higher degree of maturity.

When a department begins to display less maturity than it has in the past, the department chairperson may need to make what is called a regressive intervention and provide more direction. In a regressive intervention, the department chairperson applies a leadership style appropriate for the present lower level of maturity rather than employing the style that was effective when the department was at a higher level of maturity with regard to the task under discussion. Once the department is again able to cope with the task, the department chairperson may return to the former leadership style.

Keep in mind that, according to this conceptualization, there is no one most appropriate leadership style. The best leadership style varies for different departmental situations. Some academic departments may be best served by one kind of leadership style at any particular time; other departments or even the same departments under different circumstances may be better served by another style.

The Autocratic-Democratic Model

The style of a chairperson may range from autocratic to democratic across a broad spectrum or continuum. As departments evolve, mature, grow, and perhaps even decline, one can see that the style of the chairperson must change to suit the changing needs of the department. While one's style may be a matter of personal choice or preference, an autocratic chairperson may be most appropriate for a young and relatively immature department. At such a time an autocratic chairperson can set a course for the department and give it direction. For example, a prominent department in a large college began its existence with an extremely autocratic and authoritarian chairperson who personally molded the fledgling department. The first chairperson was succeeded by a less autocratic, more democratic type who continued with the plan of the original chairperson, but who allowed the faculty a much greater degree of participation in policy-making decisions. The department now has a national reputation, elects its chairpersons on a rotating basis, and arrives at crucial decisions in a democratic manner. If the evolutionary history of a department follows the expected pattern, an autocrat may be desirable in its formative years. This may conceivably be true even when the individual members are mature scholars and the department itself is new, or is strife-torn and divided. As the department matures, however, its individual members may expect to become more involved in the governing process. The chairperson may then decide to adopt a less autocratic and more participatory style of leadership. Unfortunately, some chairpersons choose an autocratic style because it suits their personalities rather than because it is the style best suited to the needs of the department. Such individuals are frequently too rigid to allow the faculty to become involved in policy decisions. When a chairperson cannot become less authoritarian as the department matures, he or she may need to be replaced. The average six-year period* during which an individual serves as chairperson may be related to the cycle of change in the evolution of a department.

The Gamesman Model

Michael Maccoby, in *The Gamesman*, describes four types of leadership styles of corporation executives: the spectator, the technician, the jungle fighter, and the gamesman. Maccoby assigns to each type

---

*Survey conducted in 1977 by Allan Tucker, unpublished.

characteristics that, while especially appropriate in the context of corporate affairs, are not exactly applicable to academic affairs. We use Maccoby's terminology because it is interesting and provocative, but we have altered his definitions to fit realities in the academic department. Chairpersons may be interested in seeing how closely these types resemble their colleagues or themselves. The terminology should not be taken too seriously or too literally, but rather in a light-hearted though inquiring spirit.

The spectator chairperson is a passive and acquiescent manager who flourishes in mature departments, either small or large. In the small department, the chairperson leaves the faculty alone; in the large department, the administrative hierarchy is so well developed that the faculty is generally unaware of the chairperson's presence. The spectator does very little except make sure that the department's business is conducted on time; seldom does he or she become an advocate for anything except a trouble-free life for the department. All power and authority are turned over to department committees, and generally compromises are sought on such troubling matters as curriculum reform, resource allocation, and promotion and tenure cases.

This role closely approaches the ideal of a chairperson, who serves as clerk of the court. It is often a useful role, for departments, like nations, have their cyclical movements of reform and orthodoxy, of strife and peace. The spectator chairperson functions best in a department that has just experienced a stormy period of reforms, leaving an exhausted faculty that needs serenity in order once again to focus its attention on the cardinal functions of teaching, research, and service. The spectator should not, however, be left in place too long, lest the department slide into stagnation, and decline. A chairperson who assumes this role in an immature department, whether small or large, may be ineffective unless he or she has been picked deliberately by the dean or the central administration to preside over the dissolution of a unit that should never have been made a department.

The technician chairperson is a superb bureaucrat. He or she always submits staff reports on time, follows to the letter the directions given by the college, knows all the rules and regulations of the institution, the state, and the federal government, and knows how to follow those regulations to keep everyone out of trouble. The technician chairperson has read all the literature on management techniques and assiduously follows the best advice given there; even so, he or she often appears to lack vision, imagination, and courage. Such a chairperson can function well in any kind of department and has the great virtue of being able to bring order out of chaos. By virtue of knowing the rules and regulations, the technician chairperson can inhibit the zealots and pilgrims among the faculty; by the same token, he or she can use that knowledge to prod a sluggish, lazy department.

The technician chairperson is seldom the head of a high-priority department, which requires relentless pursuit of excellence. He or she is content to ensure that the department functions well in accordance with commonly accepted procedures and policies. Being able to maintain the status quo is no mean virtue, however, and many departments in transition from immaturity to maturity or from nonpriority status to priority status are often well served by the technician. Unlike the spectator, the technician does not turn over all power and authority to committees—he or she knows the rules and regulations too well to do that—but generally conducts affairs in a democratic fashion. The style of the technician is one step further removed from the Platonic ideal of the chairperson.

The jungle fighter chairperson has taken the position for two reasons: to make the department better and perhaps someday to become dean. He or she is unabashedly ambitious and understands that a strong, successful department is the best self-advertisement. Such a chairperson is sometimes brilliant, possibly dangerous, and during his or her term department life is never dull. Next to personal success, the jungle fighter chairperson wants nothing more than the department's complete victory in all major issues; he or she becomes its forceful advocate for all its positions. If this ambition were only for the department, the college dean or the central administration would find it extremely difficult to negotiate with the jungle fighter. The either-you-give-me-what-I-want-or-I'll-resign attitude in confrontation with the upper-level administration, however, seldom results in the chairperson's resignation; this approach is likely to be a brinksmanship approach, with the jungle fighter usually pulling back before superior forces.

The jungle fighter flourishes in large departments, both immature and mature, and is most successful in large, mature, high-priority departments. Such a person is capable of making truly significant —even brilliant—contributions to the department, but his or her value to the rest of the university or college depends on what priority level the department has been assigned. Although not a team player, the jungle fighter is probably the best agent of change among all types of chairpersons. He or she tends to be less democratic than the technician and plays a heavy hand in the affairs of department committees, consequently relinquishing little power or authority. Indeed, such a chairperson pretends to speak and act for the faculty at times when he or she is speaking or acting only for personal aims or for the goals of a few department members. But jungle fighters get their way more often than not. They can make a weak department strong and lay the foundation for a great department. This role is yet one step further removed from the Platonic ideal.

The gamesman chairperson is one who takes the job in order to improve the department, the college, and the institution. While not above ambition for higher office, the gamesman is not necessarily devoted to a future in academic administration. The gamesman plays life like a game and is interested in both strategy and tactics. Such a chairperson is cool and dedicated. He or she likes to win, as much for the pleasure of winning as for any other reason, but remains a sportsman and knows how to accept defeat.

The gamesman's leadership style embodies all the paradoxes inherent in the chairperson's difficult and perplexing job. He or she is strong but flexible, a manager who is sometimes managed, a leader who is sometimes led, a Janus-like advocate who can defend, at different times, the interests of the department faculty as well as the interests of the whole institution. He or she tries to reduce the number of occasions when the department's goals are perceived to be at odds with the institution's goals by convincing others that everyone's interests are best served by keeping the department strong. The gamesman is intelligent and courageous and probably has a highly developed sense of humor.

Although the terms *spectator, technician, jungle fighter,* and *gamesman* refer to an overall leadership style, a chairperson may combine in varying proportions characteristics of two or more of these types. A gamesman may become so carried away with the game that he or she becomes a jungle fighter. A spectator, confronted with a dilemma, may be forced to learn to use rules and regulations as a technician does. A jungle fighter who has been bruised in combat or who has mellowed with age may decide to forsake ambition and try being a gamesman. A real chairperson generally does not exhibit only one type of behavior; rather, his or her personality more likely reflects a melding of all these types.

A Theory of Departmental Development

Robert K. Murray, in his article "On Departmental Development: A Theory," describes a model tracing five stages of growth and evolution in a typical department. A department in the first stage of growth—especially a department in a small, undistinguished institution—has only a few members and is ruled autocratically and arbitrarily. The second stage, frequently coinciding with an increase in department size, is characterized by turmoil and power struggles, during which faculty members fight for a greater voice in decision making. This infighting often leads to the chairperson's resignation; faculty morale is low, and the department atmosphere is antagonistic. The third stage of a department's evolution is marked by "rampant democracy." A department in this stage spends an inordinate amount of time making democratic decisions and having committee meetings. Such a department is characterized by a rotating chairmanship and a sense of drift; the chairperson simply rubber-stamps the decisions of the faculty. The fourth stage is characterized by the department's large size and a split between nontenured junior professors and tenured senior professors, who make the important governance and policy decisions. The chairperson has a good deal of power but knows that his or her authority comes from the peer group of senior professors. The fifth stage, occurring in some very large distinguished departments and in a few small ones, leaves ordinary governance matters to competent secretaries and specially selected academic bureaucrats. A department in this stage of development is at the peak of prestige and influence but is beginning to collapse because of lack of organization.

A department need not evolve consecutively through all five stages. In a given institution at any given time, departments may be in different stages, and the progression from stage to stage is not necessarily smooth nor inevitable. Murray's theory does, however, provide an interesting conceptual scheme that can be used to explain the organizational problems of some departments.

Characteristics and Skills of an Effective Chairperson

The roles of the department chairperson, as we have noted, may vary considerably. Not the least important role is that which the chairperson develops for himself or herself. A chairperson who is both an effective leader and an efficient facilitator often possesses many of the following characteristics:

- good interpersonal skills; ability to work well with faculty members, staff, students, deans, and other chairpersons
- ability to identify problems and resolve them in a manner acceptable to faculty members
- ability to adapt leadership styles to fit different situations
- ability to set department goals and to make satisfactory progress in moving their departments toward those goals
- ability to search for and discover the optimum power available to them as chairpersons; ability to maximize that power in motivating faculty members to achieve department goals and objectives
- active participation in their professions; respect of their professional colleagues

The job of chairperson varies so much from department to department that a detailed standard job description is difficult to compose. Each chairperson, to a large degree, creates the role according to his or her own talents and skills within a framework that is consistent with institutional, department, and personal goals, both academic and administrative.

Chairpersons must determine what goals they can realistically set for themselves and for their departments during the period of their leadership. They must ultimately decide what roles they must and want to play, and how best to play them. Chairpersons must decide whether they want to provide leadership to their faculty members or act in the capacity of executive secretary, whose prime responsibility is to implement the faculty's wishes. Chairpersons must be sufficiently perceptive to judge the extent to which their faculty members and deans will permit them to be the kind of leaders they want to be, and they must be able to satisfy these expectations, as well as follow their own goals. Their effectiveness as chairpersons will depend on their being able to judge which roles to fulfill under any given set of circumstances and then to fulfill them.

A job description will not relieve chairpersons of the necessity or the responsibility for making such judgments; they themselves must decide the nature of the position. The elements that make the chairperson's job ambiguous and frustrating are the same elements that also make it challenging and interesting. When the position becomes only frustrating and loses its interest and challenge, it is time for the chairperson to consider seriously whether he or she can continue as an effective leader.

Determining Your Leadership Style Following the Directive-Supportive Model

Following is a list of questions to evaluate yourself in terms of how directive and supportive you perceive yourself to be in providing leadership to your faculty members. By answering the questions and following the instructions, you will be able to place yourself in one of the quadrants on the leadership style graph. This questionnaire has not been validated, nor is there any intention to try to validate it. The results, therefore, should not be taken too seriously. However, working through the exercise will help clarify the concept of leadership style and give you a general idea of your style. Those who chair departments or divisions composed of two or more distinct academic or vocational programs may prefer to determine their leadership style as applied to the group of faculty members in one of the programs rather than to the department as a whole.

How directive are you? (In each question, circle the number preceding the response that best describes your situation.)

1. How often do you review the department's goals and missions with at least one-third of your faculty members?

   1 Hardly ever
   2 Occasionally but not too often (1 or 2 times a year)
   3 Fairly often (3 to 5 times a year)
   4 Quite often (more than 5 times a year)

2. When you give an assignment to a faculty member or a committee, how much detail do you give the individual or committee on how to carry out the assignment?

   1 Hardly any detail
   2 Some but not much detail
   3 A fair amount of detail
   4 Lots of detail

3. During the period that the faculty member or committee is carrying out the assignment, how much monitoring do you do of the progress being made?

   1 Hardly any monitoring
   2 Occasional but not much monitoring
   3 A fair amount of monitoring
   4 Lots of monitoring

4. In meeting with individual faculty members to discuss their assignments, how specifically do you discuss the assignments?

   1 Not specifically at all
   2 Not too specifically
   3 Somewhat specifically
   4 Very specifically

Add the four numbers you circled above. On the leadership style graph, Fig. 3.2, place an "X" above the number on the horizontal axis that corresponds to the total of your four circled numbers. This number represents on a scale of 1 to 16 the extent to which you are directive. Draw a straight vertical line from the "X" upward.

How supportive are you? (In each question, circle the number preceding the response that best describes your situation.)

1. How many of your faculty members have come to you to relate personal accomplishments or problems during the past year?

   1 Hardly any
   2 Less than 25 percent
   3 Between 25 and 50 percent
   4 More than 50 percent

2. With how many of your faculty members have you made a point of meeting socially during the past year?

   1 Hardly any
   2 Less than 25 percent
   3 Between 25 and 50 percent
   4 More than 50 percent

3. To how many of your faculty members have you made a point of giving personal encouragement during the past year?

1 Hardly any   3 Between 25 and 50 percent
2 Less than 25 percent   4 More than 50 percent

4. To how many of your deserving faculty members have you written unsolicited informal or formal notes commending them for special achievement during the past year?

1 Hardly any   3 Between 25 and 50 percent
2 Less than 25 percent   4 More than 50 percent

Add the four circled numbers. On the leadership style graph, place an "X" to the right of the number on the vertical axis that corresponds to the total of your four circled numbers. This number represents on a

FIGURE 3.2. Leadership style graph—style determination

scale of 1 to 16 the extent to which you are supportive. Draw a straight horizontal line from the "X" to the right.

The vertical line and horizontal line which you have drawn will intersect in one of the four quadrants of the graph. For example: suppose your "directive" total was 6 and your "supportive" total was 10. The vertical and horizontal lines which you have drawn will intersect in Quadrant 3 (see Fig. 3.2). Your leadership style, according to this simple and nonvalidated test, is low directive and high supportive (see Fig. 3.3).

FIGURE 3.3. Level of maturity and appropriate leadership style*

LEVELS OF MATURITY	QUADRANT	LEADERSHIP STYLE APPROPRIATE FOR MATURITY LEVEL
Low	1	High directive Low supportive
Moderate	2	High directive High supportive
Moderately High	3	Low directive High supportive
High	4	Low directive Low supportive

*Paul Hersey and Kenneth H. Banchard, *Management of Organizational Behavior: Utilizing Human Resources*, 3rd ed. (Englewood Cliffs, N.J.: Prentice-Hall, 1977), p. 165.

Questions

1. In Chapter 2, you were asked to estimate the maturity level of your department or division. Using the directive-supportive model, what style of leadership would appear to be most effective for that level of maturity?
2. What is your leadership style, as determined by the instrument in this chapter? How does it compare with the style that would appear to be most effective for your department, given your estimation of its level of maturity?
3. The following case study describing the merging of several departments into one is presented in skeletal form to stimulate thought. Using your imagination and past experience, fill in any missing details that may be necessary to answer the questions at the end of the case study.

Gemini University, a small to middle-size institution, had four language departments: French, German, Spanish, and Russian. These departments had existed separately for more than 30 years and each had between three to seven faculty members including the chairperson. The Board of Trustees, after some study and upon recommendation of the president, combined these four departments and their faculties into a single 18-member Department of Modern Languages with one chairperson to be appointed. The faculty members of the original four separate language departments were not happy about becoming part of a single large department and resisted the idea to the very end. Although they participated in the search for a new chairperson, they were unable to reach consensus about any of the candidates. The dean, in desperation, finally offered the job to Dr. Sidney King, chairperson of the Department of Modern Languages at Apollo University for the past five years. The Modern Language Department at Apollo University was established as a single unit about 25 years ago when the university first opened its doors and now consisted of 15 faculty members. Students in this department could major in French, Spanish, German, Italian, or Russian. Dr. King was offered the position of chairperson of the new Modern Language Department at Gemini University because of his reputation as an effective chairperson of a smoothly operating department. Dr. King's interest in the new position was his desire for a change and the added incentive of a potential salary much larger than what he was now receiving.

a. Without knowing anything about the personalities, strengths, or weaknesses of the faculty members or the dean, try to imagine conditions and circumstances that might generate the worst possible problems for the department. How might Dr. King go about resolving some of these hypothetical problems that would be generated?

b. How and from whom might he find out what the problems *really* are?

c. From the information provided in the case study, what would be your guess as to the maturity level of the new Department of Modern Languages at Gemini University? Give reasons for your answer.

d. Using the directive-supportive model, what quadrant might best represent the leadership style that would be most appropriate or effective for a new chairperson coming to the new department? What leadership style would probably be least effective? Give reasons for your answer.

e. What would be your guess as to the maturity level of the Department of Modern Languages at Apollo University? Give reasons for your answer.

f. Using the directive-supportive model, what quadrant might best represent Dr. King's present leadership style? Give reasons for your answer.

g. Because Dr. King was a successful and effective chairperson at Apollo University, can it be assumed that he will be equally successful and effective at Gemini University? Give reasons for your answer.

References

ABRELL, RONALD L. "Educational Leadership Without Carrot and Club." *The Clearing House*, February 1979, pp. 280–285.

ARGYRIS, CHRIS; CYERT, RICHARD M.; RAILEY, STEPHEN K.; AND MAEROFF, GENE I. *Leadership in the 1980's*. Cambridge, Mass.: Institute for Educational Management, Harvard University, 1980.

ASTIN, ALEXANDER W., AND SCHERRI, RITA A. *Maximizing Leadership Effectiveness: Impact of Administrative Style on Faculty and Students*. San Francisco: Jossey-Bass, 1980.

BALDRIDGE, J. VICTOR, ET AL. *Policy Making and Effective Leadership: A National Study of Academic Management*. San Francisco: Jossey-Bass, 1978.

BLAKE, ROBERT R., AND MOUTON, JANE S. *The Managerial Grid*. Houston: Gulf, 1964.

BOBBITT, H. RANDOLPH, AND BEHLING, ORLANDO C. "Organizational Behavior: A Review of the Literature." *Journal of Higher Education*, January-February 1981, pp. 29–44.

BOGUE, E. GRADY. "Administrative Malpractice: The Limits of Common Sense." *Educational Record*, Winter 1978, pp. 77–86.

BROWN, DAVID G. *Leadership Vitality: A Workup for Academic Administrators*. Washington, D.C.: American Council on Education, 1980.

COHEN, MICHAEL D., AND MARCH, JAMES G., eds. *Leadership and Ambiguity: The American College President*. Carnegie Commission on Higher Education. New York: McGraw-Hill, 1974.

CORSON, JOHN J. *The Governance of Colleges and Universities*. New York: McGraw-Hill, 1960.

HERSEY, PAUL, AND BLANCHARD, KENNETH H. *Management of Organizational Behavior: Utilizing Human Resources*. 3rd ed. Englewood Cliffs, N.J.: Prentice-Hall, 1977.

JOHNSON, F. CRAIG. "Data Requirements for Academic Departments." In *New Directions for Institutional Research: Examining Departmental Management*, no. 10, edited by John C. Smart and James R. Montgomery. San Francisco: Jossey-Bass, 1976.

MACCOBY, MICHAEL. *The Gamesman*. New York: Simon & Schuster, 1977.

MILLETT, JOHN D. *New Structures of Campus Power: Success and Failures of Emerging Forms of Institutional Governance*. San Francisco: Jossey-Bass, 1978.

MURRAY, ROBERT K. "On Departmental Development: A Theory." *The Journal of General Education*, October 1964, pp. 227–36.

NATIONAL TRAINING LABORATORIES INSTITUTE FOR APPLIED BEHAVIOR SCIENCE. *Reading Book: Laboratories in Human Relations Training.* Washington, D.C.: National Education Association, 1969.

PALMER, RUPERT E., JR. "The Chairman as Servant: Or, How to Lead a Department from a Position of Weakness." *ADE Bulletin*, May 1979, pp. 38–40.

RICHMAN, BARRY M., AND FARMER, RICHARD N. *Leadership, Goals, and Power in Higher Education: A Contingency and Open-Systems Approach to Effective Management.* San Francisco: Jossey-Bass, 1974.

SMART, JOHN C., AND ELTON, CHARLES F. "Administrative Roles of Department Chairmen." In *New Directions for Institutional Research: Examining Departmental Management*, no. 10, edited by John C. Smart and James R. Montgomery. San Francisco: Jossey-Bass, 1976.

ZORN, JENO C. "The Chairman's Return." *Educational Record*, Spring 1978, pp. 121–133.

4

Delegation and Department Committees

Delegating Responsibility

One of the first questions that a newly appointed department chairperson asks is, "How can I effectively fulfill all my responsibilities as chairperson and at the same time not reduce my teaching, research, and service activities?" Chairpersons who singlehandedly try to carry out all their administrative tasks and simultaneously maintain their previous levels of professional activity are bound to find that the workload is impossible to manage. At some point they must decide to what extent they wish to retain their commitment to teaching, research, and professional activities. Some chairpersons give up most or all of their teaching and research in order to fulfill their administrative and leadership tasks. Others, by carefully delegating many administrative tasks to faculty members and department committees, manage to schedule sufficient time for some teaching and research. Then there are those chairpersons who continue to carry out all their customary teaching, research, and service activities, paying attention to administrative tasks only when absolutely necessary. Chairpersons usually choose the model most suited to their talents, abilities, and professional objectives.

Academic vice-presidents and deans are not seriously concerned with the extent to which the chairperson personally carries out the department's administrative activities—so long as the tasks are carried out. Nor do deans and academic vice-presidents apply pressure on department chairpersons to conduct research. Faculty members, however, often expect chairpersons to continue their research and scholarly activities even while administering the department. Some chairpersons who are no longer actively engaged in research complain openly about the difficulties and frustrations of the chairperson's job and indicate repeatedly to their colleagues that they can hardly wait to return to the classroom or laboratory. The sincerity with which these statements are made cannot be overlooked. In the 1977 survey of department chairpersons, however, 90 percent responded that they would serve an additional term in the position if invited to do so. For those who envision a career in the area of university administration, the relinquishing of research activity may simply mark the beginning of a new career interest. On the other hand, many chairpersons try to maintain their earlier activities simply for love of their discipline or in anticipation of returning to their former roles when their time as chairperson is over.

Some chairpersons are appointed by the dean and serve at the dean's pleasure; others are appointed by the dean from a list of candidates recommended by a faculty search committee; and still others are elected by their colleagues to serve for one or more terms. In some departments, the position of chairperson rotates among its members. In many cases, chairpersons receive extra compensation and other perquisites, such as full-time summer appointments and more luxurious office space. The material and psychological rewards of the position are intended to compensate for frustrations encountered in the job, such as abrasive incidents with both deans and faculty members, longer hours, and reduced time for teaching and research. Occasionally the frustrations cause chairpersons to resign, especially when the dissatisfactions outweigh the benefits. The department whose chairperson serves a fixed term, usually two or three years, gives the chairperson an option to exit gracefully after a full cycle or two of experience.

Clearly the role of chairperson involves many tasks that are quite time-consuming. In their study of chairpersons at one state university, Gerald W. McLaughlin, James R. Montgomery, and L. F. Malpass found that chairpersons considered the following tasks most demanding: providing informal leadership for faculty members; representing the department to the central administration; allocating financial resources; maintaining faculty morale; encouraging organizational improvement; managing academic programs; planning for the long term; advising students; and encouraging faculty members' professional development.

Even though these tasks were considered most demanding, they provided some satisfaction. Still other tasks were perceived as providing no satisfaction at all. These included maintaining student records, serving on college and university committees, managing facilities, and preparing and presenting budgets. Especially onerous were tasks governed by federal, state, and university laws and administrative rules and requiring much detail work.

Incidentally, chairpersons in the study cited above reported that they worked an average of fifty-five hours per week. They spent an average of twenty-six hours on department leadership and administrative tasks, ten hours on teaching and student counseling, nine hours on research and professional development, and four hours on college and university activities. Several of the chairpersons polled had been in office for five years, and their schedules indicated the extent to which they had adapted their professional lives to their administrative role.

A national survey of chairpersons of medium-sized to large university departments, conducted by John C. Smart and Charles F. Elton and reported in their article "Administrative Roles of Department Chairmen," revealed that the types of roles that the chairperson assumed were related to the department's academic discipline. For example, chairpersons in the basic disciplines, whether the sciences or the humanities, spent more time in the "faculty role" than did those in applied sciences departments. They spent relatively more time recruiting, selecting, and evaluating department faculty members; encouraging their professional development and research and publication efforts; maintaining a healthy department climate by reducing conflicts among the faculty members; and providing informal leadership for the faculty members.

Chairpersons of social science departments—such as anthropology, political science, psychology, and sociology—spent more time in the "instructional role." They spent more time than others teaching and advising students; managing clerical and technical personnel in the department; and maintaining accurate student and department records.

Chairpersons of departments of pure and applied science—such as biology and agriculture departments—spent more time in the "research role" than did chairpersons of the nonscience departments, such as English, history, and communications. They spent relatively more time obtaining and managing grants, gifts, and contracts; recruiting, selecting, and supervising graduate students; and managing department finances, equipment, and grants. Chairpersons in this group also showed low commitment to the instructional role.

The "coordinator role" was not predominant among chairpersons of any particular discipline but was most often associated with chairpersons of education departments. Those in the coordinator role spent more time than their colleagues soliciting ideas to improve the department, planning and reviewing the curriculum, and assigning teaching, research, and other duties to faculty members. They also spent more time coordinating department activities with external groups, representing the department at professional meetings, participating in college and university committee work, and interacting with university administrators on behalf of the department. Education chairpersons also spent less time in the faculty role. Perhaps this emphasis on coordinating is related to the fact that education professors spend a great deal of time supervising practice teaching and working with public school personnel; this coordinator role may be carried over when the professor becomes a chairperson.

Whatever the reasons for favoring one of the roles described above, the chairperson must still attend to those tasks that are part of other roles. These tasks may be secondary, but they cannot be totally neglected. To chairpersons who complain of having insufficient time for filling all their roles, university administrators often respond by suggesting that they learn better time management skills. In fact, administrators often suggest that the busiest faculty member be chosen chairperson because busy people manage their time successfully. Many books offer valuable techniques for organizing and managing one's time, and these are helpful for those who are not skillful at getting tasks scheduled and accomplished. Effective time management, however, will not significantly reduce a chairperson's work; such a reduction is possible only if the chairperson learns to delegate tasks. The extent to which chairpersons learn to delegate tasks will determine the amount of time they will have available for teaching, research, and other activities of their choice.

Some chairpersons, as we have noted, continue to carry out all their customary teaching, research, and service activities, but they do this at the expense of administrative tasks; in effect, the administrative tasks are assumed only when absolutely necessary. The attitude that characterizes this kind of administration is that nothing deserves attention until a crisis erupts. The chairperson sees the job as a chore and never bothers to learn about either the intricacies of leadership or the techniques of organization and delegation.

The crisis-fighting approach to department administration leads to an accumulation of unopened mail, unsubmitted reports, missed deadlines, and unattended faculty concerns. The result is a department with low morale and an unfavorable work environment. Often, in the face of faculty disapproval or even rebellion, the chairperson assigns more and more responsibility to the clerical staff. The staff, then, may take on airs of administrative authority, thus further antagonizing faculty members. In such a case, the department chairperson is not really fulfilling his or her responsibility. If a chairperson wants to have time for teaching and research and still effectively lead the department, he or she must learn to practice the art of delegation.

How, then, does a chairperson become an organizer and coordinator of tasks and activities? By delegating tasks and responsibilities to staff members, to faculty members, or to committees. The ability to delegate functions, tasks, and responsibilities requires a trust and confidence in peers and staff members, a trust that occurs when there is consensus within the department about goals, objectives, policies, programs, and priorities. Delegation also requires a willingness to accept the results of the delegated effort, even if these results are not as extraordinary as those the chairperson might have achieved working alone. A chairperson who is compelled to oversee every detail and to operate with "zero defect" standards is often unable to tolerate the work of those who seem less competent.

The chairperson's responsibilities for the completion of a certain task do not end once the task has been delegated. The work of others must be evaluated, checked, and occasionally endorsed. To evaluate something, however, usually takes less time than to do it. The chairperson, by careful delegation, can save between 60 to 90 percent of the time he or she might devote to a single task, especially if the instructions are clear and precise and if those delegated are in tune with the chairperson's style and thinking. Although not every task can be assigned to any person, many detailed but routine rasks can be easily relegated to secretaries, graduate student assistants, and staff associates.

Often, the chairperson can find faculty members who will willingly perform some administrative chores. Department tasks that provide growth and development opportunities are useful governance training for junior faculty members, and they should be given credit for service to the department. For example, these tasks could be made a part of the assigned workload, or the faculty members could be rewarded with some perquisite or a special title. A chairperson must be careful not to overload the unpromoted, untenured junior faculty member to the point that his or her career is threatened.

Senior faculty members who are having difficulty adjusting to the department's changing teaching or research goals or who are in an unproductive phase of their career might also welcome the opportunity to contribute to the department by assuming some delegated responsibility. In delegating tasks to senior faculty members, the chairperson must be sure that these persons are both willing to accept and competent to perform the assignment. Great tact and delicacy may be required in enlisting the efforts of senior faculty members.

Committee Structure

Department committees are useful to the chairperson because he or she can delegate certain tasks to them. They also help provide a logical order to the department decision-making process. Moreover, the faculty is more likely to accept decisions that are made or recommended by a committee, especially if the process for selecting committee members has been approved by the faculty. Much of a department's work is accomplished through committees, and the chairperson should understand how they work and the various ways in which they can be organized.

In a survey of fifteen selected academic departments at Ohio State University, reported in her article "The Internal Organization of Academic Departments," Doris Ryan found that the number of committees per department ranged from sixteen to none, with an average of seven.*
The larger the department, the more committees it had; small departments often operated, in their entirety, as a single committee.

The size of a committee is clearly related to the tasks that it is assigned, as well as to the department structure. Large committees frequently occur in large departments that have formal subgroups, especially when each subgroup desires representation on those committees. For example, in a large psychology department, the clinical psychologists, who were not represented on the admissions committee, argued that the experimental psychologists, who dominated the selection process, were rejecting many good applicants. Generally, committees consisting of three to nine members seem to be more productive than larger committees. An odd number of members eliminates ties when voting.

There are two general types of committees—standing and ad hoc. A standing committee operates on a permanent basis. Although its membership may change, it continues to operate from year to year unless some administrative decree terminates its activities. Two examples of standing committees that operate on a permanent basis are admissions committees and faculty evaluation committees. Ad hoc committees, on the other hand, are formed for specific tasks and cease operation when their tasks are completed. Ad hoc committees may include search committees and others that respond to immediate needs. The frequency with which committees meet depends on the tasks assigned to them; some meet on a regular schedule, others on call.

Committee functions may logically be divided into three categories: developing policies, performing administrative activities, and providing technical advice. The policy-making function consists of developing rules, regulations, and criteria for governing certain department activities, such as evaluating faculty performance, admitting students, determining equitable workloads for faculty, assigning space, and so forth. The administrative function consists of making decisions on specific issues or recommending positions to the department chairperson. These administrative functions, all based on predetermined policies

*Doris W. Ryan, "The Internal Organization of Academic Departments," *Journal of Higher Education* (June 1972): 467.

and criteria, include reviewing the applications of persons seeking admission to a program and making a decision as to whether they should be admitted; evaluating the performance of faculty members; recommending equitable workloads for specific faculty members; and assigning space to faculty members.

A committee may be established for the sole purpose of developing policies and criteria to govern a single activity, and a second committee may be appointed to implement those policies. In some instances, a single committee is charged not only with developing such policies, procedures, and criteria, but also with implementing them. For example, a faculty evaluation committee may be required not only to develop department policies and criteria for evaluating the faculty but also to evaluate individual faculty members. Similarly, an admissions committee may be required not only to develop policies, procedures, and criteria for admitting students, but also to act on applications for admission.

Committees that provide technical advice are usually composed of faculty members with special expertise for addressing particular problems. These committees are usually ad hoc and are given assignments such as designing and planning new facilities, deciding what types of equipment should be purchased, developing core and specialized curricula for specified programs, and so forth.

Members of these committees may be appointed by the department chairperson, elected by the department, or chosen by a combination of both methods. Similarly, the committee chairperson may be appointed by the department chairperson, elected by the committee members, or elected by the department. In some cases, the department chairperson may also be the committee chairperson, a voting member of the committee, or an ex officio member, or he or she may not be a member at all. How these matters are handled depends on the department's nature and size and the tasks that must be accomplished.

The department chairperson must provide sufficient guidance and direction for the committee. The committee's charge should be clear and precise, and the committee should be apprised of its responsibilities, including what criteria must be followed, under what constraints it must operate, what its members can and cannot do, and what deadlines must be met. Most committees operate in an advisory capacity to the chairperson or to the department. Some advisory committees, however, are perceived as having a decision-making responsibility. One example is the admissions committee, whose task is so important that wise chairpersons rarely overrule its recommendations. In any event, an advisory committee should know that it operates in an advisory function. For committee members to work hard on some problem and then have their work ignored or rejected is disheartening, especially if they think that they are part of a decision-making rather than an advisory committee.

Sometimes chairpersons do not give clear guidance to committees. When a committee is not given a specific charge, criteria to follow, or deadlines to be met, it often accomplishes little or nothing at all. Possibly this result is just what the chairperson desired. Occasionally, a chairperson is pressured to do something that he or she is reluctant to do. Leaving the matter to a committee without giving it guidance, direction, or deadlines—especially if the committee members are at odds with each other—will give the chairperson time to let things simmer.

Some department administrative tasks can easily be delegated to committees, especially when the chairperson is willing to accept a decision that is arrived at fairly. Sometimes, however, the chairperson wants the department to take a certain course of action, which, if he or she proposed it, would arouse some opposition. In such a case, a chairperson could form a committee to recommend to the department that particular course of action.

Can there be any degree of certainty that a committee's conclusions will coincide with the chairperson's ideas? Some administrators use the following strategy. First, they discuss their ideas informally with individual faculty members to identify those who are or who might be sympathetic to the plan. These chairpersons do not use hard-sell tactics and are careful not to show undue eagerness to implement the action. Second, they select a committee of faculty members who are sympathetic to the plan and who also enjoy the respect of their colleagues. An appointed committee of this kind, properly instructed and charged, will usually come up with conclusions and recommendations that are consistent with the chairperson's original plan. If committee members or other faculty members suspect the Machiavellian nature of the chairperson's procedures, they may firmly resist adopting the intended action, regardless of its merits. Many faculty members consider machinations of this sort questionable; nevertheless, many chairpersons have been known to use such tactics. Our description of these tactics, however, is not intended to be an endorsement of them.

An elected committee may not be as predictable in terms of the recommendations it will make. If the chairperson wants an elected committee to recommend a certain course of action, he or she should talk to the committee members individually to gauge their feelings and attempt to persuade them to his or her way of thinking. If the chairperson cannot obtain the support of the committee, he or she might temporarily abandon the issue. Some chairpersons have been known to appoint two committees to work independently on the same problem in order to have a choice of recommendations. Faculty committees and departments as a whole almost always react negatively to a fresh proposal when it is introduced at a formal meeting, especially if the chairperson introduces it without having done any groundwork or having issued previous warning. And a negative reaction is not easily changed. A wise chairperson, therefore, will informally prepare committee members or department members before presenting a new concept at a formal meeting.

The work of department committees may be summarized as follows:

- Committees may function in policy-making, administrative, or technical roles.
- Committee members may be appointed, elected, or both.
- Committees may function in an advisory or decision-making capacity.
- Committees may meet regularly or on call.
- Committees may be permanent or ad hoc.
- The department chairperson may be the committee chairperson, a voting member of the committee, or an ex officio member, or not serve on the committee at all.
- The optimum number of members should be an odd number between three and nine.
- The charge to the committee should be clear and precise.

A department should, on occasion, examine the number and functions of its committees. Their value has been emphasized, but to overburden the faculty with a plethora of committees is counterproductive; only those committees that are necessary should be formed. Some large departments even have a committee to control the tendency of committees to multiply needlessly.

Following is a representative, though far from inclusive, list of department committees and a brief summary of the main functions of each. Few departments have all these committees, and some may not have any.

- *Admissions committee*—usually reviews applications of students for admission to the department and makes recommendation to admit or to deny admission
- *Graduate policy and programs committee*—determines admission and graduation requirements and standards; monitors quality of graduate programs
- *Student recruitment committee*—develops and implements methods of publicizing to prospective students the department's program and professional opportunities within the field
- *Seminars and symposia committee*—arranges and publicizes lectures, seminars, and symposia for faculty members and students within and outside the department
- *Governance committee*—at request of chairperson, considers the

structure and functions of department committees; makes recommendations or advises chairperson concerning a broad range of department business

- *Field liaison committee*—establishes and maintains relationships with outside agencies and organizations; coordinates service activities of department faculty
- *Curriculum committee*—develops and monitors curriculum, including core and required courses
- *Promotion and tenure committee*—reviews the records of faculty members eligible for promotion or tenure and recommends appropriate action; in some departments, establishes the standards and criteria for these decisions
- *Faculty evaluation committee*—reviews records of faculty members for purposes of annual evaluation and merit increases; in some cases, establishes criteria for these reviews
- *Faculty development committee*—develops, implements, and monitors procedures that contribute to the professional advancement of faculty members
- *International students committee*—develops and implements procedures for meeting special needs of foreign students
- *Faculty assignment committee*—schedules classes; develops and implements procedures for ensuring that the department's work is equitably divided
- *Student advisory committee*—a student-directed and student-run committee, concerned with student welfare; nominates student members to certain faculty committees
- *Search committee*—develops and implements procedures for recruiting new faculty members and recommends appropriate appointments
- *Examination and grading committee*—sets standards for and reviews the grading system; administers qualifying and comprehensive examinations for graduate students
- *Off-campus program committee*—recommends and supervises courses and programs offered off campus
- *Placement committee*—develops and implements procedures for placing graduates of the program
- *Planning committee*—assesses the department's future needs and develops short- and long-range plans for consideration by the chairperson and the department; sometimes plans new buildings and facilities

Well-organized departments sometimes develop rules and guidelines for the operation of their committees; other committees operate on the basis of unwritten rules. More energy is sometimes spent in developing bylaws for committees than in dealing with the issues. Following is an example of committee guidelines that were adopted by a large department in a large university. This example is not offered as a model but only as an illustration for chairpersons interested in formalizing their department's committee structure. Note that the guidelines stipulate the committee's purposes and duties, describe how members are selected, outline operating procedures, and provide for a periodic evaluation of the committee's activities.

Appropriate guidelines could be drawn up for each committee within the department. The guidelines need not be lengthy or complex, but the charge should be clear.

GUIDELINES FOR THE FACULTY EVALUATION COMMITTEE

Purposes and Duties
1. To design faculty evaluation criteria and procedures for use within the department.
2. To communicate the evaluation criteria procedures to the faculty in a timely fashion.
3. To implement the evaluation procedures for department promotion and tenure, annual evaluation, and merit, and for master's and doctoral directive status.
4. To advocate review and monitor procedures that contribute to professional advancement of untenured and junior members (e.g., to establish conditions suitable for research, writing, and publishing).

Committee Memberships
1. Each of the three degree programs in the department will elect three faculty members as representatives on the committee to serve for a one-year term.
2. The committee chairperson will be named by the department chairperson from among those elected.

Committee Procedures
1. The committee will meet as frequently as may be required to do its work.
2. All candidates for promotion, tenure, and merit, as well as candidates for master's and doctoral directive status within the department shall be reviewed by the committee.
3. The committee will make a brief report of its work to the faculty at the end of the winter quarter.
4. The department chairperson will explain and discuss with the committee the reasons for any action that is contrary to the committee's recommendations. The committee members will inform the faculty of such instances.

Review
The committee will be responsible for conducting a yearly review of its procedures. If necessary, the committee will propose recommended changes to the governance committee.

The many tasks that confront department chairpersons can be extremely time-consuming. To avoid being totally consumed by these tasks and to find sufficient time for desired scholarly activities, chairpersons must learn to delegate some of their tasks. Some chairpersons cannot bear the thought of sharing their responsibilities with colleagues; they fear that other persons are unable to do the job as well as they themselves. Delegation, however, is the only solution to the chairperson's problem of finding time to do all that he or she must do or wants to do. Chairpersons who recognize this fact are continually looking for the right person or committee to whom some department tasks can be entrusted.

Questions and Exercises

List the ten most time-consuming activities that you personally performed during the past year in your capacity as department chairperson (refer to the list of the chairperson's tasks and responsibilities on pages 2–3). Beside each activity that you list, indicate which of these tasks must be performed only by you; which could be delegated to a person in the department, such as a student assistant, secretary, or faculty member; and which could be delegated to a committee. If you think the task could be delegated, write the title of the person or the name of the committee to whom it could be delegated.

1. a. How many time-consuming tasks did you list?
   b. How many of these tasks could you delegate to a person or to a committee?
   c. How many could you not delegate to a person or a committee? Explain why not.
2. How many committees does your department have?
3. Which ones help you most with your administrative responsibilities?
4. Do you believe that your department has the right number of committees? Too many? Too few?
5. Which committees would you add, eliminate, or change? Give reasons.

References

AMERICAN SOCIETY OF ASSOCIATION EXECUTIVES. "So You're on a Committee." Washington, D.C.: ASAE, 1976.

ANDERSON, G. LESTER. "Organizational Diversity." In *New Directions for Institutional Research: Examining Departmental Management*, no. 10, edited by John C. Smart and James R. Montgomery. San Francisco: Jossey-Bass, 1976.

BALDRIDGE, J. VICTOR, ET AL. *Policy Making and Effective Leadership: A National Study of Academic Management.* San Francisco: Jossey-Bass, 1978.

BARNARD, DOUGLAS P., AND HETZEL, ROBERT W. "A Process for Committeeship." *The Clearing House*, September 1978, pp. 32–34.

COHEN, MICHAEL D., AND MARCH, JAMES G., EDS. *Leadership and Ambiguity: The American College President.* Carnegie Commission on Higher Education. New York: McGraw-Hill, 1974.

DRESSEL, PAUL L., AND SIMON, L.A. "Allocating Resources among Departments." *New Directions for Institutional Research*, no. 11. San Francisco: Jossey-Bass, 1976.

JOHNSON, F. CRAIG. "Data Requirements for Academic Departments." In *New Directions for Institutional Research: Examining Departmental Management*, no. 10, edited by John C. Smart and James R. Montgomery. San Francisco: Jossey-Bass, 1976.

MCLAUGHLIN, GERALD W.; MONTGOMERY, JAMES R.; AND MALPASS, L. F. "An Investigation of Department Heads at a State University." Paper presented at the 1973 American Educational Research Association Conference, New Orleans, Louisiana.

MILLETT, JOHN D. *New Structures of Campus Power: Success and Failures of Emerging Forms of Institutional Governance.* San Francisco: Jossey-Bass, 1978.

RICHMAN, BARRY M., AND FARMER, RICHARD N. *Leadership, Goals, and Power in Higher Education: A Contingency and Open-Systems Approach to Effective Management.* San Francisco: Jossey-Bass, 1974.

RYAN, DORIS W. "The Internal Organization of Academic Departments." *Journal of Higher Education*, June 1972, pp. 464–82.

SMART, JOHN C., AND ELTON, CHARLES F. "Administrative Roles of Department Chairmen." In *New Directions for Institutional Research: Examining Departmental Management*, no. 10, edited by John C. Smart and James R. Montgomery. San Francisco: Jossey-Bass, 1976.

5

Recruiting and Affirmative Action*

In the past, during times of expanding enrollments, increasing budgets, and no affirmative action regulations, the recruitment and selection process was much less complex than it is today. An expanded enrollment would automatically create an increased number of faculty positions, and in certain fields the number of available positions would often exceed the number of qualified faculty members to fill them. When minorities and women were hired, it was primarily due to personal values held by enlightened presidents, deans, and department chairpersons. If after one or two years, newly employed faculty members did not perform as well as expected, they would be advised to seek employment elsewhere. This was called "counseling them out." These "counseled out" individuals offered little resistance because they knew that they would have no difficulty in finding employment at another institution. Turnover among faculty members in those days was quite high, as was faculty mobility, and the process for screening and selecting new faculty members was quite informal.

There were times when a position needed to be filled rather quickly and the faculty member's area of specialization within the discipline was not a key factor in his or her selection. This resulted in continual modification of department goals to fit faculty members' areas of specialization and interest rather than the overall mission of the institution. Departmental goals were changed every time one or two new faculty members were hired.

Today the situation is different. Enrollments are not expanding but rather contracting or remaining the same. Budgets are not increasing and the number of available faculty positions is decreasing. There is

*Some elements of this chapter are drawn from a research report prepared in 1982 for the Institute for Departmental Leadership, Florida State University, by John S. Waggaman.

71

very little voluntary turnover, and mobility has slowed down to a snail's pace. Faculty members are no longer willing to be counseled out because they have few places to go. Moreover, it is becoming increasingly difficult to terminate faculty members whose performance is barely marginal. Some department vacancies are reclaimed by the central administration of the institution and never returned to the department. Therefore, when a department does have a vacancy which it is permitted to fill, every care should be taken to insure that the person selected to fill it is the best person for the job in terms of the department's future as well as its present. It is well to remember that whoever is selected for the position, bad or good, may be with the department for a long time.

Recruitment Within the Context of Departmental Planning

Recruitment of faculty members should not be an ad hoc affair carried out in isolation but rather an integral part of a long-range departmental plan which includes a clearly defined set of departmental goals. After a department's goals have been reviewed and updated, they can be used to assess the current extent to which the existing faculty members possess the skills and interests required to meet the needs stated in the goals. Where there are some unmet needs, the chairperson and the appropriate faculty committee can begin to consider the kind of person who might be sought in the recruitment process.

A department should develop and keep current an inventory of existing faculty specializations and competencies including skills in teaching, research, service, student advising, and mentoring of graduate students. This human resource inventory can serve the chairperson as a planning tool and, when measured against the department's goals, can provide guidance in determining which skills or competencies need to be added and which are no longer necessary and should be phased out. An important part of the inventory is a job description for each faculty member. Job descriptions should include data about average assignment, subjects taught, whether applied or basic research is conducted, and the range of services and other activities that are carried out or expected.

The department should also keep a list of those specialties and commitments which clientele groups such as students, private industry, and government agencies have grown to expect from the department. The combined use of the human resources inventory, the list of clientele expectations, and the goal statements of the department allows the chairperson to see which areas of specialization are presently over- or understaffed, which current areas are not addressed, and which areas may need to be addressed in the future. The strength or weakness of each department specialty is linked to the quality of performance of each individual faculty member. An analysis of faculty evaluation data can help the chairperson determine whether there are areas of weakness. Depending on the goals and resources of the department, a decision can then be made to strengthen, retain as is, or phase out certain areas of weakness.

The department should attempt to anticipate the occurrence of any position vacancies and include this information in its inventory. Vacant faculty positions emerge for many reasons, such as retirement, recruitment by another institution, noncontinuation of contract, illness, or death. A sensitive department chairperson will often have many clues that members of the faculty are in various stages of career development which may lead them to leave their current position. Personal health and lifestyles of individuals sometimes provide early warning signals of future disabilities. Making reliable estimates when vacancies are likely to occur requires that the chairperson thoroughly understand a great variety of circumstances that precede the departure of faculty members.

Having a variety of information available allows the chairperson to anticipate the course of events prior to the occurrence of a vacancy, and to avoid hasty, ill-conceived measures that might jeopardize the attainment of departmental goals. The numerical decline of the traditional college age group, poor economic conditions which limit parental support, and the reduction of federal aid to students all augur little or no expansion in enrollment, and indeed a real possibility for decline, at many institutions. There will probably be few vacancies in the 1980s. It is therefore especially important that recruitment efforts be consonant with departmental goals and that the recruitment process be well organized and conducted fairly within equal employment guidelines so that the best qualified candidate may be selected. If the recruitment process becomes an integral part of a long-range departmental plan and dates of vacancies are anticipated, the occurrence of a vacancy will not be the occasion for departmental crises, confusion, or despair over missed opportunities.

Affirmative Action

Before beginning a discussion of recruiting, it is important to consider the question of equal employment opportunity, including affirmative action. It is well known that institutions of higher education were once bastions of white, male supremacy. Most faculty members

are aware of the deleterious effects of discrimination and are committed to bringing about positive change in the structure of employment in
higher education.

The elimination of discrimination based on race, color, religion,
sex, age, national origin, or handicap is an integral part of the ethical
belief system of most American academics. In spite of the fact that there
is a shared moral objection to discrimination, the simple continuation
of traditional hiring practices within the university tends to perpetuate
the underrepresentation of women, minorities, and others in academe.
The federal government and the federal courts have established
guidelines and given instructions on how discrimination in higher education may be avoided. These guidelines address the problems of inad-
vertent as well as intentional discrimination. Affirmative action may be
defined as the process whereby qualified individuals with minority
status are actively sought to fill vacancies, and if found, given preference over equally qualified nonminority persons. Some departments in
state universities stipulate the percentage of women and minorities to
be attained over a specific period of time. To reach these goals, some officials feel so pressured that they may, after advertising a vacancy, defer
filling the available position until a woman or minority candidate is
found who can be successfully recruited and employed. Such a practice is itself a violation of fair employment criteria since, once a position
is announced and an open search is conducted, the best available person should be selected for the job, regardless of sex, age, race, religion,
etcetera.

Many institutions have made extraordinary efforts to remove ves-
tiges of discriminatory practice. Nevertheless, allegations of discrimination continue to be made in courts, in grievances, and in published
reports. Department chairpersons should be aware that each new appointment of a white male to the faculty may be seen over time as evidence of discrimination. That is, the effect of existing practices has
been seen to lead to discriminatory outcomes. In contrast to this point
of view, some courts have ruled that a clear intent to discriminate must
be found before any special change in recruitment is required. Affirmative action does not mean that institutions are required to hire less
qualified minority members over better qualified nonminority individuals.

Many grievances concerning discrimination have found their way
into state and federal courts. Court cases generally concern alleged discrimination against women and minority members in matters of hiring
practice and salary allocation. The outcome of many of these court
cases has led universities to establish their own formal guidelines
which must be followed in all cases of hiring. Guidelines vary from institution to institution, and chairpersons should be familiar with affir-

mative action procedures in their respective institutions. Good records of recruiting efforts should be kept in anticipation of possible litigation.

Because the department is the locus of the recruitment process, it should be seen as the heart of the equal employment effort and should assume the responsibility for making a serious effort at locating minority and women candidates. It has a moral obligation to eliminate all departmental policies and practices that could result in discrimination and to take whatever corrective action is appropriate.

The department also has a moral and professional responsibility to increase the size of the pool of minority and women candidates by recruiting more of them to Ph.D. and professional programs and preparing them to assume faculty positions. Chairpersons can have a special role in this endeavor since they are in a position to influence the distribution of graduate fellowships and teaching and research assistantships.

Obtaining Clearance before the Recruiting Effort

The chairperson cannot assume that just because a vacancy has occurred in the department he or she will automatically receive permission to fill it. The central administration at most institutions has the power to sweep the unfilled position from the department and reallocate it to a more favored department—one which is deemed to have greater need. This practice is becoming more common as enrollments decline and few if any new positions are created. It is also possible that the administration may feel the need to use the salary money allocated to the vacated position for other exigencies, such as a demand from the state or governing board to turn back a percentage of the allocated budget. In such a case, the departmental faculty may have to assume heavier teaching loads or cancel courses. A chairperson who desires to fill a sudden vacancy, or for that matter any vacancy, must be prepared to justify the need for the position. In any event, before beginning a formal recruiting effort, clearance for the recruitment must be obtained from the dean of the school or college.

Restructuring the Position

The occurrence of a vacancy presents a good opportunity to restructure the position and to bring it in line with the department's long-range goals. What area of specialty is desirable from the department's point of view? Should it be the same as or different from that of the preceding occupant? The department may recognize a need for a different set of disciplinary skills in some new academic specialty or research area. Should interdepartmental responsibilities be built into the position? What are the salary constraints? Is it better to replace a senior professor with another of equal rank or stature, or for the same money to hire one or possibly two promising junior scholars whose potential is as yet unproven? If the salary constraints are severe, would a part-time or temporary appointment meet the needs? If a change in enrollment or faculty workload is imminent, would it be more prudent to recruit a person for a fixed contract period with no assurance of an additional appointment? A department with large aspirations and a need for new positions may find its opportunities severely restricted by financial constraints. This problem needs to be identified as early as possible so that the chairperson can present the administration with the best arguments for new positions.

When a vacancy occurs and the requirements of the new position are in the process of being developed, the chairperson should circulate copies of the tentative job description to the departmental faculty so that they will be able to react to it. Perhaps a faculty member already in place has a mind to develop the very same specialty which is being sought. If it is learned that one of the current faculty members is interested in developing the desired specialty area, the chairperson should discuss the possibility with that individual *before* the job description is completed and the recruitment process is begun. The same advice holds if the chairperson learns that a faculty member wishes to teach the courses formerly taught by the person who vacated the position. This may be an opportunity to rekindle professional interest and energy within tired or bored faculty members by rotating them through different teaching assignments; assuming, of course, that they are qualified and other faculty members have no serious objections.

Affirmative Action Considerations

While the position description is being developed, and before any advertising or other active recruiting is undertaken, a copy of the latest affirmative action guidelines should be obtained from the office responsible for monitoring affirmative action in the institution. These guidelines often contain everything a chairperson needs to know about affirmative action procedures. It may be a requirement of the college or university that the department maintain a file of the recruitment activities in order to demonstrate that the process has been carried out fairly. Such a file should be started at the very beginning of the search and at a minimum should contain the following information which becomes a part of the department's affirmative action documentation.

1. the name and title of the person who will appoint a search and screening committee if one is to be constituted; if no committee is to be appointed, an exact description of the recruitment process should be included
2. the size and composition of the committee
3. the manner in which the committee chairperson is selected
4. in the absence of a screening committee, the name of the person responsible for seeing that the search is carried out properly and in a timely manner
5. the name and title of the staff person who maintains the documents and files of applicants
6. instructions to the file keeper concerning the removal of photographs and any other inappropriate information from the files
7. arrangements for obtaining and recording information about the race and sex of nominees and candidates to demonstrate that recruitment took place from a nondiscriminatory pool of applicants.

If the information suggested above is kept on file, the department will be able to document its response to any questions that may arise.

The Search and Screening Committee

It is a commonly accepted practice to constitute a search and screening committee whose task is to find applicants for a vacant position. The functions of the committee include: (1) seeking and finding qualified individuals who are interested in applying for the position; (2) receiving, reviewing, and evaluating the applications of the candidates; (3) interviewing qualified candidates; and (4) recommending the top candidates to the chairperson and dean. In searching for qualified individuals the committee is charged with the responsibility for actively seeking out and recruiting blacks, women, and other minority members. The committee also must use objective screening procedures, which insure fair and equitable treatment of all applicants, thus providing a basis for a legal defense against charges of discrimination, arbitrary, capricious, and unreasonable behaviors, or constitutionally impermissible activities. The size of the search committee is dependent on several factors but is usually made up of from three to seven individuals. When the duties of the vacant position cross departmental lines or involve close interaction with other departments or areas, the committee needs representation from those other departments or areas. If there are no black, female, or other minority members within the department who can be appointed to the committee, the appointer must seek such individuals elsewhere. If the vacancy is for a senior faculty member it may be desirable that the committee include senior faculty members from other areas. Often the search committee includes a student who is majoring in the specialty or area which the candidate will teach. The committee needs a chairperson, one who ordinarily is a member of the department in which the vacancy exists. Sometimes the committee elects its chairperson, but usually he or she is appointed by the department chairperson or the dean.

The function of the search and screening committee, like most departmental committees, is advisory. One of its first tasks is to review the job description for currency and completeness. The department chairperson should lead this review and revision, thus insuring that the committee members will be fully aware of the department's expectations for the next holder of the position. Having completed the review and made the necessary revisions, the committee can then prepare the vacancy announcements.

Position Vacancy Announcement

Two kinds of announcements need to be prepared. The first is a short statement used to advertise the position. The second is a longer detailed description which can be sent to all those who respond to the advertisements and to individuals who are thought to be possible candidates. In addition, copies may be sent to departments in other institutions and to members of professional associations.

The short statement, used as an advertisement, might include the following ingredients:
1. the name of the department and institution
2. the academic rank or ranks of the open position
3. minimum degree and experiential requirements for the applicant
4. description of special characteristics or expertise desired
5. brief description of teaching, research, and service responsibilities
6. whether the position is tenure-earning or for a fixed period of time
7. employment period—academic or calendar year
8. salary range or statement that salary is competitive
9. name, title, and address of person to whom inquiry should be made
10. closing date for application.

The longer detailed position description should repeat all the information contained in the advertisement, together with clear instructions on how to make application and submit credentials, and should be expanded to include all relevant information which the applicants need to know. The degrees offered by the department should be listed and if the department's name is ambiguous, the disciplines taught should be spelled out. If the position is nontenure-earning but the contract is renewable, it should be so stated, and the availability of any possible supplementary salary such as summer employment or overload work should be mentioned. If the location of the institution is not well known, a geographic description might be in order. General information about the institution need not be included in the short or long announcements; however, descriptive brochures, if available, might be sent to those who request them. If interviews will be held at a professional conference such as the Modern Language Association or the American Educational Research Association, specific dates and places need to be mentioned. Equal opportunity employers should state that fact in their advertisements. Generally, institutions that receive federal assistance or whose students receive federal aid fall into this category. A church-sponsored college that restricts its hiring to members of its faith should so indicate.

Instructions on applying and submitting credentials should be clear and precise. Applicants are usually asked to submit a letter of application, three or more letters of reference, and a current resumé or vita. In some cases the committee may wish to ask for a copy of the applicant's placement file from the institution that granted his or her advanced degree. Other materials or documents such as publications may be required as well.

It may be desirable to ask the candidate to include a written statement expressing his or her special qualifications in the letter of application. In some cases the applicant may be asked to state the earliest date employment could begin. When the salary is open, it may be appropriate to ask the candidate what expectations he or she holds and whether special conditions must be met before the applicant will accept the position.

The applicants need to be informed as to how many and what sorts of letters of reference are required. General letters of reference from a placement file are sometimes submitted by the applicant but are really not as useful as those expressly written for the purpose. Letters of reference should be current and are most valuable when they address the candidate's suitability for a particular position. Full mailing addresses and telephone numbers of the referees should be requested when references are to be checked.

If information not appearing on a standard resumé or vita is desired, it should be asked for. If there is interest in evaluating the quality as well as the quantity of publications, copies of recent published materials should be requested. If the position is in the field of music or the arts, specific instructions should be given concerning the shipment of tape recordings, photographs, slides, or artworks.

In their application materials, candidates should not be requested to submit information concerning their race, national origin, sex, age, possible handicap, family plans, maiden name, or any other items precluded under the affirmative action guidelines. However, for statistical purposes such information may be requested under separate cover by the person responsible for monitoring affirmative action procedures. The data thus gathered may not be linked to the individuals' applications.

Closing Dates

The closing date contained in the advertisement is the date after which no further applications are accepted. The practices surrounding this general rule may vary from institution to institution. In some cases, all the information requested must be postmarked by the announced closing date. In other cases, only the letter of application needs to be received by the closing date, while the supporting materials may be accepted up to the time the committee meets to evaluate the applications. Either way, the committee must decide on the policy it will follow and should so inform the applicants. Some position vacancies are announced with an application deadline listed as "open." If a desirable candidate applies for the position, it cannot be filled until another advertisement is published which announces a closing date. The closing date should not be sooner than one week after the publication of the announcement.

If no attractive candidates apply for the position by the time of the closing date, or a superior candidate appears after the closing date, the position must be readvertised with a new deadline before the latecomer or any other applicant may be considered. If the rank, salary, or other important aspect of the position is changed after advertising has begun or is completed, the changed position should be readvertised for at least two more weeks. Furthermore, no position should be filled, nor should a firm commitment be made to any candidate, before the application deadline date.

Where to Announce the Vacancy

In order to meet affirmative action guidelines and to conduct a meaningful search for possible candidates, search and screening committees must often go to great lengths in locating a variety of potential sources. Many institutions are regional in character and draw their faculty largely from residents of their own geographical area or from graduates of nearby universities. The composition of the faculty, then, frequently reflects the manpower situation of that region, which may not include many qualified minority or women candidates. In such cases, the committee must look beyond the traditional area in its effort to attract a wider variety of applicants. Even quite cosmopolitan departments may need to increase the numbers and kinds of institutions from which they have traditionally recruited faculty. An accurate record of these search efforts should be kept for accountability purposes.

Job registries are published by various agencies such as state departments of education, state postsecondary or higher education coordinating councils, and statewide equal employment job agencies. Such registries may have wide circulation, and departmental position vacancies should be listed with them. Departments in private institutions should check to see if their statewide or regional association of private universities and colleges maintains such a job registry and should announce their openings in it. Many disciplines and professions have active state and regional associations which publish position openings in their newsletters and journals, and search committees should take advantage of these opportunities. In addition, it may be possible to obtain membership lists or even purchase mailing labels from these associations in order to send announcements to the members. Of course, announcements should always be mailed to departments in the discipline that have graduate programs of quality.

Large, comprehensive institutions generally advertise in publications of national professional associations such as The American Psychological Association and The American Association for the Advancement of Science. In the last several years, *The Chronicle of Higher Education* has been used extensively to advertise position vacancies. The more specialized the desired competency, the greater is the need to consult the appropriate national discipline association. Here, too, one might be able to obtain a set of mailing labels to be used to contact a targeted set of potential candidates. Recognized leaders in the field are often able to suggest names of qualified individuals who may be ready for a change.

Most professional associations are committed to the principles of affirmative action and many maintain, as a service to colleges and universities, a list of qualified women and minority members who might be willing to consider a position vacancy. Professional associations, therefore, are a source of information that should not be overlooked. Announcements should also be sent to colleges and universities that predominantly serve blacks or women. The committee chairperson should work with the departmental staff to build a mailing list of institutions, departments, associations and key individuals who can be helpful in identifying a broad range of potential candidates.

Position Changes Which Need Not Be Advertised

In general, all instructional and research positions of a continuing nature which are half time or more need to be advertised following affirmative action guidelines. However, some positions do not need to be advertised, even in institutions with stringent guidelines. Following are examples, drawn from a list developed by the State University System of Florida, of positions "not required to be advertised."

1. promotion from assistant to associate professor
2. selection of chairperson or assistant chairperson, when the existing faculty serve on a rotating basis; however, external recruiting for a chairperson should be advertised
3. a principal investigator or recipient of a contract or grant
4. an existing position whose funding source has changed but whose duties remain the same, for example, a shift from a grant or contract to a regularly funded general budget; should the duties be redefined, the position needs to be advertised
5. visiting scholars or exchange professorships
6. positions less than half time during a term
7. "adjunct" or visiting or other temporary faculty who are not appointed for more than a year.

Record Keeping and Affirmative Action

Throughout our discussion we have mentioned the importance of keeping records of the search and screening process. Here is some additional information, along with a summary of what has been stated earlier. The records should be kept in a specific location, known to the departmental secretary, the department chairperson, and the search committee chairperson. A record of all mailings announcing the position should be maintained. When written inquiries about the position are received, they should be dated and stamped. When responding to these inquiries, a statement should be included explaining that persons found eligible to be considered for the position will be sent a survey form asking for information about their race and sex along with other data, which will be aggregated to document the affirmative action efforts of the committee.

When each application is received it should be dated and placed in an individual folder. Each applicant's folder should contain a checklist which can be used to determine quickly whether the file is complete. The application folders should be grouped alphabetically by last name. On the day after the application period closes, the head secretary should compile a master list of all persons who have made inquiry about the position vacancy. In preparation for the first meeting of the search committee following the closing date, someone should be assigned the task of inspecting the files and placing a mark beside the names of all persons whose files are incomplete. At this first meeting, the search committee should confirm that those files are indeed incomplete and retire them from further consideration for the time being. No photographs of candidates should be included in the files. They should be removed by the secretary opening the mail, labeled or tagged, and kept together in a separate file. If too much extraneous material is submitted by an applicant it should be pulled by the search committee chairperson and filed by the secretary along with the pictures. It is advisable that all records be kept for at least three years for each recruitment effort. The committee chairperson should contact the individual designated as the institutional affirmative action officer at the planning stage of the recruitment effort and stay in constant touch with this person to assure compliance with national and state policy as well as institutional regulations. It is also important that the affirmative action officer be sent copies of the advertisement and the long position vacancy announcement. In some instances this person must approve the advertising copy before it is sent out; the same approval may be required for the long announcement. Some institutions have developed a handbook containing a checklist of all the procedures that must be followed in the recruiting process. One or two copies of such a handbook, if available, should be obtained for members of the search committee early in the process.

Separating Ineligible from Eligible Applicants—The First Screening

The search committee now has the difficult task of reviewing and evaluating applicants on the basis of written information contained in each applicant's file. The committee may decide in advance to declare ineligible for consideration those applicants whose files are still incomplete by a certain date. On the other hand, the committee may decide that in the case of incomplete files, missing documents will be requested if the information thus far received suggests that the applicant has strong qualifications. Fairness would dictate, however, that if such a request were made, it should be made of every applicant with an incomplete file. The lack of a terminal degree such as a doctorate may also be sufficient reason for not considering an application. This requirement is sometimes waived for individuals who are otherwise well qualified and can certify that their degrees will be received by a certain date.

Other reasons for finding candidates ineligible may be related to the inability of applicants to meet state and institutional regulations. For example, many institutions have a nepotism rule which forbids hiring relatives or dependents of the department chairperson or dean. Often, this rule applies only to those who would be under direct supervision of a relative already employed. Some institutions follow a strict policy of not hiring their own graduates because they fear the consequences of academic inbreeding. Other objections to hiring one's own products are based on the well-known tendency of senior professors to continue to direct their former students' activities rather than accept them as equals. Conversely, there are institutions that deliberately employ selected alumni who have made names for themselves elsewhere. Such alumni, it is claimed, identify with and understand the traditions of their alma mater better than outsiders. Many institutions which forbid the hiring of their own graduates allow exceptions to be made in special circumstances, such as a need for a temporary faculty member to fill a sudden vacancy or the lack of resources to recruit an outside candidate.

Mention should be made of a class of applicants who are particularly annoying. There are individuals who state in a letter that "if you are seriously interested in me I will send . . ." an updated vita, letters of reference, or whatever to complete their applications. These persons are game players who are trying to place themselves in an advantaged position before the competition gets underway. If the committee chairperson responds with an indication of interest, it may create false expectations on the part of the applicant and raise questions of fairness to other applicants with incomplete files.

During the first screening, the files of candidates may be separated into three categories. Some candidates are clearly "ineligible" in terms of qualifications or institutional or departmental policies; others are "eligible" and still others are "marginal" in that their files may not be complete or they do not quite meet all of the criteria for eligibility. The files of those who have been declared ineligible should be set aside and a note containing the reason for the ineligibility should be inserted in each file. It is not yet appropriate to send letters of rejection to the ineligible applicants.

Evaluating the Qualifications of Eligible and Marginal Candidates—The Second Screening

Now the committee members read the files carefully and prepare for the second cut. During this review, the committee decides how well each applicant meets the criteria and the desired job qualifications listed in the position announcement. Search committees frequently develop a checklist that members can use when reviewing the application materials. Some committee members find it easier to arrive at an overall rating of individual applicants if separate ratings can be given to each of a number of items on a well-developed list. Such a list contains items concerning past experience, letters of recommendation, and every agreed upon criterion contained in the long position vacancy announcement. Several copies of the checklist, at least one for every committee member, are placed in each applicant's folder.

At present, given the condition of the academic market place, there is likely to be a veritable flood of applicants for each advertised position. A large number of these applicants may submit all the required credentials and documents but do not provide evidence that they meet the specified required characteristics. Many who do not meet the formal requirements believe they may be qualified by virtue of their special experiences in previous positions. Others want to move from where they are just to get away, and still others want a first-time, full-time job in academe. Those who do not meet the expected criteria should be declared ineligible and have the reasons for their ineligibility noted in their files. Examples of reasons are "inappropriate specialization," "wrong degree," "insufficient experience," "no teaching experience," and "too little research." It may be the case that most of the applicants are ill qualified and that the list of eligible candidates is disappointing.

The search committee may then decide to consider the "marginal" candidates, those who do not quite meet all of the criteria but nevertheless appear to have better-than-average qualifications. Marginals who are retained will be considered again in the third screening along with all other eligible candidates who are still in contention. In reviewing application materials, the committee members should keep in mind the affirmative action policies of the institution. As many women and minority candidates as possible should be retained in the "eligible" or "marginal" category for consideration in the third screening. If a committee is unable to identify a sufficient number of well-qualified candidates from the pool of "eligible" or "marginal" applicants, the committee may consider modifying the eligibility criteria. Affirmative action policies may then dictate that the position needs to be readvertised.

Formal agreement by the committee to use the advertised position characteristics as criteria needs to be taken seriously by the members and adhered to religiously unless unusual circumstances intervene. The search committee may need to decide in advance how it will proceed when it feels that equity and fairness would be served if it altered its own policies. Only rarely does a set of procedures cover all contingencies, even when expert guidance is used in their development. A search committee might agree that any of its procedures may be temporarily changed by a unanimous, or nearly unanimous, vote and submission of a written resolution explaining the perceived need.

A policy of this kind might enable the committee to consider a good potential applicant who might otherwise be excluded on procedural grounds.

The chairperson of the search committee with the help of committee members should once again screen the files of all applicants who have survived the second screening to ensure that they are sufficiently worthy to be included in the third screening. If any additional unqualified applicants are found, their files should be reviewed by the entire committee and differing interpretations should be worked out. A secret ballot may be needed to resolve a genuinely sticky case. Some of these cases might be handled by designating them as "marginals," which would automatically move them to the third stage of consideration. Those applicants who do not survive the second screening, for whatever reasons, should be noted on the master list of applicants and their files pulled from further consideration. The remaining applicants have now been judged to meet the minimum set of requirements for the position and will become the official pool of "nominees" from which the best qualified will be selected.

Selection of the Finalists—The Third Screening

Each search committee member working individually now will need to read each nominee's file and select the top six to ten candidates. The chairperson should collect a copy of each committee member's list and compile them into an aggregate table of choices. The resulting table becomes the focus of the next meeting of the committee, at which each committee member explains his or her choices and discusses their strengths and weaknesses. The chairperson next should attempt to develop a consensus about the rank order position for each nominee. The object of this meeting is to select the top three nominees, any of whom would be clearly acceptable to the faculty. The chairperson of the search committee should then draft a memorandum to the department chairperson listing the names of those nominees being recommended along with their strengths and weaknesses. If only one or two are clearly consensus nominees, then only those names should be submitted.

Checking the References

Upon receiving the search committee's memorandum and the accompanying files, the department chairperson is ready to start checking each of the recommended nominee's references. This is usually done by telephone. The number of references to be checked will depend on the kinds of responses obtained from the referees. At least three should be contacted. What should one search for in these telephone checks? Initially, level of competence, promise of career growth, ability to work with colleagues and students, outstanding achievement, other strengths, and such weaknesses as missing classes, not completing work on time, student complaints, etcetera.

If conversations with three referees do not provide clear answers to these questions, then additional ones should be called until clear answers are obtained. If comments from some referees cause other questions to be raised, or if the nominee is described as nearly perfect, then it is appropriate to "network" a larger set of referees by asking the original ones for the names and telephone numbers of two other persons who would know the nominee, and if still more information is needed, asking this second group for a third list. The department chairperson may ask members of the search committee to make some of the telephone calls.

One of the more common difficulties facing a chairperson is how to check references of nominees who don't want their current employers to know that they are contemplating a move. In such cases, recommended nominees must be informed that they are being considered and be given the opportunity to drop the names of certain referees temporarily. It may be that a nominee's colleagues, except for the department chairperson and dean, could be called at this time. Similarly, if a nominee's letters of reference were written more than two years previously, he or she should be asked to provide more current ones. Some referees have nothing positive to say about anyone, whereas others will make only laudatory comments about everyone. To obtain information that will be helpful in evaluating the candidates, it is important to be able to identify the response style of the referee and to ask questions that will elicit useful answers. A member of the search committee or the department chairperson should prepare a written summary of what has been learned in these telephone reference checks.

One of the nagging fears of a search committee, department chairperson, college dean, and the dean of faculties is that a genuinely undesirable person will be hired. The kinds of personal conduct that cause the most problems and should be listened for in these interviews are: pernicious irascibility, mental health problems, alcoholism, criminal behavior, dismissal from a college or university in the last five years, and disciplinary action in the last two or three years. Persons found to be described with any of these problems need some evidence of being fully qualified and rehabilitated to be seriously considered for appointment.

Conceivably a nominee may have to be dropped from consideration as a result of the reference checks. Minor discrepancies in important characteristics can be pursued directly with the nominee over the phone or personally if he or she is invited to visit the campus.

Before Inviting the Candidate to the Campus

Toward the end of the final screening, the credentials of those candidates likely to be invited to the campus for an interview should be verified. Institutions from which they obtained degrees can easily be contacted to verify that the degrees have been conferred. Similarly, previous titles and ranks of nominees can be checked by contacting institutions where they were formerly employed. If there is a period of time unaccounted for in the employment record of the individual or if there is a long period between degrees, it is appropriate to ask the candidate to explain these time gaps. In most instances credentials provided by the candidates will be genuine. However, when such is not the case, the situation can be traumatic and embarrassing to the department and indeed the entire university, especially if the discrepancies are not discovered until one or more years after an appointment has been made.

Once again the departmental expectations should be compared with the candidate's qualifications and career objectives. A primarily research oriented person will not be happy in a position which requires that most of his or her time be spent teaching, and conversely a primarily teaching oriented person would be unhappy in a position which requires a major research output. To mismatch people in this way would be a disservice to the candidate and to the department. Yet mismatches sometimes occur.

As soon as the final group of nominees has been checked, the support staff should send a package of materials to them *before* they are invited to the campus for a visit. The materials should include such items as a faculty handbook, an institutional catalog, a copy of the collective bargaining agreement if one exists, a minimal description of the governance of the institution, any separate statements about a continuing contract or tenure status, opportunities for career advancement, academic freedom, grievance procedures, nature of the annual contract, budgetary facts, personnel policies, fringe benefits, and patent and copyright policies. Many of the latter items are contained in faculty handbooks, faculty constitutions, or bargaining agreements.

Before extending invitations to recommended nominees, the department chairperson should confer with the dean to make sure that the original approval to initiate the recruitment is still valid. Sometimes institutions undergo financial difficulty or policy changes after the initial approval was given. In such cases, the dean may try to persuade the department to fill the position temporarily with a part-time person, or postpone filling it for one year—which is less than what was first promised. Also, under certain circumstances the dean might suggest that the search committee review the pool of applicants once again to see if a woman or minority person can be recommended—or perhaps a qualified younger person with whom students can identify more closely. A department chairperson who regularly keeps the dean up to date on the progress of the recruiting effort is likely to learn of any funding problems or policy changes that might have occurred in the interim. Moreover, a dean who is kept informed of the results of the various screenings is more likely to accept the recommendations of the search committee. In any event it is usually the dean who must authorize travel expenses for candidates who are invited to the campus for an interview. With the dean's approval reaffirmed, the department chairperson can start inviting them to visit the campus.

The invitation is usually extended in a telephone conversation and a follow-up letter of confirmation. The telephone conversation provides the department chairperson with an opportunity to find out if the candidate is still interested in the position. The chairperson also has the opportunity to ask questions that have been raised by the search committee and to make sure that the candidate understands the pay range, rank, and other vital data about the position. Some departments expect each candidate to make a formal presentation to the faculty members during the visit regarding his or her areas of expertise and interest. If such is the case, the format of the presentation can be discussed in the telephone conversation. And finally, a mutually acceptable date for the visit can be scheduled.

The Campus Visit and the Interview

If more than one candidate is to be invited to the campus, schedules should be developed so that there is at least a day's interval between visits. Each candidate should be interviewed by the department head, members of the search committee individually or as a group, faculty members with whom he or she will be working, student representatives, the dean, and perhaps a member of the central administration. It is important that candidates be made to feel welcome and at ease, and that common courtesies be extended. If possible, candidates should be met at the airport and escorted to their appointments. Otherwise, they may conclude that there is a lack of serious interest in them or that the institution is a cold and unfriendly place. If time permits, they should be taken on a tour of the city and shown appropriate residential areas and other interesting and attractive features of the community. A candidate who, for salary or other reasons, has not yet decided whether to accept the offer, may choose to do so because of the warmth and friendliness communicated by the faculty and administrators.

When conducting interviews, a recommended technique is the use of open-ended questions. Such questions elicit detailed responses from candidates rather than "yes" or "no" answers, which are neither revealing nor constructive. For example, if candidates are asked whether they enjoyed their last job, a simple yes or no is not helpful. If on the other hand, they are asked, "What did you enjoy about your last job?", their responses may provide insight into their character. Other examples of closed- and open-ended questions are:

Closed-ended Questions	Open-ended Questions
Did you apply for this position because of the research opportunities?	What was it that led you to apply for this position?
Do you feel that you are qualified for this position?	Describe your feelings on how well qualified you are for this position.
Have you ever had personality clashes with your colleagues?	All in all, how do you feel about the people you work with in your present (or previous) position?
Have you been required to demonstrate leadership?	In what ways have you been required to demonstrate leadership in the past?

An arrangement that can make the interview more effective is to have the chairperson or a member of the search committee sit through each of the scheduled sessions or meetings. This person can make the proper introductions and summarize the candidate's qualifications and interests for the benefit of those who have not had access to the application folder.

During the interview, it is important to avoid asking certain questions that violate fair employment practices. Such unlawful questions include direct inquiries about national origin, and whether one is naturalized or native born. Questions about nationality, race, or religious affiliations, or the religious affiliation of schools attended, are also unlawful. It is improper to inquire about family planning, size of family, ages of children, child care plans, and spouse's employment or salary. One may not inquire about military service in countries other than the United States or request military service records. One should not inquire about ancestry, the birthplace of applicants' parents, grandparents, or spouses, about clubs and organizations to which applicants belong, about medical history of pregnancies, and other health matters.

The overall criterion is to avoid asking nonjob-related questions, the answers to which would provide information that could be used as a basis for unlawful discrimination.

It is permissible to inquire into the place and length of current and previous addresses, to ask if an individual is or intends to become a U. S. citizen, and if the spouse is a citizen. The candidates may be asked whether they have any criminal convictions which may have a bearing on job performance, but they may not be asked about arrests. Instead of asking about family size or family responsibilities, it is proper to inquire about freedom to travel if required by the job, and ability to meet work schedules. If any candidate is asked lawful questions about convictions, ability to travel, anticipated absences, or disabilities that may affect performance, *all* candidates must be asked those questions.

Many excellent guides for effective interviewing are available. For those who prefer a handy checklist, here in paraphrased form is one taken from the *Handbook for Search and Screening Committees at Florida State University (1980).*

1. Avoid interruptions. Do not take telephone calls during the interview.
2. Treat each candidate as a unique individual.
3. Provide a good first impression of the department, college and university. Be prompt, adhere to the schedule, and provide an attractive location for the interview.
4. Listen carefully to what the candidate has to say; do not dominate the conversation.
5. Avoid unlawful questions and those not job-related.
6. Avoid entering into arguments with candidates.
7. Do not make promises that cannot be kept.
8. Conduct the interview in private and assure the candidates of the confidentiality of the information they provide.
9. Allow sufficient time for the interview, for movement between meetings, and for refreshment and restroom stops.
10. Ask questions about the candidates' ideas, philosophies, or achievements in lieu of direct questions about their attitudes.
11. Avoid lengthy notetaking during the interview. If necessary, expand notes and complete rating forms promptly after the interview.
12. Try not to turn the interview into an interrogation. Rather than launch a barrage of questions, make interesting and appropriate comments which stimulate the candidate to respond.
13. Try to avoid making hasty judgments about the candidate based solely on appearance or mannerisms—ask the candidates questions, answers to which may help dispel negative impressions.
14. Do not show impatience when the candidate does not seem to

be responding in the manner expected. Ask open-ended questions which may help the candidate to come around to the point
of information being sought.

The search committee chairperson may desire to prepare and distribute a simple evaluation form to each of the interviewers. The form
might list those characteristics to be evaluated and provide space for
written comments. Interviewers should be reminded to observe and be
prepared to comment on the behavior and mannerisms of the candidates.

- Does the candidate look better on paper than in person? If so,
  what personal characteristics contributed to a negative impres-
  sion?
- How did the candidate's energy level appear? Active? Normal?
  Lethargic?
- Did the candidate's body stance give the impression that he or she
  was nervous, relaxed, unsure, confused, defensive, or rigid?
- What was seen in the candidate's facial expressions? Openness?
  Arrogance? Puzzlement? Pleasantness? Boredom? Alertness?
- Were the expected weaknesses of the candidate confirmed by the
  interview? Were other weaknesses apparent?
- Were strengths confirmed? Were new strengths revealed? Did the
  candidate show genuine promise?
- Did the interview reveal any unexpected problems?

The chairperson of the search committee should promptly collect the
written evaluations of the interview so that the committee can use them
in its deliberations.

The Dean's Choice

The department chairperson sends the dean a memorandum containing the list of recommended candidates. A complete file with
credentials and references for each person should accompany the memorandum. Generally, a dean will prefer to receive the list in alphabeti-
cal rather than rank order. There are subtle ways in which the department chairperson can let the dean know what the search committee really felt about each candidate. The most obvious is to describe the impressions that were made during the interviews. The dean, of course,
will want to know whether any of the candidates is a woman or a
member of a minority group. After discussing the matter with the chairperson and upon due deliberation, the dean will rank order those persons who are recommended and give the chairperson permission to
make a job offer to the leading one.

The Job Offer

The chairperson usually makes the job offer by telephone. During the phone call the chairperson reiterates the proposed salary, the rank, and the date of appointment. Often, the candidate may ask for some time to make a final decision; and a week or two should be sufficient for this purpose. It is not uncommon for candidates to seek counteroffers from their current institutions, or from other institutions with whom they may be negotiating. If the chairperson at the offering institution knows or suspects that this is the case, he or she must decide whether the candidate is so valuable that additional inducements should be offered. These inducements could take the form of higher salary, moving expenses, or released time for scholarly activities. It is possible that there are no additional inducements available, and the candidate must be persuaded on the basis of intangibles such as the quality of life in the university or the community. In any event, the chairperson should insist on a decision by a fixed date.

There is always the possibility that a candidate will not accept an offer. In fact, it is possible that the top three candidates may, one after another, reject it. A desired counteroffer at the home university, a perceived better opportunity at another institution, or other conditions may lead all of them to turn the offer down. It would be unfortunate if the turndowns occur because the department is making the mistake of trying to recruit out of its league or creating negative impressions about itself.

For the candidate who does accept, several things need to be made clear. First, a letter will be sent making the formal job offer, to which the candidate should respond promptly and affirmatively. Second, a contract may be forthcoming, but only after a board of trustees or regents approves the proposed contract. If a letter of intent to employ is signed by a dean or other college official, the candidate may begin to make plans to move to the new institution. However, until the *official contract* is received and signed by the candidate, he or she is not legally bound to the new position nor can the candidate be absolutely certain of being employed at the new institution; and the candidate should be so informed. Obviously, the department chairperson or secretary should follow the progress of the appointment papers, the payroll forms, and the contract as they move through the institutional bureaucracy. A candidate who is relatively assured of being appointed needs to find housing, arrange for children's schooling, etcetera. The department should arrange for one or two faculty members or their spouses to help the candidate identify a desirable residential area. The new faculty member should be encouraged to move to to the area two weeks or a month before the term begins, if possible. This will give the new person time to adjust to the community as well as to the new institution and department.

Terminating the Search

After a search has been completed, letters need to be sent to the original applicants. It is important to indicate only that a person was found who best met the needs of the department. Written comments about the rejected person's capabilities could result in misinterpretation, arguments, and lawsuits and therefore should not be included in the notification. The chairperson should be thoroughly conversant with the requirements for compiling, submitting, and storing the records of each recruitment effort. Some institutions will not process appointment papers for the selected candidate until the affirmative action file of the search is complete. Generally, a three-year holding period is sufficient for records of a search, and a specific place may be designated for final disposition of these records.

In the event the search was unsuccessful it is still necessary to compile a complete set of records. These can be helpful later if the search is reopened. At present it seems necessary to notify each of the former applicants when a search is reopened and to ask them whether they wish to be considered again. It is apparent from actual experience that such a communication tends to raise the hopes of many persons who were previously judged unqualified or unsuitable. Many applicants evidently are not sophisticated enough to realize that if they were not called or invited to campus during the first search they stand little chance the second time around. On the other hand, if the second search specifies lower criteria for the position, some of the previous applicants may qualify as candidates or nominees. Also, it may be the case that other former applicants who in the meantime have had articles and books published may have upgraded their qualifications. If the initial search is unsuccessful, it is important not to send out letters of rejection until a decision has been made to terminate the search. If the search is to be reopened, all former applicants must be notified and the search process must begin again at its first phase.

In summary, recruitment should be an integral part of a long-range departmental plan which includes a clearly defined set of goals. As part of the planning process, departments should keep an inventory of current faculty specializations and competencies as well as a list of other areas which need to be developed, including projected time frames for their development. A central part of any recruiting effort is the commitment to principles of equal opportunity and affirmative action. Clearly written affirmative action procedures need to be developed and followed and careful records of the process need to be kept. Departments should make special efforts to expand the traditional pool of qualified applicants so that more women and minority members are considered.

A search committee must be established according to set criteria and should conduct its business in an orderly and planned manner. Part of its responsibility is to advertise a vacant position properly and screen all applicants. The task of the committee is less onerous if it is directed by a specified set of policies and procedures for evaluating all application materials, screening applicants, and designating those deemed best qualified. During the search process and subsequent candidate interviews, it is as important for the institution to make a good impression on potential faculty members as it is for these faculty members to demonstrate their best attributes. Choosing the right person is more important now than ever before in light of increasing economic problems, changing curricula, reduced enrollments, and the great difficulties encountered when attempting to discharge unsatisfactory and nonproductive colleagues. There is a strong likelihood that the person selected today may be a member of the department for a very long time to come.

Exercise

Assume that you have a new dean who has been appointed because of his proven ability to maximize productivity in an academic institution. He has been charged by the president to review programs of all departments and divisions and to prepare a ten-year plan which will accommodate the personnel needs of the next ten years. In carrying out his charge, the dean requests each chairperson of a department or division to submit a report containing personnel needs over the next ten years. The dean wants to know what areas of expertise are presently represented by the current faculty members, in what areas there will be a decreased need, and what new areas of expertise need to be added. He specifically asks for:

1. The names of faculty members currently in the department and their areas of expertise.
2. The best guess as to who will still be in the department in ten years; if not, when will they leave?

3. What new areas of expertise will be needed? How and when do you plan to add them? How many full or part-time faculty will be required?
4. How are affirmative action policies and procedures included in your plan?
5. How does your plan relate the mission and goals of the department and institution?

Your assignment is to prepare a report for submission to the dean including answers to his questions and whatever else you think the dean should know. You get the impression from the tone of the dean's request that the contents of this report will be given serious consideration in budget allocation.

References

BRAITHWAITE, RONALD L., AND BEATTY, LULA. "Minority Male Participation in Educational Research and Development: A Recruitment Selection Dilemma." *Journal of Negro Education, 50* (Fall 1981), pp. 389–400.

CAPLOW, THEODORE, AND MCGEE, REECE J. *The Academic Marketplace.* Garden City, N.Y.: Doubleday, 1958.

CARNEGIE COUNCIL ON POLICY STUDIES IN HIGHER EDUCATION. *Making Affirmative Action Work in Higher Education: An Analysis of Institutional and Federal Policies with Recommendations.* San Francisco: Jossey-Bass, 1975.

FLEMING, JOHN E.; GILL, GERALD R.; AND SWINTON, DAVID H. *The Case for Affirmative Action.* Washington, D.C.: Howard University Press, 1978.

FLORIDA STATE UNIVERSITY. *Handbook for Search and Screening Committees.* Tallahassee: Human Affairs Office, Florida State University, 1980.

GADDY, DALE. *Faculty Recruitment.* Washington, D.C.: American Association of Junior Colleges, 1969.

KING, CHARLES W. "Improving the Academic Level of Church College Faculties." *Improving College and University Teaching, 24* (Autumn 1976), pp. 219–20.

LEWIN, ARIE Y., AND DUCHAN, LINDA. "Women in Academia: A Study of the Hiring Decision in Departments of Physical Science." *Science 173* (Sept. 1971), pp. 892–95.

LINNELL, ROBERT H. "Age, Sex and Ethnic Trade-Offs in Faculty Employment: You Can't Have Your Cake and Eat It Too." *Current Issues in Higher Education 4* (1979), pp. 3–9.

MARCUS, LAWRENCE R. "Has Advertising Produced Results in Faculty Hiring?" *Educational Record 57* (1977), pp. 247–50.

MITCHELL, JOYCE M., AND STARR, RACHEL R. "A Regional Approach for Analyzing the Recruitment of Academic Women." *American Behavioral Scientist 15* (Nov.-Dec. 1971), pp. 183–205.

MOORE, WILLIAM, JR., AND WAGSTAFF, LONNIE H. *Black Educators in White Colleges*. San Francisco: Jossey-Bass, 1974.

PINEGREE, SUZANNE, ET AL. "Anti-Nepotism's Ghost: Attitudes of Administrators Toward Hiring Professional Couples." *Psychology of Women Quarterly 3* (Fall 1978), pp. 23–29.

ROOD, HAROLD J. "Legal Issues in Faculty Termination." *Journal of Higher Education 63* (1977), pp. 123–52.

SANDLER, BERNICE RESNICK. "You've Come a Long Way Maybe—Or Why It Still Hurts to be a Woman in Labor." *Current Issues in Higher Education 4* (1979), pp. 11–14.

STECKLEIN, JOHN E., AND LATHROP, ROBERT L. *Faculty Attraction and Retention*. Minneapolis: Bureau of Institutional Research, University of Minnesota, 1960.

WAGGAMAN, JOHN S. "Faculty Recruitment, Retention, and Fair Employment: Obligations and Opportunities." ASHE-ERIC/Higher Education Research Report No. 2. Washington, D.C.: Association for the Study of Higher Education, 1983.

"Why Women Ph.D's Advance More Slowly." *Science News 20* (Nov. 7, 1981), p. 294.

6

Department Decision Making and Bringing about Change

Every department, at some time or another, has to make decisions. The matters to be decided vary considerably, ranging from issues of great import to more transient ones. Departments must make decisions about larger issues—such as priorities, goals, and the allocation of department resources—as well as smaller issues, including the extent to which the department should become active in off-campus programs, the allocation of travel funds, and the teaching load of department faculty members.

The examples listed above are familiar ones. The list could be expanded to include decisions about personnel problems, budgetary problems, interpersonal problems, organizational problems, and so on. A study of the decision-making process reveals that most decisions are based on the use of a simple problem-solving model. Ordinarily when a person becomes aware that a problem exists, the first step is to identify and clarify the nature of the problem. Then a list of possible solutions can be formulated. (The possibility of doing nothing is frequently the first item on the list.) Thinking about solutions generally leads to a consideration of the possible consequences of each alternative. A person decides which solution seems most likely to produce the desired results and then proceeds to carry it out.

In the academic department, there are times when several decisions must be made simultaneously and other times when only a single, though difficult, decision must be made. Within this context, some chairpersons come to think of themselves as firemen, rushing about trying to extinguish small fires before they become conflagrations. Others fail to see the first signs of impending difficulties and react only after a crisis has occurred. Although the chairperson's personality greatly influences his or her approach to decision making, he or she can consciously adopt methods that seem best suited to the problem.

The chairperson must take the lead in deciding if things are to change or stay the same in the face of the exigencies of academic life. The questions of how to decide and who is to be involved in the decision-making process are difficult and perplexing. Most administrators recognize the desirability of involving faculty members and students in the problem-solving and decision-making processes. Nevertheless, many problems do not permit a great deal of faculty or student participation, simply because they must be dealt with swiftly. In any event, the question of the degree of faculty and student involvement in department decision making is one that most chairpersons must address.

The degree of faculty and student involvement in department decision making is often related to the chairperson's attitude and style. (A chairperson's mode of operation is probably also related to personality variables that need not be discussed here.) The chairperson's style of department leadership can range across a broad continuum, from extremely authoritarian or autocratic to extremely democratic.

The variety of styles within these extremes has been described by Robert Tannenbaum and Warren H. Schmidt in their article "How to Choose a Leadership Pattern." Summarized below is their list of leadership styles. Notice that the styles become more democratic and less autocratic, more relationship-oriented and less task- or directive-oriented, as we proceed down the list.

1. *The chairperson makes the decision and announces it.* The chairperson identifies the problem, evaluates alternative solutions, chooses one of them, and announces to the faculty which solution will be implemented. Little faculty participation is encouraged.

2. *The chairperson makes the decision and tries to sell it.* The chairperson recognizes that his or her decision may not be accepted outright by all concerned. He or she seeks to reduce any resistance by indicating what the faculty will gain.

3. *The chairperson makes the decision and invites questions.* The chairperson seeks acceptance of his or her decision by helping the faculty understand it by means of a question-and-answer session.

4. *The chairperson presents a tentative decision subject to change.* This style permits the faculty to exert some influence on the decision.

5. *The chairperson presents the problem, gets suggestions, and makes the decision.* The chairperson comes to the faculty with a problem that he or she has identified and analyzed but has not solved. He or she asks the faculty for suggestions; however, all understand that the final decision is the chairperson's.

6. *The chairperson defines the limits and asks the faculty to make the decision within these limits.* The chairperson delegates to the faculty (including himself or herself) the freedom to make the final

decision. Before doing so, however, the chairperson states the problem as he or she sees it and sets the boundaries, or areas of freedom, within which the decision can be made.

7. *The chairperson permits the faculty to make the decision within broadly defined limits.* This situation occurs when problems are vague and require a high degree of freedom of exploration if creative solutions are to be found. Only broad limits are imposed and the chairperson, if he or she participates at all, participates as an equal.

Criteria for Degree of Faculty Involvement

The continuum of leadership styles suggests that chairpersons can perform their functions in a variety of ways. Although many believe, as a matter of principle, that faculty and student involvement in decision making should be maximized, the truth of the matter is that not all faculty members and students can be, should be, or should even wish to be involved in every decision a chairperson makes. Do any guidelines or rules exist that suggest when faculty members and students should be asked to participate in the decision-making process?

When problems confront a department and decisions must be made, the chairperson might ask himself or herself several basic questions that can help determine the degree to which the faculty should be involved. These questions are based on three relevant criteria:

- *Expertise*—Who knows how to solve the problem? The chairperson alone? A particular faculty member or group within the department? The whole department?
- *Acceptance*—Is faculty acceptance of the decision crucial for effective implementation? Will implementation fail if the faculty refuses to go along with the decision?
- *Time*—Is there enough time to get the faculty involved in the process of decision making? Is the issue so crucial that an immediate decision is necessary?

While these criteria are logically independent of one another, they should all be considered when an important problem or issue arises. It would be possible to construct a matrix of hypothetical issues, with different values for each criterion, but instead we will discuss each criterion separately.

Expertise. Some decisions require expertise in specific areas. If the chairperson possesses such expertise, he or she is perfectly capable of making a decision alone. Lacking that expertise, the chairperson may seek it from faculty members in the department and should not hesitate to call on those who have experience and interests in areas connected with the problems to be addressed. Frequently the expertise needed for rational decision making may be found outside the department, within the institution, and is available for the asking. Sometimes simple pride or fear of asking for help can prevent a chairperson from using staff resources wisely and advantageously.

Acceptance. Some decisions, important or not, require that the department faculty accept them if they are to be carried out. Important decisions that affect the well-being or survival of the department will require the faculty's acceptance if they are to be implemented. Some decisions that are seen as unimportant are readily accepted by the faculty, who is grateful not to have been bothered with them. In such instances, the chairperson can make the decision alone or delegate the matter to a staff member. On the other hand, some seemingly unimportant decisions may require faculty involvement in order to gain acceptance. The chairperson must rely on his or her judgment to evaluate the faculty members' mood.

People willingly participate in an activity when they can see the benefits that accrue from a common endeavor, when they see the department's success as synonymous with their own. On the other hand, the most benign and rational decision can be resisted, subverted, or diverted by a group if it feels that it had no share in making the decision. What better way is there to encourage faculty members to accept and implement decisions than to have them participate in the process of making decisions?

Time. Occasionally problems arise and decisions must be made with great speed. In the context of modern bureaucratic organizations, opportunities arise that must be seized without hesitation or they will be lost. The chairperson must judge whether an immediate decision is better than no decision at all.

Implementing Change

The three criteria we have been discussing—expertise, acceptance, and time—vary in importance according to circumstance. Considering these criteria when the question of faculty involvement arises will help a chairperson decide whether, in those particular circumstances, the faculty ought to be involved. A related problem is *how* faculty members can be encouraged to participate in the decision-making process. Some are ready and eager to be involved in department problem solving, while others show little interest in sharing in the hard work that is a part of intelligent decision making. No single method of involving faculty members in the decision-making process is best. Departments vary considerably in size, tradition, role and mission, and the personalities and skills of their members. Each chairperson's decisions about the methods and techniques of faculty involvement must take into account the special, often idiosyncratic, characteristics of the department. Nevertheless, each chairperson must determine whether a matter should be brought to a meeting of the full faculty, referred to a committee, discussed informally with faculty members, or acted upon according to his or her own best judgment. These determinations depend partly on how the chairperson views his or her role and partly on his or her experience in working with each option.

Most department chairpersons, on the basis of their past experience, choose to share the decision-making process with their faculty members for the following reasons. First, faculty members will have to implement almost any decision the chairperson makes and are therefore more likely to be cooperative if they are involved in making the decision. Second, as mentioned earlier, individual faculty members often have expertise or experience to contribute to the decision-making process. Third, when conflicts do occur, resolving them in the context of open discussion is less disruptive than neglecting them altogether and possibly causing them to multiply unnecessarily. Finally, department decisions take place within the broader contexts of academe and a democratic society. The university, as an institution, has a long tradition of collegiality; the idea of a community of scholars is compatible with processes of shared decision making by equals.

Some department decisions can be implemented only by first changing a specific policy or procedure. Change, it has been said, is society's only constant. Certainly a huge number of changes have taken place in colleges and universities in recent years, and these changes reflect changes in society as a whole.

In most social groups, a creative tension exists between forces that operate to bring about change and forces that operate to resist change. Although the American education system in general and institutions of higher education in particular are conservative and resistive of change, the continuous pressures of political and social events demand responses, and these responses result in a good deal of change. During the turbulent sixties, it seemed as if the pressures for a thorough democratization of educational curriculum and governance would revolutionize the structure of higher education. The seventies showed a great decline in student unrest, and many predictions of the preceding decade failed to materialize. Nevertheless, there is now a good deal more student participation in academic affairs than occurred in the fifties and sixties—for example, students now sit on boards of regents and on many academic committees.

Economic uncertainties and declining enrollments have combined to threaten the optimistic predictions of unlimited growth in the power, size, and influence of academic institutions. In fact, in many instances, programs and institutions are themselves threatened. The demands of minorities, particularly blacks and women, have led to numerous changes in school policy and procedure. The rise of teacher militancy at the elementary and secondary level has been followed by increasing unionization in many colleges and university systems. Changes in technology have led to changes in instructional techniques; educational television and computer-assisted instruction are becoming more common. These are but a few of the many pressures toward change that come from within and outside the college. Therefore, to ask what changes will be required is more realistic than to ask whether change will be required.

Departments have been and are subjected to many pressures for change from within and without the institution. The discussion of decision making is related to the kinds of change departments will be required to make. The chairperson's role in bringing about needed change can be central in determining whether change is indeed desirable, in planning for change, and in providing leadership in the process of implementing change.

While the question of change and the problems of implementing it can be easily discussed and the need for change readily acknowledged, the actual processes of bringing about change are quite perplexing. The results of some social science research suggests that many methods used to effect changes in human behavior are quite inefficient.

Amitai Etzioni, who has investigated problems of change, argues that attempts to effect behavioral change in humans through educational and advertising methods may not be successful unless there are accompanying changes in the environment. In his article "Human Beings Are Not Very Easy to Change, After All," he cites failures in antismoking campaigns, alcohol and drug abuse programs, and traffic safety programs that depended primarily on advertising and propagandizing. He then contrasts these failures with efforts that succeeded in altering behavior when persons were removed from situations or environments that contributed to the problem in the first place. In discussing the dismal failures of the intensive educational campaigns to help disadvantaged children, Etzioni concludes that educational programs will continue to fail as long as the children's total environments are unchanged. Change has been implemented successfully when persons *willingly* enter a new social community. Etzioni suggests that the total change approach, exemplified by people who join a kibbutz or an organization like Alcoholics Anonymous, is often successful. While total change appeals to a radical perspective, it obviously works only with volunteers, and many persons will simply not volunteer for a radical revision of their social environment.

Although Etzioni's research is not primarily concerned with change in academic organizations, some of his findings are applicable to this discussion. For example, a department chairperson, the sole representative of her institution, participates in a regional or national workshop for academic administrators. She returns with enthusiasm and many ideas for implementing change, only to encounter a resistive and unyielding environment. In this case, motivating the department chairperson to desire change was in itself not sufficient to bring it about.

Etzioni's research also suggests that finding new persons to implement decisions for change may be easier than obtaining cooperation from those whose ways are set. Unless positions are available for new faculty members, chairpersons of some departments must wait for recalcitrants to retire before attempting any change. In those instances when the chairperson is the obstruction to changes necessary for the department's survival, the dean must seek ways of changing the chairperson's behavior or perhaps of changing the chairperson.

In his article "Hauling Academic Trunks," J. B. Lon Hefferlin notes that few institutions change spontaneously and suggests that the most important factor influencing change is the market conditions under which educational institutions operate. Colleges and universities and their departments must attract resources or fail in their mission. Departments compete, within and without the institution, for scarce resources. If they fail to compete, they are liable to wither away. A department's curricular offerings must attract students, and the working conditions must attract faculty members, or mediocrity and stagnation will result. Many, if not most, departments closely watch what departments at other institutions are doing and try to do the same sorts of things—i.e., they sail with the wind rather than trying to go against it.

The second most powerful factor influencing academic change, according to Hefferlin, is the institution's ethos toward change. Each college or university and its departments have their own historic orientation toward change. This orientation, whatever it is, tends to be self-perpetuating, since those in power usually choose persons like themselves to succeed them. Yet choosing innovative successors often results in meaningful change. It is easier to replace persons than to change their attitudes, and frequently curricular or structural changes in universities or colleges must take place at the time when old professors retire or leave and new ones replace them. Dwight Ladd's study *Change in Educational Policy* indicates that changes in colleges and universities do not take place unless the faculty is convinced of the desirability of change.

A third factor that influences change in higher education is the institutional structure, which can be an aid or a barrier to change. The same is true of department structure as well. The department's decision-making process may be facilitated by clear procedures, by the nature of committees within the department, and by the rules that govern curricular issues and personnel policies. Some departments have written bylaws that outline the structure, while others have a structure based on higher authority. Departments that have no formal rules or procedures often have informal rules based on precedent or tradition. A problem in most large institutions is the rigidity of the bureaucracy. Strict, bureaucratic rules and procedures certainly operate against policies that are flexible, adaptive, and responsive.

In certain areas within departments, the need for change seems to crop up with some regularity. The first is the area of department goals and objectives. The goals of colleges and universities change with societal needs and conditions, and department goals may have to be altered to remain consistent with the institution's larger goals. To avoid mere rhetoric, goals and objectives should be stated realistically within the institutional and societal framework.

A second area of change is the department curriculum. The curriculum should be consistent with the department's goals and responsive to the needs of students, the discipline or profession, the community, and the institution. While the curriculum necessarily reflects the capabilities of the faculty, it can become ossified if not monitored.

A third area of change is the department's research and service activities. Here, too, there is the question of whether the research activities of faculty members within the department are consistent with department goals. Another serious question concerns the relationship between the department's research and service activities and its curricular and instructional activities; some research and service activities might conceivably weaken the department's course offerings. Finally, departments can address the question of the quality and worth of the research carried out in the department. This question most commonly arises during considerations of promotion and tenure for faculty members, but it might be addressed more profitably in the context of a general department evaluation.

Hefferlin, in the article cited earlier, lists five techniques for implementing academic change: the administrator must determine the obstacles, provide reassurance, build on existing concerns, avoid rejection, and respect the past. Although Hefferlin is speaking of change at the institutional level, his techniques may be applied when implementing change within a department. If changes are contemplated, the chairperson should anticipate possible obstacles to implementing these changes. These obstacles may be internal or external. They may be due to apathy, indifference, or lack of information.

Change is sometimes threatening, and the threats can be real or imagined. The chairperson should think of ways to assuage fears and consider techniques of conciliation, cooptation, and confrontation in the attempt to implement changes. When discussing change, try to avoid distorting and misrepresenting ideas. The chairperson can avoid opposition by clarifying the ideas and activities being considered. The more information the faculty members receive, the more likely they are to feel reassured. Change that builds on the existing concerns of the department is more likely to gain acceptance than change that does not. Changes should address problems that the faculty sees as urgent. The task force approach to change, which allows interested faculty members to participate, is recommended as a way of channeling the concerns of faculty members.

One way to avoid rejection is to propose change for a specific experimental period. If such a proposal is rejected, an optional, parallel program can be suggested. Then, if the proposed change works well, the rest of the faculty is more likely to accept it. Optional, parallel programs work well in the area of curriculum.

Finally, change in academia may be garbed in tradition. Hefferlin cites President Lowell of Harvard, who, in 1938, said of the college president:

> If he desires to innovate he will be greatly helped by having the reputation of being conservative, because the radicals who want a change are little offended by the fact of change, while the conservatives will be likely to follow him because they look on him as sharing their temperament and point of view.*

This sage political advice can be applied to the governance of a department as well. Tradition should be respected while change is fostered.

In his article "Organizational Reform Is Not Enough," H. Bradley Sagen lists conditions that affect the adoption of academic innovation. His ideas, presented in terms of institutional changes, will be discussed here in terms of department changes. He favors incentives and institutional support for innovations. In fact, one common criticism voiced about department change is the lack of rewards for those who attempt to innovate. Sagen suggests that faculty members might be encouraged to develop new ideas, goals, and programs through such small incentives as secretarial assistance, student assistantships, and released time.

Proposed changes are also easier to implement if they do not conflict with the values held by the department faculty members. If proposed changes are compatible with the faculty members' values and beliefs, the changes should not meet with resistance. A chairperson in-

---

*J. B. Lon Hefferlin, "Hauling Academic Trunks," *Elements Involved in Academic Change.* (Washington, D.C.: Association of American Colleges, 1972), p. 10.

terested in innovations should be aware of the faculty members' academic and personal values and should be able to show that proposed changes are compatible, or at least not too incompatible, with those values. Sagen also stresses the importance of "participative involvement" in bringing about change. Compatibility of values is a necessary part of participative involvement.

Another desirable prerequisite to change is the clarification of the present situation. To know where you are going requires not only a clear idea of how you are going to get there, but also a clear idea of where you are. Sagen also recommends identifying and using faculty leaders to facilitate change. Some faculty members are admired and respected by their colleagues for their intelligence, honesty, and integrity; their opinions and attitudes carry a good deal of weight with their peers. A chairperson who can mobilize department leaders to support desired changes may find the path to change smoother than the chairperson who ignores department leaders.

Dealing with Change and Resistance to Change

Clark Kerr, a former president of the University of California, once said that changing a university curriculum is like trying to move a cemetery. His statement aptly characterizes faculty resistance to change. Though colleges and universities are characterized by massive inertia, in the long run they too must yield to the pressure of changes. Because faculty members perceive change as threatening and manipulative, chairpersons tend to shy away from talking about it directly in order to avoid provoking anxiety and resistance. Faculty members feel less anxious, however, when discussing such subjects as self-renewal, organizational development, or faculty and staff development, all of which are actually efforts for planned change. For chairpersons to act as leaders or facilitators in these efforts, they should know and understand the process of change.

When faculty members resist change, what are they really resisting? Will a plan be automatically accepted if it is logical and educationally well conceived? Not necessarily. As we noted earlier, plans for change that rely exclusively on rationality are typically not successful. A faculty member's first reaction to a proposed change is to ask how it will affect him or her personally in terms of opportunity for professional development, promotion, salary increases, and work assignments. Faculty members will also be concerned about how the change will affect their future relationships with coworkers, students, administrators, colleagues, and so forth. To ensure the greatest likelihood of acceptance, therefore, a proposed plan for change should not only be logical and well conceived but should take into consideration the personal concerns of those involved. The chairperson should seek out those who feel that they will lose status if the change occurs. If their fears are unfounded, they should be given the necessary assurances. If indeed the change may cause them to lose status, the chairperson should think about what, if anything, could be done to make up for this loss or to improve their present status. When the chairperson shows proper concern and interest, resistance may be converted to support.

Proper and frequent communication with faculty members before, during, and after a change will help alleviate many of their personal concerns. Those who will be affected by a proposed change should be provided with as much information as possible about the situation. Lack of knowledge about what is going on causes insecurity, and insecurity increases resistance, regardless of the merits of the proposed change. Information that presents the rationale for suggested changes may be sufficiently persuasive to reduce resistance or gain support for a proposed plan. Changing a person's knowledge base is frequently a prerequisite for changing attitude and behavior.

Another impediment to change often results from the requirement that plans for proposed changes must be reviewed and approved by many persons and groups in the institution's governance hierarchy. Any faculty committee or administrator may veto an idea as it travels the hierarchy from department to dean's office to president's office. Whenever a new idea for change is presented to a faculty committee for the first time, the reaction is generally negative, and after the initial rejection, committee support for the idea is difficult to obtain. In some instances, it is better to discuss the idea individually with several members of the committee before making the presentation to the committee as a whole. If individual members are persuaded that the idea has merit, they will help obtain support from the rest of the committee. Proper and frequent communication with committee members and administrators during the development of the plan can reduce resistance.

Change involves considerable risk because it will not necessarily solve a problem. Not every new approach will prove effective, and when a change fails, the innovator may be criticized or even terminated. A wrong change could stir up conflict, upset sensitive balances and relations, and waste faculty members' energy. Therefore, before the chairperson decides to implement a plan for a change, he or she could collect data that will help determine the probability of the plan succeeding without demoralizing the faculty. If the probability of success is low, the plan should not be implemented. Keep in mind also that the smaller the change, the less resistance it will generate. If a change is necessary, select one that will solve the problem in the simplest and least noticeable way. Do not amputate a leg to cure a toe infection. Remember also that if faculty members have not been involved in the planning, they will resist even the smallest change that might affect them.

What motivates faculty members to change? First, many are motivated by the desire for competence and the need to achieve. These persons are primarily interested in job mastery and professional growth and are constantly thinking of better ways of doing things. They are willing to participate in planning and implementing change for the sake of their own professional improvement and the department's improvement. Second, some faculty members are motivated to change only if they can anticipate a more tangible reward that they can share with their families. Third, some faculty members are motivated to change only when they consider the consequences of not changing—if, for example, they thought that unwillingness to change could cause them to lose privileges or face possible termination. A department with decreasing enrollments might be motivated to modify its recruitment policies, its curriculum, and its goals and activities if decreasing enrollment could lead to a reduced department budget and perhaps a reduced number of faculty positions. Faculty members' response to the need for change is generally based on a combination of all three factors, each of which may be weighted differently for different persons. But there are some faculty members who just won't change under any circumstances. The question of what to do with them is one of the challenges facing the department chairperson.

When considering the feasibility of implementing a plan for change, the chairperson should try to anticipate who will support the plan and who will resist it. The chairperson should make a list of potential supporters and the reasons for their support and another list of those who are expected to resist the plan and the reasons for their resistance. The supporting faculty members and their rationale can be thought of as "driving forces," the resisters and their rationale as "restraining forces."

Because the faculty members on each list will vary in the degree to which they support or resist the plan, the chairperson should rate the strength of each person's support or resistance on a scale of 1 to 5. When all the driving and restraining forces have been listed and the strength of each force has been rated, totals of the driving forces and the restraining forces can be calculated and then compared.

In his book *Field Theory in Social Science*, Kurt Lewin, a well-known social psychologist, has developed what is called the force field analysis theory, which says that change takes place when an imbalance occurs between the sum of the driving forces and the sum of the restraining forces. The greater the imbalance, the more acceptable the change will be. When the two sets of forces are balanced, the status quo continues. To bring about change, the driving forces must become strong enough to overcome the restraining forces, or the restraining forces must be sufficiently reduced or weakened to be overcome by the existing driving forces.

Applying Lewin's theory to the chairperson's role, we see that the chairperson should determine what kind of and how much influence is needed to attain the optimum pressure of driving forces necessary to bring about the desired change. He or she must then calculate whether there is enough support—or enough influence to obtain support—for the change. At this point the chairperson can decide whether the efforts for change are likely to be successful. If the decision is made to go ahead with the plan, a decision must also be made about the strategy to be used.

Strategies for bringing about change include the participative model and the power model. The participative, or involvement, model is used most often in organizations. In this model, new knowledge is made available to the group with the hope that the group will accept the data and develop a commitment to the desired change. The group is involved in reviewing the data and helping select or develop new methods for choosing the desired goal. In the power model, the chairperson imposes the plan for change on the faculty members in the hope that when they see how well it works, they will support it. In a university setting, the participative model is the most appropriate most of the time. The power model, however, can be more efficient and effective when the faculty's acceptance is not crucial to the implementation of the plan.

In evaluating the need for the change, the department chairperson must learn how to ask the right questions. He or she should talk to faculty members, the dean, other chairpersons, students, and recent alumni. The questions should include these: What is good about the department? What is not so good? What might happen in the future if the status quo remains unchanged? What would faculty members like to see happen in the future?

These questions will elicit mounds of useful information. Moreover, the process will generally please those who are asked to comment and will thereby earn the chairperson a measure of positive support. These interviews will result in a tentative list of proposed changes that should be considered.

In selecting and implementing plans for change, then, the following points should be kept in mind:
- select changes that are most timely and appropriate for the department's current situation

- select plans for change that have a reasonable chance of success—e.g., sufficient faculty support, sufficient resources, and so forth
- select plans that require the least drastic change to solve a problem
- develop plans for responding to the personal needs of those who will be affected by the changes
- develop strategies for communicating appropriately with those who will be affected by the change as well as those who must approve it
- develop strategies for obtaining faculty members' commitment to supporting and participating in the implementation of the plan
- be sensitive to values held by members of the department

In bringing about needed change, the department chairperson should have the ability to perform the following functions:

- provide guidance to the faculty in developing and updating department goals and objectives
- assess local, regional, and national needs for education services provided by the department
- develop action plans for the needed changes
- implement action plans for the needed changes

Examples of specific skills helpful to department chairpersons in dealing with change include these:

- ability to design and implement strategy for bringing about needed curriculum and program change
- ability to develop long-range plans and strategies—for example, strategies for timely appointment, promotion, tenure, and retirement of faculty members—that will enable a department to remain responsive to new and changing needs
- ability to identify and develop programs to meet the professional development needs of faculty members in times of retrenchment

Intervention Plans

For our purposes, an *intervention* is defined as a person's action or series of actions that causes a change in the behavior of another person or group. Literally, it is an interruption in the direction in which a person or group is moving. A department chairperson can devise an intervention plan that will move a department in the desired direction and at the same time improve faculty motivation and morale. A well-planned intervention may further the goals of collegiality and shared governance. In its simplest form, such a plan would consist of a statement of the intervention and its expected outcome. Evidence for these expectations should be specified so that a follow-up can determine whether the intervention was effective.

Some interventions seem especially appropriate to the university setting, with its horizontal structure and its traditional framework of collegiality. Nine particularly appropriate kinds of interventions are described below, with examples of how such interventions might be useful.

The first kind of intervention calls attention to a contradiction in action or attitudes. Recently a chemistry department had the opportunity to fill a vacant position at the associate professor level. In establishing the criteria for the application, the faculty members stipulated at least five years' teaching experience, significant publications in major journals, national visibility, demonstrated service in the profession, and the ability to direct graduate students. Some months later an assistant professor in the department with four years of teaching experience, two publications, a good service record to the university, and a pleasant personality applied for a promotion to the rank of associate professor. Since he was well liked and seemed to show promise as a researcher, the department members were anxious for him to be promoted. The chairperson called their attention to the discrepancy between their criteria for someone coming from outside the institution and their criteria for someone within the institution. After some discussion, they decided to ask the faculty member to wait another year and work toward coming closer to department standards. In this case, the department chairperson's intervention modified the way in which the department developed and used its human resources.

The second kind of intervention relies on the use of research findings or conceptual understandings to help faculty members broaden their perspective on a particular problem. A communications department chairperson was faced with the problem of having too many sections of an extremely popular speech course and too few instructors. The faculty's desire to maintain the twenty-to-one student-faculty ratio in the classroom was opposed by the dean, who said that he simply could not find the additional faculty positions to support so low a student-faculty ratio in a lower-division course. The chairperson looked into the research on students evaluating their peer's performance, which showed that students' evaluation of their fellow students was reliable and permitted a larger class size by reducing the amount of time the instructor spent on grading. She shared the information with the faculty members, who were convinced by the evidence. The appeal to research findings was persuasive and allowed the department chairperson both to double her class size and to maintain the faculty members' morale.

The third kind of intervention reexamines the existing methods for solving problems within the department. A new economics department chairperson wished to involve junior faculty members in the department's decision-making process. When he met resistance from the existing oligarchy, he used the occasion of a university self-study to appoint a committee composed of junior and senior faculty members to review the department's decision-making process. The committee concentrated on the methods used to make decisions and, with the input from the junior faculty members, recommended a revision of the department's decision-making processes. The committee workload was distributed more evenly and the senior faculty members' time used to better advantage.

The fourth kind of intervention focuses on lowering situational conflict within the group by improving group relationships. The faculty members of an English department were unable to modify their selection of requirements for their undergraduate general education courses. The modernist faction felt that the traditionalists were being stubborn in their devotion to the past, while the traditionalist faction felt that many of the modernists' innovations were too avant garde and that faculty members who espoused curricular revisions were merely trying to promote their own ends. Tensions had increased when the department chairperson organized a weekend retreat for the faculty members at the university convention center some twenty-five miles from campus. During the retreat, as the faculty members walked together on the beaches or sat in front of the fire, many of the superficial emotional elements of the conflict were reduced. On the last day of the retreat, the faculty members were able to resolve the problem to everyone's satisfaction.

The fifth kind of intervention allows for the adoption of two or more options rather than a single forced choice. This approach is particularly appealing to science departments and other departments that are quantitatively oriented. Although the procedures for comparing courses of action are not scientifically exact, they do add an element of logic to the decision-making process. A graduate psychology department wished to modify its comprehensive examination procedures by substituting a research project assignment for the written examination. The faculty members disagreed about the appropriateness of this course of action, so the department chairperson allowed one group of doctoral students to select either the examination or the project for one academic year. After the year's experience with both options, the faculty decided to adopt the research project as an option for students.

The sixth kind of intervention identifies significant alternatives and examines the consequences that might follow the adoption of each alternative. The chairperson of a history department found that she was unable to provide adequate office space for a growing number of faculty members and graduate students. A morale problem developed. The dean told the chairperson that she could have all the office space she wanted in a vacant house on the edge of campus. The chairperson met with the faculty members to explore the advantages of being housed in spacious quarters but away from the center of campus life and the advantages of being housed in cramped quarters but close to the center of campus life. After much discussion, they decided in favor of more cramped quarters closer to classrooms and other students. The intervention resulted in increased understanding, thus reducing the morale problem.

The seventh kind of intervention objectively applies a historical perspective to the present situation. A geology department chairperson wished to encourage faculty members to solicit research proposals from outside agencies. To this end he conducted a review of outside funding received by the department over the preceding ten years and compared it with research activities and funding both of other science departments within the university and of other geology departments within the university system. The evidence indicated that the department was missing out on some research opportunities. Faculty members began to write proposals and to receive outside funding.

The eighth kind of intervention identifies the source of the problem as something related to an institutional policy or constraint. A humanities department chairperson was challenged by a group of her faculty members for her failure to secure enough travel money for them to attend the national convention. The department chairperson met with the group and reviewed the board of regents' budgetary procedures, the university's restrictions on travel, and appropriations of travel funds throughout the university. She was able to demonstrate that while the absolute amount of travel money was ridiculously low, the department had received more than its fair share, given the institutional constraints. She also indicated that those departments that had more travel money usually obtained it from outside sources. By showing the faculty members the structure of the system, she was able to spur their requests for funds from outside agencies.

The final kind of intervention relies on one of the strongest arguments of all—tradition. Faculty members, it has been said, never like to do anything for the first time; appeals to tradition can, therefore, be particularly persuasive. An education administration department chairperson wished to encourage the faculty members to be more active in ordering books for the library. Ordering books was consuming a great deal of his time, but he knew from experience that a general request for more book orders would generate little response. He began his strategy by assigning students in his own classes to read books that he considered basic to areas in his field but that were unavailable in the library. When students reported that the library did not possess the books that were assigned, the chairperson relayed those reports to a meeting of the faculty. At the meeting, the chairperson spoke of the great libraries at the universities at which many of the faculty members had earned their doctorates. He stated that funds were available to the department for the purchase of books in their respective fields; thus a library could be built that would at least equal those they had used as students. With the expertise of the faculty mobilized, a first-class collection representing the highest tradition of university scholarship could be amassed. As a result of the discussion, the book-ordering function was taken over by a faculty committee.

The nine intervention techniques that seem especially appropriate for use in universities may be summarized as follows:

1. Call attention to a contradiction in action or in attitudes.
2. Rely on the use of research findings or conceptual understandings.
3. Reexamine the existing methods for solving problems.
4. Focus attention on lowering intergroup conflict by improving group relationships.
5. Test the adoption of two or more options, as opposed to a single forced choice.
6. Identify significant alternatives and examine the consequences of adopting each alternative.
7. Apply a historical perspective to the present situation.
8. Identify the source of the problem as related to an institutional policy or constraint.
9. Argue from tradition.

In this chapter we have discussed the need for chairpersons to obtain information from faculty members when contemplating department changes. Faculty members who have not had the opportunity to become involved in the decision-making process sometimes resist, actively or passively, the implementation of the resulting decision, regardless of its potential benefit to the department. Too much involvement, however, can be just as detrimental as too little. We have described various ways of determining the extent to which faculty members should be involved, how to involve them, and how to help them overcome some of their feelings of resistance to a proposed change. Some attitudes of resistance, if unchecked, can develop into difficult conflict situations. Dealing with potential and active conflict is described in some detail in chapter 11.

Questions

1. What are some fairly important types of decisions that you as chairperson could make for your department without involving the faculty members in the decision-making process and that they would accept without serious complaint?
2. What are some fairly unimportant types of decisions that you could make without involving the faculty members in the decision-making process and that they would not accept?
3. What types of department decisions would your faculty members prefer that you make without bothering them?
4. Following is a case study concerning a "high failure mathematics department." Please answer questions at the end of the case study. If more details are needed in order to answer the questions, please fill in the missing aspects of the case with hypothetical information based on your own experience. To the extent possible, apply the suggested methods in the chapter as well as your own ideas in attempting to reduce the resistance to the change.

   The department of mathematics in a middle size university has an unusually high failure rate in freshman level mathematics courses. In a meeting called to discuss the problem, the dean of arts and sciences points out that he has received numerous complaints from the dean of engineering because too many students were failing the mathematics courses required to enter full-time study in the college of engineering.

   The mathematics faculty feels that the high failure rate simply reflects inadequate preparation on the part of entering students. The director of institutional research counters this suggestion by revealing that many students who ranked in the top quartile of the College Board Examination were included in the large number of failing students. The dean of engineering is threatening to develop mathematics courses within the college of engineering if the situation persists any longer. The mathematics chairperson wants the faculty to see that a problem exists. He recognizes that they must develop a plan for changing the grading policy or the structure of the freshman mathematics courses, otherwise engineering students might be required to take their mathematics courses in the college of engineering.

   a. How can the chairperson get the department to recognize that the present situation cannot continue?
   b. What type of faculty members might resist making any changes?
   c. What might be the concerns of those who oppose change?
   d. What can be done to alleviate their concerns?

    e. How might the chairperson involve faculty in developing a plan for solving the problem?

    f. Review the nine interventions described in this chapter. Is one or more of them appropriate in this case? Which one(s)? If none is appropriate, design another intervention strategy that might work.

    g. How might the chairperson handle faculty members who adamantly refuse to consider changing the grading policy or the course structure?

5. Do you currently have a specific problem in your department, the solution to which requires a change that will be resisted by some faculty members?

    a. Knowing your faculty members as you do, can you identify in your mind:

        i. those who would immediately support your idea.

        ii. those who would have an open mind and could be persuaded.

        iii. those who generally follow the opinion of the majority when a consensus has been reached.

        iv. those who would adamantly oppose the idea.

    b. What interventions would seem to have the most positive effects on faculty members in your department? See interventions listed in this chapter.

    c. What procedures and strategies would you use to win over those faculty members who might create opposition?

References

ARGYRIS, CHRIS. "Interpersonal Barriers to Decision-Making." *Harvard Business Review*, February 1966, pp. 84–97.

ARGYRIS, CHRIS, AND SCHON, DONALD A. *Theory in Practice: Increasing Professional Effectiveness*. San Francisco: Jossey-Bass, 1974.

BERGQUIST, WILLIAM H., AND PHILIPS, STEVEN R. "Components of an Effective Faculty Development Program." *Journal of Higher Education*, March 1975, pp. 177–211.

BIRNBAUM, ROBERT. "Using the Calendar for Faculty Development." *Educational Record*, Fall 1975, pp. 226–30.

BROWN, DAVID G., AND HANGER, WILLIAM S. "Pragmatics of Faculty Self-Development." *Educational Record*, Summer 1975, pp. 201–6.

BUHL, LANCE C., AND GREENFIELD, ADELE. "Contracting for Professional Development in Academe." *Educational Record*, Spring 1975, pp. 111–21.

BURNS, TOM, AND STALKER, G. M. *Management of Innovation*. New York: Methuen, 1961.

CARTWRIGHT, DORWIN. "Achieving Change in People: Some Applications of Group Dynamics Theory." *Human Relations,* November 1951, pp. 381–92.

CARTWRIGHT, DORWIN, AND ZANDER, ALVIN, eds. *Group Dynamics: Research and Theory.* 3rd ed. New York: Harper and Row, 1968.

CHAMBERLAIN, PHILIP C. "Resistance to Change in Curriculum Planning." In *The Academic Department or Division Chairman: A Complex Role,* edited by James Brann and Thomas A. Emmet, pp. 250–62. Detroit: Balamp, 1972.

CLEARY, ROBERT. "University Decision Making." *Educational Forum,* November 1978, pp. 89–98.

COCH, LESTER, AND FRENCH, JOHN R. P., JR. "Overcoming Resistance to Change." *Human Relations,* August 1948, pp. 512–32.

CONRAD, CLIFTON F. "A Grounded Theory of Academic Change." *Sociology of Education,* April 1978, pp. 101–12.

ETZIONI, AMITAI. "Human Beings Are Not Very Easy to Change, After All." *Saturday Review,* 3 June 1972, pp. 45–47.

FLORIDA BOARD OF REGENTS. *Comprehensive Development Plan of the State University System of Florida.* Tallahassee: Board of Regents, 1970.

GROUP FOR HUMAN DEVELOPMENT IN HIGHER EDUCATION. *Faculty Development in a Time of Retrenchment.* New Rochelle, N.Y.: Change Magazine Press, 1974.

GUEST, ROBERT H.; HERSEY, PAUL; AND BLANCHARD, KENNETH H. *Organizational Change through Effective Leadership.* Englewood Cliffs, N.J.: Prentice-Hall, 1977.

HAMMONS, JAMES O., AND WALLACE, TERRY H. SMITH. "Sixteen Ways to Kill a College Faculty Development Program." *Educational Technology,* December 1976, pp. 16–20.

HEFFERLIN, J. B. LON. *Dynamics of Academic Reform.* San Francisco: Jossey-Bass, 1969.

———. "Hauling Academic Trunks." In *Elements Involved in Academic Change,* edited by Charles U. Walker, pp. 1–10. Washington, D.C.: Association of American Colleges, 1972.

KOWITZ, ALBERT C., AND KNUTSON, THOMAS J. *Decision Making in Small Groups: The Search for Alternatives.* Boston: Allyn & Bacon, 1960.

LADD, DWIGHT R. *Change in Educational Policy: Self-Studies in Selected Colleges and Universities,* with commentary by Katharine McBride. New York: McGraw-Hill, 1970.

LAWRENCE, PAUL R. "How to Deal with Resistance to Change." *Harvard Business Review,* May–June 1954, pp. 49–57.

LEVINE, ARTHUR. *Why Innovation Fails: The Institutionalization and Termination of Innovation in Higher Education.* Albany: State University of New York Press, 1981.

LEWIN, KURT. *Field Theory in Social Science,* edited by Dorwin Cartwright. Westport. Conn.: Greenwood, 1975.

LINDQUIST, JACK. *Strategies for Change: Academic Innovation and Adaptive*

Development. Washington, D.C.: Council for the Advancement of Small Colleges, 1980.

LIONBERGER, HERBERT F. *Adoption of New Ideas and Practices.* Ames, Ia.: Iowa State University Press, 1960.

LIPPITT, RONALD, ET AL. *Dynamics of Planned Change: A Comparative Study of Principles and Techniques.* New York: Harcourt Brace, 1958.

MARROW, ALFRED J.; BOWERS, DAVID G.; AND SEASHORE, STANLEY E., eds. *Strategies of Organizational Change.* New York: Harper and Row, 1967.

MCGANNON, BARRY JAMES, S. J. "Guide to Academic Planning—St. Louis University." In *The Academic Department or Division Chairman: A Complex Role,* edited by James Brann and Thomas A. Emmet, pp. 269–96. Detroit: Balamp, 1972.

MILGRAM, STANLEY. "Group Pressure and Action against a Person." *Journal of Abnormal and Social Psychology,* August 1964, pp. 137–43.

MILLER, RICHARD I. *Evaluating Faculty Performance.* San Francisco: Jossey-Bass, 1972.

NATIONAL TRAINING LABORATORIES. *Explorations in Human Relations Training.* Washington, D.C.: National Education Association, 1969.

NEUMAN, YORAM. "The Perception of Change in University Departments." *Research in Higher Education,* 1979, 11(1), pp. 45–48.

RICHARDSON, RICHARD C., JR. "Staff Development: A Conceptual Framework." *Journal of Higher Education,* May 1975, pp. 303–11.

RONKEN, HARRIET O., AND LAWRENCE, PAUL R. *Administering Changes: A Case Study of Human Relations in a Factory.* Boston: Harvard University Press, 1952.

SAGEN, H. BRADLEY. "Organizational Reform Is Not Enough." In *Elements Involved in Academic Change,* edited by Charles U. Walker, pp. 20–29. Washington, D.C.: Association of American Colleges, 1972.

STEELE, CLAUDE M., AND GREEN, STEPHEN G. "Affirmative Action and Academic Hiring: A Case Study of a Value Conflict," *Journal of Higher Education,* July 1976, pp. 413–35.

TANNENBAUM, ROBERT, AND SCHMIDT, WARREN H. "How to Choose a Leadership Pattern." *Harvard Educational Review,* March-April 1957, pp. 95–101.

TRINKHAUS, JOHN W., AND BOOKE, ALVIN L. "The Curriculum Change Process: Participants, Strategies and Tactics." *Research in Higher Education,* 1980, 13, pp. 307–19.

VON HADEN, HERBERT I., AND KING, JEAN MARIE. *Educational Innovator's Guide.* Worthington, Oh: Charles A. Jones, 1974.

WALBERG, HERBERT J., ed. *Evaluating Educational Performance: A Sourcebook of Methods, Instruments, and Examples.* Berkeley: McCutchan, 1974.

WERGIN, JON F.; MASON, ELIZABETH J.; AND MUNSON, PAUL J. "Practices of Faculty Development: An Experience-Derived Model: Virginia Commonwealth University." *Journal of Higher Education,* May 1976, pp. 289–308.

7

Faculty Development: Encouraging Professional Growth

The case can be made that the department chairperson's most important function is to foster the growth and development of faculty and staff members within the department. Experts in staff and personnel development contend that an organization's effectiveness depends heavily on an ongoing, self-renewing program of human resources development. In the same way, an academic department's effectiveness depends largely on *faculty development*, a term coined to denote self-renewing activities for faculty members. In this regard, one vital question emerges: To what extent should the department chairperson help faculty members acquire the requisite knowledge, skills, and attitudes for maintaining their effectiveness, improving their approach to fulfilling responsibilities, and making satisfactory adjustments to the changes in their environments?

Although the need for staff or personal development has been recognized in the past, such development has been mainly a "background" activity. Sometimes it was relegated to the chairperson, for whom it was probably a minor concern. Occasionally, sabbaticals were granted to those who could afford to survive on a reduced income for a limited time. More recently, centers for the improvement of instruction have been established to help faculty members improve the quality of their instruction. By and large, however, faculty development has been allowed to happen naturally through ongoing professional activity, such as attending or participating in conferences or consulting with old friends and colleagues.

In times of expanding resources and faculties, the need for a deliberate faculty development effort was perhaps not as acute or obvious as it is now. New ideas were imported with the everflowing stream of new faculty members. With the influx of new and energetic talents, it was easy to cover up or overlook maturing but nonproductive faculty members. But circumstances have changed. Colleges and universities are now faced with steady-state or declining budgets, a population of maturing faculty members who hold tenure and have little chance of obtaining more rewarding positions at other institutions, and the mixed opportunities of unionization. In addition, enrollment is declining and a growing number of nontraditional students demand that their rights and expectations be upheld.

How then should institutions of higher education respond to these powerful forces that demand change? Before addressing this question, colleges and universities must first identify the nature of such forces and formulate a reasonable guess as to how these forces may affect university systems, institutions, departments, and ultimately the faculty, which actually delivers the services. Then the question may be raised: What is the department chairperson's responsibility in enhancing faculty members' continuing development to meet emerging institutional needs, their own needs, and the needs of students?

A Case for a Deliberate Development Effort

The following trends that have begun to emerge may well compel college faculty members, as individuals and as department members, to reexamine their professional careers:

- a decline in the growth of higher education due to the decline in the 18–22-year-old population
- a decline in the level of public support, resulting in an economic crunch for universities and for students
- an emerging awareness of new skills and understandings that will be required for effective functioning in a changing society
- the decreased mobility of faculty members and administrators
- a high percentage of tenured faculty members, most of whom are in their forties and fifties
- a buyer's market for students with regard to educational opportunities
- an increasing number of students who are not awed by a teacher's authority and who are willing to bring legal action if they don't get what they pay for
- an increased demand for accountability by parents, members of governing boards, legislators, and the general public

Four trends from this list deserve special consideration in light of their effect on faculty members; namely low mobility of faculty members and administrators; decline in the growth of higher education; decline in public support for higher education; and the demand for new knowledge, skills, and attitudes in a changing society.

Low Mobility of Faculty Members and Administrators. After several years of unprecedented growth, higher education enrollments are now leveling off and quite possibly even declining. This trend, coupled with an overabundance of Ph.D.'s, has resulted in fewer faculty vacancies and, therefore, in less mobility for existing faculty members. Unless enrollment increases significantly, there will be little need for "new hires" before 1990. Without regular faculty turnover, the responsibility for updating curricula will increasingly rest with existing staff members. As a result, a deliberate faculty development effort may be required to assist faculty members in refreshing and upgrading their command of their disciplines.

Decline in the Growth of Higher Education. How can colleges and universities be sure that enrollment growth will not increase again soon? They can be quite sure within specified time periods, as long as they include present census data as a point of reference. For example, the number of children born in 1970 can help institutions determine the number of eighteen-year-olds in the year 1988. But how many of these eighteen-year-olds will attend college? According to U.S. Office of Education enrollment projections, total enrollment in higher education will peak about 1980, begin to decrease, and then bottom out about 1988. Although this projection takes into account the increasing number of high school graduates pursuing postsecondary education, this increase cannot compensate for the plunge in the number of college-age youth through the 1980s. The increasingly severe national economic picture, coupled with the absence of a military draft for the next ten years, would reduce even further the number of college-age youth who actually attend college during this period.

Given existing demographic data and trends, it is clear that fewer and fewer youth and young adults will attend colleges and universities in the years ahead. What is not so clear is whether older adult learners, many of whom need or want to continue their education at the college or university level, will fill the gap left by the younger students. Many urban universities and community colleges have discovered that they are now enrolling more adult part-time learners than recent high school graduates.

In addition, this "new clientele" for higher education is composed of different kinds of learners, with wide ranges of abilities, interests and life experiences. They may have more experience than the instructor and be as knowledgeable in some subjects. They often challenge time-tested and traditional ways of perceiving how knowledge is organized and may not want credit or degrees for their efforts. Adult learners may also desire learning that is relevant to current issues and problems, since most are not in training for a position or job. Finally, they may wish to be involved in educational decision-making processes, such as needs assessment, goal setting, selection of content and method, and evaluation.

The major question facing higher education today may well be, "To what extent can faculty members learn to relate effectively to the learning needs, styles, and personal attributes of adult students, a potential clientele larger than the total number of persons now enrolled in the education system, from kindergarten through graduate school?" To address such changes, a faculty development effort may include activities that familiarize faculty members with research about learning characteristics of adults.

Decline in Public Support for Higher Education. Unfortunately, public confidence in higher education is declining at the same time that financial support is eroding. If universities and colleges could count on a constant level of financial support in the face of declining enrollment, this situation would be tolerable. The public, however, is telling higher education to do more with less. This adaptation will be difficult because of the relative affluence of the past decade. With the curtailment of institutional funds to support many valued activities, faculty members may be required to develop skills in obtaining funds from external sources to support these activities. For example, one strategy would be to initiate a deliberate effort to help faculty members acquire skills in grantsmanship to support their research interests.

Demand for New Knowledge, Skills, and Attitudes. Perhaps the most compelling reason for planned renewal efforts can be derived from analyses and forecasts made by futurists, such as Alvin Toffler, Herman Kahn, and Daniel Bell. For example, Toffler forecasts negative psychological and sociological consequences brought about by accelerating social change and details these negative consequences under the now familiar concept of "future shock." Toffler is highly critical of current education and refers to it as "a hopeless anachronism" because of its orientation toward the past rather than the future. He argues that education appropriate for an industrial age is no longer adequate for the postindustrial age. As he puts it, "For education the lesson is clear: its prime objective must be to increase the individual's 'copeability'—the speed and economy with which he can adapt to continual change. And the faster the rate of change, the more attention must be devoted to discerning the pattern of future events."* In Toffler's view, a curriculum is required that effectively helps students learn how to learn, how to relate to others, and how to clarify their values so that they can effectively choose among competing alternatives.

Approaching the problem from another perspective, the futurists Kahn and Bruce-Briggs envision a traumatic future for the human race.

---

*Alvin Toffler, *Future Shock* (New York: Random House, 1970), p. 357.

In *Things to Come: Thinking about the Seventies and Eighties,* they point out the irony that technology—the means of production that has raised our standard of living so dramatically—may also be responsible for a series of environmental and economic disasters. They predict a world-wide crisis around 1985 brought on by thoughtless use of technology. Perhaps Toffler is correct in advocating values clarification and the opportunity to choose among competing alternatives as appropriate curricular goals. Values based on consumption and growth may have to be changed to values based on conservation and more humanistic concerns if these predicted disasters are to be averted.

Daniel Bell, in his book *The Coming of Post-Industrial Society,* describes several changes that create strain as society moves from an industrial to a postindustrial age. The sources of strain include the inclusion of disadvantaged groups into society; the growth of global economic interdependence and the creation of international societies; the increasing substitution of political decision making for market decision making; the creation of fully urbanized societies and the erosion of an agricultural population; and the introduction of a multitude of technological products. According to Bell, the "elite" approach to higher education must change to accommodate the ever-increasing number of students from lower- and working-class backgrounds. Bell sees the university as becoming society's primary institution for the dissemination of required survival skills. Many of these skills can be deduced from his analysis: the ability to codify, store, and retrieve theoretical knowledge for the purpose of solving human problems; ability to coordinate human behavior in complex systems; ability to engage in participatory decision making; ability to play; ability to regulate individual and group behavior; and ability to resolve conflict. Bell posits that decision-making processes will be political in nature in the postindustrial society. As a result, tension and conflict will probably increase, and conflict resolution will become a necessary skill.

Analyses by these futurists provide much food for thought. Observation of recent trends and events lends credibility to many of their forecasts. We need only examine the advent of legislative mandates for minimum contact hours, collective bargaining by public employees, land use legislation, affirmative action programs, energy control legislation, and pollution control legislation to find evidence of the new kinds of decision-making processes and interest groups described by Bell. Clearly, each of these trends has critical significance for the role of faculty members in higher education.

In response to such dramatic changes in society, renewal activities for faculty members may include an introduction to the concepts of global interdependence, to techniques in values clarification, and to principles of attitude development and change. Nevertheless, perhaps the most compelling rationale for a deliberate faculty development effort is the severe curtailment and ineffectiveness, due to these trends, of the informal and spontaneous forces that have fostered faculty growth, development, and change in the past. Faculty members must now accept greater responsibility for conducting and managing their own change and renewal processes. Without these processes, stagnation and irrelevance in both teaching and research may well increase.

State of the Art

Given a case for a deliberate faculty development effort, what are some of the ways in which such efforts have been conducted? One salutary effect of the student unrest of the mid- and late 1960s was that it drew attention to the quality of college teaching. Not surprisingly, the American Council on Education chose as the theme for its 1966 Annual Meeting the topic of improving college teaching. Papers and commentaries on "teaching the teachers" were presented there; proceedings of the conference were published the following year. Interestingly enough, Calvin Lee, who edited the papers (*Improving College Teaching: Aids and Impediments*) noted that only two paragraphs were devoted to the teaching of older teachers, but at least the matter was raised.

Several relevant monographs on the topic have appeared since then, however. *Career Development of the Effective College Teacher*, by Kenneth E. Eble, appeared in 1971 through the sponsorship of the American Association of Colleges and the American Association of University Professors. Jossey-Bass, in its New Directions for Higher Education series, featured a collection of essays by Mervin Freedman entitled *Facilitating Faculty Development*. Perhaps the most cogent and provocative statements regarding the teaching of older teachers can be found in the book *Faculty Development in a Time of Retrenchment*, by the Group for Human Development in Higher Education. The work that resulted in this latter monograph was supported at various times by the Carnegie Corporation, Lilly Endowment, and the HAZEN Foundation. As a matter of fact, the Lilly Endowment has committed funds to several liberal arts schools for the purpose of establishing faculty development programs. The question no longer seems to be whether or not but when and how.

When we examine the existing literature on faculty development, we find that nearly all of it focuses on only one of the faculty members' roles—teaching. Yet in most institutions faculty members serve as researchers, curriculum developers, information analysts, disseminators of knowledge through the mass media, theory builders, providers of service, problem solvers, consultants, advisors, and counselors. Some also serve as administrators, managers, and members of government committees. Thus, faculty roles and responsibilities span far more than the teaching function itself. The term *faculty development*, as used in this chapter, therefore, refers to establishing activities and procedures that assist faculty members in acquiring knowledge, skills, and attitudes that enable them to become more effective in performing all functions related to professional academic life.

What, then, are some activities that could aid a department faculty development effort? The following list includes only a few of the many possible activities, some of which may already be available at some institutions. Two criteria govern the selection of the activities listed here: faculty members can engage in such activities without great cost to the university and without the assistance of elaborate service facilities or massive bureaucratic effort; and little effort beyond individual initiative is required in order to participate. The list was adapted from a list compiled by David G. Brown and William S. Hanger.*

SUGGESTED SELF-DEVELOPMENT ACTIVITIES FOR FACULTY
MEMBERS
- A. New experiences
  1. Exchanges and sabbaticals
     a. Exchanges within your college or university
     b. Exchanges between colleges and universities regionally, nationally, and internationally
     c. Short visits to neighboring colleges or universities
     d. Exchanges with government, industry, or foundations
     e. Joint appointments
     f. Assignments in other universities or institutes
     g. New, unusual, or unfamiliar committee assignments
  2. Special assignments in administrative posts
     a. Work in dean's office
     b. Work in contracts and grants office
     c. Prepare a grant proposal for a faculty development project sponsored by your institution
- B. Development of expertise
  1. Research practices
     a. Submit articles, monographs, books, book reviews, or poetry for publication
     b. Attend research colloquia within and outside the department
     c. Team with a colleague from outside the department to write a grant proposal or article
     d. Join a research center or institute

*David G. Brown and William S. Hanger, "Pragmatics of Faculty Self-Development," *Educational Record*, Summer 1975, pp. 202–6.

e. Participate in local, regional, or national conferences
f. Participate in consortia activities
g. Read literature in your field

2. Developments in peripheral areas
   a. Audit courses given in your field or a related field
   b. Enroll in a new degree program
   c. Take a continuing education course
   d. Enroll in an undergraduate short course
   e. Attend a dissertation defense in another discipline
   f. Read literature about higher education (e.g., *Chronicle of Higher Education, Journal of Higher Education, Educational Record, Change, Higher Education and National Affairs,* and so forth)

C. Instructional development
   1. New techniques and materials
      a. Organize or participate in instructional improvement seminars or luncheons
      b. Visit classes conducted by colleagues
      c. Sponsor a session at a professional conference or convention on teaching techniques within your discipline
      d. Develop and use audio-visual aids
      e. Experiment with one of the new teaching technologies—computer-assisted instruction (CAI), individually guided instruction (IGI), instruction television (ITV), simulation and gaming
      f. Talk with book salesmen or equipment dealers
      g. Write and distribute to students clear objectives for the courses you teach
      h. Vary teaching techniques—for example, if you teach primarily by lecturing, introduce some discussion techniques
      i. Try the case-study method
   2. New skills and knowledge about the teaching and learning processes
      a. Take a psychology course or education course in language development or cognitive development
      b. Seek out colleagues familiar with objective test design, criterion-referenced assessment, evaluation strategies, performance testing
      c. Make an item analysis of your tests
   3. Curriculum development
      a. Develop a new specialty area
      b. Attempt to assess and evaluate the effectiveness of a series of courses or a program
      c. Learn about competency-based education
   4. New teaching experiences
      a. Prepare to teach a new course in your discipline or in a related discipline
      b. Teaching a continuing education course
      c. Teach an in-service workshop for practicing professionals

    d. Take over a colleague's class in another discipline when he or she is away

    e. Teach an intensive short course

    f. Teach a high school class or a graduate seminar for a few days

    g. Team teach with a colleague or student

5. Evaluation

    a. Have students evaluate your teaching effectiveness

    b. Form a student feedback committee to advise you on teaching effectiveness

    c. Invite a teaching specialist to sit in on your classes and offer constructive criticism

    d. Xerox your lecture notes and have peers react to them

    e. Videotape your lectures and have colleagues critique them

    f. Develop a peer evaluation system with your colleagues

D. Service

1. Advisement

    a. Solicit current information about employment possibilities for students majoring in your discipline

    b. Study counseling techniques and human development theories

    c. Advise a campus student group (fraternity or sorority, political group, campus newspaper, service clubs, and so forth)

    d. Keep up with rules and regulations regarding curriculum options outside your discipline

    e. Help with registration advisement or drop-add advisement

    f. Learn to recognize abnormal behavior patterns persons use when coping with stress or anxiety

    g. Find out about community mental health services and how to make referrals

    h. Learn about campus services available to students

2. Interaction with students

    a. Entertain students in your home

    b. Live in a residence hall for two days

    c. Host a foreign student

    d. Attend an intercollegiate athletic event

    e. Lead a group of students to Europe, Mexico, Asia

    f. Participate on a faculty intramural team

3. Community involvement

    a. Run for local office

    b. Serve on local or state government committees and councils

    c. Do volunteer work with a hospital board or local charity

    d. Consult

    e. Participate in academic fairs, workshops, or other activities with elementary and secondary teachers or counselors

4. Work for the college or university

    a. Assist the admissions office in recruiting students

    b. Prepare attractive materials or publications for recruiting students to your field

      c. Call on prospective donors of gifts and bequests asking for time, money, equipment, artifacts

      d. Serve on an admissions committee

E. Personal development

  1. Personal knowledge

      a. Enroll in a skill development course such as typing, book-keeping, auto repairs

      b. Enroll in a continuing education course

      c. Enroll in a leisure education course

      d. Join a group to watch a public television course

      e. Participate in an "outward bound" program

      f. Try to attend a dozen special lectures on campus next year

      g. Analyze how you spend your free time

      h. Attend a personal growth group (assertiveness training, stress management, interpersonal communication, and so forth)

      i. Join a book club

  2. Cultural experiences

      a. Attend an artist series on campus

      b. Travel to a foreign country

      c. Learn a new foreign language or sign language

  3. Career development

      a. Schedule brown-bag sessions to discuss life and careers of important or interesting persons

      b. Organize a panel on nonacademic career opportunities related to your discipline

      c. Develop a contract with your department chairperson that allows you to pursue a special area of interest in the year ahead

      d. Work at another profession or develop new sources of income that complement but do not detract from academic responsibilities

  4. Physical development

      a. Jog with a group of colleagues

      b. Form a faculty intramural team

      c. Learn a new sport

The Question of the Chairperson's Role

In all likelihood, when aspiring faculty members assumed their roles as chairpersons, no clause was included in their contracts or job descriptions that alluded to responsibilities regarding faculty development. The question naturally follows, "How much responsibility should a chairperson have in ensuring that faculty members continue to upgrade their knowledge and skills as researchers and instructors?" Below are three short scenarios describing possible role models for the ways in which chairpersons might respond to this issue.

The Caretaker

Chairperson Smith, fifty-five years old, has been a department chairperson for four years. The faculty members in his department are all tenured; half are associate professors, and the other half are full professors. Most are between the ages of thirty-five and fifty-five, and they are generally satisfied with their lot professionally. Smith has noticed lately, however, that many of them are beginning to invest more of their effort in nonprofessional activities—such as camping, jogging, and community affairs—and that department productivity in research and student credit hours is beginning to fall off.

Smith recognizes the need for faculty development in general but feels that each person should assume complete responsibility for finding activities that foster his or her own growth and development. He does, however, have a good reputation for helping faculty members who come to him for advice, and he encourages them to pursue their own initiatives, particularly in research. Merit pay is awarded primarily on the single criterion of research productivity. Smith sees his role as chairperson mainly as that of a caretaker who manages routine administrative duties. He plans to resume eventually the role of full-time faculty member.

The Broker

Chairperson Jones, fifty years old, has been department chairperson for three years. Approximately 20 percent of the department faculty members are untenured. Ten percent are assistant professors; 30 percent are associate professors; and 60 percent are full professors. Their ages range from thirty to sixty; forty-five is the median age. Jones has stated that the primary criterion for determining merit pay should be effective teaching, but the department's tenure and promotion committee clearly rewards those who demonstrate productivity in research. The department enrollment has held steady over the past several years and probably will continue to do so since the department's admissions standards are now somewhat selective. Should applications decline, the department would simply decrease admissions standards to compensate. The faculty morale is good, but none of the faculty members are exerting unusual efforts—such as serving on editorial boards or establishing clearly focused research programs—to distinguish themselves nationally.

Jones's view of her role regarding faculty development is that of facilitator and broker. She is familiar with services available to faculty members within the institution and in the community. During the annual evaluation conferences, she reviews with the faculty members their career objectives, suggests resources to help them, and often makes referrals to the contracts and grants office, the instructional design center, and, for personal and career problems, the campus or community counseling centers. But she definitely sees her role as helping faculty members realize their personal and professional goals by encouraging them to seek help from specialized services outside the department. To this end, she maintains a complete file of brochures pertaining to faculty development services and opportunities for growth, such as sabbaticals and exchange programs. Jones has stated publicly that she does not seek a higher administrative office, but she has indicated to close associates that if she were nominated for the position of dean, she would accept the nomination.

The Developer

Chairperson Adams, forty-five years old, has been chairperson for three years. The department faculty members are all tenured; 65 percent are associate professors, and 35 percent are full professors. The median age is forty. The faculty members are highly competitive and ambitious. Adams, who entertains the goal of some day assuming greater administrative responsibility as a dean, seeks to help his department gain a strong regional and perhaps even a national reputation. The department's goals are to increase the number and quality of students enrolled in the program, to have each faculty member in the department establish a focused research program, and to have each member demonstrate service to the profession and the community in ways that will enhance the first two goals.

As a result, Adams has established and organized a rather sophisticated faculty development effort. He has established a committee on research that coordinates and encourages grant-writing efforts and publication. A seminar on grantsmanship is held once a year, and a colloquium in which faculty members report their research efforts is held once a month. A curriculum committee is also active; it coordinates matters concerning the content of the curriculum and encourages new delivery mechanisms as well. To expand enrollments, the curriculum committee plans an outreach effort to offer, through the continuing education office, special interest courses to the community. Through this effort the department hopes to enroll many students in full-credit courses or degree programs. The chairperson realizes that the faculty members have had little experience in conducting programs like that planned by the curriculum committee and feels that a series of seminars is necessary to help them acquire the requisite skills for the new program.

Thus Adams views his role regarding faculty development as that of developer. He actively helps faculty members acquire skills and knowledge to implement department goals. The faculty members realize that by contributing toward department goals, they, in turn, will be more able to attain individual professional goals. Adams has also established a reward system that recognizes achievement in these areas and requires that faculty members demonstrate how they have helped the department achieve its goals.

Whether a department chairperson acts as a caretaker, broker, or developer or wishes to assume some other role depends on several factors, such as his or her career goals, self-image, or leadership skills. These factors then interact with the collective will of the department faculty. Does the department want to be led by a caretaker, broker, or developer? A department's capability to survive and grow in an era of declining resources may well depend on the chairperson's ability to lead within the constraints of the faculty's expectations and aspirations.

If the idea of a faculty development program seems attractive, the chairperson and each department faculty member should ponder the following questions: What important trends will affect the department in the next five to ten years? What should be the department's response to these trends? Where does each faculty member want to be, with respect to his or her own life and career, five or ten years from now? Tentative answers to these questions can provide the foundation on which to build a faculty development program and a serious commitment to professional development.

Planning a Development Program

Once the faculty has decided to explore the possibility of establishing a deliberate faculty development effort, a first step in planning is to analyze how local, regional, and national trends might affect the department. One planning technique that is helpful in analyzing how trends may affect a department is the matrix method. One dimension of the matrix lists important trends, while the other identifies components of a program, such as curriculum, faculty members, students, and research (see Fig. 7.1). Intercepts in the matrix show how the trends will affect particular program components. Using a five-year planning horizon might be helpful—i.e., project how the trend will affect the program component five years from now. Information organized in this way can provide a basis for establishing priority goals and activities in the area of faculty development. Figure 7.1 presents hypothetical data on how certain local and national trends may affect a department in a school of education.

PROGRAM COMPONENTS

	Curriculum	Faculty Members	Students	Research
More adult learners	1. Ways of crediting prior experience will be developed. 2. More evening classes will be required. 3. More in-service training will be required. 4. Practical application will be emphasized.	1. Faculty members may be required to teach on evenings or on weekends. 2. Faculty members must become knowledgeable about how adults learn. 3. Faculty members may be threatened.	1. New services may be required (e.g., babysitting). 2. There may be less collegiality among students.	1. Research moneys will be available to address problems of adult learners.
Energy shortage	1. Delivery systems must rely on low-cost dissemination. 2. Ways of learning through media at home or at work will be explored.	1. Faculty members may be required to go to students rather than vice versa. 2. Instruction may take place through media and correspondence.	1. Skills in independent learning may be crucial. 2. Transportation costs to schools may be prohibitive for commuter students.	1. There will be less mobility to travel to conventions. 2. There will be more emphasis on journals to keep informed. 3. Funds will be available to explore ways of disseminating information through low-cost media.
More working women	1. Ways of coping with sex bias will be included in curriculum. 2. Ways of removing stereotyping will be included in curriculum materials.	1. Faculty members may be required to adjust teaching methods to working mothers or single parents. 2. Faculty members' values regarding the career woman, dual-career families, and single-parent families may be tested.	1. More men may pursue elementary education as a career. 2. More women may pursue math and science as careers.	1. Studies in processes of stereotyping will be encouraged. 2. Studies in the educational development of children from dual-career families will be encouraged.

TRENDS

FIGURE 7.1. Sample of matrix analysis: trends affecting an education department, 1980–85.

Anyone using the matrix technique must be able to identify those trends that would exert the strongest influence. Otherwise, one may plan to scratch where no itch develops. Assuming, though, that the predictions resulting from this analysis are correct—or at least defensible—gaps between the existing state of affairs and the desired state of affairs become readily apparent.

Initiating a Development Program: Six Caveats

After analyzing important trends and ways in which it could effectively respond, the department should consider strategies for change. Certain caveats should be kept in mind when initiating faculty development activities.

1. *Aim for cooperation.* For faculty development to become an ongoing process, it must be a cooperative effort involving the faculty members, department chairpersons, and other administrators. Lack of support at any of the three levels could result in wasted effort.

2. *Think big, but start small.* A well-planned activity for a small group of interested faculty members is more likely to be successful than a large-scale, general effort, which may suit no one. A low-profile, low-key approach keeps expectations at realistic levels and provides a better basis to begin working with faculty members. A hard-sell approach tends to alienate or intimidate many faculty members and thereby creates difficulties in working with them later. A small group of satisfied and motivated volunteers will soon set an example for their colleagues.

3. *Involve faculty members in planning development activities.* This approach will help ensure content validity for the participants and enhance their commitment to follow through. The cliché "Begin where the people are" is as pertinent when working with the faculty as with any other group of adult learners. The goals to be achieved should be set by the faculty members themselves, not by other persons in the academic hierarchy. Given adequate performance counseling, faculty members should assume the ultimate authority for determining the direction and nature of change.

4. *Be eclectic in approach.* When planning a faculty development program, the department may be tempted to concentrate on a single new technique. No single technique is suitable for everyone, however, and a variety of possible techniques would enable faculty members to choose some that suit their own style and needs.

5. *Start where the chances of success are high.* First impressions are crucial, and a few small but highly successful efforts will soon pave the way for more ambitious projects and activities.

6. *Institutionalize faculty development efforts.* A meaningful program of faculty development must address itself to the question of long-term efforts and how these efforts can be formalized to ensure longevity, adaptability, and relevance.

Strategies for Initiating a Development Program

If the chairperson has decided to begin a faculty development program and has determined his or her level of responsibility for administering it, he or she should analyze some of the conditions that would foster or inhibit the implementation of a program. Two approaches, described below, may be appropriate for initiating a faculty development program.

1. *Faculty development as a means to individual development.* This strategy begins with an activity in which a reasonable number of faculty members have agreed to participate. Determining the topic could be accomplished through the use of a questionnaire administered by a department faculty development committee. After collating the data, the committee would set priorities and consult with the chairperson for endorsement of its plans. The advantage of this strategy is that the faculty members assume the responsibility for determining areas in which they would like to improve.

2. *Faculty development as a means to department development.* Another strategy is to make faculty development a means to help the department achieve its goals. The department determines its goals by analyzing perceived trends that will affect its future. In addressing these trends and the changes required to meet them, the department should consider whether the faculty is currently qualified to meet the new demands. A faculty development program then is anchored to department goals agreed upon by the faculty. This approach addresses the matter of motivation—i.e., why faculty members should participate in an organized faculty development effort. The faculty members can then collectively monitor their progress in attaining department goals. Obviously, when faculty members perceive a faculty development effort as a means for enhancing both their individual goals and a department's goals, an optimum state of affairs exists.

Conditions That May Inhibit Faculty Development

Faculty development programs have met resistance for various reasons. The chairperson should be aware of common problems that impede the implementation of a program.

- The faculty members' personal goals may not be congruent with the goals of the department or the college. In this case, faculty members may fail to identify with any effort to alter the status quo.
- Faculty members often perceive development activities as unnecessary infringements on their already crowded schedules. They need to be convinced of the value of deliberate efforts toward professional growth.
- Even when faculty members become aware of the need for such involvement, they often have little idea of where to go or whom to ask for assistance.
- Some chairpersons see as a barrier the lack of funds to buy books or materials, to pay for travel, or to hire consultants. Some programs require little or no funding, however, and the chairperson should encourage development efforts even when moneys are not available.
- Physical isolation from colleagues deprives some faculty members of opportunities for stimulation and learning.
- In some departments a spirit of apathy exists, and faculty members are indifferent to the idea of continuing their professional growth. Other departments may have faculty members who feel that they have already achieved perfection and therefore see no need for organized development activities.

Many of the conditions that inhibit development efforts may be overcome by proper leadership on the part of the chairperson.

Assessing Readiness for Involvement

Before embarking on a faculty development effort, a chairperson may wish to obtain an indication from the faculty members regarding their interests. Identifying interest areas could be accomplished through a questionnaire listing areas of development and relevant activities. The following list includes some possible activities that department chairpersons can adapt for use with their faculty members:*

AREAS OF DEVELOPMENT AND POSSIBLE ACTIVITIES FOR
FACULTY MEMBERS
    A. Professional development
        1. Acquiring visiting professorships
        2. Locating and applying for sabbaticals
        3. Getting published

*This list is part of the Professional Seminars and Workshops Questionnaire, prepared by the Institute for Departmental Leadership, Florida State University, with the cooperation of the Instructional Systems Institute.

4. Preparing grant proposals
5. Establishing your own research program
6. Exploring professional exchanges with business, industry, and government
7. Setting up joint appointment possibilities
8. Conducting an effective committee meeting
9. Exploring techniques for department curriculum planning

B. Instructional development
1. Developing course objectives
2. Preparing and using media in the classroom
3. Preparing and delivering a lecture
4. Stimulating class discussions
5. Preparing classroom tests
6. Using computers for testing students
7. Using atypical classroom procedures
   a. Keller Plan (using student tutors to teach subsections of large lecture courses)
   b. Personalized systems of instruction
   c. Competency-based education
   d. Self-instructional systems
8. Evaluating students' writing skills

C. Personal development
1. Managing time efficiently
2. Improving relationships with colleagues
3. Improving relationships with department chairpersons
4. Learning about faculty career patterns
5. Using assertiveness techniques with students and peers
6. Training in stress management
7. Dealing with job frustrations
8. Overcoming boredom
9. Developing effective communication skills
10. Exploring local recreational opportunities
11. Improving your physical health
12. Managing the dual-career family
13. Countering sexism in higher education
14. Exploring tax-deductible professional activities

D. Service
1. Becoming a consultant for government, private industry, or other consumers
2. Exploring consultation techniques
3. Getting appointed to state, regional, and national professional committees
4. Teaching special interest courses
5. Evaluating your service contribution to the university
6. Finding opportunities for public speaking
7. Learning to speak effectively
8. Planning and conducting workshops and conferences
9. Advising students about courses and careers

10. Recognizing, coping with, and referring troubled or disruptive students
11. Exploring career possibilities for students in your discipline
12. Participating on department committees
13. Securing public support for your program

Staff, or professional, development activities existed long before the term *faculty development* was coined. Nevertheless, before a chairperson expends a great deal of energy in organizing a deliberate faculty development effort, he or she should determine whether faculty members perceive a need for it. Not surprisingly, most faculty members consider themselves "above average" teachers, and some openly claim to be among the best. With such perceptions of perfection, it is no wonder that faculty members are sometimes unresponsive to efforts to induce them to improve their teaching skills. Faculty members must perceive a need to change before they will commit themselves to participating in a faculty development effort, whether in teaching or some other professional area. Without a cogent rationale, however, such efforts will probably not elicit much faculty response.

This chapter has highlighted three critical factors that chairpersons should consider before embarking on a deliberate faculty development effort: (1) the significant local, regional, and national trends that may require of the faculty members new skills for serving their students; (2) the chairperson's own perceptions of his or her role in the area of faculty development; and (3) the extent to which individual faculty members' goals can be met by meeting the department's goals. Unless faculty members themselves can be convinced of the need to be involved in some form of faculty development and are willing to participate in a program, however, the probability of success for these types of activities is not great.

Questions and Exercises

1. In view of the changes that may well affect higher education in general, select three trends or changes that are likely to have the most effect on your department during the next five years.
2. For each trend you cited above, how would your department's curriculum, faculty, students, and research programs be affected? Construct a matrix similar to the one shown in this chapter.
3. a. From the list of faculty development activities suggested in this chapter and from your own experience, list three activities that would be appropriate for helping faculty members in your department acquire knowledge and skills to cope more effectively with each of the three trends you listed in question 1.

    b. Having read the three scenarios in the chapter describing ways in which a chairperson could approach faculty development, formulate an approach that would have the best chance of success in your department.

4. To what extent is faculty development an individual responsibility of each faculty member versus a departmental responsibility?
    a. What if any should be the role of chairpersons who believe it to be an individual responsibility of each faculty member?
    b. What should be the role of chairpersons who believe it to be a departmental responsibility?

5. To what extent should faculty members be required to submit a yearly plan for their professional development?

6. To what extent should a faculty member's involvement in professional development activities be included in the criteria used for annual performance evaluation?

7. To what extent should faculty members be expected to engage in individual professional development activities at their own expense?

8. To what extent should departmental funds be used to support an individual's professional development activities:
    a. when it is an integral part of a current plan for implementing departmental goals. Give examples of faculty development activities that might fall into this category.
    b. when it has potential for contributing to possible future plans for implementing departmental goals. Give examples of faculty development activities that might fall into this category.
    c. when it is primarily for the benefit of the individual without benefiting the department. Give examples of faculty development activities that might fall into this category.

References

Bailey, Stephen K. "People Planning in Postsecondary Education: Human Resource Development in a World of Decremental Budgets." In *More for Less: Academic Planning with Faculty without New Dollars*, edited by James N. Nesmith, pp. 3–11. New York: Society for College and University Planning and Educational Testing Service, College and University Programs, 1975.

Bell, Daniel. *The Coming of Post-Industrial Society: A Venture in Social Forecasting.* New York: Basic Books, 1973.

Bennis, Warren G. *Organization Development: Its Nature, Origins, and Prospects*, edited by Edgar Schien et al. Reading, Mass.: Addison-Wesley, 1969.

BERGQUIST, WILLIAM H.; PHILIPS, STEVEN R.; AND QUEHL, GARY H. *A Handbook for Faculty Development*. Washington, D.C.: Council for the Advancement of Small Colleges, 1975.

BOYER, RONALD K., AND CROCKETT, CAMPBELL, eds. "Organizational Development in Higher Education." *Journal of Higher Education*, May 1973 (special issue), pp. 339–51.

BROWN, DAVID G., AND HANGER, WILLIAM S. "Pragmatics of Faculty Self-Development." *Educational Record*, Summer 1975, pp. 201–6.

CHICKERING, ARTHUR W. *Education and Identity*. San Francisco: Jossey-Bass, 1969.

CROW, MARY LYNN; MILTON, OHMER; MOOMAW, W. EDMUND; AND O'CONNELL, WILLIAM R., JR., eds. *Faculty Development Centers in Southern Universities*. Atlanta: Southern Regional Education Board, 1976.

EBLE, KENNETH E. *Career Development of the Effective College Teacher*. Washington, D.C.: Association of American Colleges and the American Association of University Professors, 1971.

———. *Professors as Teachers*. San Francisco: Jossey-Bass, 1972.

FELDMAN, KENNETH A., AND NEWCOMB, THEODORE M. *The Impact of College on Students*. 2 vols. San Francisco: Jossey-Bass, 1969.

FREEDMAN, MERVIN. *Facilitating Faculty Development*. San Francisco: Jossey-Bass, 1973.

GAFF, JERRY G. *Toward Faculty Renewal: Advances in Faculty, Instructional, and Organizational Development*. San Francisco: Jossey-Bass, 1975.

GAGNE, ROBERT M., AND BRIGGS, LESLIE J. *Principles of Instructional Design*. 2nd ed. New York: Holt, Rhinehart, & Winston, 1979.

GROUP FOR HUMAN DEVELOPMENT IN HIGHER EDUCATION. *Faculty Development in a Time of Retrenchment*. New Rochelle, N.Y.: Change Magazine Press, 1974.

KAHN, HERMAN, AND BRUCE-BRIGGS, B. *Things to Come: Thinking about the Seventies and Eighties*. New York: Macmillan, 1972.

LEE, CALVIN B. T., ed. *Improving College Teaching: Aids and Impediments*. Washington, D.C.: American Council on Education, 1966.

MAGER, ROBERT F. *Preparing Instructional Objectives*. 2nd ed. Palo Alto, Calif.: Fearon-Pitman, 1975.

MORRIS, CELIA. "A Call for Faculty Reform." *Change*, Winter 1973–1974, pp. 13–15.

NELSON, WILLIAM C., AND SIEGEL, MICHAEL C. (eds.). *Effective Approaches to Faculty Development*. Washington, D.C.: Association of American Colleges, 1980.

NOONAN, JOHN F. "Curricular Change: A Strategy for Improving Teaching." In *The Expanded Campus: Current Issues in Higher Education 1972*, edited by Dyckman W. Vermilye. San Francisco: Jossey-Bass, 1972.

O'CONNELL, WILLIAM R., JR., AND MEETH, L. RICHARD. *Evaluating Teaching Improvement Programs*. New Rochelle, N.Y.: Change Magazine Press, 1978.

SELDIN, PETER J. "Fostering Faculty Talent." *Change*, September 1976, pp. 10–13.

SMITH, RALPH B., AND OVARD, GLEN F. "Professional Development: A New Approach." *Improving College and University Teaching*, Winter 1979, pp. 40–43.

STONE, JAMES C., ET AL. *Toward Excellence in Teaching, Too.* Berkeley: University of California Press, 1974.

TOFFLER, ALVIN. *Future Shock.* New York: Random House, 1970.

WILSON, ROBERT C.; GAFF, JERRY G.; DIENST, EVELYN R.; WOOD, LYNN; AND BAVRY, JAMES L. *College Professors and Their Impact on Students.* New York: John Wiley & Sons, 1975.

8

Faculty Evaluation

Evaluation of faculty performance is one of the chairperson's most difficult and important responsibilities. Probably no other activity has more potential for strengthening or weakening the department over a period of years. One of the most important components of faculty evaluation is communication with each faculty member regarding what is expected and what will be evaluated. This communication can be in the form of a contract, a written memorandum of understanding, or an official assignment statement. A verbal understanding not in writing may not be enough. Handled properly, evaluation can improve faculty morale and result in a strong, effective department. Handled improperly, evaluation can destroy morale, decrease the chances for the department's success in meeting objectives, and place the chairperson on the receiving end of a long succession of grievances. Most colleges and universities have or should have official documents that provide specific information about the evaluation process, such as how often evaluations will be conducted, who will do the evaluating, in what form the evaluations will be submitted, who may use them, how they will be used, and what may be placed in the faculty member's personnel file.

A necessary condition for effective evaluation is clear, specific criteria. In addition, there must be a reasonable, definitive assignment of activities and an ongoing system of performance counseling. If faculty members' assignments are sufficiently clear and if discussion between chairperson and faculty members regarding performance becomes a regular activity, evaluation will no longer be seen as a dreaded annual exercise. In effect, the process could become no more than a report of a faculty member's performance—a report that would hold no surprises for either the faculty member or the chairperson.

This chapter will focus on four questions: Why is evaluation necessary? What should be evaluated? Who should do the evaluating and what should be the process? How should performance be evaluated? Examples of different procedures used to evaluate faculty performance are presented. No single procedure is advocated as being better than another. It should be noted, however, that each of the procedures described in the following pages is used by at least one department at some institution.

Why Is Evaluation Necessary?

Every department chairperson who has held the position for at least a year has been faced with the need to evaluate staff and faculty members. Evaluation is required by the dean, the collective bargaining contract (if the institution has one), the vice-president, the president, the board of trustees, and even the faculty. One basic purpose of evaluation has always been to provide faculty members with some measure of how well they are performing in their professional role so that they can improve their performance. Sooner or later, however, all evaluation activity must serve as a basis for decision making in matters of promotion, tenure, salary increases, and other benefits. In times of limited resources and static or declining university growth, competition becomes intense and decisions are sometimes challenged. State legislators, parents, and citizens are requiring more accountability with regard to the quality of teaching, benefits from research, and time away from campus for service.

Faculty members themselves are no longer satisfied with an arbitrary and paternalistic evaluation by a department chairperson. They insist on a more formal evaluation based on specific criteria, and this desire seems to increase as the discretionary funds available for merit raises decrease. Faculty members also want the option to appeal in the event that they disagree with the evaluation. Leaders in education, therefore, need to find ways to perform evaluations that are reliable and acceptable to students, to the faculty, to faculty unions, to university administrators, and to state legislators and other groups responsible for providing financial support.

What Should Be Evaluated?

The central academic functions of most universities and baccalaureate granting colleges include teaching, research, and service. The amount of effort allotted to each of these functions varies from institution to institution. The main functions of community colleges are teaching and service. Community college faculty members are not expected to conduct research as part of their workload and hence research is not evaluated. Some of their professional efforts, however, are devoted to special projects and could fall into a general category called "special assignments." Community college department chairpersons and division directors may wish to ignore those sections in this chapter dealing with research and include instead a category of "special assignments" as a performance area to be evaluated along with teaching and service. A department committee or the department as a whole will have little difficulty in developing a list of activities to be evaluated under each of the broad areas of performance as determined by the institution. Questions about the minimal level of performance quality and the kinds of evidence that will be accepted for the evaluation, however, are considerably more difficult.

One point that has emerged in the last several years, especially at those institutions that have faculty unions, is the importance of evaluating only what has been formally assigned. Penalizing faculty members for failing to complete unassigned duties or for failing to accomplish more than what has been assigned has created legal problems in some instances when faculty members were not subsequently promoted or awarded tenure. It behooves chairpersons, therefore, to anticipate what activities within each major category will be evaluated and to include them in the formal assignments.

Receiving an assignment does not necessarily mean that a faculty member is called into the chairperson's office and told "This is what you are assigned to do this year." The most common practice is for the faculty member to tell what courses he or she plans to teach, and what other activities are planned. The chairperson may make suggestions, and when a plan is agreed upon by the faculty member and the chairperson, the plan is written up as the faculty member's assignment. The word "assignment" seems to have a negative connotation in the minds of some academics because of its perceived authoritarian implication. Nevertheless, it is a term commonly used in official faculty contracts. Such contracts often stipulate that faculty may be evaluated only on activities contained in the formal assignment. Regardless of semantics, however, a faculty member needs to know what is expected of him or her and upon what basis an evaluation will be made. At some institutions the "official" assignment and the expectations may not be the same. For example, the "official" assignment may contain only the amount of teaching that is expected. Although faculty members at these institutions are expected to engage in other activities such as research, these expectations are not included in the formal assignment but are called "add ons" and are often interpreted by newly appointed faculty members as voluntary. Yet, the awarding of promotion or tenure at some of these institutions is often based on the performance evaluation received for the "add on" activities. Faculty members who are denied promotion or tenure because they performed poorly or not at all in an "add on" activity sometimes file grievances. They claim that they were not explicitly informed that a recommendation for their promotion and tenure would depend on a satisfactory performance in that activity.

Performance Areas to Be Evaluated

Performance areas to be evaluated are generally listed in various official documents, such as the university constitution, the state system personnel policy manual, or a union contract. The list may vary in detail from one university to another, from one department to another within the same university, or from one faculty member to another. Most lists, however, will include the following performance areas, compiled from a variety of official documents. Note the mixture of activities, outcomes, and the quantitative and qualitative characteristics included.

Teaching.   Teaching involves the presentation of knowledge, information, and ideas by methods that include lecturing, discussion, assignment and recitation, demonstration, laboratory exercise, practical experience, direct consultation with students, and so forth. In an evaluation, the use and effectiveness of each method should be considered. The evaluation of teaching effectiveness should also be related to the written objectives of each course, which should have been given to each class at the beginning of the term. Evaluation of teaching should include consideration of:

- correlation of imparted knowledge and skills to course objectives
- stimulation of the students' critical thinking and creative ability in light of the course objectives
- the faculty member's adherence to accepted standards of professional behavior in meeting his or her responsibilities to students

In an informal sample taken in 1979, chairpersons in two major state universities in Florida listed the following as their preferred sources of evidence for evaluating teaching: (1) systematic rating by students; (2) chairperson's evaluation; (3) colleagues' opinions; (4) committee evaluation; (5) content of course syllabi and examinations; (6) informal rating by students; (7) colleagues' ratings based on classroom visits; (8) long-term follow-up of students' performance; (9) faculty member's interest in teaching improvement activities (workshops and so forth); (10) faculty member's self-evaluation or report; (11) students' examination performance; (12) popularity of elective courses (e.g., enrollment); and (13) opinions of alumni.*

*Informal survey conducted by Allan Tucker, unpublished.

Research and Other Creative Activities.   Contribution to and discovery of new knowledge, new educational techniques, and other forms of creative activity should be considered for evaluation. Evidence of research and other creative activity should include, but not be limited to, published books; articles and papers in professional journals; paintings and sculpture; works for performance (musical compositions, dances, plays, and so forth); papers presented at meetings of professional societies; and current research and creative activity that has not yet resulted in publication, display, or performance. Evaluation of research and other creative activities should include consideration of:

- quality and quantity of productivity of both short-term and long-term research and other creative programs and contributions
- recognition by the academic or professional community of work accomplished (for judgments pertaining to the decision to award tenure, evaluation should be sought from qualified scholars in pertinent disciplines both within and outside the university)

Special Assignments.   Community colleges may use this category in lieu of research. Each institution must determine for itself what projects or activities should be included under this category and what criteria and evidence will be used in evaluating the activities.

Service.   Service should include, but not be limited to, involvement in department, college, and university committees, councils, and senates; service in appropriate professional organizations; involvement in organizing and expediting meetings, symposia, conferences, and workshops; participation in radio and television; and service on local, state, and national governmental boards, commissions, and other agencies. Only those activities that are related to a person's field of expertise or to the university's mission should be evaluated. Evaluation of service should include consideration of:

- contribution to the orderly and effective functioning of the academic administrative unit (program, department, school, college) and the whole institution
- contribution to the university community
- contribution to local, state, regional, and national communities, including scholarly and professional associations

Other University Duties.   Reasonable duties other than those usually classified as teaching, research or other creative activity, or service are occasionally assigned to faculty members. The performance of these duties—which might include academic administration, academic advising, career counseling, or the supervision of interns—should also be evaluated. A dean or director may be the best person to conduct the evaluation of these activities, so the chairperson should consult them about correct procedures.

Evaluation Based on Assignments

If evaluations are to be based on assignments, then the assignments must specify what constitutes successful and acceptable completion. Such specification requires an understanding of the difference between activities and outcomes, for both may be evaluated. Typically, faculty members are paid for participating in an acceptable set of professional activities, such as conducting classes, preparing syllabi and other materials for classes, advising and counseling students, serving on department and institutional governing committees, reviewing manuscripts, collecting and analyzing data, conducting research, and so on. Simply assigning activities without some idea of what is expected or what constitutes satisfactory completion of the assignment, however, makes it difficult to differentiate the performance of faculty members, especially when they are given similar activity assignments—the same number of courses to teach, the same percentage of time to conduct research, and so forth.

Outcomes are the results of activities. Whereas activities emphasize process, outcomes focus on achievements and end products. Examples of simple outcome assignments made by department chairpersons include preparing and duplicating for students a research bibliography on subject X for course Y; completing the first draft of the third chapter of a book manuscript on topic Z; and reviewing the professional literature on subject R for inclusion in a consulting paper for government agency A. All these outcomes are clearly observable.

Examples of complex outcome assignments would be completing manuscript M and finding a publisher for it; submitting a completed proposal for funding and having it accepted in principle; and completing a consulting project by a specific deadline date and arranging for publication of the final report. These outcome assignments are "complex" because they include more than one condition that must be met. Two other complex outcome assignments, drawn from the literature of educational performance objectives, are teaching introductory course S so well that at least 75 percent of the students believed it was worthwhile and teaching course R so well that 85 percent attain a grade of C or higher on the final exam. Some controversy surrounds the idea that outcomes can be clearly specified, particularly when an arbitrary figure—such as 85 percent—appears in the statement. Such figures should be specified only after careful thought about what constitutes a satisfactory outcome; they should not be included merely to give an appearance of precision. Note that faculty members can meet these kinds of performance objectives by lowering standards.

Outcome assignments, if properly made, lend themselves more easily to an objective evaluation of performance quality than do activity assignments, which usually focus on quantity rather than quality of performance. Chairpersons who try to evaluate faculty performance on the basis of outcomes usually consult in advance with their faculty members to determine what each person plans to accomplish during the year and to stipulate the intended outcomes. The chairperson and the faculty member together develop the annual assignment, incorporating as far as possible the faculty member's plan. Some chairpersons and faculty members claim that faculty members generally resist a request to provide an advance list of the individual activities, projects, and outcomes that they plan for the coming year. They do not object, however, to submitting a detailed list of their accomplishments and their performance outcomes during the past year in order to prepare for an annual performance evaluation.

An interesting exercise for chairpersons would be to review some lists prepared by faculty members of their accomplishments of the past year, changing the tense of the verbs from past to future. By doing so, chairpersons can see what the anticipated outcome of assignments made at the beginning of the year might have been. Would these faculty members have been able to anticipate their accomplishments one year in advance? Would it have been helpful to them and to the department if they had been required to think in terms of intended accomplishments? Each person has his or her own opinion on these issues, and the arguments on both sides would provoke an interesting discussion.

Chairpersons who wish to specify desired outcomes in faculty members' annual assignments should obtain the following information about each person's activities. As far as teaching is concerned, the chairperson should know what level of effectiveness the faculty member plans to attain in helping students reach stated course objectives; what innovations are anticipated; how much effort will be expended in preparing for class; and what level of satisfaction will be expected from the students. If research or creative activity is part of the faculty member's assignment, the chairperson should know what progress can be expected by the end of the year and what kind of evidence (short of a published article or book) is acceptable to demonstrate that progress has been made; whether a grant proposal will be written by the end of the term; whether a rough draft of an article for publication will be completed; whether a special seminar or recital will be given; whether a specified amount of progress can be expected on a research project; and whether a library literature search will be completed by the end of the year. If a service assignment is made, the chairperson should know what outcome is expected; whether attendance at committee meetings is all that is expected; whether, if the assignment is on an ad hoc department committee, a report is due and who has responsibility for writing the report; whether contacts with potential students are part of a service assignment; and, if so, how many contacts are expected. These are the kinds of questions that department chairpersons should consider in making faculty assignments on which evaluations are based.

Obvious and specific procedures are necessary for interpreting whatever evidence is deemed appropriate for a faculty evaluation. For example, there must be procedures for reading and interpreting student ratings of teachers and some basis for assigning an overall quality rating, i.e., for stating whether the faculty member's teaching is "outstanding," "very good," "satisfactory," "weak," or "unsatisfactroy." Similarly, standard procedures for interpreting all other evidence are also needed, so that a chairperson can demonstrate the extent to which the final evaluation is based on objectively assessed evidence.

Who Should Do the Evaluating and What Should Be the Process?

Evaluation of a faculty member's performance is usually derived from some or all of the following sources: the faculty member's chairperson or other administrator; the faculty member's self-evaluation; the faculty member's peers; professional colleagues at other universities (in matters of promotion and tenure); students; and other university officials.

The department chairperson is usually the person responsible for collecting evaluations about each faculty member from these sources. Even though a faculty committee may have assisted the chairperson in the evaluation, most universities hold the department chairperson responsible for the official evaluation. Each faculty member should be told who will perform the official evaluation, the nature of the process, the performance criteria to be used, and so on. Similarly, all persons involved in submitting evidence or making judgments should be informed of their particular roles. One point cannot be overemphasized: the chairperson's official evaluation rests on his or her informed judgment of all the appropriate evidence. The evaluation process gains substantial legitimacy in the eyes of the faculty members if they have been able to participate in the development of department goals and objectives.

Another way to involve faculty members in their own evaluation is to have each of them prepare a "brag sheet" describing his or her activities and accomplishments. Faculty members should be afforded the opportunity to describe in detail what they consider their important contributions to the department, the institution, the profession or discipline, and the community. Sometimes they cannot easily enumerate their outstanding accomplishments on a standardized form. Therefore, the self-evaluation could be written in narrative form, which would allow them the freedom to describe their achievements in their own words. Faculty members feel more confident that their actions are appreciated and valued if they have the opportunity to describe them adequately. On the other hand, the chairperson, when reading the brag sheets, should be able to distinguish between rhetoric and reality.

Students are often invited to participate in the institutional evaluation of faculty members. At some institutions they also conduct their own evaluation of teaching faculty members and publish the results for the benefit of fellow students. The results of these evaluations are quite interesting, to say the least.

How Should Performance Be Evaluated?

The questions of what should be evaluated and who should do the evaluating are relatively simple to answer compared with the question of how performance should be evaluated. The art of evaluating the performance of faculty members is not that well developed. Experts who are invited to make presentations on how to evaluate such performance will adequately explain why evaluation is important, what should be evaluated, who should do the evaluating, and what procedures should be followed to obtain maximum involvement of appropriate faculty members, students, and administrators in the evaluation process. Usually, however, these experts are unable to provide a magic formula that will make the evaluation process more simple or less painful.

The evaluation system that a department uses will depend on a variety of factors—the institution's requirements, the school or college's procedures, and so forth. The chairperson must remember, however, that basically four kinds of personnel decisions based on performance evaluation data must be made each academic year: (1) promotion decisions; (2) tenure decisions; (3) annual assessments; and (4) recommendations for merit pay. Two or more of these decisions may use the same evaluation data and thus may be scheduled simultaneously, but at most institutions these decisions are distinct in terms of legal requirements. Moreover, each personnel decision should be based on evaluation data that represent more than the subjective and arbitrary response of a chairperson or a committee of peers. Therefore, as these decisions become more complex, the chairperson should seek to implement or improve quantitative evaluations rather than avoid them.

Not every faculty member in a department is outstanding, but the difficult task for the chairperson is to differentiate among the members, most of whom perform their assigned duties at least satisfactorily. The department faculty members should help determine the specific criteria to be used for personnel decisions, whether these decisions are related to promotion, tenure, annual assessment, or merit recommendations. The chairperson must work with the faculty to delineate the particular evaluation criteria used in each part of the evaluation. The chairperson should also state how the criteria will be applied to the evidence in each person's evaluation folder.

In thinking about devising a system for evaluation, the chairperson and the faculty members together must confront several questions: First, what constitutes 100 percent of a full-time workload for a given term or year? Does a 100 percent assignment demand all of a faculty member's professional time and effort, regardless of the number of hours worked? Or does it consist of a specified number of hours, say forty hours per week? Is a formal definition of what constitutes 100 percent of a full-time workload even necessary? Will a faculty member's teaching duties alone make up 100 percent of his or her assigned full-time workload, with research and service activities considered as "add-ons"? If so, will such additional activities be required or voluntary? Will the performance of these additional activities, even though they are not part of a formal assignment, be evaluated for promotion and tenure purposes? Will a subjective evaluation be made of each faculty member's overall worth to the department without separate evaluations of the performance in each activity and regardless of whether the activity was formally assigned?

After the chairperson and the faculty members have thought through these questions and arrived at answers that are acceptable to them as a department, they must consider further questions. If each faculty member is expected to engage in some teaching, research, and service activities, will this expectation be stated formally in an assignment contract? If activities in these three areas are formally or informally assigned, will each faculty member receive a separate performance rating for each area? Will a faculty member's overall performance evaluation be determined by simply averaging the three ratings? Or will the ratings also take into consideration the amount of time and effort expended in each area? Is good teaching just as important to the department as good research? If a faculty member receives an "outstanding" rating for research and a "poor" rating for teaching, will the "poor" rating for teaching pull down his or her overall evaluation?

Some evaluation procedures are more complex and quantitative than others. The more quantitative the system, the more objective it is perceived to be. For some reason, the use of numbers is supposed to dilute the subjectivity of human judgment. In reality, this is not necessarily the case, especially in evaluating the quality of performance. Much to the surprise of some chairpersons, however, there are faculty members in some departments who insist on the use of detailed quantification. Quantification involves the use of arabic numbers rather than descriptive words to express human judgment. Numbers can be added, averaged, and otherwise subjected to statistical treatment. Descriptive words cannot. But human judgment is still the only basis upon which many qualitative evaluations can be made. When evaluations are based on human judgment, the evaluator in effect becomes the evaluation instrument. The number and range of experiences in a given field, together with common sense and good judgment, contribute to the degree of precision of the human evaluation instrument.

Examples of Evaluation Processes and Performance Ratings

Simple Subjective Evaluation of Overall Contribution to the Mission of the Department

In this type of evaluation the chairperson bases his or her evaluation on the faculty member's performance of department activities without necessarily listing the activities and without prescribing what percentage of time or effort of full-time workload is to be spent on each activity and without a separate detailed scrutiny of each activity performed. The chairperson reviews each faculty member's performance over the past year, including the self-evaluation report, and then asks the question, "How valuable, in my opinion, is this faculty member to the department?" This process is repeated for all the faculty members, and then they are ranked according to how much the chairperson values their contributions to the department. In the process of ranking, the chairperson assigns a number to each subjective evaluation and by so doing gives a quantitative measure to each faculty member's performance. This simple type of evaluation, as well as the types described later, may be done by the chairperson alone, with or without the help of consultants; by a department committee headed by the chairperson; by a department committee without the chairperson's participation; or by the entire department.

At this point, the matter of rating faculty members as "above average" should be mentioned. Every department chairperson must face the fact, difficult as it may be to acknowledge, that all the members of his or her department are not necessarily "above average." If the evaluations of all faculty members in a single department are averaged, the evaluation of some faculty members will be below that average. To evaluate faculty members as "above average" or "below average" does not make sense unless the group with which they are being compared can be clearly specified. Is the reference group another department in the same school or college, another department in the institution, or a similar department in another university? To give ratings higher than faculty members deserve simply because everyone else is doing so is not good policy.

Performance ratings can range from simple to complex. A chairperson might simply rate the faculty members as "O.K." or "not O.K.," "merit" or "no merit," or "acceptable" or "not acceptable." Faculty members can also be rated on a three-point scale, such as "high merit," "low merit," and "no merit." The difference between a rating of 73 percent and 75 percent, however, may be insignificant in determining whether the performance of one faculty member should be rated higher than another's.

An evaluation procedure based on a four-point scale is also suggested for use.* This approach is helpful because the scale is familiar to anyone who has graded academic performance. Simply translate the value terms "outstanding," "very good," "satisfactory," "weak," and "unsatisfactory" to the numbers 4.0, 3.0, 2.0, 1.0, and 0 (see figure 8.1 for performance rating key). For example, if the performance of a teaching activity is evaluated as "very good," the faculty member would receive a performance rating of 3.0. This scale will be used in subsequent discussions of more complex systems of evaluation, but it should be remembered that other schema can be used with equal effectiveness.

Before a number system is adopted to designate levels of performance as "outstanding," "very good," "satisfactory," and so forth, the chairperson and the department should have some idea of what those ratings imply. In terms of performance, what is the difference between being "outstanding" and just "satisfactory"?

Separate Evaluation of Each of Several Components of a Faculty Member's Activities

The question of value at the next level of complexity takes into account the faculty member's contributions in each of the three major performance areas—teaching, research, and service. In this system, the faculty member's performance in each area is rated separately on a four-point scale, and his or her ratings are averaged. Figure 8.2 shows the performance ratings, by area and based on the four-point scale, of three faculty members.

*Developed by Allan Tucker.

LEVEL OF PERFORMANCE	PERFORMANCE RATING
Outstanding	4
Very Good	3
Satisfactory	2
Weak	1
Unsatisfactory	0

FIGURE 8.1.   Performance rating key.

In our example, Jones comes out with an average rating of 3.33, which can be interpreted as somewhere between "very good" and "outstanding." Smith's average rating is "very good," and Brown's is "satisfactory." If this type of evaluation were being done by a committee rather than the chairperson, each committee member could give each department member a separate rating for each area of performance. These ratings could then be averaged to produce a committee rating for each performance area.

The system described above is used in departments that are not particularly concerned with the percentage of full-time workload that is assigned to any given activity. These same departments probably consider teaching, research, and service equally important in achieving department goals and do not rate outstanding researchers higher than outstanding teachers.

Weighting the Evaluation of Each Component Activity Proportionately to Effort Expended

Faculty members in some departments are not satisfied with a laissez-faire system of assignment. They want evaluations to take into account the percentage of full-time workload that is assigned to each of the three major performance areas; in addition, they want the evalua-

FIGURE 8.2.   Rating of faculty members, by area of performance, using four-point scale.

Area of Performance	FACULTY MEMBERS		
	Jones	Smith	Brown
Teaching	4.0	2.0	2.0
Research*	3.0	4.0	1.0
Service	3.0	3.0	3.0
Total of Ratings	10.0	9.0	6.0
Average Rating	3.33	3.0	2.0

*Community colleges may wish to use "special assignments" as an area of performance instead of "research."

tions to count activities that fall under a fourth category called "other." The fourth category generally includes assignments such as administrative duties, career counseling, supervision of interns, and so forth. Such calculations are not difficult.

Subsequent discussion will make use of the following terminology:

- *Performance ratings* (PR)—These ratings are based on a four-point scale and are used to differentiate "outstanding, "very good," "satisfactory," "weak," and "unsatisfactory" performance (see figure 8.1).
- *Rating points* (RP)—Rating points are calculated for a given area or activity by multiplying the performance rating for that activity by the percentage of full-time workload assigned to that activity. For example, if 60 percent of a faculty member's full-time workload is assigned to teaching and if her rating for that assignment is "outstanding," she would receive 240 rating points (4 × 60).
- *Rating point average* (RPA)—The rating point average is calculated by totaling the rating points obtained for the areas of performance being evaluated and dividing that total by the sum of the percentages of the full-time workload assigned to the several areas or activities being rated.

    For example, Faculty Member A is rated 4.0 for his teaching assignment, which constitutes 60 percent of his full-time workload. He therefore would receive 240 rating points (4 × 60) for the area of teaching. He is rated 3.0 for his research assignment, which constitutes 30 percent of his full-time workload. For the area of research, therefore, he would receive 90 rating points (3 × 30). His assigned percentage of full-time workload for service was 5 percent; his assigned percentage of full-time workload for "other," which consisted of supervising interns, was also 5 percent. For each of the latter two areas he was rated 3.0 and thus received 15 rating points (3 × 5) for each. The total number of rating points for the four areas—teaching, research, service, and "other"—therefore was 360 (240 + 90 + 15 + 15). The sum of assigned percentages of full-time workload for the four areas was 100 percent (60 + 30 + 5 + 5). The rating point average (RPA) for this faculty member was 3.6 (360 ÷ 100). (The calculations used to derive the RPA also appear in figure 8.3.) Since "full time" constitutes 100 percent of a faculty member's workload, the sum of the percentages assigned to the several areas cannot exceed 100 percent, and since 4.0 is the highest performance rating that can be given to any area, a rating point average can never be greater than 4.0.

Following are examples of assignments and ratings given to two other faculty members in the same department, Faculty Member B and

Area of Performance	I Performance Rating	II Assigned % of Full-Time Workload	Rating Points (RP) (I × II)
Teaching	4.0	60	240
Research*	3.0	30	90
Service	3.0	5	15
Other	3.0	5	15
Total	13.0	100	360

$$\text{Rating Point Average (RPA)} = \frac{\text{Total of Rating Points}}{\text{Total of Assigned Percentages}} = \frac{360}{100} = 3.6$$

*Community colleges may wish to use "special assignments" as an area of performance instead of "research."

FIGURE 8.3. Rating of Faculty Member A's performance, by area of performance and by percentage of full-time workload assigned to each area.

Faculty Member C. Forty percent of Faculty Member B's full-time workload was assigned to teaching, for which she was rated 2.0; 40 percent was assigned to research, for which she was rated 4.0; 10 percent was assigned to service, for which she was rated 3.0; and 10 percent was assigned to "other" (in this case, administrative duties), for which she was rated 2.0. Sixty-five percent of Faculty Member C's full-time workload was assigned to teaching, for which he was rated 1.0; 20 percent was assigned to research, for which he was rated 1.0; 10 percent was assigned to service, for which he was rated 4.0; and 5 percent was assigned to "other" (in this case, career counseling), for which he was rated 3.0. Figures 8.3, 8.4, and 8.5 show how the rating point averages (RPAs) can be calculated for each faculty member.

FIGURE 8.4. Rating of Faculty Member B's performance, by area of performance and by percentage of full-time workload assigned to each area.

Area of Performance	I Performance Rating	II Assigned % of Full-Time Workload	Rating Points (RP) (I × II)
Teaching	2.0	40	80
Research*	4.0	40	160
Service	3.0	10	30
Other	2.0	10	20
Total	11.0	100	290

$$\text{Rating Point Average (RPA)} = \frac{\text{Total of Rating Points}}{\text{Total of Assigned Percentages}} = \frac{290}{100} = 2.9$$

*Community colleges may wish to use "special assignments" as an area of performance instead of "research."

AREA OF PERFORMANCE	I PERFORMANCE RATING	II ASSIGNED % OF FULL-TIME WORKLOAD	RATING POINTS (RP) (I × II)
Teaching	1.0	65	65
Research*	1.0	20	20
Service	4.0	10	40
Other	3.0	5	15
Total	9.0	100	140

$$\text{Rating Point Average (RPA)} = \frac{\text{Total of Rating Points}}{\text{Total of Assigned Percentages}} = \frac{140}{100} = 1.4$$

*Community colleges may wish to use "special assignments" as an area of performance instead of "research."

FIGURE 8.5.   Rating of Faculty Member C's performance, by area of performance and by percentage of full-time workload assigned to each area.

Had Faculty Member A's ratings been averaged without regard for the percentage of full-time workload assigned to each area, he would have received a rating of 3.25 (13 ÷ 4). Taking the percentage of full-time workload assigned to each area into account, his rating point average is 3.60. Faculty Member B, who would have received an average rating of 2.75 (11 ÷ 4), receives a rating point average of 2.90 when consideration is given to the percentage of full-time workload assigned to each area. Faculty Member C, who would have received an average rating of 2.25 (9 ÷ 4), now receives a rating point average of 1.40 when percentage of full-time workload assigned to each area is considered.

Keeping in mind that human judgment is a factor to be reckoned with in the assessment of faculty members' performance, the chairperson must address the question of the quantity of work completed in the amount of time assigned to the effort. For example, if a faculty member receives an "outstanding" rating for assigned research that constitutes 10 percent of a full-time workload, should that person receive an "outstanding" rating for the same effort and end product if research constitutes 30 percent of a full-time workload?

*Weighting the Evaluation of Each Component Activity
Proportionately to Its Importance to Mission of the Department*

So far we have discussed two types of evaluation: (1) a simple type based only on performance rating without regard for percentage of full-time workload assigned to each area and (2) a more complex type that takes into account separate performance ratings for each area and the percentage of full-time workload assigned to each of the areas rated. We have not yet considered the question of priority of performance areas.

Some departments prize research more highly than other performance areas and wish to reward good research more highly than good teaching or good service. On the other hand, some departments with enormous undergraduate teaching loads are primarily concerned with encouraging and rewarding their outstanding teachers. Such departments not only evaluate faculty members in terms of their assigned duties, as already illustrated, but also assign priority factors to the various areas according to the priority given to each. If a department wishes to encourage its members to do more research, for example, it could reward its more productive members by assigning larger percentages of their full-time workload to research, or it could assign a higher priority factor to the research portion of the assignment.

Figures 8.3, 8.4, and 8.5 describe a department that assigns a priority factor of 1 to each performance area; in this way the department indicates that it believes all areas to be of equal importance and that "outstanding" performance should be rewarded equally, regardless of area. A department that wishes to give more priority to research than to other assigned areas can do so in several ways within the four-point system. A chairperson, after consulting with department members, could arbitrarily decide that research is 1.5 times as important as any other area and accordingly multiply each faculty member's assigned percentage of full-time workload devoted to research by a priority factor of 1.5.

Consider Faculty Member B, who in figure 8.3 was assigned 40 percent of her full-time workload to research and received a rating of 4.0 for research. If Faculty Member B's assigned percentage of full-time workload for research is multiplied by a priority factor of 1.5, her adjusted assigned percentage of full-time work-load for research becomes 60 percent (40 percent × 1.5). Figure 8.6 shows these calculations. When Faculty Member B's percentage of full-time workload assigned to research (40) is multiplied by the area priority factor for research (1.5), her rating point average rises from 2.90 to 3.08.

If a priority factor is applied to the percentage of full-time workload assigned to a given performance area for one faculty member, then the same priority factor has to be applied to that performance area for all faculty members. The adjustment described in figure 8.6 would result in a lower rating point average for Faculty Members A and C. Faculty Member A's would drop from 3.60 to 3.50, and Faculty Member C's would drop from 1.40 to 1.35. These differences might affect the distribution of merit money. Note that the higher the priority factor in any activity, the greater will be the change in the rating point averages.

A chairperson who does not want to assign a priority factor that could be considered arbitrary might conduct a survey of the faculty members, asking each to indicate on a ten-point scale the value that

FIGURE 8.6. Rating of Faculty Member B's performance, by area of performance and by percentage of full-time workload assigned to each area, taking into account the area priority factor.

Area of Performance	I Performance Rating	II Assigned % of Full-Time Workload	III Area Priority Factor	IV Adjusted Assigned % of Full-Time Workload (II × III)	V Adjusted Rating Points (I × IV)
Teaching	2.0	40	1.0	40	80
Research*	4.0	40	1.5	60	240
Service	3.0	10	1.0	10	30
Other	2.0	10	1.0	10	20
Total	11.0	100	N/A	120	370

$$\text{Adjusted Rating Point Average (RPA)} = \frac{\text{Total Adjusted Rating Points}}{\text{Total Adjusted Assigned \%s}} = \frac{370}{120} = 3.08$$

*Community colleges may wish to use "special assignments" as an area of performance instead of "research."

should be given to each assigned area. For example, on a form similar to figure 8.7, each faculty member would circle the number that, in his or her opinion, reflects the priority of the performance area to the department's mission.

The average of the faculty members' responses for each performance area would be the priority factor for that area. In figure 8.7, therefore, the department has given a priority factor of 8 to teaching, 10 to research, 5 to service, and 5 to "other." In figure 8.8, Faculty Member B's assigned percentages of full-time workload have been adjusted by multiplying the assigned percentages by the department priority factor for each area.

By the same method of calculation, Faculty Member A's rating point average would become 3.58 and Faculty Member C's 1.25. Note that the effect of applying priority factors, while not great, has increased the rating point average (RPA) of the department's best researcher, Faculty Member B, from 2.90 to 3.10, thus raising her evaluation on the four-point scale from "satisfactory" to "very good." This adjustment, however, has not greatly reduced the other faculty members' rating point averages.

In the calculations thus far, performance ratings have been used for the major categories of teaching, research, service, and "other." Each of these major categories may be broken down into several components. For example, the area of teaching can be divided into these components: amount of teaching; fulfillment of educational objectives; use of innovative techniques; and student evaluations. Each component could then be rated individually on the four-point scale, and from these individual ratings a composite rating for the area of teaching could be calculated. The areas of research and service can also be broken down into component activities and rated accordingly.

Evaluation Using the Point System

Some departments have developed a point system to help in the evaluations. They have a comprehensive list of all activities in each area, and a specific number of points is awarded for the completion of

FIGURE 8.7. Faculty rating of the priority of performance areas to the department's mission.

Teaching	1	2	3	4	5	6	7	⑧	9	10
Research*	1	2	3	4	5	6	7	8	9	⑩
Service	1	2	3	4	⑤	6	7	8	9	10
Other	1	2	3	4	⑤	6	7	8	9	10

*Community colleges may wish to use "special assignments" as an area of performance instead of "research."

FIGURE 8.8. Rating of Faculty Member B's performance, by area of performance and by percentage of full-time workload assigned to each area, taking into account the area priority factor.

AREA OF PERFORMANCE	I PERFORMANCE RATING	II ASSIGNED % OF FULL-TIME WORKLOAD	III AREA PRIORITY FACTOR	IV ADJUSTED ASSIGNED % OF FULL-TIME WORKLOAD (II × III)	V ADJUSTED RATING POINTS (I × IV)
Teaching	2.0	40	8.0	320	640
Research*	4.0	40	10.0	400	1600
Service	3.0	10	5.0	50	150
Other	2.0	10	5.0	50	100
Total	11.0	100	N/A	820	2490

$$\text{Adjusted Rating Point Average (RPA)} = \frac{\text{Total Adjusted Rating Points}}{\text{Total Adjusted Assigned \%s}} = \frac{2490}{820} = 3.09$$

*Community colleges may wish to use "special assignments" as an area of performance instead of "research."

each activity. For example, some departments award a certain number of points for publications in refereed journals and fewer points for those in nonrefereed journals. In some fields there exists a well-known and generally accepted hierarchy of journals and publications in the most prestigious journals are awarded more points than publications in less prestigious journals. A small number of points might be given for submitted publications and a larger number of points for accepted publications. A certain number of points may be given for papers presented at national meetings and a smaller number for papers presented at regional or local meetings of professional societies. The number of points given for the publication of a book might differ according to the publisher's prestige.

In the area of service, questions about allocation of points may be complex and difficult. Consideration might be given to the number and importance of committees on which the faculty member serves. A department might award more points for chairing a committee than for serving on it and might vary the number of points for service on national, regional, and state committees. The number of points earned by each faculty member for each activity is then totaled. The department must then determine how to translate these totals into performance ratings. This system is mentioned as a matter of information but is not necessarily advocated for use.

Following is an example of a point system for evaluation developed by a small, primarily research-oriented department. The system specifies the number of points to be awarded for each activity included in the areas of teaching, research, and service.*

SAMPLE OF POINT SYSTEM FOR FACULTY EVALUATION
  A. Teaching
     1. Teaching load
        a. Graduate courses—each 0.50 points × number of credit hours
        b. Undergraduate courses—each 0.30 points × number of credit hours
        c. Directed individual study, supervised research, or supervised teaching—each 0.10 points
     2. Students' evaluation of faculty member; evaluation of peer or supervisor may also be conducted according to this form
        a. 90th percentile ranking—20 points
        b. 75th–89th percentile ranking—16 points
        c. 60th–74th percentile ranking—12 points
        d. 50th–59th percentile ranking—8 points
     3. Supervisory committees or positions
        a. Director of doctoral committee—5 points for each Ph.D. granted during faculty member's evaluation period; 3 points for each ongoing doctoral committee

*Point system used by a small, primarily research department at Florida State University until 1978.

        b. Member of doctoral committee—2 points

        c. Director of master's committee—3 points for each master's degree granted during faculty member's evaluation period; 2 points for each continuing student

        d. Member of master's committee—1 point

        e. Graduate student advisor—1 point for every three students

        f. Laboratory director—10 points

B. Research and scholarly activity

    1. Publications

        a. Writing

            1) Article for refereed national journal—5 points

            2) Article for nonrefereed national journal—3 points

            3) Article for state journal—2 points

            4) Book with major publishing company—15 points

            5) Revised book—7 points

            6) Section of book with major publisher—5 points

            7) Book with local publisher—5 points

            8) Section of book with local publisher—2 points

        b. Editorial activities

            1) Editor of book—7 points

            2) Editor of national professional journal—15 points

            3) Editor of state professional journal—10 points

            4) Associate editor or reviewer for national journal—10 points

            5) Associate editor or reviewer for state journal—5 points

            6) Manuscript reviewer for major publisher—2 points each manuscript

            7) Reviewer for federal agency—5 points

    2. Research projects

        a. Author of R&D project funded by outside agency—15 points

        b. Author of R&D project funded by university—10 points

        c. Author of R&D project submitted to outside agency but not funded—5 points

        d. Author of R&D project submitted to university but not funded—3 points

    3. Papers and speeches

        a. Presented at national or international meeting, by invitation—10 points

        b. Submitted to national or international meeting—5 points

        c. Presented to regional or state meeting, by invitation—5 points

        d. Submitted to regional or state meeting—3 points

        e. Presented at another institution, by invitation—5 points

        f. Presented at local meeting—1 point

C. Service

    1. Committee activities

        a. Chairperson of university committee—10 points

        b. Member of university committee—5 points

        c. Chairperson of school or college committee—5 points

    d. Member of school or college committee—3 points

    e. Chairperson of area or program committee—3 points

    f. Member of area or program committee—1 point

    g. Member of faculty senate—7 points

    h. Chairperson of search committee—5 points

    i. Member of search committee—3 points

2. Professional activities

    a. Chairperson of national committee—5 points

    b. Member of national committee—3 points

    c. Chairperson of regional or state committee—3 points

    d. Member of regional or state committee—1 point

    e. Officer at regional or national level—10 points

    f. Officer at state level—7 points

    g. Leader for in-service training—3 points

    h. Organizer for workshop—5 points

    i. Member of professional association—1 point

    j. Attendance at professional meeting—1 point each

3. Consulting (each visit—2 points)

This point system was used until the department was merged with several others that were less research oriented. The resulting larger department felt that this system was too rigid and too specific and abandoned it.

This system is highly quantitative in that it assigns a number of points for each activity. It is also qualitative, however, in that it allocates more points to good teaching performance than to average teaching performance, more points for papers published in prestigious journals than for papers published in lesser journals, and more points for membership on important committees than for membership on less important committees.

Another system of point allocation used by some departments rates faculty members' teaching performance on a ten-point scale, with "outstanding" performance receiving a full ten points and "poor" performance receiving no points at all. The average score for faculty members in the department is fixed beforehand at five points. Thus a department with ten members will have a total of fifty points to be divided among all the faculty members for teaching performance. This system is sometimes called the "constant sum" method. If a rater gives three faculty members ten points each for teaching performance, there would be only twenty points left to be divided among the other seven members. The same method is used for evaluating research and service.

This rating system, by limiting the total number of points that can be allocated, keeps a department from giving high ratings to all its members. In practice, if a small committee does the rating, the result will be sharp differentiations between faculty members, with some receiving high scores and others receiving low scores. When a large number of persons does the rating, the result will be a regression towards the mean, and the system loses much of its discriminating force.

The Evaluation Folder

The rules and regulations governing faculty members usually require that an official evaluation folder be established for each member. The folder is to be accessible only to the faculty member and to administrators who must make evaluative decisions. It may contain any information that will be used in the evaluation process, including summaries of performance counseling actions as well as annual formal evaluations prepared by the department chairperson.

In this age of due process, a faculty member may challenge any item placed in the evaluation folder and, by mutual agreement, the item may be removed from the folder. Also note that anonymous material, except systematic student evaluations and committee summaries, may not be placed in the folder. Some state laws may give even greater protection to personnel files.

Linking Merit Increases to Rating Point Averages

The following example will focus only on the allocation of moneys for merit increases. Assume that cost-of-living increases and other types of salary adjustments, if any, have already been made. The four-point system can link merit increases with performance evaluations in several ways. In this example, merit is divided into several levels—"high merit," "medium merit," "low merit," and "no merit." The department has seven members. They have been evaluated using the four-point system, and their rating point averages are as follows: Faculty Member A—3.8; Faculty Member B—3.4; Faculty Member C—3.2; Faculty Member D—2.8; Faculty Member E—2.6; Faculty Member F—2.5; and Faculty Member G—1.9.

The first question the department must address is, "Where should the lines be drawn to differentiate the levels of merit?" In this example, the lines will be drawn as follows: "high merit"—3.5–4.0 RPA; "medium merit"—3.0–3.4 RPA; "low merit"—2.5–2.9 RPA; and "no merit"—0–2.4 RPA. This merit level key is shown in figure 8.9.

Three units of money are allocated for "high merit," two units for "medium merit," and one unit for "low merit." The number of faculty members in each merit category and the number of merit units are illustrated in figure 8.10.

	RPA
High merit	3.5–4.0
Medium merit	3.0–3.4
Low merit	2.5–2.9
No merit	0–2.4

FIGURE 8.9. Merit level key.

Assume that $3,900 has been made available to the department for merit increases. The total number of merit units in the example is 10, and each unit is therefore worth $390 ($3900÷10). The amount of merit raise that each faculty member in the department will receive is shown in figure 8.11. If the department had decided to draw the lines differently, the money would have been allocated differently. The fewer the merit units, the greater would be the dollar value per unit. The fewer the faculty members earning merit raises, the greater would be the amount of money per faculty member deemed meritorious. In some departments, less than 50 percent of the faculty receive merit money. Determining policy in the allocation of merit money is a vexing matter and the subject of some controversy.

At institutions that have faculty salary schedules, merit moneys are often allocated not in dollars, but in units. The central administration takes upon itself the responsibility of determining the dollar value of each unit and specifying the number of units each department will receive. At such institutions, the chairperson has the responsibility for determining only the number of units to be awarded to each faculty member. The process used could be the same as described above.

In this chapter we have described a wide variety of procedures for evaluating faculty performance. The art of evaluating the quality of performance has been a perplexing problem ever since there have been faculty members. In most cases, quality is still best measured in terms of the opinions, values, and perceptions held by students, peers, alumni, and other persons who have actually observed or been the beneficiaries of the performance. Quality of performance is best described with words and phrases, but words and phrases cannot be added, multiplied, or averaged. To overcome this difficulty, numbers are often assigned to various words and phrases that describe quality of performance. Numbers can be processed mathematically for the purpose of yielding a final number that supposedly represents a faculty member's overall evaluation. This final number can then be transposed into words or phrases that describe the quality of the overall performance. The number, regardless of how sophisticated the mathematical process that yielded it, still represents a collection of human judgments. At-

FIGURE 8.10. Calculation of number of merit units available for distribution.

	Rating Point Average	Number of Faculty Members		Merit Units Per Faculty Member		Total Merit Units
High merit	3.5–4.0	1	×	3	=	3
Medium merit	3.0–3.4	2	×	2	=	4
Low merit	2.5–2.9	3	×	1	=	3
No merit	0–2.4	1	×	0	=	0
				Total	=	10

Faculty Member	Number of Merit Units		Value of Merit Unit		Merit Raise
Faculty Member A	3	×	$390	=	$1170
Faculty Member B	2	×	$390	=	$ 780
Faculty Member C	2	×	$390	=	$ 780
Faculty Member D	1	×	$390	=	$ 390
Faculty Member E	1	×	$390	=	$ 390
Faculty Member F	1	×	$390	=	$ 390
Faculty Member G	0	×	$390	=	$ 0

FIGURE 8.11.   Calculation of merit raises.

tempting to quantify the quality of faculty performance, nevertheless, does force the evaluator to examine more carefully all facets of the faculty member's professional life. Quantification makes it easier to compare faculty members in terms of their performance and contribution to the department.

Questions and Exercises

1. *Evaluating Teaching Performance*
   Following is a partial list of the characteristics of a good teacher. Please answer the questions which appear at the end of the list.
   • Is the teacher enthusiastic in presenting material?
   • Does the teacher show concern with whether students learned the material?
   • Does the teacher encourage students to express opinions?
   • Does the teacher encourage class discussion?
   • Does the teacher present material at the right speed?
   • Does the teacher organize the course well?
   • Are students told what is expected of them?
   • Is the teacher a good lecturer?
   • Does the teacher have any bad speaking habits?
   • Has the teacher prepared a syllabus?
   • Are the material and the syllabus up to date?
   • Does the teacher keep punctual office hours?
   • Do examinations reflect course objectives?
   • Is the grading done fairly?
   • How well do students learn in the class?
   • How attentive are the students in the class?
   • How well does the teacher make use of audio visual aids?
   • Does the teacher try to be innovative?

- In the case of laboratory classes, how well organized are the classes?
a. Which of the above items can be evaluated quantitatively and which can be evaluated only on the basis of human judgment?
b. If you were responsible for obtaining evaluations about the quality of teaching performance, whose evaluation or judgment would you seek? Would you be willing to settle for just one person's judgment or would you want judgments from more than one person? How many? Why?
c. Should individuals whose evaluation judgments are sought have special qualifications? What should be the qualifications?
d. When evaluations are based on human judgment, the evaluator in effect becomes the evaluation instrument. What can or should be done to sharpen or hone the instrument? Can individuals be trained to be good evaluators?
e. How important is it for those whose teaching performance is to be evaluated to agree on who should evaluate their teaching? Give reasons for your answer.
f. Identify the faculty member whom you consider the most valuable to your department. Also identify the faculty member whom you would consider the least valuable. Using the four-point scale and the format described in this chapter, calculate the rating point average (RPA) of each of the two faculty members. Assume that all activities—teaching, research, service and so forth—are of equal importance to the department's mission, and that for each faculty member you have either formally assigned percentage of full-time workload to each activity or you know the percentage of effort devoted to each activity.
2. *Evaluating Research Productivity*
   In evaluating the research productivity of a faculty member, one could give an overall evaluation based on general impression or one could list some characteristics of good research and judge the extent to which each is present in the research being evaluated.
   a. One of the end products of research is a published research paper. List some characteristics of good research that could be considered in evaluating the quality of the published research paper.
   b. In the case of a faculty member who is conducting research but has not yet published a paper on it, what interim accomplishments or milestones toward the completion of the project could be considered in evaluating the faculty member's research efforts?
   c. In an annual faculty evaluation, should a faculty member re-

ceive credit toward a merit increase or promotion for an above satisfactory research effort even though a paper has not yet been published? Give reasons for your answer.

d. In the case of the performing or visual arts, what criteria can be used to evaluate interim or final accomplishments?

e. What should be the qualifications of individuals selected to evaluate the quality of research?

f. If more than one qualified individual evaluates the quality of a research paper, can it be assumed that all will give the paper the same rating? Give reasons for your answer.

g. Who should decide who is or is not qualified to evaluate research?

h. How important is it for those whose research is to be evaluated to agree on who should evaluate their research? Give reasons for your answer.

3. *General Questions*

   Which of the following would be most desirable? Please give reasons for your answer.

   a. The department receives exact instructions from some office in the institution on how to carry out faculty evaluations including the instrument, criteria, and procedures. The department is expected to follow the instructions without deviation.

   b. The department is given general criteria and a framework within which it must develop its own instrument and procedures for carrying out faculty evaluations.

   c. The department is instructed to develop its own criteria, instrument, and procedures for carrying out faculty evaluation. It receives no guidance whatsoever from the office of the dean or academic vice-president.

4. *Case Study*

   The following abridged case study on "A Discrepancy in Rating between Two Evaluation Procedures" is presented as a basis for thought. Please answer the questions at the end of the case study.

   The chairperson of a certain department has rated Professor Smith as being more productive than Professor Jones for each of the past four years. His method of evaluation was based primarily on his overall impression of these two faculty members. This year, however, on the advice of his faculty, he decided to follow a more complex evaluation system which required that each of the three primary activities—teaching, research, and service—be broken down into its component activities, that each component activity be rated separately using numbers rather than descriptive words, and that the numbers be treated statistically so that an overall numerical rating could be determined for each faculty member. The chairperson was surprised to find that Professor Jones came out with a higher overall rating than Professor Smith. But in his heart, the chairperson felt that Smith was the more productive professor.

a. Give reasons that might account for the discrepancy.
b. What must the chairperson do to resolve his inner conflict?

References

ALLEN, PAUL M.; BARNES, WILLIAM D.; REECE, JERALD L.; AND ROBERTSON, E. WAYNE. *Teacher Self-Appraisal: A Way of Looking over Your Own Shoulder.* Worthington, Oh.: Charles A. Jones, 1970.

ARGYRIS, CHRIS AND SCHON, DONALD A. *Theory in Practice: Increasing Professional Effectiveness.* San Francisco: Jossey-Bass, 1974.

ASTIN, ALEXANDER W., AND LEE, CALVIN B. T. "Current Practices in the Evaluation and Training of College Teachers." *Educational Record,* Summer 1966, pp. 361–75.

BRASKAMP, LARRY A.; ORY, JOHN C.; AND PIEPER, DAVID M. "Student Written Comments." *Journal of Educational Psychology,* 1981, 73(1), pp. 65–70.

CADENHEAD, KENNETH, AND NEWELL, LAURA. "Personalizing Teacher Education." *Educational Technology,* March 1973, p. 51.

COOK, MARVIN J., AND NEVILLE, RICHARD F. "The Faculty as Teachers: A Perspective on Evaluation." ERIC Clearinghouse on Higher Education, Report no. 13, Washington, D.C.: George Washington University, 1971.

DENT, PRESTON L., AND NICHOLAS, THOMAS. "A Study of Faculty and Student Opinions on Teaching Effectiveness Ratings." *Peabody Journal of Education,* January 1980, pp. 135–43.

EBLE, KENNETH E. *Professors as Teachers.* San Francisco: Jossey-Bass, 1972.

ECKARD, PAMELA J. "Faculty Evaluation: The Basis for Rewards in Higher Education." *Peabody Journal of Education,* January 1980, pp. 94–100.

"EVALUATING ADMINISTRATIVE/SUPERVISORY PERFORMANCE." *Educational Research Service,* circular no. 6. Washington, D.C.: Educational Research Service, 1972.

GAFF, JERRY G.; WILSON, ROBERT C.; ET AL. *The Teaching Environment: A Study of Optimum Working Conditions for Effective College Teaching.* Berkeley: Center for Research and Development in Higher Education, 1970.

GRAY, CHARLES E. "The Teaching Model and Evaluation of Teaching Performance." *Journal of Higher Education,* November 1969, pp. 636–42.

HILDEBRAND, MILTON. "How to Recommend Promotion for a Mediocre Teacher without Actually Lying." *Journal of Higher Education*, January 1972, pp. 44–62.

HILDEBRAND, MILTON, AND WILSON, ROBERT C. *Effective University Teaching and Its Evaluation*. Berkeley: Center for Research and Development In Higher Education, 1970.

HIND, ROBERT R. "Evaluation and Authority in a University Faculty." Ph.D. dissertation, Stanford University, 1968.

HIND, ROBERT R.; DORNBUSCH, SANFORD M.; AND SCOTT, W. RICHARD. "A Theory of Evaluation Applied to a University Faculty." *Sociology of Education*, Winter 1974, pp. 114–28.

LINDMAN, ERIC L. "The Means and Ends of Accountability." *Proceedings of the Conference on Educational Accountability*. Conference sponsored by the Educational Testing Service, Chicago, Illinois, June 1971.

MAGER, ROBERT F. *Preparing Instructional Objectives*. 2nd ed. Belmont, Calif.: Fearon-Pitman, 1975.

MARSH, HERBERT W.; OVERALL, J. U.; AND KASLER, STEVEN P. "Validity of Student Evaluations of Instructional Effectiveness: A Comparison of Faculty Self-Evaluations and Evaluations by their Students." *Journal of Educational Psychology*, April 1979, pp. 149–160.

MCKEACHIE, WILBERT J. "Student Ratings of Faculty: A Reprise." *Academe: Bulletin of the AAUP*, October 1979, pp. 384–397.

MILLER, RICHARD I. *Evaluating Faculty Performance*. San Francisco: Jossey-Bass, 1972.

MORGAN, HENRY H., AND COGGER, JOHN W. *The Interviewer's Manual: Fair and Effective Interviewing*. 2nd ed. New York: Drake-Beam & Associates, 1980.

NATIONAL CENTER FOR HIGHER EDUCATION MANAGEMENT SYSTEMS. *Faculty Activity Analysis: Interpretation and Uses of Data*. TR 84. Boulder, Colo.: NCHEMS, 1974.

————. *Faculty Activity Analysis: Overview and Major Issues*. TR 24. Boulder, Colo.: NCHEMS, 1971.

————. *Faculty Activity Analysis: Procedures Manual*. TR 44. Boulder, Colo.: NCHEMS, 1973.

NATIONAL SCIENCE FOUNDATION. *Systems for Measuring and Reporting the Resources and Activities of Colleges and Universities*. NSF 67-15. Washington, D.C.: National Science Foundation, June 1967.

SCOTT, ROBERT A. *Lords, Squires, and Yeomen: Collegiate Middle Managers and Their Organizations*. AAHE-ERIC/Higher Education Research Report no. 7. Washington, D.C.: American Association for Higher Education, 1978.

SCOTT, W. RICHARD; DORNBUSCH, SANFORD M.; BUSCHING, BRUCE C.; AND LAING, JAMES D. "Organizational Evaluation and Authority." *Administrative Science Quarterly*, June 1967, pp. 93–117.

SELDIN, PETER. *Successful Faculty Evaluation Programs; A Practical Guide to Improve Faculty Performance and Promotion/Tenure Decisions*. New York: Coventry Press, 1980.

SMITH, ALBERT B. *Faculty Development and Evaluation in Higher Education*.

ERIC/Higher Education Research Report no. 8. Washington, D.C.: American Association for Higher Education, 1976.

SMITH, RICHARD, AND FIEDLER, FRED E. "The Measurement of Scholarly Work: A Critical Review of the Literature." *Educational Record*, Summer 1971, pp. 225–32.

VAN HADEN, HERBERT I., AND KING, JEAN MARIE. *Educational Innovator's Guide*. Worthington, Oh.: Charles A. Jones, 1974.

WALBERG, HERBERT J., ed. *Evaluating Educational Performance: A Sourcebook of Methods, Instruments, and Examples*. Berkeley: McCutchan, 1974.

9

Performance Counseling and Dealing with Unsatisfactory Performance

The Importance and Purpose of Performance Counseling

Performance counseling offers the chairperson a valuable communications tool that, properly used, can significantly enhance relations with faculty members and improve the department's chances for attaining its goals. *Performance counseling* is here defined as a regular although not necessarily formal contact between the chairperson and individual faculty members for the purpose of discussing successes and failures in completing assignments and duties. It is a two-way communications device that affords chairpersons and faculty members an opportunity to express their concerns and needs. Failure to provide this opportunity can become a grievance issue in the case of faculty members whose performance has been labeled deficient at evaluation time. At many institutions, performance counseling is required by state law, institutional policy, or collective bargaining agreement.

Some department chairpersons shirk the responsibility of providing performance counseling because they view this activity as nonprofessional or even degrading. They regard faculty members as professional peers and feel that infringing on or criticizing a fellow faculty member's professional activities is unjustifiable. This attitude is particularly prevalent in institutions in which department chairpersons serve on a rotating basis; it also exists in departments in which the chairperson's academic rank happens to be lower than that of his or her peers. Both chairpersons and faculty members will find performance counseling more acceptable, however, when they see that it can pave the way for more palatable decisions about promotion, tenure, and salary increases.

Chairpersons are also reluctant to provide performance counseling because it demands a complete understanding of department goals and objectives, the ability to make specific assignments for faculty members, and experience in assessing what constitutes acceptable performance standards. Meeting these requirements is no small matter and requires a great deal of thought and maturity. Further, the skills involved cannot easily be taught, because they require an intuitive judgment that not all chairpersons possess equally.

Perhaps the most important advice that can be given to performance counselors is, "Avoid distorting the record." Chairpersons often tend to look for strong points that can offset weak points or to gloss over problems, especially those considered minor. Another distortion results when justifiable criticisms are turned into compliments. For example, a faculty member who gives unreasonably difficult examinations and fails an excessive number of students may be described by the chairperson as a teacher who "demands a high standard of excellence from students"! Such distortions merely avoid the issues and undermine the counseling approach, if not the entire evaluation procedure.

Dealing with Unsatisfactory Performance

One of a chairperson's most difficult and unpleasant duties is to inform faculty members that their performance has been unsatisfactory. Nevertheless, unsatisfactory performance must be dealt with, since bad situations often deteriorate even more if left unattended. Because chairpersons are colleagues of the faculty members whose performance is deemed inadequate, the problem of how to confront those colleagues is often perplexing. Some basic principles, practices, and techniques can be useful when attempting to remedy certain situations.

Unsatisfactory performance is handled most effectively if it is identified early. Early detection of an unhealthy situation allows time for diagnosis and remediation. How, then, does a chairperson recognize a developing problem that requires attention? First, the faculty member's performance must be compared with predetermined standards of satisfactory performance (see chapter 8 on faculty evaluation). In this discussion we will assume that the department has developed criteria that are used to determine whether or not a faculty member's performance is acceptable in the areas of teaching, research, service, and other assigned duties.

Some unsatisfactory behaviors, such as unethical or illegal conduct, must simply be stopped to prevent irreparable harm. Other problems that occur because of rule or policy infractions generally are easily handled *provided* the chairperson adopts a strong managerial position. Institutional policy statements, faculty constitutions, or collective bargaining agreements may give the chairperson significant authority in such matters. For example, most institutions require that faculty members who accept outside employment report such employment before beginning the work. Such activity may well affect performance, especially if the faculty member is off campus one or more days per week. A faculty member's failure to follow this rule should be dealt with directly and firmly if the violation appears to be intentional.

Another example of unacceptable behavior is a faculty member's failure to hold office hours as required by university regulations or to meet scheduled classes. Repeated behavior of this type simply cannot be tolerated. The chairperson's job is *not* to be a policeman but to correct actions that are not in the best interests of students and the department. The effective chairperson may initially make light of the problem, but direct action, through informal as well as formal means, is appropriate if the situation does not improve.

Unsatisfactory performance, like most behavior, usually has a discernible cause or cluster of causes. The chairperson must learn to search for possible causes before attempting to discuss unsatisfactory behavior with a faculty member. Most instances of unsatisfactory performance on the part of faculty members can be linked to the presence or absence of elements in one or more of the following groups of factors.
1. knowledge of subject matter and skills in teaching and conducting research
2. psychological and physical characteristics
3. personal or family situations
4. working conditions.

Knowledge of Subject Matter and Skills in Teaching and Conducting Research

A faculty member may perform poorly in teaching a certain course because he or she was trained in another area and does not possess the requisite knowledge to teach the assigned course. Other persons may have the knowledge but lack pedagogic skills or are unable to organize course content, manage field experiences, and so on. Poor performance in research productivity may be due to a faculty member's inability to conduct independent research. The research completed for his doctoral dissertation may have been suggested by his adviser and carried out under continuing direction and supervision which is now not available to him.

Psychological and Physical Characteristics

Aptitude. Certain faculty members may not only demonstrate incompetence but also lack the aptitude to improve their skills or acquire new ones. For example, a biology professor whose training was in taxonomy lacked the detailed knowledge of biochemistry and physiology necessary for teaching courses in modern biology. No matter how hard he tried, he was unable to master the new material.

Physical Stamina. Occasionally there is a faculty member who has a low energy level or perhaps a minor heart ailment and may not have the stamina required to conduct long seminars or travel long distances to teach off-campus courses. The chairperson may not be aware of this situation.

Social Skills. There are faculty members who lack the social skills necessary to maintain good relations with colleagues, students, and staff. Quality of performance can suffer if proper relationships are not maintained.

Maturity. Some faculty members have difficulty in adjusting to new situations. When a change is needed in a department program to accommodate the new needs of students or society, certain faculty members are not sufficiently flexible to modify their work habits. Some faculty members are unable or unwilling to carry out assignments that may not be their first choice and thus do not perform at their best.

Judgment. At most colleges and universities, each faculty member faces more activities than he or she can possibly do in the time available. Some faculty members lack the necessary judgment for deciding which activities should receive high priority in terms of what is best for the department and for their own professional development. These faculty members may spend more time on activities that are only tangentially related to their formal assignments and that are considered of little importance to the mission or goals of the department.

Attitude. Some faculty members do not have the appropriate attitude to carry out certain assignments. For example, some extremely competent scholars seem temperamentally incapable of teaching undergraduate general education courses. Although very successful with graduate courses in their specific fields, they lack patience and understanding with students whose major interests may lie elsewhere. Other faculty members are resentful of duties that they consider demeaning. Such duties may include undergraduate counseling, off-campus teaching, service on certain committees, attendance at official functions, and so forth. These negative attitudes often lead to poor performance.

Reliability and Dependability. There are faculty members who find difficulty in meeting commitments they have made. This lack of dependability may range from never being on time or not coming to scheduled meetings or classes, not keeping promised office hours, not turning in grades on time, or not turning in required reports.

Personal and Family Situations

There are many problems faced by faculty members that are unrelated to their work except when stress from these problems affects performance. Examples are physical and mental problems, marital problems, problems with illness in the family, problems with difficult children, financial problems, and so forth.

Working Conditions

Lack of Incentives.   Some faculty members are not motivated to perform well because of insufficient incentives. These incentives may include adequate financial rewards, public recognition for achievements, and perquisites such as travel expenses for professional meetings or even parking space.

Lack of Appropriate Facilities and a Pleasing Environment.   A faculty member's performance may suffer because of inadequate physical facilities and resources such as laboratory equipment, office space, libraries, and classroom environments. Dissatisfaction with the social and physical climate of the community at large may also affect the quality of his or her performance.

Insufficient Orientation in Terms of What Is Expected.   A faculty member may never be explicitly told by the chairperson or any other designated faculty member what her duties are and how she will be evaluated. For example, a faculty member who felt that teaching was her main responsibility received a poor evaluation because of her lack of research activity. She was not told that all members of her department were expected to conduct research. Another faculty member thought that teaching off-campus courses fulfilled his service responsibilities. He was never told that membership in committees was expected and therefore refused to serve on them. As a result, his overall evaluation in the area of service was unsatisfactory.

Conflict with the Chairperson.   In some instances a faculty member's poor performance may be directly related to counterproductive interaction with the department chairperson. The faculty member may receive insufficient encouragement, praise, direction, or supervision. As a result, he or she may perceive a lack of concern on the chairperson's part. Other chairpersons may supervise too closely, thereby causing undue anxiety and tension.

In attempting to deal with a faculty member whose performance is considered unsatisfactory, the chairperson should first learn as much as possible about the personal and environmental matters that may be affecting the faculty member's behavior. Some of these circumstances may be known to the chairperson from personal observation, some from observations of other faculty members. In most instances it is advisable for the chairperson to meet with the faculty member in question to discuss the matter. The chairperson should prepare for the encounter by giving thought to the following suggestions.

First, it is difficult to tell someone that his or her performance has been unsatisfactory without provoking a defensive reaction. Even the chairperson may become defensive when confronting a faculty member whose performance is unsatisfactory. But being defensive is counterproductive and should be minimized whenever possible. If the discussion regarding the faculty member's performance is seen as a counseling session rather than as an interview for formal evaluation, any potential conflict may be diffused. The discussion should be just that—a discussion, not a lecture. The chairperson should try to involve the faculty member, rather than reprimand him or her. As mentioned earlier, the chairperson should start a dialogue with a faculty member at the first hint of difficulty and continue the dialogue at regular intervals. In this way, discussion of instances of poor performance will arise within a context of openness and will not provoke an immediate negative reaction. The chairperson should avoid lumping all of a faculty member's shortcomings into one bundle and dumping it on the unsuspecting person without warning.

The chairperson may perceive unsatisfactory faculty performance as a personal insult or as a poor reflection of his or her leadership abilities. He or she may also feel guilty about a faculty member's shortcomings. These reactions should not be allowed to become anger or hostility toward the faculty member. The chairperson should be as self-controlled and as calm as possible, since emotional responses may get out of hand. Yet the chairperson needs to recognize his or her feelings and anxieties and not try to repress them completely. At times, however, poor performance may be caused by the chairperson's behavior. In such cases, the chairperson should admit to this possibility and not try to project an image of omniscience and infallibility.

The faculty member should be made to feel that the chairperson is genuinely interested in bringing about positive changes and is willing to spend as much time and effort as is necessary to do so. The faculty member should also be made to feel that his or her poor performance need not be shouldered alone, that it is a problem for the whole department and can be solved cooperatively for the good of the department. What must be determined, therefore, is how best to solve the problem, not who should be blamed. Problem solving requires the chairperson's empathetic understanding of the faculty member and the ability to see the other person's point of view. To relieve the faculty member's anxiety, the chairperson must point out that others have had similar problems that have been successfully resolved.

When the chairperson has achieved the proper frame of mind for performance counseling, he or she should again review the possible reasons discussed earlier to see if anything can be done to change the situation. The faculty member should be encouraged to participate in the dialogue and make suggestions for change. If the dialogue goes well, some of these suggestions may correspond to those the chairperson has thought of. At the same time, the chairperson should be flexible enough to change his or her mind when new insights emerge as the result of dialogue. Some measures within the realm of the department's authority or control include providing opportunities for retraining faculty members who lack certain competencies; providing opportunities for reassignment for those who lack the ability to gain competence or whose health requires less demanding tasks; providing more preparation time for those who are overloaded or overworked; and changing or upgrading facilities for a better research atmosphere. Faculty members who are experiencing a personal crisis may benefit from a new assignment, for the change may give them a renewed sense of importance and productivity.

Sometimes unsatisfactory performance cannot be remedied. Although an attempt should be made to resolve the problem, the chairperson must be able to recognize and accept the fact that some faculty members' performance cannot be improved.

Initiating and Conducting a Dialogue about Unsatisfactory Performance

The importance of dialogue in solving problems of poor performance has been emphasized. Following are some concrete suggestions to the chairperson about how to initiate and conduct a discussion with a faculty member. Some of the suggestions are contained in standard college textbooks on counseling, interviewing, and personnel management. Others were obtained from experienced administrators who participated in department leadership workshops.

- Do not send a memorandum to the faculty member listing his or her areas of unsatisfactory performance and asking that an appointment be made with you to discuss them. It is better to make a personal contact, during which you can invite the faculty member to meet with you to talk about his or her progress toward reaching performance expectations.

- Try to allay the faculty member's anxiety by being calm and cool. Let the faculty member know that he or she is respected as a person and that his or her abilities are appreciated, but that specific changes in performance are necessary.
- Be open-minded, tolerant, and cooperative, and encourage the faculty member to express his or her point of view. Be considerate. Listen attentively to what is being said without interrupting, and keep sufficient control over the discussion so that it does not develop into a shouting match or an abusive argument.
- Be as empathetic as possible and give credit where credit is due, but try to focus on those areas that need improvement and on the possible solutions to the problem. Personal feelings toward the individual whether positive or negative should not be allowed to stand in the way of challenging unsatisfactory performance.
- When pinpointing poor performance, be specific and descriptive, rather than ascribe a blanket negative value to the performance. Be ready to offer concrete suggestions about what needs to be done, especially when the faculty member seems unable to develop his or her own plan. At the same time, keep the plan flexible. (See Chapter 15 on Assigning and Reporting Faculty Activities.)

The meeting should result in the development of a course of action that is agreed upon by both chairperson and faculty member and that includes specific objectives and a schedule for achieving them. The chairperson should arrange additional meetings, if necessary, and keep a written record of the dialogue and its conclusions. The faculty member deserves to have a copy of the record of the meeting. A note of caution: The chairperson should not try to give psychological counseling to the faculty member or even suggest that it is needed. Experience has shown that giving this kind of advice, even when it is solicited, sometimes results in legal action against the chairperson or the university or both.

Encouraging Good Performance

A department recently hired a temporary faculty member to teach two classes. During the term, she spent an inordinate amount of time on the assigned courses and developed some innovative activities that were adopted for continued use in the class. An evaluative questionnaire completed by the students rated both the classes and her teaching "excellent." At the end of the term, the chairperson's only comment to her was, "You may be interested to know that I didn't receive any negative comments on your work this term." Needless to say, the faculty member did not feel that her efforts were sufficiently appreciated!

In facing the day-to-day problems of running a department, the chairperson can easily overlook the importance of encouraging acceptable performance. Most faculty and staff members feel encouraged when their chairperson makes the effort to identify good performance and offers a sincere comment on the work. Chairpersons must find time to compliment special efforts by faculty members. Obvious performance—such as unusually high student ratings, a published paper, a successful grant proposal, or an outstanding presentation to a group of local businessmen—is easy to identify and deserves favorable comment. The recognition of less obvious accomplishments—such as completing an assignment ahead of schedule, spending extra time with a group of students, or being available to help with an unexpected problem—can be an even greater boost for a faculty member's morale.

The chairperson should also take every opportunity to encourage actions by faculty members that will lead to successful promotions and tenure decisions and to ensure that good performance is properly documented. The chairperson's task is *not* to build the case for the faculty member but to have as much supporting evidence as possible when making a case for promotion or tenure.

Maintaining a Record of Performance Counseling

The chairperson's responsibility for maintaining a record of performance counseling, including comments on successful and outstanding accomplishments as well as problem areas, is increasingly important. This record need not be extensive or detailed, and it should not be kept secret from the faculty member involved. It can be as valuable to the faculty member as it is to the chairperson, since the faculty member soon gains a clearer picture of the performance standards expected by the chairperson. The performance counseling record is a valuable document when decisions about promotion, tenure, and salary adjustments are made. When promotion, tenure, or salary adjustments must be denied, the chairperson must be able to document that a reasonable effort has been made to assist the faculty member to improve poor performance. Summaries of performance counseling actions should go in the faculty member's evaluation folder.

The department chairperson, then, should establish a regular pattern of performance counseling with department faculty members. This effort may be formal or informal, but the real purpose of the counseling is to establish a close working relationship with faculty members and to encourage actions that the chairperson feels will benefit both the faculty member and the department. Counseling must be based on clear, definite assignments and on reasonable standards of performance in each major academic area—teaching, research, and service. The chairperson must document performance counseling activities as accurately and as quantitatively as possible without overreacting with either positive or negative comments.

The improvement in faculty members' performance as a result of performance counseling can play a significant role in promotion, tenure, and salary adjustment decisions. Performance counseling may also prove to be important to the chairperson as a way of establishing and maintaining meaningful communication with faculty members.

Questions and Exercises

1. Identify one or two faculty members in your department or in another department who have performed unsatisfactorily in teaching, research, service, or some other area that is important to the department.
2. For each faculty member so identified, ask yourself the following questions:
   a. In what way was the performance in each case unsatisfactory? Against what criteria was each performance compared?
   b. Are you familiar with any personal factors that may have contributed to the poor performance of the faculty member concerned, such as lack of competence, lack of mental or physical ability to carry out assigned data, lack of understanding of what is expected, or lack of proper attitude? Give examples.
   c. Are you familiar with any environmental factors that may have contributed to the poor performance of the faculty member concerned, such as lack of acceptance by colleagues, lack of incentives, lack of appropriate facilities, or lack of adequate leadership. Give examples.
   d. To your knowledge, did the faculty members in question receive any kind of performance counseling? What kind, if any?
   e. Assuming that you have decided to provide these faculty members with performance counseling, how would you go about it? Prepare a mental script that you would use with each faculty member. Under what circumstances would you meet with each of them? Anticipate their response. What kind of assistance would you offer them? How would you motivate them?
3. Following is a list of situations that call for some performance

counseling. Expand each situation into a scenario based on your experience and/or imagination. Assume that you are the chairperson who will deal with the faculty members in question. What would you say to them? Under what circumstances would you meet with each of them? Anticipate their response. What kind of help could you offer them?

a. Dealing with the faculty member whose teaching performance is unsatisfactory. Assume that the faculty member in this instance has never been counseled before regarding this problem.

b. Dealing with the faculty member whose research output is inadequate. Assume that the faculty member in this instance has been counseled once before regarding this same problem.

c. Informing a nontenured assistant professor who has been in the department for three years that his contract will not be renewed the following year. Assume that the assistant professor has received no performance counseling prior to this meeting.

d. Dealing with a productive faculty member whose morale is low because his application for promotion was denied.

e. Dealing with the faculty member who is productive in areas not related to the department's mission. His efforts need to be redirected.

f. Counseling with the faculty member who casually visits your office to talk about an apparent simple problem while underneath is a considerably more fundamental problem.

g. Counseling with the faculty member who has been the subject of gossip about improper behavior but there is no hard evidence.

h. Rewarding the high performer who may not receive promotion and who sees others performing at a barely acceptable level.

4. Perhaps you could persuade one or two of your colleagues to role-play with you. One of you could be the chairperson, another the faculty member who is being counseled, and a third person could be the observer and critic of the role playing.

5. The following case study of "An Unsuccess Story" is presented for thought. Please answer the questions at the end of the case study.

This case is based on an actual incident that occurred after a chairperson attended a department leadership seminar sponsored by the Institute for Departmental Leadership, Florida State University.

When Harry Casper, a social science department chairperson, returned home from a workshop on collegial administration for the 1980s, he decided to test his new knowledge. The first problem he wanted to approach was the issue of inequitable workloads among the faculty members. This problem was uppermost in his mind because it was time to work out the class schedule for the next term. After several days of effort he developed an assignment plan using several ideas that were discussed at the workshop. He designed a basic system of points for various activities and a form for recording the planned assignments. To make sure the plan was understandable and that the point weights reflected the priorities agreed upon by the faculty members, he sought out some of his colleagues to get their reactions and made a few important changes based on their suggestions.

While creating and obtaining acceptance of the plan, Casper contemplated ways of making assignments that would be equitable and at the same time allow for faculty development that could be recognized and rewarded. As he reviewed the latest student evaluations of faculty members' performance and considered those persons who were most strongly criticized, his thoughts turned especially to one faculty member, Anne Stone.

Stone, an associate professor, was the first woman social scientist recruited by the department search committee. She had been an outstanding undergraduate social science major, graduating cum laude from this very institution. She completed her doctorate at Indiana University six years ago and had continually done good research. She published regularly and had a book manuscript in process. Her otherwise good record was marred by continuous complaints about her teaching. Students reported that she was uninteresting, disorganized, unfriendly, and rarely available to those seeking advice. In fact, of the department's nineteen full-time faculty members, she always had the lowest rating for teaching.

Stone's record seemed to be getting worse, and Casper wanted to make some special assignments that would enable her to improve her performance. He began work on an assignment that would provide released time for consultation with some instructional design professionals in the university; he also would propose that she teach a few small sections of the introductory courses, as well as a reduced graduate teaching load. In all, he spent almost two weeks working out the details for her faculty development program and for each term of the next academic year's assignment. He felt a genuine sense of accomplishment, tinged with altruism, and felt that Stone would be pleased with his plan for improving her teaching and advising capabilities.

A meeting with Stone was scheduled for the Wednesday morning preceding Thanksgiving holidays. She came into his office, seeming a bit fidgety; her manner was friendly, but she showed some anxiety. Casper explained the new assignment system first, then elaborated on the special assignments that could be worked out for her growth and development as a faculty member. As he began to unfold the details of the plan, her face changed from a look of mild curiosity to one of growing anger. Her first response was to ask why Casper did not like her teaching, and he answered that his plan was based on complaints about her teaching. She responded forcefully that she was one of the best teachers in the department and that he was judging her on the basis of incomplete, unreliable, and bad evidence. Casper tried to reason with her, offering to change the plan in any way that she thought would help improve her teaching. At the end of the third exchange about the plan, Stone jumped from her chair and without another word walked out and slammed the door. Casper made some minor changes in her assignment and then prepared for the consultation with the next faculty member.

Just before the term ended at Christmas, Casper received a call from the president that surprised, saddened, and angered him. Stone had filed an official faculty grievance against him. She claimed that he was harassing her and embarrassing her by requiring that she seek help in improving her teaching from professionals who were not faculty members when she already was an accomplished and experienced teacher. An informal conference with the president's faculty grievance representative could not resolve the issues, so they were to be heard formally by a university grievance committee at the end of January.

a. Assuming that the chairperson was well-intentioned in his attempt to help Stone improve her performance, why were his efforts rebuffed?
b. What could or should the chairperson have done to have aroused a less negative response from Stone?
c. Was Casper wrong in trying to design an annual assignment for Stone that included a program to help her improve her teaching?
d. Should Casper have involved other faculty members of the department in designing an improvement program for Stone? If so, how should they have been involved?
e. How would you have handled the situation?

References

BASKIN, OTIS W., AND ARONOFF, CRAIG E. *Interpersonal Communication in Organization.* Santa Monica, Calif.: Goodyear, 1980.

BOLTON, ROBERT H. *People Skills: How to Assert Yourself, Listen to Others, and Resolve Conflicts.* Englewood Cliffs, N.J.: Prentice-Hall, 1979.

BRAMMER, LAWRENCE M. *The Helping Relationship.* 2nd ed. Englewood Cliffs, N.J.: Prentice-Hall, 1979.

CUNNINGHAM, PATRICK J. "Disciplinary Counseling: The First Step Toward Due Process." *The Journal of the College and University Personnel Association,* Summer 1980, pp. 1–6.

EGAN, GERARD, AND COWAN, MICHAEL A. *People in Systems: An Integrative Approach to Human Development.* Monterey, Calif.: Brooks-Cole, 1979.

ERICKSON, STANFORD C., AND COOK, JOHN A. *Support for Teaching at Major Universities.* Ann Arbor: Center for Research on Learning and Teaching, University of Michigan, 1980.

FOURNIES, FERDINAND F. *Coaching for Improved Work Performance.* New York: Van Nostrand Reinhold, 1978.

HASENFELD, YEHESKEL, AND ENGLISH, RICHARD A. *Human Service Organizations: A Book of Readings.* Ann Arbor, Mich.: The University of Michigan Press, 1974.

LEAVITT, HAROLD J., AND PONDY, LOUIS R., eds. *Readings in Managerial Psychology.* 2nd ed. Chicago: University of Chicago Press, 1974.

ROMAN, PAUL M. "Employee Alcoholism and Assistance Programs: Adapting an Innovation for College and University Faculty." *Journal of Higher Education,* March-April 1980, pp. 135–49.

SHERTZER, BRUCE E., AND STONE, SHELLEY C. *Fundamentals of Counseling.* 3rd ed. Boston: Houghton Mifflin, 1980.

STEINMETZ, LAWRENCE L. *Managing the Marginal and Unsatisfactory Performer.* Reading, Mass.: Addison-Wesley, 1969.

10

Faculty Grievances and Unions

In the days of rapid expansion of colleges and universities, little attention was given to resolving problems relating to the conditions and procedures of employment of faculty members. Because the academic market was strong, faculty members who were dissatisfied with their jobs could escape their problems by changing institutions. Moreover, many faculty members were of patrician background, and their upbringing taught them to disdain strident, overt conflict. Colleagues "were done in quietly": they simply disappeared in June, to emerge at another school the following September.

By the end of the 1960s, much had changed. Students had frightened university administrators into making various reforms, and issues of war and peace had become campus concerns. Faculty members from the working class, ethnic backgrounds, and, to a lesser degree, minority cultures had joined the profession. Legislators voted to punish university communities for real or imagined transgressions, and most traditional disciplines faced declining markets. For many faculty members the idea of organizing themselves and their professions no longer seemed outlandish.

At one time, faculty members who were denied tenure or whose contracts were not renewed might have respectably transferred to other institutions. With few employment opportunities available, they now were increasingly willing to challenge negative evaluations by administrators and colleagues. They tried to retain their jobs through existing, though sometimes impotent, procedures, and their cases frequently reached federal or state appellate courts.

Some institutions changed their procedures, although most did not. A few institutions, especially those supported primarily by private sources, developed formal procedures that were included in their consitutions and faculty handbooks. Others, particularly those state universities supervised or coordinated by state boards of higher education, developed procedures that became part of state law. At some institutions where procedures were actually included in the law, faculty members still felt that they had no strong advocates to ensure that the procedures were applied impartially. When they were not satisfied with the implemenatation of the procedures and mechanisms designed for appealing individual nonrenewals, de facto tenure quotas, or layoffs, faculty members often designated unions to represent them in negotiating with the administration and in filing grievances. This cooperation frequently resulted in the development of official faculty union contracts that contained conditions and procedures of employment. Contracts at some state universities—for example, the state universities in Florida—contain the same conditions and procedures as those stipulated in the state law concerning university personnel policies.

In several states the difference between the legislation and the contracts is that the contracts are monitored by union officials who act as faculty advocates. In states with legislation but no negotiated contract, the conditions are monitored by the administration, a situation that many faculty members perceive as the fox guarding the henhouse. The spirit of the legislation appears to be remarkably similar to the spirit of the negotiated contracts. Perhaps if a mechanism were developed that carried out the legislative intent fairly, faculty members might not feel such a strong need to unionize.

Faculty personnel problems occur whether a union exists or not. In fact, although the power and influence of faculty unions are increasing dramatically in some areas of the country, the personnel problems facing faculty members have remained the same. These problems have led to formal grievances or informal complaints, depending on the procedures at any given institution.

Regardless of whether a faculty union exists, a department chairperson may confront many kinds of grievances. The following list contains examples of typical problems that have led to grievances:

- conflict with colleagues, administrators, students, or community over teaching methods, course content, research design, or subject matter
- complaints about rank or pay; claims that inequities were due to discrimination against race, sex, religion, or handicap
- dissatisfaction with status or classification; claims that existing status or classification did not reflect training, experience, or responsibilities
- disagreement over assignment; claims that assignment was made late, represented an undesired overload, constituted disciplinary action, or was made arbitrarily and capriciously
- problems concerning evaluation; claims that evaluations were

biased, that supervisors failed to notify employees of the results of their observations, that the evaluation procedures and instruments used were in violation of the contract, that the evaluation file was stacked with negative information, or that evaluation was based on materials not contained in the evaluation file

- problems concerning nonrenewal of contract; claims that employees were not notified of nonrenewal within contractual time limits, that reasons for nonrenewal were not provided on request, or that reasons provided were in violation of the contract, the law, or university rules or constitution
- problems concerning layoff; claims of failure to follow contractual guidelines for layoff or failure to pursue actively recall and placement procedures
- problems with peer review; claims of failure to conduct peer reviews so that administrative decisions would be based on consistent criteria and procedures established by the contract, the law, or university rules
- problems concerning promotion and tenure; claims that decisions were not based on established criteria, were arbitrary and capricious, or contradicted supportive materials in the evaluation folder; claims of unwillingness to overturn an erroneous review on its merits; claims of total disregard for a favorable peer review
- problems concerning reprimand or censure; objections to negative letters placed in personnel file; objections to suspension or termination
- problems concerning access to records, documents, or information; disagreements over administrative use of "relevance" or "privilege" arguments to refuse access
- problems concerning efforts to solve problems; claims that administrators failed to observe time lines, to conduct impartial meetings, or to make good faith efforts to reach a settlement or to issue decisions based on the merits of the grievance

The issues of greatest conflict between faculty members represented by a faculty union and the board of regents in one state university system have been identified in a recent dissertation. The study found that during the period from 1 January 1977 to 1 January 1978, 114 conflicts reached the second step of the formal grievance procedure—i.e, review by the chancellor of the board of regents or his or her representatives. These conflicts arose from complaints about salary inequities (24 cases); tenure and promotion decisions (24 cases); assignment of responsibilities (12 cases); nonrenewal (11 cases); evaluation (11 cases); salary schedule not established by board of regents (5 cases); sabbaticals (5 cases); academic freedom (2 cases); holidays (2 cases); failure to hold informal conferences (2 cases); and other issues (16 cases, each different).*

Most of the inequity grievances grew out of a sex discrimination clause of the contract. Once the initial inequities were rectified, this cause of grievances became of secondary importance in subsequent years. Tenure, promotion, assignments, nonrenewals, and evaluations still remained major grievance areas. Since these 114 cases reached an advanced step in the grievance process, certain matters of faculty relations clearly deserve close scrutiny. With these conflicts in mind, the chairperson may be able to anticipate personnel problems. In many cases, when the reason for a problem is understood, the potential difficulty can be resolved to everyone's benefit before it becomes critical.

Sometimes personnel problems result in formal grievances. A *grievance*, as the term will be used here, is a claim that a contract negotiated under collective bargaining has been violated or that university or college rules, state statute, federal law, or constitutional rights have been violated. When a faculty union perceives that its members have a problem, it may "find" an article of the contract that it will claim is being violated. Such a claim does not necessarily mean that a violation has occurred but that the union can be expected to interpret the contract liberally when the interests of its clientele are involved. If a faculty member's unhappiness stems from something other than a violation of the contract or of any of the above laws, rules, or rights, he or she may simply choose to write a letter of complaint to some upper-level administrator in the college or university.

An unusually large number of complaints or grievances within a department, whether based on alleged violations of a faculty contract or not, is often symptomatic of deep-seated conflict. A wise chairperson will try to create a department environment that minimizes grievances and maximizes openness and trust. In discussing how to minimize grievances, we have assumed that a better understanding of grievance procedures will lead department chairpersons to adhere to the spirit and letter of the faculty contract (if one exists) or of current university rules and regulations governing faculty personnel. Unfortunately, some department chairpersons are not cognizant of these rules and regulations or choose to ignore them. As faculty members expend greater efforts defending their rights, it is increasingly important for chairpersons to understand the faculty contract or other operative personnel rules and regulations, as well as alternatives for dealing with personnel problems.

A chairperson can minimize grievances, contractual or other, by as-

---

*Chris Parnell Plyler, "The Grievance Appeals Process in the State University System of Florida: A Case Study." Unpublished doctoral dissertation, Florida State University, 1978, p. 53.

signing responsibilities in a clear and forthright manner; providing a process for faculty members to dispute and change an arbitrary or capricious assignment; regularly evaluating employees on the basis of their assignments, rather than on personality or social considerations; instructing committees engaged in peer evaluation also to evaluate a faculty member on the basis of that person's assigned responsibilities; and counseling faculty members who have performed poorly. A good personnel policy is one that is fair, provides means of improvement, and minimizes complaints and grievances.

When a faculty member files a grievance, considers doing so, or simply has a complaint or problem, the chairperson should be willing to discuss the problem with the potential grievant and his or her representative. A chairperson should not be offended if a department member feels the need for a representative when dealing with a serious career matter. Unions usually advise faculty members to have a colleague witness such discussions with supervisors. Moreover, to the chairperson, the faculty member may be a colleague, but to the faculty member with a problem, the chairperson may simply be the "boss." Even a professional may need the moral support of a colleague or grievance specialist.

Faculty members with grievances are under enormous pressure. They do not want to offend friends or administrators, but they do want a just resolution of their problem. A simple description of the grievance process does not begin to reveal the strain that a grievance creates, even among innocent bystanders in a department or college.

Resolving personnel problems is easier when the complaints are still informal. Clearly, doing whatever possible to eliminate potential causes of grievances and attempting to solve them informally is in the best interests of all persons in the university community. Possibilities of settlement may arise at informal meetings early in the grievance process and should be seriously pursued. An experienced party might be recruited to suggest solutions. Early resolution keeps the complaint within the chairperson's control; avoids time-consuming hearings, depositions, or court appearances; spares upper-level administrators the need to deal with the department's headache; and prevents the intradepartment bloodletting that often results when factions form behind protagonists.

The Grievance Procedure

If the problem is not resolved, it may become a formal grievance. When a contract exists, only matters covered by the contract may constitute the subject of a grievance. The contract encourages administrators and employees to communicate openly and to make every attempt to resolve problems before a grievance is filed. Once a grievance is filed, however, the contract stipulates three steps to be followed in the attempt to settle the grievance. The grievance procedure for the State University System of Florida will serve as our model for the three-step grievance procedure.

The first step consists of the grievant and his or her representative presenting evidence supporting the grievance to the university president or his or her representative. At this time, the "acts or omissions" leading to the grievance and the university officials involved are identified, and a solution is proposed. The president or his or her representative must give a written decision within a defined time. If the grievance is not satisfactorily resolved within the institution, the process moves to the second step, which consists of a prompt review by the chancellor of the university system or his or her representatives, who must give a decision with supporting reasons within a defined time. If no satisfactory resolution results, the third step is taken at the discretion of the union. This step consists of a process of arbitration conducted by a neutral arbitrator chosen from a preselected panel. The arbitrator's decision is binding on the board of regents, the union, and the grievant, though the arbitrator's decision may be appealed to a court of law if he or she appears to have acted outside his or her jurisdiction.

The three-step approach gives the impression that grievances are primarily resolved at one of the three official levels. Many grievances, however, never reach the first step but are worked out informally between the local union steward or chapter grievance specialist and the department chairperson or, occasionally, a dean. In addition, many grievances are worked out along the way as "settlements" that are satisfactory to both sides. Still others end in ad hoc committees, acceptable to both the administration and the faculty union, which successfully resolve the problems. The distasteful prospect of arbitration encourages both sides to strive for an acceptable settlement. The grievance procedure with the possibility of a review by a neutral party introduces an element of accountability into contract administration.

The situation is considerably different when a union contract does not exist. At universities that provide due process, usually one or several peer committees exist to deal with complaints. The committees may be appointed by administrators, chosen by senates, or elected at large. Such committees hear charges, examine evidence, and keep records. The committee members are colleagues of the grievant and rarely, if ever, have authority to change personnel decisions on their own. Their charge is to make a recommendation to a high-level management representative, who may or may not choose to follow the recommendation.

Several states have legislation modeled on the federal Administrative Procedures Act, and a considerable number of academic rules and procedures for state universities are usually included in these state statutes. Florida law, for example, provides for standard university governing policies, such as criteria for tenure and promotion, acceptable reasons for nonrenewal, and even the relationship of teaching to research and publication in the promotion criteria. The state's Administrative Procedures Act provides a mechanism for faculty members to deal with violations of those procedures.

The shortcomings of the Administrative Procedures Act in Florida, however, are typical of those throughout the country. Under this act, a party has the right to have a grievance placed before a neutral hearing officer, who is chosen on the basis of his or her expertise in the matter in question. In the absence of a collective bargaining contract, the hearing officer's ruling on whether a faculty member's rights have been violated is only a recommendation to the university. If the university does not choose to implement the recommendation, the aggrieved faculty member can litigate, but in so doing faces considerable financial costs. Moreover, in Florida the courts have rarely upheld the hearing examiner when he or she ruled against management. The unions, of course, point out that the standard grievance procedures in collective bargaining contracts culminate in neutral arbitration, which the courts almost universally support. For this reason neither management nor labor enters into litigation over arbitration decisions, except in the rare instance in which the arbitrator exceeds his or her authority.

The chances of a grievant winning his or her argument seem to be much greater on those campuses where faculty members have union contracts. Nevertheless, the chairperson may face even greater involvement in a noncontractual case because so many separate hearings may need to be conducted for a single case. The strain on the department, the loss of faculty members' time, and diversion of department administrative effort can be significant. For example, one standard noncontractual tenure grievance case was in intrauniversity system hearings for two years and in litigation for another three years. Faculty members and especially chairpersons are frequently required to take part in hearings and litigation. Although the department will not have to incur legal costs for such cases, the university will. In addition, upper-level administrators will have to take part in this unpleasant diversion. University administrators may view chairpersons who are involved in a great many grievances as problems in themselves. Chairpersons should not acquiesce to unreasonable claims made by some department members but should understand the rules under which they function and minimize grievances through sound personnel practices.

A grievant or the union will occasionally blame the chairperson for the problem leading to the grievance. The grievant will sometimes demand that the chairperson be disciplined or receive psychiatric counseling. Grievants often vent their hostility in this way, and the chairperson should not succumb to emotional reactions. Such reactions not only make resolution more difficult and final adjustment to the situation unlikely, but they also may weaken the argument for the chairperson's position. The goal of both sides is to reach an equitable settlement, but the chairperson will have to live with whatever settlement is attained. Department members may have difficulty accepting an uncomfortable situation, but the chairperson must acquiesce gracefully for the sake of the department and its development. In such instances, it helps for the chairperson to have a thick skin.

A Case Study of a Grievance Filed under a Union Contract

The following case study is based on a grievance that took place in the State University System of Florida. The procedures that were followed are outlined in a contract for 1978–1981 negotiated between the United Faculty of Florida and the Florida Board of Regents. The Florida contract is not presented as a model for other states to follow, nor is this study to be viewed as advocating or opposing the cause of faculty unions. It is presented in order to inform department chairpersons of the dynamics of a grievance process. Other states with similar contracts usually have similar, though not necessarily identical, processes. This case study should also be of interest to chairpersons in institutions that do not have union contracts, because it deals with a grievance about tenure and closely resembles cases that have occurred in the absence of a contract.

The facts of the case presented here have been slightly modified in order to protect the privacy of the persons involved. The actual case involved several steps, but it has been restructured as only a one-step case. The names of the persons have been changed, minor facts altered, and some events deleted, but the case is based on an actual incident.

A Brief Background of the Case

John O'Hara, a member of the department of educational foundations for six years, filed a grievance after being denied tenure. During his fifth year he had been promoted to associate professor, and the promotion was unanimously approved by his department's tenure and promotion committee. When he applied for tenure the next year, the same committee rejected him unanimously. When O'Hara formally asked why he had failed to receive tenure, the university president's representative responded that the department would state only that it had rejected O'Hara because a majority of the committee had voted against him.

O'Hara filed a grievance citing several documents: a letter from the department chairperson, C. B. Rhodes, a collective bargaining unit member [at certain institutions in the State University System of Florida, some chairpersons are designated as members of the collective bargaining unit and some are designated as part of management]; a letter from Jason Smith, the chairperson of the tenure and promotion committee; and a letter from James Deles, the leading scholar among the full professors serving on the committee. The initial series of letters supported O'Hara's promotion; a subsequent series supported his tenure approval. These letters were uniformly positive, praising O'Hara's qualities as both a teacher and a scholar. Deles, for example, described him as "the strongest scholar in the department." O'Hara also included letters from the same persons that were written following the department's rejection of his request for tenure. These three letters, all written in a remarkably similar style, considerably modified the earlier praise and indicated unspecified doubts about the candidate.

The file contained several other letters. Among them were two unsolicited communications to O'Hara from nationally known scholars praising his latest book and a related article of his that had appeared in the leading journal in the field. The file also included a copy of the chairperson's annual evaluation of faculty members, which rated as "excellent" O'Hara's teaching and research for each year that he had served at the university. Student evaluations of O'Hara's teaching were also quite positive. His publications list was formidable.

In the area of service, however, O'Hara had received only a "satisfactory" rating for his first three years with the department; for the last three years, he was not evaluated for service. Included in the grievance file was a statement by O'Hara pointing out that he did not understand why he had received only a "satisfactory" rating for meeting his service obligations. O'Hara noted that he had served on as many committees as anyone else in the department, had several doctoral students working under him, and had obtained more money in grants in the last four years than the three most successful grants recipients in the department had obtained in their combined academic careers. O'Hara also coached a pee-wee league softball team, an activity he felt constituted community service of a sort. He stated, however, that he was not sure what "community service" meant for someone in the field of philosophy of education. O'Hara noted that when he asked Rhodes what he should do to improve his service rating, Rhodes assured him—verbally—that O'Hara need not worry about the matter. Subsequently, he was not assigned a service obligation for the last three years.

An Informal Attempt to Deal with the Problem

A union grievance representative brought the O'Hara matter to the attention of the dean of the college of education, Carmine Calabrezi. The dean chose not to have the assistant to the president for labor relations present, indicating that on principle he would not overturn a unanimous vote of a department. In addition, Dean Calabrezi emphasized that he had utmost confidence in the department chairperson, Rhodes. Dean Calabrezi would not speak of the substance of the grievance. If Rhodes indicated to him that a serious error had taken place, Calabrezi assured the representative that he would be happy to reconsider the tenure recommendation.

The union representative then met informally with Rhodes, who also refused to discuss the substance of the case. Rhodes began by noting that the union had filed this grievance only after the dean had rejected O'Hara's tenure. Rhodes emphasized, "I'm in the collective bargaining unit, not an administrator who has to justify his decisions." After his meeting with Rhodes, the union grievance representative gave a report of "no progress" to O'Hara.

Grievance Meeting

O'Hara's grievance meeting was held on 3 April 1979. Grievance meetings at this stage in the process take on different forms at different institutions. At some universities, the president's representative meets first with the representatives of one party and then with the representatives of the other. At O'Hara's grievance meeting, the union's representative and the president's representative remained for the entire meeting.

At the meeting, O'Hara and his union representative discussed the grievance matter with the president's representative. O'Hara based his argument on documents from his personnel file and on relevant sections of the collective bargaining contract, board of regents rules, and state law. The president called on O'Hara's department chairperson, Rhodes, to testify against O'Hara's charges. The union representative asked Rhodes many questions, but Rhodes refused to cite any specific reasons for the denial of O'Hara's request for tenure other than the fact that a peer committee had unanimously made that recommendation. He also refused to answer any substantive questions regarding the case, citing the secrecy of the tenure process. In addition, he claimed that, as a collective bargaining unit member, he had no official responsibility in the matter.

The representatives of the union and the president both countered that merely citing the unanimous vote against O'Hara's tenure application was an inadequate response by the chairperson. The president's representative added that although Rhodes was a unit member, a chairperson serves in a management role when deciding about promotion and tenure matters and should be responsible enough to aid the grievant in his right to due process. The representative added that any chairperson who does not accept supervisory responsibilities should meet with the dean to redefine the chairperson's role or else resign the position. He also pointed out that if the chairperson were not able to provide the evidence on which the rejection of O'Hara's request was based, the department would have to grant O'Hara tenure. "If, Mr. Rhodes, you persist in hiding behind the argument that you are in the unit, you will be stuck with a man you claim you do not want in your department," the president's representative said.

Other members of the tenure and promotion committee appeared at the meeting or were contacted directly by the president's representative. All but one member of the committee presented the same arguments as Rhodes and refused to give any substantive reason for opposing O'Hara's request for tenure.

The one exception, Jason Smith, chairperson of the department's tenure committee, stated that he did not feel strongly about O'Hara's request for tenure one way or the other. He considered O'Hara an "overly aggressive man who cared only about research and his own career" and stated that O'Hara had little loyalty to the department. The union representative asked Smith if any criteria such as "department loyalty" or "lack of aggressiveness" were included in the qualifications for tenure drawn up by the university or the board of regents. Smith said that he was not familiar with the specifics of tenure criteria found in official documents. His vote had been based on his intuition, on information he had received from students and colleagues, on his personal impression of the grievant, and on a careful examination of O'Hara's promotion file. He also noted that because of O'Hara's overconcern with research, he had a weak service record. Smith stated, however, that he intended to vote for O'Hara's tenure next year. [In this institution, candidates could be considered for tenure during the seventh year even though they have been formally notified of nonrenewal.] Smith felt that another year of seasoning would provide O'Hara with some much needed humility.

Before examining the president's decision about O'Hara's grievance, let us review certain relevant excerpts from the contract between the

Florida Board of Regents and the faculty union, as well as excerpts from the Florida Administrative Code, the Board of Regents Manual.* Chairpersons should have some familiarity with the language of contracts, statutes, and rules that define the rights and responsibilities of faculty members and administrators. Note that the language of each is similar.

EXCERPTS FROM THE FLORIDA ADMINISTRATIVE CODE, FLORIDA BOARD OF REGENTS MANUAL, 1979

> Each faculty member, tenured and non-tenured, shall be evaluated at least once annually on the basis of his or her individual total performance in fulfilling responsibilities to the university. The basic purpose of the evaluation is faculty improvement in the functions of teaching, research, service, and any other duties that may be assigned, with the resulting enhancement of learning, cultural advancement, and the production of new knowledge. This evaluation shall precede and be considered in recommendations and final decisions on tenure, promotions, and salary for tenured and non-tenured faculty members and on retention or non-renewal for non-tenured faculty members. [6C-5.05(1)(a)]

> When first employed, each faculty member shall be apprised of what is expected of him or her, generally, in terms of teaching, research and other creative activities, and service, and specifically if there are specific requirements and/or other duties involved. If and when these expectations change during the period of service of a faculty member, that faculty member shall be apprised of the change. [6C-5.05(1)(b)]

> Tenure is that condition attained by the faculty member through highly competent teaching and research, or other scholarly activities, service, and contributions to the university and to society.... [6C-5.06(1)(a)]

> Each nomination for tenure shall be acted upon with careful consideration being given to the qualifications of the faculty member, including evaluations by colleagues and the immediate superior.... [6C-5.06(2)]

> Tenure recommendations shall be based on the institution's evaluation procedures.... [6C-5.06(4)(a)]

> [The areas of performance to be evaluated are:]
>
>   (a) Teaching....
>
>   (b) Research and Other Creative Activities—Contribution to the discovery of new knowledge, development of new educational techniques, and other forms of creative activity shall be considered and evaluated. Evidence of research and other creative activity shall include, but not be limited to: published books; articles and papers in professional journals; ... and current research and creative activity that

---

*The BOR has contended that such BOR rules, state law, and state and federal constitutions do not, as such, constitute the subjects of a grievance. The union has continually cited BOR rules and state law in grievances. The issue has not yet been decided either in arbitration or litigation. Whether the BOR or the union eventually prevails in this issue, the chairperson should understand the material involved. Also nonunit grievants will likely utilize these citations.

has not yet resulted in publication, display, or performance. The evaluation shall include consideration of:

1. Productivity, including quality and quantity of what has been done during the year, and of the faculty member's long-term research and other creative programs and contributions, and

2. Recognition by the academic or professional community of what is done.

(c) Service—Service shall include, but not be limited to, service on departmental, college, and university committees, councils, and senates; service in appropriate professional organizations; involvements in the organization and expedition of meetings, symposia, conferences, workshops; participation in radio and television on local, state, and national governmental boards, agencies and commissions. Only those activities which are related to a person's field of expertise or to the mission of the university shall be evaluated. [6C-5.05]

In evaluating the competency of a faculty member, primary assessment shall be in terms of his performance of the assigned duties and responsibilities, and such evaluation shall be given adequate consideration for the purpose of salary adjustments, promotions, re-employment, and tenure. . . . Flexible criteria for rewarding faculty members, consistent with the institution's educational goals and objectives, shall be established, which criteria shall include quality teaching as a major factor in determining salary adjustments, promotions, re-employment or tenure. [Florida Statute 241.731, a portion of what is known as the Omnibus Education Act of 1973]

[Although not a part of the statute proper, the Title of the bill conveys the legislative intent] that no denial of promotions, salary adjustments, re-employment or tenure be solely for failure to do research, publish, or perform other scholarly activities. . . . [Laws of Florida, Chapter 73–338]

ARTICLES FROM THE FLORIDA BOARD OF REGENTS–UNITED FACULTY OF FLORIDA AGREEMENT, 1978–81

Article 8
APPOINTMENT

8.4 When first employed, each employee shall be apprised of what is expected, generally, in terms of teaching, research and other creative activities, and service, and specifically if there are specific requirements and/or other duties involved. If and when these expectations change during the period of service of the employee, that employee shall be apprised of the change.

Article 9
ASSIGNMENT OF RESPONSIBILITIES

9.1 The professional obligation is comprised of both scheduled and non-scheduled activities. The parties recognize that it is a part of the professional responsibility of employees to carry out their duties in an appropriate manner and place. For example, while instructional activities, office hours, and other duties and responsibilities may be required to be performed at a specific time and place, other non-scheduled activities are more appropriately performed in a manner and place determined by the employee.

9.2 Employees shall be apprised in writing, at the beginning of their employment and at the beginning of each year of employment thereafter, of the duties and responsibilities in teaching, research and other creative activities, service, and of any other specific duties and responsibilities assigned for that year.

9.3 Except for an assignment made at the beginning of an employee's employment, the person responsible for making an assignment shall contact the employee prior to making the final written assignment. Such contact shall also take place prior to changes which become necessary in an assignment, and such changes shall be specified in writing. The employee shall be granted, upon request, a conference with the person responsible for making the assignment to express concerns regarding:

  (a) the employee's qualifications and preferences; and

  (b) the character of the assignment, including the number of hours of instruction, the preparation required, whether the employee has taught the course in the past, the number of students and time required by course, whether travel to another location is required, the number of preparations required, the employee's assignments in other quarters, and the availability and adequacy of materials and equipment, secretarial services, student assistants, and other supportive services needed to perform the assignments.

An employee may request which three of four quarters the employee wishes to work and this request shall be honored where appropriate. Available assignments to a fourth quarter shall be offered equitably and as appropriate to qualified employees in sufficient time to allow voluntary acceptance or rejection.

9.4 ... No employee's assignment should be arbitrarily and capriciously imposed. If an employee believes that the assignment has been so imposed, the employee should, prior to the effective date of the assignment, take the matter up with the individual who has the responsibility for making the assignment. If that discussion does not resolve the dispute, the employee may discuss the matter with the dean or other appropriate administrator. If no satisfactory resolution is accomplished after consultation with the dean or appropriate administrator, UFF may, prior to the effective dates of the assignment, refer the matter to a neutral umpire acceptable to both parties or, failing agreement, to a member of the Arbitration Panel in accordance with the procedures in Article 20.11. The umpire shall determine whether or not the employee's assignment has been arbitrarily and capriciously imposed. Upon a finding that the assignment has been so imposed, the President or designee shall take appropriate corrective action. ...

Article 10
ANNUAL EMPLOYEE PERFORMANCE EVALUATION

10.1 Employees' performance shall be evaluated at least once annually and they shall be advised of the quarter during which such annual evaluation will be made. Personnel decisions shall take such annual evaluations into account, provided that personnel decisions need not be based solely on written employee performance evaluations.

10.2 The employee, if assigned teaching duties, shall be notified at least two weeks in advance of the date, time, and place of any direct classroom observation or visitation made in connection with the employee's annual evaluation.

10.3 The evaluation shall be in writing and shall be discussed with the employee prior to being placed in the employee's evaluation file. The evaluation shall be signed by the person performing the evaluation, and by the person being evaluated, who may attach a concise comment to the evaluation. A copy of the evaluation shall be made available to the employee.

10.4 Those persons responsible for supervising and evaluating an employee shall endeavor to assist the employee in correcting any performance deficiencies reflected in the employee's annual evaluation.

10.5 The annual performance evaluation shall be based upon assigned duties, and shall take into account the nature of the assignments, in terms, where applicable, of:

(a) Teaching effectiveness, including effectiveness in presenting knowledge, information, and ideas by means or methods such as lecture, discussion, assignment and recitation, demonstration, laboratory exercise, practical experience, and direct consultation with students. The evaluation shall include consideration of effectiveness in imparting knowledge and skills, and effectiveness in stimulating students' critical thinking and/or creative abilities, and adherence to accepted standards of professional behavior in meeting responsibilities to students.

(b) Contribution to the discovery of new knowledge, development of new educational techniques, and other forms of creative activity. Evidence of research and other creative activity shall include, but not be limited to: published books; articles and papers in professional journals; musical compositions, paintings, sculpture; works of performing art; papers presented at meetings of professional societies; and current research and creative activity that has not yet resulted in publication, display, or performance. The evaluation shall include consideration of the employee's productivity, including the quality and quantity of what has been done during the year, and of the employee's long-term research and other creative programs and contributions; and recognition by the academic or professional community of what is done.

(c) Service on departmental, college, and university committees, councils, and senates; service in appropriate professional organizations; participation in meetings, symposia, conferences, workshops; participation in radio and television; and service on local, state and national governmental boards, agencies and commissions. Evaluation of service shall include consideration of contribution to:

(1) the orderly and effective functioning of the employee's academic unit (program, department, school, college) and/or the total university;

(2) the university community; and

(3) the local, state, regional and national communities, and scholarly and professional associations.

(d) Other assigned university duties, such as advising, counseling, and supervision of interns, or as described in a Position Description, if any, of the position held by the employee.

(e) Such other responsibilities as may be appropriate to the assignment.

Article 11
PERSONNEL EVALUATION FILE

11.1 There shall be one file in which all written materials used in the evaluation process are maintained. When evaluations and personnel decisions are made, the only documents which may be used are those contained in that file. Employees shall be notified upon request of the location of the personnel evaluation file and the identity of the custodian.

11.2 An employee may examine the evaluation file upon reasonable advance notice, during the regular business hours of the office in which the file is kept, and under such conditions as are necessary to insure its integrity and safekeeping. Upon request and the payment of a reasonable fee for photocopying, an employee may obtain copies of any materials in the evaluation file and may attach a concise statement in response to any item therein. A person designated by the employee may examine that employee's evaluation file with the written authorization of the employee concerned and subject to the same limitations on access that are applicable to the employee.

11.4 In the event a grievance proceeds to arbitration, the Board, UFF, the arbitrator, and the grievant shall have the right to use copies of materials from the grievant's evaluation file relevant thereto in the arbitration proceedings.

11.5 No anonymous material shall be placed in an evaluation file, except for student evaluations which are part of a regular evaluation procedure of classroom instruction.

11.6 Evaluative materials or summaries thereof prepared by peer committees as part of a regular evaluation system may be placed in an evaluation file when signed by a representative of the committee.

11.7 Materials shown to be contrary to fact shall be removed from the file. This section shall not authorize the removal of materials from the evaluation file when there is a dispute concerning a matter of judgment or opinion rather than fact. Materials may also be removed pursuant to the resolution of a grievance.

11.8 Except as noted above, only university and Board officials responsible for the supervision or evaluation of employees shall have access to such files except under order of a court of competent jurisdiction.

Article 15
TENURE PROCEDURE

15.1 A tenured employee may be terminated only for cause in accordance with the provisions of Article 16, Termination and Other Actions, or laid off only in accordance with the provisions of Article 13, Layoff and Recall.

15.3 Except for employees who, by virtue of prior service credited at time of appointment, are eligible for consideration earlier, an employee shall normally be considered for tenure during the fifth year of continuous service in a tenure-earning position or, at the option of the employee and with the concurrence of the appropriate administrative officials, during the sixth such year in a tenure-earning position. Part-time service of an employee employed at least three academic quarters out of four in any 12 month period shall be accumulated. For example, one year (at least three quarters) of half-time service shall be considered one-half year of service for purposes of tenure eligibility. By the end of six full years of service within the State University System, an employee eligible for tenure shall either be awarded tenure or given notice that further employment will not be offered. The notice shall be accompanied by a statement of reasons by the President or representative why tenure was not granted.

15.4 The decision of the Board to award or deny tenure shall be made by September 15 and the employee shall be notified in writing by the President within five days of the decision of the Board. An employee being considered for tenure prior to the sixth year may withdraw from consideration on or before April 15 without prejudice.

15.5 The performance of an employee during the entire term of employment at the institution shall be considered in determining whether to grant tenure.

Grievance Finding

A grievance report was drawn up by a member of the president's committee, which acted in lieu of a single representative. After reading the report, the president sent a letter to O'Hara indicating that he would recommend to the Board of Regents that O'Hara be granted tenure. The president cited the following reasons for his decision:

1. The documentary evidence indicated that without any doubt John O'Hara had fulfilled two of the three standard criteria for tenure, those of teaching and research, in an exceptional manner. These cri-

teria, it should be noted, had been cited to all chairpersons by the dean of faculties in a memorandum dated 8 October 1976. [The established criteria for promotion and tenure are cited in Florida Statutes 241.731, the Florida Administrative Code Section 6C-5.06, and the BOR/UFF Collective Bargaining Agreement, Articles 10 and 15.]

2. Neither the members of the tenure and promotions committee nor the department chairperson could or would adequately explain their negative votes. They could not explain how O'Hara failed to meet the existing criteria for tenure. Only one member of the tenure committee even discussed the substance of the grievance, and that member's only relevant argument was that O'Hara's service record had been weak. O'Hara had been rated "satisfactory" in the area of service for three years and had not been given a service assignment during the next three years. If he had not performed the service responsibilities well, this weakness should have been noted on the evaluation forms. In addition, the chairperson should have counseled O'Hara about the matter and given him an opportunity to improve in that area.

3. Senior faculty members in the department had repeatedly rated O'Hara's performance in both research and teaching as "excellent," ratings that were recorded on the evaluation forms used for considering his requests for promotion and tenure. O'Hara had letters in his file from program leaders indicating strong support for his candidacy. In addition, he had received two "high merit" raises. [Criteria for such salary adjustments are the same as for promotion and tenure under Florida Statute 241.731.] The tenure committee could not adequately explain the inconsistency of O'Hara's continued high ratings and the negative tenure vote. If the committee had not changed the criteria on which its earlier judgments had been based, then this judgment was clearly inconsistent, arbitrary, and capricious. If the criteria had in fact changed, O'Hara had not been informed of the changes. Failure to inform him of such changes is in violation of Florida Administrative Code 6C-5.05 (1)(6) and Article 8.4 of the BOR/UFF agreement.

4. Before the vote on the tenure application, the department chairperson had at no time informed O'Hara of any inadequacies in his performance of his teaching, research, or service responsibilities. Following the tenure vote, the tenure committee and the department chairperson evaded O'Hara's request to cite specific inadequacies on his part so that he could work to overcome these immediately. By not informing O'Hara of his inadequacies, if in fact they existed at all, the department and the chairperson clearly violated both Florida Administrative Code/BOR Rule 6C-5.05 (1)(a), which states that those being considered for tenure shall be evaluated in order to improve "the functions of teaching, research, service," and Article 10.4 of the BOR/UFF Collective Bargaining Agreement, which states that "persons responsible for

supervising and evaluating an employee shall endeavor to assist the employee in correcting any performance deficiencies. . . ." To refuse to reveal the inadequacies of the candidate clearly contradicts the purpose of the evaluation, namely faculty improvement.

Rhodes, the department chairperson, had the specific responsibility of ensuring that the department tenure committee not act in an arbitrary and capricious manner. Clearly, Smith, who chaired the tenure committee, had little knowledge of the official criteria. In addition, Rhodes, who had the responsibility of ensuring that O'Hara knew of his performance inadequacies in time to correct them before the tenure vote, had been totally unresponsive and continued to insist that a peer committee vote should not be overruled on any grounds. This argument was rejected since it would deny O'Hara his due process in any grievance or appeal process following a peer committee vote. In addition, Rhodes argued that the BOR/UFF Agreement provisions were new and that therefore it was unnecessary to follow them this year. When it was pointed out to him that these provisions had recapitulated long-standing Board of Regents rules, university rules, and state law, he claimed that these rules had not been traditionally followed. In all, Rhodes' approach to the tenure process and the appeal procedure seemed to be at best cavalier. O'Hara should not be penalized because of his chairperson's poor judgment and inadequate leadership.

5. Rhodes' position that as a chairperson in the bargaining unit he had no responsibility in the matter was rejected. This argument is not unique. Some members of the state university system collective bargaining unit who supervise and evaluate other members have filed grievances stating that they should no longer have the obligation to evaluate members of their own bargaining unit. The viewpoint is invalid since the collective bargaining contract was never intended to change the assignment of any unit members. The collective bargaining agreement also gives the administration the right to make assignments and to determine the types of duties and responsibilities. Faculty members in the unit have, of course, traditionally taken on management roles such as the evaluation of peers for tenure and promotion purposes. Chairpersons should continue in a similar manner.

The president concluded that the administration of the department of educational foundations violated both the letter and the spirit of the BOR/UFF Collective Bargaining Agreement, Florida Statute (241.731), Board of Regents rules, and reasonable standards of academic administrative judgment. He would add O'Hara's name to the recommended tenure list and officially forward it to the Board of Regents.

After the case was completed and the decision rendered, other facts that revealed the source of O'Hara's actual problems with his colleagues came to light. O'Hara's tenure was opposed primarily because his peers resented his large grants and because he made little effort to include any of them in his bounty. In fact, he did invite several members from another department within the university to join him in his work. Although O'Hara had rejected collaboration with his department colleagues, he had nevertheless fulfilled all the requirements for tenure. Incidentally, O'Hara had never been specifically told of the department's resentment, and neither the union's representative nor the president's representative had even surmised the crux of the problem.

Other Case Studies

Following are brief descriptions of other grievances filed under a variety of conditions. Some of them have been resolved; others have not. These abbreviated case studies are examples of the kinds of grievances chairpersons might face, regardless of whether a union contract exists.

Grievance Heard before a Faculty Senate Committee

The following grievance was processed through university procedures at an institution that had no collective bargaining contract.

Three associate professors in the classics department argued that the dean had rejected their promotion requests even though each of them had fulfilled all the department's requirements for promotion. In a subsequent memo, the dean noted that the classics department promotion committee did not recommend any of the three applicants for promotion and that the chairperson supported the committee's recommendation. In response to the grievants' requests for the reasons for not being promoted, the dean replied that the information he had received from the department chairperson indicated that none had adequate publishing records.

In the formal grievance the candidates for promotion pointed out, with substantial supporting evidence, that the publishing records of previously promoted candidates were rarely stronger than their own records and often appeared somewhat weaker. In addition, they noted that the only senior woman in the department was promoted, even though she had a publishing record considerably weaker than any of theirs. They claimed that she was promoted because of affirmative action pressure. The grievants also pointed out that the classics department consisted mostly of full professors; that the department's promotion and tenure committee was made up entirely of full professors; that full professors in the department taught half as many hours as associate professors; and that many in the department believed that if the associate professors were promoted, the full professors would have to increase their teaching loads in order to maintain department productivity.

The faculty senate was asked to establish an intrauniversity committee to hear the grievances and to make a recommendation to the university president. The committee established by the senate consisted of four full professors and one assistant professor. In addition to the points already discussed, it considered the following counterarguments: the associate professors were hired as part of a quality improvement program that was designed to upgrade the department; they were involved in developing the changes in promotion and tenure criteria; and the allegations that the full professors were motivated by selfish, personal considerations were untrue.

The committee rejected the grievance. The grievants then threatened a lawsuit, alleging that the senate committee was stacked against them. To avoid an acrimonious public airing of the controversy, the university president agreed to promote two of the associate professors and to consider the third application the following year.

Grievance Heard before a State Hearing Officer

The following dispute occurred at a state university that had no collective bargaining contract. The case was eventually heard before a state hearing officer.

The university hired Howard Gibson to serve as director of the university art gallery and as assistant professor of fine arts. At the time the department chairperson, Roger Smythe, assured Gibson that an assistant gallery director would be employed within six months. The assistant director, however, was never employed. In addition to administering the gallery and teaching, Gibson was expected to create and display his own works on the same basis as other members of the art department. Some of his associates asserted that Gibson had the heaviest workload in the department.

Four years after Gibson's appointment, the art department evaluated its untenured faculty members. Gibson was not formally informed that this evaluation was going to take place; therefore he did not submit any of his material. He later indicated that he thought the session was being held only to review the files of those faculty members being considered for tenure. The committee voted 7 to 2 in favor of abolishing Gibson's position. The chairperson's report to the dean stated: "The position is simply too big for any one person to handle. Since the administration cannot provide the funds for the department to employ an assistant galley director, we must do away with this aspect of our program entirely." Gibson's contract was then not renewed.

After the nonrenewal, several students circulated a petition that endorsed Gibson's retention and that received considerable student support. Four members of the department's evaluation committee, each of whom had voted to abolish Gibson's position, stated that they had never intended to recommend nonrenewal of his contract and would have voted against the measure if they had understood that it would result in his termination. Nevertheless, the university administration acted in accordance with Smythe's recommendation, and Gibson was sent a notice of nonrenewal. He filed a grievance that resulted in a formal hearing, with a state-appointed hearing officer serving as an umpire. The officer's decision was not binding but merely served as a recommendation to the president.

Smythe, the chairperson, was the administration's chief witness and the defender of his department's recommendation. The university administration depended on Smythe's verbal and documentary evidence in putting together its case. The chairperson was rigorously cross-examined by the grievant's attorney. Members of Smythe's department, some students, and some upper-level administrators attended the meeting. Charles Jones, university attorney, represented the administration in the hearing. Jones requested and received from the department chairperson evidence in support of Gibson's termination.

Gibson's attorney was extremely successful in buttressing the argument that his client had not been properly informed of the nature of the evaluation. He also had several committee members testify that their vote to abolish the position of gallery director was not a vote to abolish Gibson, whose abilities they respected and admired. The hearing officer's decision was in Gibson's favor. He asserted that the grievant's rights to due process were violated in several ways and that even though the university had the right to abolish the position of gallery director, it did not have the right to terminate Gibson's employment in a manner inconsistent with established university practice. The university accepted the recommendation of the hearing officer and renewed Gibson's contract.

Potential Grievance at a Private University with No Collective Bargaining Contract

Mary Ellis, a member of the social work department, complained to her chairperson that she had been discriminated against. First, she had received no merit pay during the previous four years. Although she admitted that she had not published a great deal, Ellis pointed out that the department's thrust had been toward teaching and service and that she excelled in both areas. In addition, Ellis's publishing record was no weaker than those of other department members who had received higher salary increases. She therefore felt she was entitled to merit pay.

Ellis also protested that she had not been treated fairly in her teaching assignments. Although her course load was not heavier than that assigned to other department members, she was denied her request to teach late afternoon courses. Late classes in her department constituted an overload and provided extra pay. The late afternoon courses were applied courses taken by students already employed in the field, and Ellis did not have expertise in the applied area.

Ellis basically supported her department's democratic tradition of forwarding to the dean, directly and unchanged, the salary recommendations of an elected committee. An elected committee also determined the annual assignment. Ellis claimed, however, that faculty members with Master of Social Work degrees dominated all key department committees and received "high merit" raises at the expense of faculty members with Ph.D.'s in fields other than social work. Ellis holds a Ph.D. in sociology.

Discussing the matter with the dean, the chairperson asserted that since Ellis's degree was in sociology and her background was strong in research methodology, he expected her to have a stronger publication record than her colleagues. The dean suggested that the chairperson review Ellis's case carefully, since there seemed to be some merit to her argument. The dean further stressed the need for documenting the facts of the case in the event of a formal grievance, which could conceivably end up in court if the problem were not satisfactorily resolved. He urged the chairperson to advise Ellis about what she might do to upgrade her expertise so that she could teach some applied courses. He also suggested that the chairperson assign a research role as part of Ellis's workload.

The chairperson followed the dean's advice and met with Ellis several times to discuss her concerns. Ellis made an earnest attempt to heed the chairperson's suggestions and qualified for a merit raise the next year.

Potential Grievance under a Union Contract

Bosley Cowpens had been an assistant professor of history for five years. The department tenure committee voted 7 to 2 against his being granted tenure in the department, and he contemplated filing a grievance. Although the department placed a high priority on research, Cowpens had only a mediocre publishing record. His record showed improvement, but the improvement did not satisfy the department committee. He claimed that his publication record for the last two years was equal to the record of two senior tenured professors. The department had thirty members, sixteen of whom were tenured. On the basis of student evaluations, Cowpens's teaching record was below the department average. Moreover, on numerous occasions he had failed to meet his classes, and a letter of reprimand concerning his unexcused absences was on file. He did, however, have a small but loyal following among the students. His service record showed an enormous amount of time and effort spent on the United Fund campaign but very little service to the profession or department.

Cowpens claimed that the real reason for his failure to gain promotion was his iconoclastic behavior on committees. The promotion and tenure committee called his behavior abrasive and reported that he had withdrawn from committee work whenever he had quarreled with other members. The chairperson had discussed his previous unsatisfactory annual evaluations with him, but Cowpens had refused to accept the substance of the evaluation. He was kept on, according to the chairperson, in the hope that his performance would improve, but the degree of improvement had not been deemed satisfactory. The chairperson kept records of his discussions and his attempts to counsel Cowpens and informed him of his record keeping.

Cowpens insisted that he was being denied tenure because he was not a team player and because of personality differences with other faculty members. He also insisted that his community service deserved to be recognized and that his teaching was as good as that of many other department members.

The department union representative, a close friend of Cowpens, expressed his willingness to support the assistant professor if he wanted to file a grievance. The chairperson feared that Cowpens, if he were not granted tenure, would file a formal grievance and would receive union support. Nevertheless, the chairperson was determined to support the findings of the tenure committee. He felt confident that the department committee was properly constituted, had followed established procedures, and was justified in its decision.

The chairperson then met with the university (not the department) union representative to discuss the issue. Despite the fact that Cowpens was counting on union backing, the union, in this instance, decided not to support a faculty member whose case was so weak and informed Cowpens accordingly. Cowpens received notice of nonrenewal of his contract. A grievance was never filed.

By anticipating the kinds of personnel problems that are occurring in postsecondary education, by understanding the nature of grievance mechanisms and the chairperson's role in them, and by becoming familiar with the way rulings, recommendations, and settlements occur, chairpersons can prevent many potential grievances. Personnel problems, however, will be with us as long as there are bosses and workers, managers and employees, and administrators and faculty members. Thus there will always be grievances, whether a collective bargaining contract exists or not. Formal bargaining may result in a greater number of officially filed grievances, but unofficial grievances have always existed.

Chairpersons will no doubt see some changes in their roles as a result either of collective bargaining or of conscientious support of state law and institutional personnel rules. (The latter often emerges when a collective bargaining contract seems probable.) Chairpersons will give greater attention to formal evaluations and personnel decisions and will thus be faced with more paperwork. They will have to provide evidence and appear at various kinds of hearings, while administrators will be transmitting more rules and directives to the department level. Chairpersons will assume the task, often avoided in the past, of counseling less productive department members and suggesting ways to improve their work. If chairpersons avoid such tasks or attempt to reject them because they see themselves as faculty members and not administrators, the administration will shift the position of chairperson upward into the management bureaucracy.

Such trends have not occurred solely because of collective bargaining. For example, institutions of higher education, with or without collective bargaining, have become increasingly centralized. In addition, chairpersons have always had both academic and administrative responsibilities; they were sometimes colleagues and sometimes bosses. Thus some chairpersons have always perceived themselves as centaur-like creatures—half man and half beast. Whether the beast is the management half or the employee half depends on the chairperson's philosophy.

Questions

1. Give examples of unfair treatment of faculty members at the hands of the chairperson in the areas of workload, evaluation, and financial matters, in which the chairperson *may not be aware* that he or she is treating a faculty member unfairly.
2. Give examples of unfair treatment of faculty members at the hands of the chairperson in the areas of workload, evaluation, and financial matters, in which the chairperson *may be aware* that he or she is treating a faculty member unfairly.
3. Give examples of treatment perceived by faculty members to be un-

fair in the areas of workload, evaluation, and financial matters, in which upon investigation it was found that the treatment *was really not unfair.*

4. In some departments, committees are designated to make decisions in the areas of workload, evaluation, and financial matters. What might a chairperson do in the event that he or she believes that the committee decision is unfair to a faculty member?

5. The following questions are based on the O'Hara case:
    a. Distinguish between a grievance and a complaint according to the definitions given in the chapter.
    b. How was the union contract violated in O'Hara's case?
    c. What instructions should the department chairperson have given the tenure and promotion committee about its charge as well as about the contract?
    d. What might the chairperson have done in order to avoid the situation? What should have been his reaction to the 9–0 vote against O'Hara?
    e. What effect will the retention of O'Hara now have on the department?

6. The following questions are based on the Gibson case:
    a. How might Chairperson Smythe have countered the argument that the department committee members did not understand what they were voting on?
    b. If the university had no clear policy or rules regarding evaluation and review of faculty members, on what grounds could Gibson have filed a grievance?

7. The following questions are based on the Ellis case:
    a. As department chairperson, how would you have attempted to resolve this problem?
    b. What specific measures might a chairperson institute within a department in order to keep this type of problem from occurring?

8. The following questions are based on the Cowpens case:
    a. If Cowpens had filed a grievance, he probably would have lost. If you were the chairperson, what arguments would you use to persuade Cowpends to resign?
    b. Under what altered circumstances might Cowpens have won a grievance?

9. If a college or university has no faculty union and its board of trustees prefers not to have one, what can the administration do to bolster the faculty members' feeling of security so that they might not feel the need for union representation?

10. If a college or university has a faculty union and wants to keep

grievances to a minimum, how should administrators and department chairpersons deal with faculty problems on a continuing basis so that faculty members will not feel the need or the urge to file grievances?

References

ANGELL, GEORGE W. (ed.). *Faculty and Teacher Bargaining: The Impact of Unions on Education.* Lexington, Mass.: D. C. Heath, 1981.

BENEWITZ, MAURICE C., AND MANNIX, THOMAS M. "Grievance Procedure in Higher Education Contracts." *Community and Junior College Journal,* December 1974–January 1975, pp. 22–24.

BERGMANN, THOMAS J., AND O'MALLEY, JOHN T. "The Department Chairperson in Campus Governance." *College and University Personnel Association,* Fall 1979, pp. 7–17.

BERNSTEIN, MERTON C., ET AL. "Arbitration of Faculty Grievances: A Report of a Joint Subcommittee of Subcommittee A and N." *AAUP Bulletin,* Summer 1973, pp. 168–70.

BETTEN, NEIL, AND OLDSON, WILLIAM. *Contract Administration: From Grievance to Arbitration.* Tallahassee: UFF/Florida AFL-CIO Publications, 1978.

EDMONDSON, WILLIAM FRED. "Grievance Arbitration and Its Role in the Settlement of Professional Negotiation Disputes in Higher Education." Ed.D. dissertation, University of Mississippi, 1973.

ELLIS, JOHN M. "Grievance Procedures: Real and Ideal." *New Directions for Higher Education,* Autumn 1974, pp. 63–76.

FERGUSON, TRACY H., AND BERGAN, WILLIAM L. "Grievance Arbitration Procedures and Contract Administration." *Journal of College and University Law,* Summer 1974, pp. 371–91.

KELLEY, EDWARD P., JR., AND RODRIGUEZ, ROBERT L. "Observations on Collective Bargaining: Implications for Academic Management," *Liberal Education,* March 1977, pp. 102–117.

LESLIE, DAVID W. "Impact of Collective Bargaining on Conflict Resolution Practices." Research Summary no. 2. Washington, D.C.: Academic Collective Bargaining Information Service, 1975.

MANNIX, THOMAS M. "Community College Grievance Procedures: A Review of Contract Content in 94 Colleges," *Journal of the College and University Personnel Association,* April 1974, pp. 23–40.

PLYLER, CHRIS PARNELL. "The Grievance Appeals Process in the State University System of Florida: A Case Study." Ph.D. dissertation, Florida State University, 1978.

RUFF, RAYMOND T., JR. "A Description and Analysis of Faculty Grievances and Faculty Grievance Procedures in New York State Community Colleges." Ph.D. dissertation, State University of New York at Buffalo, 1972.

SATRYB, RONALD P. "The Art of Settling Grievances: A Study in Campus Conflict Resolution." Special Report no. 27. Washington, D.C.: Academic Collective Bargaining Information Service, 1976.

―――. "Evolution of the S.U.N.Y. Grievance Procedure from the First Contract to the Second." *Journal of the College and University Personnel Association*, July/August 1975, pp. 46–52.

―――. "Faculty Grievance at S.U.N.Y.: The First Two Years under a Negotiated Contract." Special Report no. 10. Washington, D.C.: Academic Collective Bargaining Information Service, 1974.

11

Dealing with Conflict and Maintaining Faculty Morale

Conflict, according to many department chairpersons, is something that happens in someone else's department. Academicians with preconceptions about harmonious campus life are often reluctant to speak or even think about discord and dissension in their immediate environment. Those who think of conflict as abnormal or aberrant tend to shun the subject. Some chairpersons view conflict in their department uneasily and feel that it is somehow their fault. Some chairpersons are unaware that conflict exists because they are so awe-inspiring that their faculty members conceal it from them. Even though conflict is a subject academicians do not like to talk about, they need to accept the idea that it can occur.

There seems to be an inverse relationship between the degree of conflict in a department and the level of morale: the more conflict, the lower the morale; the less conflict, the higher the morale. Although this discussion focuses primarily on types of conflict that may occur in an academic department, it also touches on promoting and maintaining good morale. Reducing conflict will not automatically raise faculty morale, but a good level of morale cannot exist in a department where energies are consumed by serious conflict.

The chairperson ought to be concerned about conflict within the department, because once it occurs, it tends to fester and grow. Conflict is divisive; it pits individual faculty members against each other and wastes time and effort that are best used in more creative endeavors. It often develops a dynamic and logic of its own. A conflict can polarize a department, forcing members into competing groups. In extreme cases, destructive and hostile behavior can destroy a department's effectiveness. Chairpersons who learn to identify and diagnose conflict at an early stage and who help their departments deal with it effectively fulfill one of the most difficult requirements of their role.

The term *conflict* is used here in a variety of ways. In psychology the term refers to the inner struggle between desires requiring immediate gratification and desires that can only be met by deferring the immediate in order to gain long-term benefits. For the purposes of this discussion, the term *inner conflict* will be used to describe tension, anxiety, turmoil, and frustration that can impair a person's activities but that do not emerge as interpersonal conflict. Webster's definition —"competitive or opposing action of incompatibles"—reflects a more common understanding of the term. Generally a disagreement becomes a conflict when it goes beyond the normal intellectual differences that characterize academic life. Serious conflict is often accompanied by feelings of fear, anxiety, or anger, and is often evidenced by intemperate or abusive language and overtly hostile actions.

Conflict may be defined either as an incident or as a process. As an incident, it occurs as a disagreement between two persons or parties in which the first acts in a way that the second perceives to be detrimental to the latter's interests and designed to force some undesired action. As a process, conflict is manifested in a series of actions by two persons or groups in which each person or group tries to thwart the other's purposes or prevent satisfaction of the other's interests. In essence, conflict is a struggle for control of another person's behavior.

Types of Conflict

Departments are made up of intelligent persons who are often ambitious, strong-willed, and competitive. Even though academicians are usually committed to the use of reason in problem solving and to the model of collegiality in interpersonal relations, conflict often arises either through personality clashes or as a result of institutional demands on faculty members. Conflict within departments can usually be categorized as one of four distinct types: (1) inner conflict; (2) conflict between employer and employee; (3) conflict among faculty members; and (4) conflict between faculty members and students.

Inner conflict concerns a person's feelings. It does not consist of a set of observable behaviors but has to do with frustrations and anxieties that a person feels and that can affect his or her normal functioning. For example, a faculty member who has long been a successful teacher but whose research skills are undeveloped fails to get promotions or merit increases as the department becomes more research oriented. He feels that the rules have been changed in the middle of his game and is angry and bitter. He withdraws from social contacts with other faculty members.

Disputes arising over matters such as promotion, tenure, merit pay, perquisites, work assignments, annual evaluations, and working conditions can usually be classified as employer-employee conflicts. These may involve faculty members and administrators, staff persons and administrators, or other types of employees and supervisors. Chairpersons who try to increase productivity by asking their faculty members to teach more or larger classes without discussing the matter with them beforehand can find themselves embroiled in employer-employee conflicts.

Conflict among faculty members can be the result of minor personality clashes or perceived inequities. Frequently such conflict arises when the egalitarian workload model is violated either by allocating varying awards for similar workloads or by allocating similar rewards for varying workloads. In the academic context, sorting out conflicting claims is extremely difficult, especially when the privileges of rank are considered. Many institutions have an uncodified, unwritten tradition that allows the senior faculty lighter course loads and more graduate courses. A more serious kind of conflict among faculty members is related to academic matters—e.g., what activities are worthwhile and what methodologies and techniques are best. Conflicts concerning the practice of the discipline are very difficult to resolve and sometimes lead to a kind of academic warfare in which entire factions are banished from the department.

Conflict between faculty members and students commonly begins either with student complaints about a faculty member's teaching performance or grading practices or with a faculty member's charge of cheating or plagiarism. Student complaints about faculty members sometimes grow into wholesale protests or demonstrations, especially when students feel that their right to due process has been violated.

In all types of conflict the disagreement can concern territory, clientele, and intergroup relations. Debates over humankind's territorial nature aside, conflict often does involve territory or "turf." Administrators, faculty members, and students at times all identify certain subjects, courses, or areas as exclusively their own and attempt to defend them against encroachment by others. Territorial disputes can break out over such seemingly trivial matters as the decision to assign some persons to windowless offices. Disagreements can arise when a new clientele is identified—as, for example, when a department adopts an off-campus program and faculty members argue with each other about who must teach in the program. Faculty members might also quarrel over a particularly able student, with whom they all may want to work, or a particularly poor student, with whom no one may want to work. Students may protest being assigned to particular faculty members.

Conflict in intergroup relations is often ideological. It may develop when various factions argue about what constitutes the proper methodology of a discipline. Intergroup conflict can occur when students organize and press demands. Student activism usually involves more than a department, however, and thus will not be discussed here. Other frequent sources of intergroup conflict in the academic environment involve relations between one department and another or relations between the university and the department. Neither of these sources of conflict is especially relevant to this discussion, but they are mentioned because the chairperson may be involved in such disputes. When departments are reviewed by policy councils or as part of accountability procedures, the chairperson may be thrust into the role of leading the struggle for the department's survival.

Attitudes toward Conflict

The way a person acts in a conflict situation may well be related to his or her attitude toward conflict. These attitudes vary considerably from person to person. Institutions in general and colleges and universities in particular also have "attitudes" toward conflict that are represented in institutional policy and procedure. Social theorists have, since antiquity, developed different views on the matter that are still with us.

Let us examine two extreme views and see how they are reflected in present-day approaches. The first, the "Rousseauian" perspective, assumes that men and women are innately good, but that this goodness is perverted by society. Hence, conflict is unnatural. If society's unjust conditions and institutions were removed and humanity's natural goodness allowed to emerge, conflict would disappear. The opposite view—which might be called an "original sin" view or, in a more secular context, a Hobbesian view—assumes that each person attempts to maximize his or her goods and opportunities until he or she is stopped by someone else who is doing the same thing. In this view, conflict is natural as well as normal. Improving social conditions will not reduce conflict and might even increase it. Conflict is regulated by strict rules and procedures and accompanying sanctions.

These two views are, of course, mutually exclusive. While neither is intended as an empirically verifiable description of reality, these and similar attitudes toward conflict are prevalent. From these examples we can say that a person's behavior in conflict situations is related to his or her attitudes and beliefs about the nature of conflict and its role in human affairs.

J. Victor Baldridge, in *Power and Conflict in the University,* identifies three models of university governance based on attitudes toward conflict. The first governance model, the *collegial model,* views conflict as abnormal. This view holds that a true community of scholars would eliminate conflict altogether. When disagreements arise, they are solved by deliberation and reason, not by negotiation and arbitration. Moreover, professors are civilized men and women, not brawlers, who prefer to live in an atmosphere of harmonious consensus.

The second model, the *bureaucratic model,* also views conflict as abnormal. This model of governance, however, assumes that conflicts will occur but that they will be controlled by bureaucratic sanctions. Although the bureaucratic model does not adequately describe traditional faculty behavior in most colleges and universities, it seems to be increasingly appropriate in large systems where collective bargaining is practiced and where guides to organizational behavior are increasingly codified.

The third model, the *political model,* accepts conflict as a normal part of organizational life. This model assumes that contention among competing interests precedes almost any policy change. In the language of the model, the social structure of the university is not a homogeneous community of scholars. Instead, the professional community is said to be pluralistic, fractured into subcultures and divergent interest groups, and composed of fairly autonomous professional practitioners. The general style of decision making and policy development involves negotiation, political influence, and bargaining (i.e., making trade-offs). Political influence is attained by persuading and mobilizing persons of like opinion into an interest group or faction. It assumes neither a community of professional interests nor agreement about the ends of higher education beyond the need to preserve academic freedom.

To view the collegial, bureaucratic, and political governance models as ideal types, abstracted from reality, is helpful. Most institutions have elements of all three models within them, and members of the institutions often behave in ways that are consistent with the model to which they personally subscribe. Comparing the governance models to the attitudes toward conflict, the collegial model seems compatible with the Rousseauian "natural goodness" attitude; the bureaucratic model, which assumes that people must be constantly watched and supervised, is compatible with the Hobbesian model, which sees people as inherently selfish.

The three models also emphasize communication and its role. The collegial model stresses the importance and value of communication in consensual decision making. The bureaucratic model emphasizes the need for clear channels of communication to avoid mistakes and get the messages through. The political model rejects the view that conflict is due to misunderstandings and communications breakdowns and labels such belief "the communications fallacy." Indeed, the political model, while admitting the desirability of authentic communication, denies that communication is in itself sufficient to reduce conflict. Even though two disputants may clearly understand each other, such understanding well may lead to increased rather than reduced hostility, as may a clear communication that one side is losing and the other winning. In fact, the perception of "them" winning and "us" losing almost always precedes conflict. The political model sees conflict resolution essentially as a trading off of advantages and favors in a process called "rational selfishness."

A continuum reflecting the various stages of conflict within a department—from an anarchic state of total conflict at one end to a bland and blissful state of total cooperation at the other—can easily be constructed (see figure 11.1).

FIGURE 11.1.   Department conflict continuum

Total Conflict	Controlled Conflict	Competition	Collaboration	Total Cooperation

One interesting aspect of this continuum is the central position of competition. Friendly competition lies to the right of center; unfriendly competition lies to the left of center. On the continuum, the balance point is the competitive state, and the implication is that life in an academic department goes on in a state of nonconflictual competition. Conflict can be constructive when it enables antagonists to make their beliefs and dissatisfactions explicit, thus clearing the air. In such a case, a step toward problem solving has been taken, and, it is generally agreed, conflict ought to be reduced to problem solving.

Stages of Conflict

Another way of understanding conflict is to view it as a series of stages that make up a conflict episode. This theory permits taking a developmental view of conflict and treating the separate stages individually. Each stage, it should be noted, contains the elements of the preceding stages as well as elements of its own.

The first stage is called *latent conflict*. In this stage the conditions are being set for future conflict. Common sources of conflict include competition for scarce resources, drives for autonomy, divergence of individual goals, incompatible role expectations, and the frustrations of a person or group resulting from events beyond its control.

Latent conflict, deriving from the causes mentioned above, exists in almost every department in every college and university in the country. We need hardly discuss competition for scarce resources, which has characterized academic affairs for the last decade. Drives for autonomy or independence can be interpreted in several ways: faculty members can become frustrated when they feel that they have no role in the department's decision-making process; a department chairperson may desire more authority than the administration is willing to delegate; a faculty member may claim the right to teach anything she sees fit, even while teaching a section of a colleague's course. (Faculty members who pursue their own goals without regard for others in the department are common figures, often creating dissension and frustration by their tactics.) Faculty members serve as teachers, researchers, providers of service, and, sometimes, as administrators, and the demands of these many roles can often lead to frustration and conflict. So too can the role expectations of the faculty of professional schools when it clashes with the liberal arts faculty at promotion committee meetings. Finally, of course, many academicians feel they are losing control of their professional lives.

This stage of conflict is called "latent" because the conditions that lead to conflict are present but, for a variety of reasons, are suppressed. Some persons avoid conflict, perhaps because it can be painful and threatening, and ignore or withdraw from a situation that promises to erupt. Clearly, within any department there are many examples of latent conflict.

The next stage of conflict is called *perceived conflict*. In this stage, one element from the latency stage emerges as problematic. The persons involved are aware of a disagreement but do not yet feel tense or anxious. This stage is sometimes called the "semantic" conflict stage, because the perception of conflict comes from information that may be erroneous or incomplete. At this stage, *if* the perception really comes from misinformation, improved communications may nip a crisis in the bud. If the information, once clarified, proves the perception correct, however, the conflict can rapidly move on to the next stage, *felt conflict*. Felt conflict moves beyond intellectual awareness to a personalized feeling of anxiety and tension. Some persons at this stage withdraw and become uncommunicative. Nevertheless, once tension, unease, and anxiety emerge, the progression to open conflict is simple.

The stage of open conflict, often called the *manifest conflict* stage, is marked by open aggression, generally verbal but occasionally physical. Instances of faculty members engaging in physically aggressive behaviors are few but not unheard of. Occasionally, a frustrated student will attack a faculty member whom he sees as having prevented him from achieving his goals.

The final stage is *conflict aftermath*. Every conflict ultimately comes to an end. The conflict may not have been satisfactorily resolved, but hostilities have simply ceased. Sometimes one side is clearly victorious. Sometimes an external party may intervene and impose a settlement. Sometimes a genuine solution satisfactory to every party is achieved. Unfortunately, many a conflict aftermath merely sets the stage for a new conflict.

Understanding conflict as a process that encompasses several stages can help the chairperson recognize the importance of maintaining department morale. The subject of maintaining morale will be discussed in some detail here because low morale is often an indication that conflict is moving from the latency stage to a higher stage. Moreover, much conflict, especially inner conflict, comes from the perception that the interests of human beings are pitted against the interests of the system. The feeling that the system, whatever *system* means, is becoming larger, more powerful, and more oppressive, and that the person is powerless to do much to oppose it contributes to the anxiety and frustration that lead to conflict.

Diagnosing and Dealing with Conflict

A number of factors that affect department morale have been identified. The chairperson has little control over many of these, but he or she can nevertheless try to minimize the feelings of dissatisfaction that lead to inner conflict. Two of these factors are the salary and working conditions of the department members. Faculty members can easily become depressed about the fact that their income declines in inflationary times. They also resent the imposition of heavier teaching loads or larger classes. Although the chairperson cannot magically produce salary increases for the entire department, he or she can reduce resentment by showing that, compared with departments elsewhere, the department is not doing as badly as its members think. If the department actually is in a poor position compared with similar departments in other institutions or other departments in the university, the chairperson can boost morale by showing that he or she is actively lobbying for a fair share of the funds available. Similarly, faculty members often feel that they are being discriminated against with respect to the allocation of travel funds. Again, the chairperson should be able to show them that they are no worse off than anyone else in the college or the institution.

Another factor that contributes to low department morale is the sense of ever-increasing bureaucratization—the proliferation of meaningless rules and regulations and increasing outside pressure on the department. The chairperson can raise department morale by showing that he or she opposes the proliferation of administrative trivia. When the chairperson is seen as the defender of the department's welfare, he or she helps create a climate of solidarity within the department. Faculty members will come to feel that by sticking together in the face of adversity they can overcome some of the difficulties that appear insurmountable.

A common source of frustration and inner conflict for faculty members is the feeling that they are losing control over crucial department decisions affecting their future. One way to reduce feelings of alienation and powerlessness is to establish a set of policies within a department that permit the faculty to participate in the decision-making process. There should be formal means for allowing debate over department policy and procedures, such as faculty meetings that allow open discussion and debate. Written reports on policy decisions should contain evidence that a variety of points of view have been reviewed. In this way, the chairperson can show that minority opinions have been considered and respected.

Conflict can be reduced when the lines of authority and responsibility in the department are clarified. For example, a chairperson assigned a faculty member the task of making up teaching schedules for the entire department but failed to inform the department members that he had given this responsibility to one of their colleagues. When the schedule was distributed, the faculty members were confused and resentful. Had the chairperson informed the faculty that he had delegated this task and had he instructed the schedule maker to consult with each member of the department, this conflict would have been avoided. Whenever a chairperson delegates administrative responsibility to faculty or staff members, the lines of authority must be clarified.

Department meetings should allow open confrontation over controversial issues. Confrontation need not lead to destructive conflict. Free debate and free expression can ensure a fair hearing for diverse viewpoints about significant issues. Debate can also bring out conflicts at an early stage of development, allowing them to be dealt with before they become critical. The chairperson can help develop an atmosphere of commitment to orderly change within the department. Autocratic methods should not be advocated, and both majority opinions and minority rights should be respected and upheld.

This discussion of minimizing latent and inner conflict has emphasized what a chairperson can do to identify conflict before it becomes destructive. Chairpersons are advised to establish an atmosphere that prevents conflict from escalating, since conflict is difficult to resolve once the department is polarized. A chairperson who does not hear of conflicts—particularly a chairperson of a large department, where the probability of their existence is high—should ask whether there is something about his or her administrative style that causes the faculty, staff, and students to avoid discussing difficult situations. Perhaps the chairperson is perceived as too authoritarian or unyielding. If so, the chairperson might begin to visit briefly but regularly with every member of the faculty and staff. These visits, which may be held once a month, should be on a one-to-one basis and should not be held in the chairperson's office. Meetings on neutral ground, such as a faculty club or restaurant, or on the faculty member's turf, such as his or her office or home, are much less threatening. The purpose of the meetings is not to solve problems but to listen and look for the emergence of latent or inner conflict.

One skill the chairperson can learn is the technique of "active listening," developed by Thomas Gordon, which is useful for discovering latent conflict. Active listening is an extremely effective communications technique that is used by many thousands of parents. Academicians have some difficulty with the technique because the listener does not lecture, teach, give logical arguments, judge, criticize, question, interpret, analyze, or diagnose. In other words, all the logical and conceptual skills that are indispensable to a university career are temporarily put aside. Active listening consists of the listener (or receiver) "feeding back only what he feels the sender's message meant—nothing more, nothing less."*

By listening patiently and "feeding back" the feelings of the speaker, chairpersons may promote a good relationship between themselves and their faculty, facilitate problem solving, and, in general, foster a cooperative spirit in the department. To be an effective listener, the chairperson must want to be helpful, believe in the speaker's sincerity, and be willing to accept the speaker as a fellow human being. A chairperson who gets good results by listening quietly, with an occasional empathetic grunt and a few gestures showing he understands the speaker's feelings, would be well advised to read Gordon's book in order to perfect the listening technique.

Occasionally, conflict in a department may be related to a faculty member's mental state. Recent research has examined and brought to the public consciousness the existence of "life crises" that most people undergo. The chairperson should be sensitive to each faculty member's

---

*Thomas Gordon, *Parent Effectiveness Training* (New York; London; and Scarborough, Ontario: New American Library, 1970 and 1975), p. 53.

state of mind. Reading some of the literature on life stages, such as Levinson's *The Seasons of a Man's Life* or Sheehy's *Passages,* can help the chairperson understand some of the personal crises that can lead to unhappiness and consequent strife within a department. Many personal crises, such as divorce or a death in the family, can temporarily impair or disrupt a faculty member's normal functioning. The chairperson can arrange for substitutes in the classroom and on committees. But how long can a chairperson cover for a faculty member? There are no hard and fast rules. Some persons take longer to recover from crises than do others. The chairperson who is thoroughly aware of university rules and policies on leaves of absence and sick leaves can support faculty members in times of personal adversity.

Academicians, like all professionals, may suffer from serious personality disorders or develop patterns of behavior that are disruptive or dangerous. The chairperson must be able to distinguish between a person who is frustrated or temporarily disabled and one who is chronically disabled. When a faculty member is in constant conflict with colleagues or students, the chairperson must exercise judgment. Sometimes the chairperson may wait patiently in the belief that the crisis will be temporary. At other times the chairperson may decide to suspend the person from work. A decision such as this is a painful one: it may ease or erase conflict in a department, but only at the expense of that faculty member's professional life.

The matter of faculty members who behave erratically is complicated by the legal and the psychological aspects of the issue. To suggest to a colleague that he or she is sick and needs help may result in a charge of character assassination and a lawsuit. Chairpersons must remember that they have no legal or professional authority to counsel a department member. When someone with no training attempts to counsel an emotionally unstable person who is incapacitated by inner conflict or actively engaged in a dispute, serious and unpleasant consequences may result. If a faculty member needs to be referred to a counselor or psychiatrist, the chairperson should discreetly discuss the matter with the dean and the legal staff before proceeding.

Thus far, we have discussed situations in which the chairperson has been dealing with inner conflict, latent conflict, and feelings of powerlessness against the system. We have not discussed in detail manifest or overt conflict. But conflicts, despite strenuous efforts to control them, do emerge and, in most cases, are destructive and costly. There is, of course, no clear blueprint of what to do when conflict occurs. The chairperson who is aware of the stages of a conflict episode and who has a finger on the department's pulse will not be surprised if conflict does emerge, because he or she will have been watching it develop. Yet there is more to dealing with conflict than simply not being surprised by it, since some persons who are not surprised by events are still unable to handle them.

Much department conflict can be managed effectively by an astute chairperson. What does *conflict management* mean? For our purposes, it means the shaping of conflict in such a way that it is reduced to a process of problem solving. In many cases, this transformation can be accomplished if the chairperson is able to develop a clear idea about the basic attitudes of the disputing parties toward, first, the conflict they are engaged in and, second, the stakes involved. This understanding is important because attitudes toward conflict influence persons' behavior and because conflict over low stakes is much easier to resolve than conflict over high stakes.

Analyzing the participating parties' attitudes to the conflict need not be complicated. The chairperson should know whether they feel that the conflict was avoidable and whether they feel that some agreement or compromise is possible. If disputants feel agreement is possible, they can generally be persuaded to convert their dispute into an opportunity for problem solving. If, on the other hand, they feel that an agreement is impossible, they may engage in a fierce struggle to the bitter end, especially if the stakes are high. Generally, if the stakes are high, the conflict will be much more vigorous, and the possibility exists that the conflict will not be settled amicably.

Chairpersons can settle a dispute if they can make the opposing parties believe that an agreement is possible or if they can get the parties to lower the stakes in their dispute. For example, an anthropology department was engaged in a bitter dispute between its structuralists and its functionalists. Each side was accusing the other of not being "real" anthropologists and was preventing the promotion and tenure of young faculty members in the enemy camp. The stakes were the survival of each faction in the department. The chairperson, even though a member of one of the factions, was able to persuade the groups that they could live with each other and that their ideological differences need not lead to the expulsion of half the department. In this case, the stakes were not lowered, but the attitudes were changed.

The question of what "high" stakes are, compared with "moderate" or "low" stakes, is somewhat subjective but certainly includes such matters as promotion, tenure, and status in the department. Low stakes might include a large office, allocation of a typewriter, and travel funds. Nevertheless, serious conflicts have erupted over the last three examples. Someone once said that the reason academic politics is so sordid is that the stakes are so small. Low stakes for one person may be high stakes for another.

The question of whether parties to a conflict think the conflict was avoidable is of little concern here. Some persons believe that conflict is avoidable but that, if it should occur, an agreement is impossible. Research indicates that such persons often tend to withdraw from the conflict when it occurs. Generally, however, if persons see conflict as inevitable, agreement as impossible, and stakes as high, they are likely to engage in the most bitter of conflicts. Sometimes attempts to lower stakes and change attitudes do not succeed, and the results can be serious indeed.

When diagnosing a conflict, a chairperson must exercise analytical ability. He or she must use good judgment in deciding whether to intervene and strive to reduce conflict or channel it creatively. If the chairperson can identify an emerging conflict, uncover the faculty's attitudes and beliefs about the nature of conflict, and assess the stakes involved in the conflict, he or she will be better equipped to decide what to do in a particular situation. Often, the best decision is not to act. When intervention obviously will not improve the situation or even make it worse, the chairperson's best strategy is to remain aloof from the conflict while staying alert to the situation and sensitive to the conditions that produced it. For example, two senior faculty members have been bickering for years. Their differences do not impede the operation of the department, and the chairperson does not attempt a peace-making role. On the other hand, if the quarreling department members attempt to pressure the rest of the faculty to choose sides and build up factions within the department, some intervention is called for.

As stated earlier in this discussion, the chairperson should try to transform conflicts into opportunities for problem solving. It may be useful here to make a conceptual distinction between *conflicts* and *problems*. A problem exists when a set of expectations is not being fulfilled; a conflict exists when one or more persons is intentionally or unintentionally thwarting the needs or wants of another person or persons. For example, several faculty members taught an introductory graduate seminar on a rotating basis. Students who took the course from a particular faculty member had great difficulty passing the department qualifying examination. This difficulty caused conflict between the students and the faculty members, as well as among the faculty members themselves. The chairperson arranged a meeting of all the teachers of the course. Instead of permitting them to dwell on their differences, he limited the agendum to a discussion of what the students were expected to know at the completion of the course and what the examination should cover. By concentrating on the problem rather than on the dispute and by reaching a mutually satisfactory solution, the chairperson defused the conflict.

The chairperson can resolve some conflicts by acting as clarifier. An emerging conflict may be reduced if the chairperson can show the parties that their expectations are based on incorrect information. For example, conflict in a department over inequitable teaching loads may be reduced if the chairperson supplies precise information about who teaches what. On the other hand, such information, if it gives evidence of real inequities, may widen the conflict.

When the chairperson receives reports of a conflict, he or she would be wise to begin a discreet inquiry into the situation before taking any overt action. For example, two faculty members were engaged in a bitter feud because one believed the other had misrepresented her ability and record to a Washington funding agency and thus was responsible for its rejection of her grant proposal. By conducting a few interviews, the chairperson was able to clarify the situation. Discreet inquiry was also effective in a case involving rumors of sexual misconduct by a faculty member. When the chairperson met with some graduate students, he discovered evidence of a pattern of sexual exploitation in which the faculty member threatened the careers of students unless they granted him favors. In some instances when rumors of misbehavior were ignored, the university was later subjected to adverse publicity and legal action.

The department as a whole or committees within the department can be used to settle or reduce conflict. For example, a bitter quarrel over who was to teach a certain course threatened to disrupt the activities of a statistics department. The department referred the problem to a committee and asked its members to develop a set of criteria and procedures for determining who would teach specific courses in the department. The decision of who was to teach each course, including the one in question, would henceforth be made on the basis of established policy.

Some conflicts are caused primarily by problems that the chairperson may be able to identify but not be authorized or suited to address. In such cases, the use of an outside authority may be required. For example, a faculty member's alcoholism was ignored and even concealed by his colleagues and chairperson until a committee of graduate students spoke with an attorney about the man's chronic absenteeism and erratic behavior. The chairperson then discussed the matter with the dean, and they contacted a staff member who was an effective alcoholism counselor. Together they worked out a program of action that they offered to the faculty member.

Occasionally a chairperson will encourage an emerging conflict in the belief that getting things out in the open will help correct misunderstandings and ultimately result in a more positive relationship. Some chairpersons may even induce conflict in order to discover the intensity of feelings about a particular issue. Only a skilled conflict manager should attempt to introduce a dispute into the department. The potential for damage is high and probable outcome too unpredictable.

When thinking about the kind of strategy to use to reduce a conflict, the chairperson should examine the values held by the opposing parties. He or she should be aware that intervention might unwittingly lend support to one party's values. Examining values is especially important when the department has no clear priorities or goals. In such instances, the chairperson, by supporting a value or goal, is causing a conflicting value to be downplayed or rejected. The chairperson then becomes a party to the conflict rather than a mediator, part of the problem rather than part of the solution. In departments that have no clear-cut goals, the value supported by the chairperson establishes priorities and creates a latent conflict situation. For example, in a department that had established no priorities concerning the value of research or teaching, the faculty members began to argue about the relative merits of generating large numbers of student credit hours rather than publishing research. The chairperson sided with the advocates of teaching large classes. By so doing, he established a priority that would later cause conflict between the disaffected researchers and the rest of the department.

Although it is often wise to adopt a neutral stance toward conflict in the department, the chairperson must sometimes become embroiled in a conflict because the role demands it. On such occasions, one of the parties in conflict may perceive the chairperson's action as partisan or punitive. Thus far we have emphasized the chairperson's role as a problem solver, but there are times when the attempted solution to a conflict requires that the chairperson make a decision that arouses someone's anger and hostility. Indeed, on occasion traditional ways of reducing conflict are not successful and a party to conflict must be warned, disciplined, or reprimanded. Chairpersons should know what authority they have to order persons to desist from certain behaviors. They should be aware of institutional rules and regulations and know the extent of their legal powers as chairpersons.

In some cases of conflict the best action is to intervene immediately. If equipment, students, or faculty or staff members are threatened with danger, the chairperson must act quickly and effectively. In the rare case of hostile or threatening behavior, the chairperson and the staff should know how to contact police or security officers. The chairperson should also know what to do in the case of fire, storms, and accident. Thefts should be reported promptly, since they may be part of an organized and systematic activity that the police might be able to identify and stop.

Some disputes can be settled only by consultation with a dean or other official. Such disputes include quarrels between departments, quarrels between a department and the administration, and quarrels between a department and a university committee. With chairpersons vigorously advocating the claims of their own departments, quarrels can escalate into conflict. In such an event, the dean or the academic vice-president must try to settle the fight. For example, a school of education offered statistics courses to its own students, while a statistics department offered courses to the university in general. When many arts and sciences students began to take courses in the school of education, the statistics department pressed for a regulation that would prohibit crossing college lines for statistics courses. Each department began accusing the other of proselytizing, so the chairpersons decided to cool things down by taking the problem to the academic vice-president. Another example: When the graduate policy committee suspended a department's authorization to grant graduate degrees, the department claimed it was treated unfairly. Again, the chairperson took the problem to the dean. In both instances, the chairpersons were part of the conflict, but they used their knowledge of the dynamics of conflict to arrive at a solution.

The chairperson is sometimes called on to appear as an expert witness or as an independent observer in proceedings that arise as a result of conflict. During grievance procedures and in the course of official hearings, the chairperson may be required to present evidence or give testimony about the conduct of department members. The chairperson should keep journals or records that recount in detail the actions of the parties in a dispute, especially if he or she intervenes in the conflict. The chairperson should take into account the legal aspects of building a case history or record and should comply with requirements of due process and with laws respecting privacy. Ordinarily, if a file is being kept, the person or persons who are the subject of the documentation should be informed of its existence. The file should not simply document the errors or misdeeds of persons or parties; it should also record the steps taken to resolve the dispute or transform it into an opportunity for problem solving.

A conflict poses a more difficult dilemma for chairpersons when none of the possible interventions seems likely to resolve the whole problem. On occasion a chairperson may hesitate to intervene in a conflict for fear of losing his or her effectiveness as chairperson, alienating powerful members of the department, or possibly losing his or her position. Suppose that two very influential faculty members who generally disagree about each other's principles and practices and who both are extremely vindictive have joined forces to deny junior faculty members the opportunity to teach certain courses and the opportunity for released time to do research. The two faculty members are politically strong enough to threaten the chairperson's position. The junior faculty members have approached the chairperson and asked for assistance in the conflict. What should the chairperson do?

Another hypothetical dilemma: The short-tempered dean of the college is a tenured faculty member in a certain department. He thinks of himself as a superb teacher and insists on teaching a required undergraduate course. In fact, he has the deserved reputation of being one of the worst teachers in the university. The students are outraged at the poor quality of instruction and the lack of organization in the course and are vigorously protesting. In addition, one of the younger faculty members in the department is upset because he feels he is more qualified than the dean to teach this particular course. What can the chairperson do about his own dean?

The chairperson's role in dealing with conflict and maintaining morale is crucial to the smooth operation of the department. He or she must be aware of the conditions in the department that might give rise to conflict and be prepared to use analytic ability, good judgment, and creativity in order to handle conflict effectively. He or she must be able to recognize and analyze a conflict when it occurs and to exercise good judgment when deciding whether or not to intervene. The kind of intervention depends on the facts and dynamics of the situation. The chairperson must be creative and deal with each situation individually. In the case of recurring conflict, the irrational and emotional elements of the situation can be defused if the chairperson can find or get the department to develop a regulation or policy covering that type of conflict. As a general rule, conflict that can be reduced to an opportunity for problem solving has the greatest chance of being settled. This transformation requires that the chairperson explore the limits of his or her own creativity. Although no formula exists that can be applied to all conflict situations, the following guidelines can be of help to the chairperson.

- Keep in touch with the feelings and attitudes of faculty members. Through frequent meetings, the chairperson can discover latent conflict situations before they emerge.
- Be aware of the four stages of conflict episodes in order to be able to deal with them at the earliest opportunity.
- Use techniques of active listening to raise morale and to understand the perceptions of faculty members who may be engaged in conflict.
- Structure the department in such a manner that conflicts can be discussed, aired, and dealt with through normal governance procedures.
- Be sensitive to faculty members with personal problems but do not necessarily get involved. Intervene only if the operation of the department is impaired.
- In cases of conflict, determine what conflicting values are held by the parties.

- Do not take sides in a conflict that does not concern the welfare of the department.
- Do not intervene in conflicts unless you have reason to believe that intervention can help the situation.
- Find out whether disputants perceive the stakes as high or low. If they are perceived as high, try to reduce them.
- Find out whether parties believe the conflict is amenable to solution. Try to persuade them that solutions are possible.
- Try to change any conflict to an opportunity for problem solving.
- Be prepared to make discreet inquiries about reported potential and actual conflict.
- When appropriate, use department committees to establish policies and procedures that govern situations in which conflicts have occurred and may occur in the future.
- As soon as possible, clarify misconseptions that may cause conflict.
- Communicate clearly with the faculty about any unprecedented action that might cause conflict.
- Be prepared to be called as a witness to or observer of a conflict. Keep records of action and involvement in conflicts.
- Do not violate laws or institutional regulations when dealing with conflict.

We have briefly discussed, from both a theoretical and a practical point of view, conflict as it occurs in academic departments. Chairpersons of academic disciplines other than the social sciences may be unaware of the great amount of research conducted by sociologists and psychologists on the problems of identifying, analyzing, and resolving conflict. Knowing how to deal with conflict can be useful in managing families, schools, churches, businesses, legislatures, and international affairs. Chairpersons, in order to be effective, must continually be alert to the possibility of conflict in their departments. They must be sufficiently wise to determine whether they should get involved. If they decide to become involved, they must select the strategy that has the best chance of solving or diffusing the conflict.

Questions

1. What factors or influences outside the university have caused latent conflict among the faculty members in your department?
2. What factors or influences *within* the university but outside the department have caused latent conflict among your faculty members?
3. What kinds of issues, situations, or relationships that exist within your department have contributed to latent or emergent conflict?

4. a. Review one or more conflicts in your department or in another department that have been constructive. How were they resolved?

   b. Review one or more conflicts in your department or in another department that have been destructive. How were they resolved?

5. Do any serious conflicts exist in your department at the present time? What are they?

6. In this chapter we have discussed morale in general terms. Identify factors that at one time or another have lowered morale in your department. How did you react to those factors? Do you think your reaction was appropriate?

7. Identify factors that have raised morale in your department. Did you have any influence over these factors?

8. What elements in the governance structure of your department serve to minimize conflict?

9. Pages 233–4 contain a list of guidelines for helping resolve conflicts. For each guideline on the list, think of two or three examples of conflict situations and stages of conflict for which the particular guideline might be helpful. Try to find a colleague or two who are willing to join you in this exercise.

10. Described below are five skeleton sketches of conflict situations in a department. Assume that you are the chairperson who must resolve each of the conflicts. Use your experience and imagination to expand each sketch into a more comprehensive case study by adding more details. Try to interest one or two of your colleagues in joining you in this exercise.

    1. Half the faculty of a department have signed a letter to the dean, asking for the chairperson's resignation.
    2. A faculty member has a personal problem that is affecting his performance and relations with others in the department.
    3. Students complain, with some justification, that an instructor's grading practices are discriminatory.
    4. Faculty in a department have polarized into two camps and are feuding. Students are suffering because of the conflict.
    5. Two faculty members are fighting with each other. Their areas of specialization overlap and they are competing for resources.

In developing the hypothetical case study try to include the following:

• Background information describing the history and development of the conflict.

• A description of the personality and character of the individuals involved. Be specific about their roles and status.

- Give details of various incidents in the conflict.
- Using information from the chapter in the text, analyze the conflict in terms of the stakes involved and the attitudes of the actors.
- Describe your reasoning about whether or not to intervene.
- Describe the strategies you will use to try to reduce or settle the conflict, if you decide to intervene. Which strategies from those described in the text can be applied?
- Describe how you anticipate the conflict will be resolved.

References

BALDRIDGE, J. VICTOR. *Power and Conflict in the University: Research in the Sociology of Complex Organizations.* New York: John Wiley & Sons, 1971.

BALDRIDGE, J. VICTOR, et al. *Policy Making and Effective Leadership: A National Study of Academic Management.* San Francisco: Jossey-Bass, 1978.

BARZUN, JACQUES. *The American University: How It Runs, Where It Is Going.* New York: Harper & Row, 1968.

BENNETT, DUDLEY. *TA and the Manager.* New York: The American Management Association, 1978.

BLAKE, ROBERT R.; SHEPARD, HERBERT; AND MOUTON, JANE. *Managing Intergroup Conflict in Industry.* Houston: Gulf, 1964.

GORDON, THOMAS. *Parent Effectiveness Training.* New York; London; and Scarborough, Ontario: New American Library, 1975.

GORDON, THOMAS, AND BURCH, NOEL. *T.E.T.—Teacher Effectiveness Training.* New York: David McKay Co., 1975.

GOULDNER, ALVIN W. "Cosmopolitans and Locals: Towards an Analysis of Latent Social Roles." *Administrative Science Quarterly,* December 1957, pp. 281–306; and March 1958, pp. 444–80.

HERSEY, PAUL, AND BLANCHARD, KENNETH. *Management of Organizational Behavior: Utilizing Human Resources.* 3rd ed. Englewood Cliffs, N.J.: Prentice-Hall, 1977.

HOBBS, WALTER G., AND ANDERSON, G. LESTER. "The Operation of Academic Departments," *Management Science,* December 1971, pp. 134–44.

JENKS, CHRISTOPHER, AND RIESMAN, DAVID. *The Academic Revolution.* Garden City, N.J.: Anchor Books, 1969.

LEVINSON, DANIEL J. *The Seasons of a Man's Life.* New York: Alfred A. Knopf, 1978.

LOEWENBERG, PETER. "Love and Hate in the Academy." *The Center Magazine,* September-October 1972, pp. 4–11.

LUTHANS, FRED, ed. *Contemporary Readings in Organizational Behavior.* 2nd ed. New York: McGraw-Hill, 1976.

LUTHANS, FRED. *Organizational Behavior.* 2nd ed. New York: McGraw-Hill, 1976.

McCONNELL, T.R., AND MORTIMER, KENNETH P. *The Faculty in University Governance*. Berkeley: Center for Research and Development in Higher Education, University of California, 1971.

PETERSON, MARVIN W. "Faculty and Academic Responsiveness in a Period of Decline: An Organizational Perspective." *The Journal of the College and University Personnel Association*, Spring 1980, pp. 95–104.

PONDY, LOUIS R. "Organizational Conflict: Concepts and Models." In *Contemporary Readings in Organizational Behavior*, edited by Fred Luthans. 2nd ed. New York: McGraw-Hill, 1976.

SHEEHY, GAIL. *Passages*. New York: Dutton, 1976.

SNOW, C.P. *The Masters*. Lib. rep. ed. New York: Charles Scribner's Sons, 1960.

TANTER, RAYMOND, ed. "Why Fight? Conflict Models for Strategists and Managers." *American Behavioral Scientist*, July-August 1972 (special issue).

TEGER, ALLAN I. *Too Much Invested to Quit*. Elmsford, N.Y.: Pergamon Press, 1980.

12

Avoiding Legal Pitfalls: Sensitivity to Faculty and Student Concerns

We often cast the department chairperson in the role of mediator, conciliator, advocate, and judge, so it should come as no surprise that the role of the chairperson involves legal obligations and risks of legal liability. As an employee of the institution, the chairperson nominally acts as agent for the principal; his or her acts, when committed within the scope of employment, are attributable to the college or university. Although the incidence of individual liability is remote, the acts of the chairperson may result in costly and unnecessary litigation for the institution, consuming time and diverting efforts that could otherwise be directed to essential educational objectives.

"Lawyers," Supreme Court Justice Oliver Wendell Holmes is said to have remarked, "spend a great deal of their time shoveling smoke." It might also be suggested that when the smoke clears, little of substance is left to guide conduct and protect against liability. Courts have decided relatively few cases that directly affect the role of the department chairperson, and of the cases resolved, subtle distinctions make unerring generalization difficult.

While it is undoubtedly true that the law has recognized few principles that would serve to guide the administrator, some generalized legal notions relating to the department chairperson's role can be identified. From the limited case law available, one can draw conclusions that may not always apply in a given circumstance but that so closely parallel standards of appropriate administrative practice that they deserve elaboration.

Learning by example may be a desirable method for conveying the meaning of legal principles applicable to the department chairperson. The opinions of judges, based as they are upon the facts of a particular controversy, offer a case study approach to the analysis of legal issues and permit the extrapolation of guidelines for the department chairperson. However, these legal generalizations require a few initial qualifications. First, the department chairperson must look to state statute, regulatory standards, institutional policy, and, where appropriate, collective bargaining agreements in order to clarify the legal obligations unique to each state jurisdiction. Second, applicable legal standards vary depending on the institutional type involved, particularly where an institution is exclusively private or pervasively religious in character in contrast to state-supported public institutions and land grant colleges.

Judicial Restraint

Judges are reluctant to intervene in matters outside their area of expertise or susceptible to resolution through expeditious administrative process. Since the responsibilities of the department chairperson relate both to academic decision making and administrative procedure, judicial restraint is particularly appropriate as a basis for limiting judicial review of the chairperson's decisions. As a corollary to this principle, the department chairperson should welcome the development of administrative procedures which permit review of his or her decisions and advise those who are adversely affected by these decisions to initiate the review process in the event they are dissatisfied. Furthermore, it is a wise chairperson who emphasizes the central role of academic policy implementation in his or her actions and who takes care to harmonize decision making with the educational objectives of the department and the institution. The chairperson who always assumes the correctness of his or her decision making forgets that "assumption is the mother of all foulups."

Rational Relationship and the Rule of Reasonableness

In general, courts indulge a presumption in favor of the chairperson's exercise of authority on behalf of an institution. The presumption assumes that the chair has acted reasonably, in good faith, for motives consistent with the bonafide purposes of the institution. Such a presumption, however, is not irrebuttable and may be subject to judicial review when facts are presented from which a judge may infer the lack of a rational relationship between the actions of the chairperson and the bonafide purposes of the institution.

If the court is initially persuaded that such actions leave some doubt about the reasonableness or the rational relationship between actions and institutional policy, the burden of proof may shift from the person or persons who allege the impropriety to the department chairperson. Under this circumstance the chair's obligation is to go forward with a showing that his or her action was both reasonable and warranted.

Once the burden of proof has shifted to the chairperson, both argument and evidence are required in order to establish substantial proof in support of the propriety of the chair's action. It is extremely helpful for the chairperson to provide an evidentiary record corroborating the "reasonableness" of his or her action. A personal notebook detailing the basis for a particular administrative decision, anecdotal records substantiating observations and evaluations, written memoranda establishing that proper notice has been provided are among the sources of evidentiary material on which the chairperson may need to rely at some later date. Such a record, which may be accessible to both the person bringing the suit and the institution, should reflect the chair's concern for fair dealing and adherence to the academic and professional standards of the institution.

Legal Liability

Legal liability can be established only where a complaint properly alleges and a plaintiff proves the elements of a legal claim. "Plaintiff" is the title given to the individual who brings suit. Plaintiffs, whether students or employees, must demonstrate that a duty was owed to them, that the duty was breached, and that the breach of duty is the principal cause of an injury for which the court should grant relief. Depending on the nature of the injury, the court may grant relief in the form of an award of damages or an order enjoining or compelling some institutional practice.

It is a popular maxim among lawyers that what really matters is the name a litigant succeeds in imposing on the facts—not the facts themselves. It is possible to categorize the differing allegations that might be argued as a basis for the chairperson's and the institution's legal liability. Among the various types of liability that may be associated with the role of the department chairperson, five types are of particular importance because of the frequency with which they appear in litigation. The types of liability most likely to involve the performance of a department chairperson would include allegations of arbitrary and capricious action, breach of contract, denial of constitutional rights, discriminatory practice, and unintentional or intentional breach of a common law duty which resulted in injury to the individual.

Arbitrary and Capricious Action

Courts have long recognized that behaviors motivated by bad faith, arbitrariness, or capriciousness may be actionable at law. Evidence that a student or faculty member has been treated radically different from others tends to establish arbitrary and capricious action, particularly when the department chairperson fails to follow recognized institutional procedures, when irregularities in the application of standards are discovered, or when there is a lack of uniformity in the administration of standards.

Typically, where a court does discover evidence of arbitrary or capricious action, the court will turn to the institution for a justification of its policy. Courts generally follow a "rule of reasonableness" under such circumstances, inquiring whether the chairperson's action can be shown to have employed some understandable, unified standard. Obviously, the failure to establish and maintain such standards leaves the chairperson open to a charge of impermissible abuse of discretion and breach of a duty of good faith or fair dealing.

This is not to suggest that every deviation from accepted policy constitutes arbitrary or capricious conduct by the chairperson. Exceptions to the uniform application of a standard are widely recognized in law, but it is an unwritten presumption that a justification accompany the exception to policy. The most often encountered situation is one in which exceptions to a policy have been permitted, then the policy is suddenly enforced by the chairperson with adverse and injurious consequences for the person affected.

Clare Booth Luce's observation that "no good deed goes unpunished" seems apt for such a circumstance. The benevolent chairperson who has granted exceptions to a rule or policy suddenly finds that the enforcement of the policy can conceivably be legally enjoined as arbitrary. Courts will insist upon a rationale for the disparity in treatment, and it behooves the chair to clarify every exception to a rule of policy, adopting the exception whenever later cases present the same or conspicuously similar circumstances.

Nowhere is the allegation of arbitrary or capricious treatment more likely to appear than in cases involving students. Usually, the denial of the degree or dismissal for academic deficiencies engenders the litigation. In an illustrative case, a law student whose cumulative grade point fell below required standards for graduation was informed that he could continue for a fourth year, but that regardless of whether he improved his overall average, he would not be given the degree. He refused to accept the conditions, but did enroll and managed to bring his cumulative average up to the requisite graduation standard in his fourth year. Despite his improvement, he was denied the degree.

While the court recognized that the law school had absolute discretion to deny the request for readmission to a fourth year, it took cognizance of the institution's previous practice of allowing other probationary students to enroll and correct deficiencies during a fourth year. In some cases these students had met requirements and been awarded the law degree. The imposition of a condition that the student could not be granted a degree even if he satisfied degree requirements was deemed by the court as arbitrary and a manifest abuse of discretion.[1]

In another case, a student successfully alleged a cause of action for arbitrary treatment when singled out from other students and compelled to meet special requirements not originally outlined in order to complete a degree.[2] Similarly, a student dropped from medical school for failing to pass a second-year final examination successfully challenged the dismissal by establishing that the examination had been incorrectly administered and that other affected students had been granted the opportunity for reexaminations.[3]

Allegations of arbitrary and capricious treatment have seldom been sustained where the department has applied clear, unambiguous academic policies relative to retention and graduation. In a case that proves the rule, a student sought to invest the department's minimum grade point policies with an alternative meaning which the court described as "frivolous" and inconsistent with the institution's uniform application of academic policy.[4] In another, the student was unable to establish that a faculty adviser's interpretation of the procedure for awarding grade changes should prevail over the express written policy of the school. In the latter instance, the court was particularly impressed by the extent to which the institution had accorded the student procedural due process in the administrative appeal of the dismissal decision.[5]

Breach of Contract

A contract is an agreement between parties involving mutual understandings relative to specific considerations and obligations. The law in every jurisdiction prefers to enforce the express, written agreements of the parties, but oral understandings and actions of the parties during the performance of the contract have frequently influenced the court's interpretation of a contractual obligation. The department chairperson is seldom considered to be a principal party to a contract involving faculty, staff, or students and does not normally act as an agent for the institution in the negotiation of a contract agreement. However, the chair is often responsible for the administration of a contract and must faithfully execute the obligations the institution has agreed to assume. The acts of the chairperson may also influence the determination of whether a contract can be implied between the institution and another party.

When it comes to the obligations of a contract, brevity and ambiguity are often concomitants. Since ambiguity is often the source of contract disputes, it is not surprising to see considerable detail in express agreements, whether they be college catalogues, graduate bulletins, or collectively negotiated agreements. For the department chairperson, the administration of any contract often involves rigorous attention to detail as well as a fine eye for resolving ambiguities in a fashion consistent with institutional policy and the intent of the parties.

Courts consider college bulletins, program guides, and brochures as contracts that create mutual obligations between institution and student. Fundamental fairness to the parties involved in a lawsuit requires that the court consider the extent to which a contractual relationship did exist between parties and the potential harm when one party has breached a duty under terms of the contract. As a consequence, the oral representations of faculty advisers, deans, and chairpersons have been relied upon as a basis for initiating a suit for breach of contract. However, courts do not appear to apply contract standards rigorously, choosing to resolve many ambiguities in favor of the institution and often abstaining from resolving substantive matters of academic policy.

Two contractual situations that are particularly relevant to the relationship between student and department chairperson have received significant consideration by courts. Where department or college programs constitute a contractual inducement to enroll and students can be said to have reasonably relied upon these contractual terms in undertaking a field of study, students may sue to enforce specific compliance with the proposed program or seek an award of monetary damages for their reliance on the contract. In a second situation, oral and written representations related to degree and program requirements, often the result of inaccurate or improper advisement, have been the basis for suits in which students seek award of the degree or program modifications consistent with the alleged contractual obligation.

An illustration of the first instance involved students enrolled in the school of architecture at Ohio University. The school had lost accreditation, but its faculty and college administrators repeatedly assured students they would obtain an accredited degree. Provisional accreditation was secured when institutional representatives gave assurances to accrediting officials that the institution would work toward meeting all requirements for accreditation. Subsequently, this provisional accreditation was withdrawn when the university elected to phase out the architecture program in response to institution-wide financial problems.

The students enrolled in the architecture program sued, alleging that an implied contract based on the oral representations of university faculty and administrators was breached when the university failed to maintain accredited status.

The reviewing court recognized a contractual obligation because the faculty and staff of the school continually conveyed the promise that the institution would work toward full accreditation. Since students acted upon this promise and continued to enroll, pay fees and tuition, and attend classes, the court concluded that the students had acted reasonably in reliance upon these promises and that the institution breached the implied contract when it withdrew funding and support for the program. In recognizing that college governing boards have the authority to discontinue programs, the court qualified this authority by emphasizing that contractual commitments that have been undertaken must be honored or, alternatively, damages for breach of contract awarded unless the institution can show financially exigent conditions so overwhelming as to permit a defense of impossibility of performance.[6]

A student's reliance on the oral representations of faculty advisers or written academic policies has often been the basis for contract suits. In one representative case, the student sought the award of a master's degree when he relied upon a faculty member's erroneous advice relative to the scoring of a final comprehensive examination. When the college applied a higher standard than the professor had indicated, the student was denied the degree and sued to force the institution to make the award of the master's. Although the student asserted that he would have passed the examination using the criteria articulated by the professor, the court found this a highly speculative contention. Showing a characteristic judicial reluctance to intervene in academic policy and noting that the institution had offered the student a reexamination without prejudice, the court refused to require the award of the degree.[7]

Any contract between a student and the institution implicitly requires the student to demonstrate academic competence and the institution to act fairly and in good faith. Even though courts are extremely reluctant to compel the award of a degree, it is important for the institution to meet its obligations and avoid irreparable injury to the student. Statements guaranteeing special service such as remedial or tutorial programs for the disadvantaged or specifying academic procedures which the student must follow are frequently recognized as actionable contract claims by courts.[8] Although the judicial branch is reluctant to interfere by requiring award of an academic degree, the courts will not defer to the professional educator when it comes to the contractual obligation to provide student services expressed or implied by the institution or its representatives.

Obligations specified in employment contracts, whether collectively or individually negotiated, are generally interpreted with greater emphasis on strict construction by courts. The department chair would be well advised to avoid commitments to faculty and staff that are beyond the chair's authority and to seek consultation with other administrators before resolving ambiguities in employment contracts. As chairpersons, doing nothing may seldom be appropriate, but saying nothing, particularly when it relates to interpreting the institution's obligation under a contract, is often the wisest course until clarification can be obtained.

A department chairperson who failed to take appropriate action under tenure denial of a contract was held to have violated the contractual obligation of a private college in Tennessee. The contract of employment specified that once a faculty member was given a contract to teach for the fourth consecutive year the institution must give notice within ten days after the beginning of the second semester of the fourth year if a decision has been made not to grant tenure. The court noted that the institution had an affirmative duty under the contract provision to provide timely notice if the faculty member was not to be continued. Since the department chair did not provide notice of tenure denial until three months after the start of the second semester, contractual notice had not been provided and the faculty member could be considered to have acquired tenure.[9]

Alternatively, a department chairperson's letters and off-hand statements can often be incorporated as part of a contract provision. In a case from New Hampshire, a professor was considered to have violated his contract when he failed to give adequate notice of his sabbatical leave plans. When the professor signed his employment contract, a letter attached to the agreement stipulated that he would be expected to take a year's sabbatical at half-pay rather than a one-semester sabbatical at full pay unless he notified his administrative representative prior to a date set in the letter. Several times after the date for notification passed, the professor was requested to inform the college of his sabbatical plans. Finally, the professor was advised by letter that he would be on a one-year sabbatical at half-pay and that if he objected, he should notify the college president.

The basic issue in this case was whether the professor failed to perform a condition of his employment contract when he postponed notice to the department of his plans for sabbatical leave until after the deadline stipulated in the chairperson's letter. The court held that the letter attached to the contract was binding and incorporated material elements of the contract of employment. Further, the request for notice of sabbatical plans within a specified time was a reasonable request of the department. The professor's failure to give timely notice, particularly after repeated requests to do so, constituted a breach of the terms of the sabbatical leave provisions, and the college could compel the full-year leave at half-pay.[10]

Despite the protection of employment rights guaranteed by a contractual obligation, an institution may act to dismiss an employee prior to the end of a contract term if good cause to do so can be established. In public institutions, good cause most often includes dismissal for insubordination, incompetence, or immorality. Other grounds are sometimes inferred, including neglect of duty, persistent misconduct, and conditions that compel lay-offs such as financial exigency or declining enrollment.

In most cases, the role of the department chairperson in instances of faculty dismissal, reprimand, or lay-off will be that of investigator and information gatherer. In such a role, the chair will find it hard to avoid the position advocated by the man who sought reelection to a judgeship on the basis that he had always endeavored to "seek a balance between impartiality on the one hand and partiality on the other."

The formal administrative processes established for dismissal or lay-off of employees will normally specify the standards to be applied in these adverse employment decisions. The chairperson should endeavor to conduct a confidential inquiry, providing reasonable disclosure to the employee under scrutiny and emphasizing that the inquiry is limited to an investigation of conduct that may be reasonably expected to have an adverse effect on the employee's performance on the job or on relations with students and colleagues. Immoral behavior should be shown to have some nexus with job-related activity, such as a negative impact on classroom performance or students. Insubordination should relate to a repeated refusal to obey reasonable institutional rules or adminstrative directives and should be tied to the chairperson's previous notification and warning to the employee that the behavior must be corrected. Incompetence, always a most difficult ground to establish, usually involves a burden of proof in which periodic evaluations, anecdotal records, and complaints by students and colleagues create a cumulative record of deficiencies that the employee is unable or unwilling to remediate.

Denial of Constitutional Rights

Public colleges and universities are obligated to respect the federal constitutional rights of students and employees. In recent years, the doctrine of state action has extended this obligation to ostensibly private institutions who receive substantial federal or state funds for programs. (A program at a private institution may receive so much federal or state financial support as to be "infected" with a public purpose and liable for the denial of constitutional rights.) The protections of federal constitutional law must often involve the guarantees of due process under the fourteenth amendment and the right to free speech and association secured by the first amendment.

Due Process.   Under the fourteenth amendment, an employee's interest in public employment may be constitutionally protected. Procedural fairness must be observed whenever the public university threatens an employee's property rights or liberty interest. Property rights are those entitlements which are recognized as part of a contract of employment, such as a right to continued employment. Liberty relates to the employee's interest in protecting his or her reputation and securing other job opportunities. Due process entitles the individual to notice of the reasons for the institution's action and an opportunity for a hearing on disputed issues of fact. Due process procedures are designed to mitigate arbitrary or capricious official action, but because a liberty or property interest must be established by the employee before any process becomes due, official action may be allowed to stand if a protectable interest is not found.

To compel due process protections, a faculty or staff member might show that a certain property interest is sufficient to justify court intervention. Typically, whether a legitimate claim of entitlement to continued employment exists will be defined in reference to employee contracts, negotiated agreements, institutional regulations, and state laws. Faculty in public institutions who are dismissed or otherwise denied property rights during the contractual term of employment are entitled to due process of law. This view is consistent with the decision in *Perry v. Sindermann*,[11] in which the Supreme Court ruled that a teacher who had held his faculty position for four years in reliance upon a de facto tenure arrangement could establish a legitimate claim of entitlement worthy of due process protection. The Court cautioned, though, that "if it is the law (of the state) that a teacher . . . has no contractual or other claim to job tenure, the . . . claim would be defeated."[12]

The faculty member involved in the *Perry* case was able to establish de facto tenure by coupling the institution's lack of a formal tenure system with oral and written representations by various deans and department chairpersons that satisfactory performance would be rewarded with continuing employment. The faculty member submitted the statements of his administrative superiors as proof that a contract existed which granted him a long-term property right tantamount to tenure. Numerous appellate decisions have distinguished the *Perry* case by emphasizing that an established system with published standards and procedures for granting tenure would not allow for a de facto grant of tenure.

Assurances of tenure given a faculty member by a department head would not appear to create a sufficient expectation of continued employment to guarantee due process protection provided the assurances are clearly contradicted by published tenure policies. A promise by a department chair that a new professor would receive tenure "as a matter of course" or assurances by tenured colleagues that a professor is progressing satisfactorily and would eventually receive tenure would not create an implied right to tenure when the nontenured faculty member is given notice of a formal tenure process.[13] Since formal tenure standards preclude reliance on the assurances that a new employee may receive, it is wise for the department chairman to lobby for the adoption of such a formal, written policy to put new faculty on notice of the existence of such a policy and to avoid statements that might reasonably be construed to create a genuine expectation of continued employment. With regard to the creation of a property right to continuing contract, the chair might well rely on the evidentiary proposition that "If you don't say it, he or she (the faculty member) can't repeat it."

A liberty interest may be infringed when the results of administrative action impose a stigma or other disability on the employee that forecloses the individual's freedom to take advantage of other employment opportunities or otherwise injures good name, reputation, or standing in the community. In *Board of Regents v. Roth*,[14] the conditions that would impose such a stigma were expressed as "a charge that (the employee) had been guilty of dishonesty or immorality."[15] Roth, hired to teach for one year at the university, was informed without explanation that he would not be rehired. He alleged that the true reason for nonretention was his criticism of the university and insisted that a due process hearing was required in which the university must justify its nonrenewal decision. The United States Supreme Court held that Roth failed to establish a violation of first amendment free speech rights, and no fourteenth amendment liberty interest was denied because the university had made no charges against Roth that would bar him from employment at another institution.

There is no legal obligation on the part of the department chairperson to give reasons for nonrenewal of contract unless there is a stipulation in state law, institutional regulations, or negotiated contract requiring that reasons be given. Although it is a general rule that timely notice be given if the employment contract is not to be renewed, the employee does not have a federal constitutional right to reasons for nonrenewal. However, the department chairperson would be well advised periodically to evaluate and confidentially to inform the faculty or staff member of his or her performance in order to avoid any possible allegation of arbitrary treatment. Giving reasons for a nonrenewal decision is permissible and appropriate provided the reasons are communicated to the employee in confidence and have to do with job-related concerns, such as inability to cooperate with colleagues, poor evaluations of teaching, declining enrollments, and budget constraints.

In *Roth* no reasons were given for the professor's nonrenewal, but in *Beitzell v. Jeffrey*[16] a faculty member who was denied tenure was unsuccessful in claiming the denial of a liberty interest. The faculty member's chairperson had submitted a memorandum to a grievance committee which described the professor's professional behavior as "irresponsible" and indicated that other faculty had expressed concern about the faculty member's drinking. The departmental committee had voted against a recommendation for tenure after a discussion that included references to the professor's lack of adequacy as a teacher and adviser and to his drinking. In all communications relative to the decision not to grant tenure, the department chairperson maintained a high level of confidentiality, disclosing the basis for the committee's decision to the professor, and forwarding his memorandum to the grievance committee only when the professor's attorney insisted that the memo become a public record in the grievance proceedings. The appellate court observed that the professor failed to show that the personal aspects of these discussions, including references to drinking habits, became public as a result of the actions of the department chairperson. Since the chairperson did not make the charges public, the university could not be said to have stigmatized the former employee in such a way as to interfere with his ability to take advantage of other employment opportunities.

The requirement that a stigma seriously damage the faculty member's ability to take advantage of other employment opportunities, coupled with the requirement of public disclosure of the reasons for the employment decision, has limited the number of cases in which faculty have successfully claimed a right to due process based on a denial of a liberty interest. A charge of inadequate teaching performance would appear to be insufficient to establish a stigma denying a liberty interest; rather, a showing that the institution made public charges that the employee had been guilty of dishonesty or immorality would seem required.[17]

The extent of process which is due a faculty or staff member depends on a balancing of the public institution's interest in efficient operation of the system against the weight of the property of liberty interest of the individual. The seriousness and permanence of an adverse employment decision will influence the requirements for notice and/or hearing and the extent to which administrative appeal and review are necessary. Generally, where the faculty member has established a property or liberty interest worthy of due process, minimal elements afforded to the employee would include the following:

1. The employee must be advised of the cause or causes for the adverse employment decision in sufficient detail to fairly enable the employee to show any error that may exist.
2. At a reasonable time after notice of cause, the employee must be accorded a meaningful opportunity to be heard in his or her own defense.
3. A hearing should be granted before a tribunal that both possesses academic expertise and has an apparent impartiality toward the charges.

Generally, the institution's formal grievance procedures established for administrative review of employment decisions accord the minimal elements of due process. The department chairperson is often charged with the responsibility of providing notice to the employee, informing the employee of the charges, procedures, and consequences of any action which might be taken and outlining the route of appeal. Failure to provide timely notice to the employee has resulted in a court-ordered continuation of employment, specifically when the college or university has promulgated rules on notice of nonrenewal and the chairperson, as agent of the institution, fails to notify within the period established for notice of nonretention.[18] Similarly, a department chairperson's failure to discuss his renewal recommendations with a non-tenured faculty member, when college procedural rules specifically required such notice to the individual faculty member under consideration for renewal, has resulted in continuation of employment for the affected employee.[19] Both these results indicate the importance of adhering to procedural safeguards in employment situations, whether those procedures are developed by the institution, required by negotiated agreement, or extrapolated from state or federal law.

While courts have regularly expressed reluctance to intervene on behalf of students in the academic decision-making process, adherence to procedural safeguards of due process has been a basis for judicial scrutiny of administrative action. As guardians of process, courts first consider the nature of the property right or liberty interest, then assess the requisite amount of procedural due process required. While disciplinary standards of due process have long been codified as part of the public institution's honor code or student judicial review board, academic standards involving students remain largely within the province of the faculty and department chairperson in the academic department.

Courts have applied few restrictions on the discretion of academic decision makers relative to due process in academic affairs. The principal case on the amount of due process required in such circumstances is *Board of Curators of the University of Missouri v. Horowitz*,[20] a case in which the United States Supreme Court ruled that no hearing need be afforded to a medical student who was fully informed of academic deficiencies in her clinical performance and given adequate opportunity to correct those deficiencies prior to dismissal. For purposes of this case, the Court assumed that the student could demonstrate the existence of a protected liberty or property interest but held that the school had met its obligation by informing the student of her unsatisfactory performance, warning of the consequences of a failure to improve, and giving her sufficient time to improve.

Academic decisions are recognized by courts as generally more subjective and evaluative, requiring subject matter expertise and an assessment of cumulative information not easily reviewable by judges. In contrast to disciplinary actions, which are adversarial, associated with the resolution of factual questions and determination of standards of proof, academic judgments are typically nonadversarial, subjective judgments involving specialized knowledge. What seems required under such circumstances is adequate notice of deficient performance, specifying the inadequacies that must be remedied and giving reasonable opportunity to correct deficiencies. Such a notice could be challenged where reasons given were arbitrary and capricious, but otherwise no right to an adversarial hearing is automatically conveyed by constitutional standards of academic due process.

In *Horowitz*, the stigma of dismissal was the principal basis for the medical student's contention that she had been denied a liberty interest without due process of law. While the Court recognized that a stigma foreclosing any opportunity to transfer and matriculate at another medical school might result, it refused to grant the student a hearing. However, if the decision to dismiss for academic deficiencies is a subterfuge for a dismissal decision unrelated to academic performance, the student may be able to compel a due process hearing to clear his or her good name. A student engaged in a required course for teacher certification was administratively dropped when he refused to withdraw after being advised of his academic deficiencies. In a note outlining the student's academic deficiencies, the supervising faculty member expressed the opinion that the student was in need of psychological help. The note was not disclosed to anyone besides the student and the associate dean, who advised the student of his academic deficiencies and instituted the administrative drop. Was the note a stigma which necessitated a due process hearing?

A federal district court reasoned that the administrative and supervisory record of the student's academic deficiencies was sufficient to justify removing the student from the course and, ultimately, denying teacher certification. Among the deficiencies noted were charges of failure to develop and follow lesson plans, failure to detect and correct grammatical errors, inability to accept criticism, and difficulty in focusing on day-to-day matters relative to student learning styles and teaching details. No evidence tended to show that the dean's decision was predicated on that part of the note which referred to the student's alleged psychological problems. Furthermore, there was no publication or dissemination of the note's contents beyond the student, supervising teacher, and the dean. The district court concluded that no stigma was created, and found that the decision to drop the student was substantiated by identified academic deficiencies of which the student had periodic notice during the course; thus no hearing was required.[21]

The observance of procedural safeguards could be influenced by the nature of the property interest claimed. While the contract between student and institution will usually meet the requirement for some legitimate claim of entitlement to due process, this property right would appear to grant nothing more than periodic notice of academic progress. However, the denial of some property rights extended to students would require even more due process, including a right to a hearing. At least one court has extended a right to a limited hearing, creating an exception to the *Horowitz* standard. Recognizing a graduate student's property right to remain in good standing in order to receive an assistantship, and taking cognizance of the university's policy requiring consideration of the student's motivation and attitude toward academic work in any dismissal decision, a United States district court granted a student an opportunity to explain the reason for his poor scholarship in order that the university could take into account circumstances that might have influenced the student's motivation and attitude. The court's view of the hearing required was limited to granting the student an opportunity to explain mitigating factors relative to his performance; it would not appear to extend to a right to an adversary proceeding at which he could contest evaluations.[22]

The situation in which minimum grade point average is the sole determining factor in academic decisions would not admit to any right to a hearing, unless institutional policy extended due process protection going beyond that provided by the fourteenth amendment. In one such instance, a student dismissed from a private institution was granted due process rights to notice and a hearing on the dismissal because the institution's policy required these elements of due process.[23] Although fourteenth amendment standards do not normally apply to private colleges, how much due process is granted to the student will depend not only on constitutional guarantees but also on those property entitlements a student is granted by contract with the institution and by reference to institutional rules.

A former student's right to due process, including written notice and the specification of reasons, was recognized by a state court when the student sought readmission to a program in medicine after more than a year's leave of absence. The student had completed two years of the program with a B plus average but was forced to reapply after his one-year medical leave of absence had lapsed by two months. He reapplied, submitting statements of fitness from physicians and psychiatrists, but was denied admission without explanation. The court ruled that the student was entitled to complete his education unless the institution could show specific circumstances preventing his continuation. Two years of matriculation in good standing created a property right to due process which was not forfeited by a one-year and two-month hiatus from matriculation.[24]

Although courts consider the nature of the property right protected by due process, they do not challenge the institution's right to apply reasonable academic standards nor do they require successful completion of preconditions for receipt of a degree. A graduate student pursuing his doctorate repeatedly failed his written examinations, but was granted review after alleging personal bias on the part of a faculty member. After a long and elaborate review and evaluation, including readers selected from outside the university, the graduate school determined that the student passed the written examinations and directed the department to administer the student's orals. Two years had elapsed in the appeal process, and the student sought to waive the orals and receive the degree. The court rejected any entitlement to a degree and refused to intervene in the circumstances. The court's holding emphasized that the student's refusal to sit for the orals constituted a deficiency in establishing a property right worthy of due process.[25]

Free Speech and Association.   In the public sector the first amendment provides some protection to individuals in the exercise of speech and association. In colleges and universities, these protections are often confused with notions of "academic freedom," but it is probably more accurate to characterize these rights as constitutional protections. Largely because United States courts have been reluctant to recognize an entitlement beyond the grant of free speech and association available to every citizen, few courts have recognized a right to "academic" freedom which transcends the protections already granted by the first amendment.

To protect the right of the employee to constitutionally guaranteed first amendment freedoms, courts have elaborated a series of tests which balance the rights of the individual against the state's interest as employer. Typically, a faculty member would be required to show that his or her conduct was constitutionally protected, and that it was the exercise of this constitutionally protected right that was the primary or motivating factor in the department chairperson's decision to deny some employment benefit or invoke some penalty. In the specific case of a faculty member, even when a faculty member could have been discharged for no reason whatever, with no constitutional right to a hearing on the administrative decision, he or she may establish a claim for reinstatement if the decision not to rehire was made on the basis of that faculty member's exercise of first amendment freedoms.

The application of free speech constitutional protections is illustrated in a case involving a nontenured teacher whose contract was not renewed following her sixth year of teaching in a junior college. The official reason for nonrenewal, "declining enrollment and poor evaluation of her work," was appropriate enough, but the faculty member introduced evidence that the real reason for nonrenewal was retaliation for her vigorous support of her husband's candidacy for the college board of regents and her efforts to promote a faculty association. The court noted that the department chairperson admitted advising the teacher to have her husband withdraw from the election, voiced objection to her activity on behalf of the teachers' association, and recommended nonrenewal to discipline the teacher for trying to create ill will and lack of cooperation with the administration. This evidence supported a jury verdict awarding damages after a finding that the teacher had not been rehired because of her exercise of constitutionally protected rights.[26]

In similar cases involving allegations that a faculty member was discharged for a constitutionally impermissible reason, courts have insisted that the plaintiff first establish that the conduct is constitutionally protected. A questionnaire soliciting the views of faculty on a broad range of subjects, some of which were related to evaluating administrative efficiency and effectiveness, has been held to be protected under the first amendment. When the university refused to review a nontenured teacher's contract solely because he helped construct and circulate the questionnaire, the court held that this refusal denied free speech and ordered reinstatement.[27] An avowed Marxist, openly critical of textbooks and politically active on behalf of the Progressive Labor Party, was reinstated by a federal court when it was determined that the administration's ostensible reason for nonrenewal, alleged student complaints, had never been discussed with the professor nor verified by the department chair. After finding that the teacher had never used his classroom to proselytize nor deviated from required curriculum, the court concluded that the teacher's nonrenewal was attributable to his exercise of free speech and held that the administration had acted in a constitutionally impermissible fashion.[28] In another case, an untenured faculty member's circulation of memoranda critical of university practices, characterized by a department chair as evidence of frustration and hostility, was sufficient to raise an inference that the teacher may have been denied renewal for his criticism of his employer. If the faculty member's criticism was the primary or motivating factor in the nonrenewal, then a claim of a denial of free speech would be substantiated.[29]

The department chairperson can withstand a charge of denying free speech and association if it can be shown that the employee could have been disciplined notwithstanding the exercise of constitutionally protected rights. It is permissible for a teacher to be denied salary increases when the actual basis for denial is unsatisfactory scholarship rather than public criticism of university projects.[30] Similarly, it would be considered reasonable for a chairperson to deny summer teaching and offer a relatively small salary increase to a professor in order that the lowest paid faculty members might be provided additional compensation as an inducement to keep highly competent but underpaid young faculty, despite allegations that the denial of salary increases and summer teaching was in retaliation for the professor's opposition to departmental policy.[31] In one instance, a faculty member who was not renewed after protesting a reassignment challenged the department chair's recommendation not to renew on the basis that his criticism of the chair's directives and the faculty member's reassignment was protected free speech. However, the record supported the testimony of the department chairperson that the decision not to renew had been reached some months before the teacher's protests and criticisms of the chairperson. The reviewing court concluded that the decision not to renew could not have been predicated on the faculty member's exercise of free speech, and upheld the nonrenewal.[32]

Given extraordinary circumstances, even the constitutional exercise of free speech will be balanced against the interests of protecting the campus from substantially disruptive or materially interfering conduct. While the difference between advocacy, which enjoys constitutional protection, and action, which may not be so protected, is difficult to assess, there are times when courts recognize the authority of the chairperson and the institution to act despite the potentially "chilling" effect on the exercise of free speech. An illustrative case involved a tenured assistant professor, dismissed for playing a prominent role in unauthorized protest activities. The professor contended that his dismissal was in retaliation for his exercise of free speech and assembly rights granted by the constitution. The facts were that the professor tried to stop a motorcade bringing officials to a campus ceremony, led student demonstrators in raucous catcalls to disrupt the ceremonies, and encouraged demonstrators to leave their seats and enter the stadium field, thus creating a danger of violent confrontation. The court upheld a finding that the professor's actions went beyond advocacy of ideas and that he engaged in a course of conduct which interfered and disrupted the regular operation of the school in a manner which left him outside the protection of the first amendment.[33]

Students, like faculty and staff, enjoy a constitutionally protected right to the reasonable exercise of free speech and association in the public higher education setting. The leading case on the subject is *Healy v. James*,[34] a decision in which the United States Supreme Court recognized that students may organize and demand recognition as a valid student group unless the institution's agents can show a compelling state interest that would overcome the constitutional right to freedom of association. The case arose when a local student group was denied recognition by a state college president because of the group's avowed political activism. While the president sought to deny recognition on the basis that similar student groups had interrupted classes and fermented disruption on other campuses, the court took notice that the students had promised to abide by reasonable campus restrictions on advocacy and action and disassociated themselves from the national organization (Students for a Democratic Society). Adopting the view that the students' right to speech and association was of paramount constitutional importance, the Court required that the student group be recognized in the absence of strong evidentiary proof that the students acting in concert could reasonably be predicted to substantially disrupt or materially interfere with the operation of the institution.

The department chairperson is more likely to be a student's advocate than a detractor when it comes to the rights of free speech and association. Universities and colleges have long been recognized by courts as institutions in which the free exchange of ideas is vital, and any actions that "chill" the right to expression are given close scrutiny by courts. It should be noted that a faculty committee had recommended college recognition for the student group in *Healy*, a recommendation that influenced the Court's decision to reverse the president's action denying recognition. The chairperson's principal obligation in such circumstances would be to insure that academic or disciplinary action taken by the department against a student or students is free of any hint that the institution sought to penalize the individual for the exercise of free speech or associational rights.

Discrimination

Congress has enacted several federal statutes designed to extend and elaborate the prohibitions against invidious discrimination contained in the equal protection clause of the fourteenth amendment. This plethora of federal statutory entitlements prohibits discrimination on the basis of race, sex, religion, age, national origin, and handicap in programs receiving federal financial assistance.[35] The laws protect employees and "participants in, or beneficiaries of" programs that receive federal financial assistance. Methods available for enforcement of these laws include federal agency reporting and regulatory standards, compliance reviews, affirmative action agreements, institutional self-regulation, and suits by private parties.

It may be small comfort to the department chairperson, but the legal standards applied to a proof of discriminatory practice remain consistent across most of these statutes. In the principal cases, the burden is on the party alleging discrimination to establish the existence of an intent to discriminate prohibited by law. The crucial issue for resolution of most allegations of discrimination remains a showing that the defendant was motivated by a discriminatory animus.

Generally, this discriminatory animus must be shown to have been overt. Evidence of an expressed intent to exclude a handicapped student or give preferential treatment to a male employee in relation to a female of equivalent skills and ability would be compelling for a court. While statistical proof of disparities between men and women and between blacks and whites relative to salaries, hiring practices, or admissions would contribute to a case for discrimination, the department chair can be most effective in negating a charge of discriminatory practice by scrupulously avoiding any overt action that might be characterized as exhibiting a discriminatory intent and by showing a willingness to investigate and intervene in situations where discrimination within the department is alleged.

This is not to suggest that federal law prohibits any form of discrimination. Courts recognize that it is the nature of the academic process to evaluate and discriminate on the basis of factors that relate reasonably to an institution's valid educational mission. It is for the department chair, in concert with colleagues and institutional representatives, to justify the standards that will be applied to that process of discrimination. Particularly where the discriminatory processes of the institution appear to have a substantial deleterious effect on members of an identifiable sex or race, however, the justification offered by the institution may be judicially required to go beyond a simple showing of a reasonable relationship, extending to a proof that the practice is necessary, essential, or compelled to realize valid institutional objectives.

Most cases alleging discrimination against students have involved the admission policies of the institution. Since admission policies may often include departmental criteria, the chairperson has a responsibility to insure that reasonable standards are applied. The department's authority to establish admission criteria is seldom challenged by the courts, but the established criteria or the way in which criteria are applied should avoid discrimination on the basis of race, sex, or national origin, nor should the criteria exclude "otherwise qualified handicapped individuals."

While courts have struck down admissions quotas based upon race, they have been quick to point out that race may be used as one of several factors which may be considered in insuring an institution's legitimate interest in a diverse student body. The celebrated decision of the United States Supreme Court in *Bakke vs. Regents of the University of California*[36] struck down a medical school admissions program which allocated a number of admission slots to minority and disadvantaged students through application to a separate minority admissions council. In declaring the university's policy discriminatory, the court did sanction an alternative strategy for the admission of minority and disadvantaged students by adopting the view that race could be given additional weight as one of a number of factors to be considered in an admissions policy applied uniformly to all applicants. The key element in any such admissions system would be a set of admissions criteria reasonably related to the institution's educational goals and uniformly applied to all students. The high court suggested that insuring a diverse student body would be an appropriate justification for a "weighted" admissions program.

In a more recent decision by the high court, *Southeastern Community College v. Davis*,[37] the justices refused to require that a hearing-impaired student be admitted to a clinically oriented educational program in nursing. The Court's rationale emphasized that provisions of the Rehabilitation Act of 1973 did not require the admission of a handicapped applicant where it could be demonstrated that the handicapping condition would require substantial modification of the curriculum of the college and that the likelihood of placing the handicapped graduate in a job related to the training offered was remote. In a similar decision by a federal court of appeals, an applicant to medical school who was denied admission due to a history of psychological disorders was unable to obtain court-ordered relief. Recognizing the *Davis* case as controlling, the court noted that the applicant's disability had not responded to treatment and would seriously impair her ability to practice medicine; consequently, she could not be considered an "otherwise qualified handicapped person" under the law.[38] While handicap may not normally be used to exclude the individual from an educational program, a department may consider handicap when substantial revision of the educational curriculum to accommodate the person would be necessary or when it is unlikely that the training could effectively be utilized by the handicapped individual in seeking later employment.

For the department chair in an institution receiving some form of federal financial support, the primary constitutional and statutory provisions governing issues of employment discrimination focus on the equal protection clause of the fourteenth amendment, Title VII of the Civil Rights Act of 1964,[39] and Title IX of the Education Amendments of 1972.[40] In recent years, faculty alleging a discriminatory animus on the part of colleges and universities have relied on the provisions of Title VII rather than on the rigorous proof of official intent to discriminate required under the fourteenth amendment or on the as yet unresolved standards to be used in Title IX proceedings.

Title VII of the Civil Rights Act of 1964 prohibits employment discrimination against individuals on the basis of race, color, religion, sex, or national origin. Employment practices resulting in disparate treatment of a person or class protected by the act constitute one form of discrimination; however, the employer can justify the discriminatory practice by articulating a legitimate, nondiscriminatory reason for the employment decision such as an occupational qualification bearing a reasonable relationship to the job in question. Legal controversy in most of these cases has alternated between the employee's burden to establish a prima facie case and the defendant employer's burden to articulate some legitimate nondiscriminatory reason for the allegedly discriminatory practice.

The principal case involving disparate treatment in higher education is *Board of Trustees of Keene State College v. Sweeney*,[41] a case which involved allegations of sex discrimination in the denial of promotion to a female associate professor. Dr. Sweeney was successful in establishing a prima facie case of sex discrimination by a statistical showing that the promotion of women at Keene was substantially confined to the lower ranks. The college sought to demonstrate that its decision not to promote Sweeney to full professor was based upon legitimate factors, citing insufficient service to the college, primarily in committee work, and personality considerations which allegedly interfered with her teaching and relationships with colleagues. The United States Supreme Court ruled that once the college articulated a legitimate nondiscriminatory basis for its adverse employment decision, the burden of proof shifted once again to Dr. Sweeney, who must establish that the articulated reason offered by the college was a subterfuge or pretext for a discriminatory practice.[42] Sweeney carried this burden. She demonstrated that her complaints concerning discrimination had largely been ignored by her department head and the administration and that the "personality variables" which were a basis for denial of promotion had not been introduced when she was granted tenure at the college two years previous to the initial denial of promotion. Sweeney had been promoted to full professor two years after the initial denial of promotion. Reasons cited for promotion by the department chair emphasized her committee service, excellence in teaching and community service, factors cited as negative performance indicators during the initial promotion decision, yet Dr. Sweeney's qualifications had not changed in any significant way in the interim between promotion decisions.

Disparate treatment in the *Sweeney* case was manifest in administrative indifference to the concerns of women faculty, statistically significant differences in hiring and promotion practices, inconsistent application of promotion and tenure criteria, and a preoccupation with trivial criticisms as a justification for the promotion decisions. In another case, disparate treatment was established by a showing that a female faculty member was evaluated for tenure using criteria different from those applied to male candidates and that personnel advisement practices of the department discriminated on the basis of sex.[43] Similarly, a department chairman's imposition of degree requirements not initially required nor reasonably related to a position as athletic administrator and coach were held to be evidence of a discriminatory animus.[44]

The college or university must demonstrate that its employment decision (whether related to hiring, promotion, award of tenure or benefits, demotion, or termination) is based upon legitimate factors and not on explicit or implicit considerations prohibited by Title VII. Such a proposition does not rule out peer review, nor does it hold that consideration of teaching, research, and service (essentially subjective criteria) are inappropriate to the employment decision. What is important is that there be no differential treatment in the employment decision-making process. Uniformity of procedures and criteria for evaluation are essential. The articulation of a rationale for employment decisions that bears a reasonable relationship to departmental, college, and institutional objectives is extremely important. The articulated basis for adverse employment decisions should relate to legitimate, performance-related reasons, which might include negative student evaluations, unwillingness to assume responsibility for teaching or service assignments, refusal to accept student advisees, and the like.

While statistical evidence of a disparity in hiring and promotion may be sufficient to establish a prima facie case of discrimination, it must often be coupled with overt discriminatory treatment in order to require a legal remedy. Evidence that a chairperson engaged in or condoned differential treatment of employees or made compliance with unwanted sexual overtures a condition of employment or advancement in employment would substantially strengthen a case of employment discrimination. Coupled with evidence of a statistical disparity, even the slightest manifestation of an overt discriminatory intent may be actionable. In these latter situations, evidence that the chairperson had difficulty cooperating with racially or sexually identifiable employee groups, ignored the employee's expressed concern for alleged discrimination, or demeaned an employee because of the employee's race or sex could be influential in proving discriminatory animus.

Another aspect of Title VII focuses on employment practices that are "fair in form, but discriminatory in operation." This provision most often calls into question employment practices that involve testing and evaluation. A plaintiff or class of plaintiffs must establish that the effect of an employment practice is to exclude a disproportionate number of those who represent a particular minority or sex. While nothing in Title VII prohibits the use of tests and rating or evaluation procedures, the act does require that these devices or mechanisms bear a valid relationship to job performance.

Title VII was not made applicable to education institutions until 1972. When coupled with the relatively recent use of evaluation systems and measurement devised in employment settings, it is not surprising that few cases involving the application of disparate impact standards have appeared in higher education. Two principal considerations relative to disparate impact standards are worthy of consideration by the chairperson. First, any blanket application of an evaluation instrument or test may disregard the obvious fact that teaching assignments and subject-matter specializations vary substantially. Some formal analysis of the faculty member's job, coupled with the development of a rating system that reasonably relates to the subject matter area involved are prerequisites to the validation of an evaluation instrument for faculty. Second, the development and use of a formal evaluation or rating instrument should be carefully devised to avoid cultural bias and should be subjected to preliminary validation before wide-scale implementation. Ultimately, the chairperson may be required to justify the necessity of such a test if it can be shown to have a disproportionate impact on a protected minority.

Common Law Liability

Once described as a "brooding omnipresence," the common law consists of duties and obligations as defined by court cases. While previous discussion has centered upon those duties of the department chair that relate to constitutional, statutory, or contractual provisions, there exists a judicially imposed set of standards which in some cases predate constitutional laws. These duties may loosely be categorized as falling under the law of torts, a category of civil wrongs not actionable under general principles of contract or constitutional law, but recognized as meriting relief under judge-made standards.

Two classes of tort law liability are particularly relevant to the department chair despite a paucity of actual case law involving the liability of the chairperson. First, there are those tort law cases involving the negligent breach of a duty of care. Typically, these cases involve a determination that the chairperson could have reasonably foreseen a danger to another person to whom the chair owed a duty of reasonable prudence. Second, there are those cases which involve an intentional or willful act, the injurious consequence of which could only have been intended by the person who so acted. The two forms of intentional tort of particular relevance to the department chairperson are defamation and fraudulent misrepresentation.

Negligence: Duty of Reasonable Prudence.   A department chairperson provides services to several constituencies (students, staff, faculty) which imply obligations beyond those recognized under contract or constitutional mandate. The provision of service implies a duty to act with reasonably prudent care in foreseeing possible dangers to the individual and in mitigating any potential risk of injury. The meaning to be attached to "reasonably prudent care" is subject to the evaluation of a lay jury or judge using the hindsight available only after an injury has occurred; hence a definitive statement of meaning is difficult. However, it is possible to extrapolate at least three common law duties that may apply to the department chairperson under certain circumstances.

Consistent with the chair's responsibility for scheduling and employee assignment, a duty to act with reasonably prudent care to *assign appropriate faculty or staff* can be inferred. A risk of injury might not be anticipated in a history class, but it could reasonably be foreseen if a chemistry lab program were over-enrolled and inadequately staffed. Under such circumstances, the failure to assign employees with the requisite training to provide proper instruction and adequate supervision might ultimately be construed as a breach of reasonably prudent care by the chairperson. The chair's duty to act with reasonable care in assigning faculty or staff would generally require consideration of the foreseeable dangers attendant to an activity and provision of a level of supervisory expertise consistent with reducing that risk to within acceptable limits.

As the administrator most often charged with implementing faculty and administrative policies, the role of chairperson may carry a *duty to promulgate reasonable rules for the safety of others*. If a danger can reasonably be foreseen, then action to mitigate the risk often takes the form of a rule or regulation to guide the conduct of others. The chair might be charged with a duty to promulgate and inform staff, faculty, and students of an office or building security policy designed to protect against intruders. Where previous acts of vandalism or assaults have occurred on the campus, the chair's negligence in failing to develop and disseminate a security policy might be construed as the proximate cause of any injury in which an assailant gained entrance and attacked a building occupant or invited guest.

In most circumstances the chairperson's obligation extends no further than insuring that proper notice of a safety hazard has been provided to others. The *duty to notify of dangerous conditions* may involve dissemination of the institution's policy on building security, arranging for posting of radiation warnings, or informing other administrative personnel of a building hazard which needs to be corrected in order to insure the safety of those who can reasonably be anticipated to use the facilities. Notice to others through memoranda or posting of conspicuous signs is generally considered to relieve the chair of responsibility in the event of a later injury and offers concrete evidence that the chairperson took positive steps to alleviate any foreseeable danger to persons or property. It is worth pointing out that a policy of *immediate* notification is a convenient method for transferring liability to another party, who, once aware of a dangerous condition, may be said to have assumed an obligation to act reasonably in relationship to the danger.

Intentional Torts: Defamation. A former faculty member sued for libel and slander based on a letter read at a faculty tenure committee meeting which accused the former professor, a married man, of having attempted to seduce a young woman who was a student in one of his classes. The author of the letter was unnamed, the accusations were unverified, and the professor was not afforded an opportunity to see or respond to the letter. Charging defamation, the professor alleged that his professional reputation and standing in the community had been injured, that the letter referred to a rumor that had been discredited months earlier, and that he was denied tenure as a result of the reading of the letter. These allegations constitute the basic elements of a defamation.[45]

A defamatory statement is one which injures reputation or standing in the community. The communication may be written (libel) or oral (slander). It has been considered defamatory to report that a faculty member drinks liquor excessively,[46] is a racist,[47] or has falsified credentials. An accusation that a professor has attempted to seduce a student, when coupled with a corresponding denial of an employment opportunity (promotion or tenure), has been recognized as a defamation.[48]

Department chairpersons are regularly compelled to appraise faculty and students. To protect against the risk of legal liability for defamation, two defenses are available. First, the chairperson may establish the truth of the allegation, coupling this proof with evidence that the alleged defamatory communication was made in good faith without malice or intent to injure. Since the burden of establishing that the defamation is true may prove too demanding, an alternative is to establish that the communication was qualifiedly privileged. This latter defense is conditioned upon the absence of malice in circumstances where the law recognizes that the communication was uttered in a reasonable manner, limited in scope, for a proper purpose.

Qualified privilege was the appropriate defense to a charge of racism when black medical students sought to grieve the allegedly discriminatory practices of a professor in the university's medical school. The professor contended that the students had libeled him when they filed a written grievance charging him with willful acts of discrimination. The court found that a qualified privilege existed since the students had acted in good faith to redress a grievance and had limited their communication to university officials who had an interest or duty to respond to such a concern.[49]

A defense of conditional privilege may be overcome by evidence that there was excessive publication of the defamation, or that the communicator acted out of malice. While the court in question recognized that a prima facie case of defamation had been established by the faculty member accused of seducing a student, the case was remanded for a determination of whether malice had prompted the reading of the letter. The court was unwilling to find an inference of malice in a showing that the letter was false, adopting the position that it may have been appropriate to provide information of a mere suspicion or a rumor when the communication is made to faculty who have a legitimate interest in the matter.[50]

Intentional Torts: Fraudulent Misrepresentation.   While a student or employee's reliance on statements made by university administrators may be a basis for a contractual obligation, there are few cases in which the agent's representations have been construed as attempts to fraudulently induce the individual to pay fees or perform services. Cases of fraudulent misrepresentation are rare, confined primarily to proprietary institutions in which inducements were considered gross and the defrauded person was unable or unlikely to be sufficiently informed to know better.[51]

Nevertheless, as recruiting practices and marketing strategies signaling increased competition for students and faculty proliferate, it is advisable to exercise caution in representing the program of an institution. Courts seem particularly protective of students who have been induced to enroll in programs that provide placement assistance bordering on a guarantee of employment or mislead students into believing they have special aptitude through the use of inappropriate testing and bogus courses. A public community college lost a jury verdict to a student who complained that he was induced to enroll in a one-year welding technology program through representations of faculty and administrators. These representations induced him to believe that certain classes would be taught, specific equipment would be available, and program completion would prepare the student for employment in the trade. The representations were false in that several courses were not offered, machines and materials were not available at the college, and the year-long course of study was not sufficient to prepare him adequately for employment as a welder. A jury verdict awarded $125,000 to the student, but it was overturned by the trial judge and appellate court on the grounds that Oregon statute law grants governmental immunity for state college officials in the exercise of their role as counselors.[52] (No such defense would be available to a private college official.)

Conclusion

It may be argued that this chapter raises more questions than it answers. For the conscientious department chairperson, the answer to what constitutes a "reasonably prudent person" or "good faith" behavior may appear ambiguous, vague, and uncertain. As in any situation involving the use of case study, the ability to generalize from individual cases is limited and the applicability of a particular standard may be subject to variables which remain undetermined. If the chair's quest is for certainty and unerring guidance, then an inquiry into the law of the case is nothing more than a modern quest for a yet to be discovered holy grail.

What the case law does convey is a sense of the issues that occupy courts in the administration of justice. Some sensitivity to how liability may be determined provides a conceptual framework for the department chairperson in assessing the risk of liability. The outcome of particular cases may provide an intuitive guide to factually related circumstances. There are no absolutes, but a sufficient number of qualified answers gives rise to a few guiding generalizations.

When risk of legal liability exists, consultation with legal counsel is often an appropriate preventive measure. Particularly when the institution employs in-house counsel or has a competent attorney on retainer for consultation, the chairperson is advised to seek advice before undertaking any action that would deny identifiable rights or result in injury. Often, the effort to obtain advice of counsel coupled with the chair's conscientious effort to act on that advice will serve as evidence of good faith and further limit the risk of individual liability.

The corollary to consultation with legal counsel is consultation with appropriate and knowledgeable colleagues. Appropriate colleagues are those whose formal status in the administrative hierarchy of the institution creates a measure of responsibility for supervision and articulation of the department chairperson's role. Knowledgeable colleagues are those with the experience and training to inform the chairperson on institutional objectives and traditional past practices or procedures. Observing existing standards, remaining consistent with past policies, and informing a superior of this intention prior to action is no guarantee against a lawsuit, but it is one of the best ways of making your problem the institution's problem and thus avoiding individual liability.

In addition to observing the traditional policy and procedures of the institution, the chairperson should strive to identify and implement those often illusive "best professional practice standards" related to the chairperson's role. The appropriate standard of conduct for a chairperson is a factual question which neither an attorney nor a judge can resolve without the aid of expert testimony or the opinion of other administratively competent academicians. In this sense the guidance upon which a chairperson might wish to rely in order to avoid legal liability is contained in those chapters of this text which suggest a best practice standard. While it might appear self-serving for the chairperson to explain his or her conduct on the basis of practices proposed by a treatise on the department chairperson, courts have shown extraordinarily deferential attitudes when a chair's action is consistent with recognized professional practice.

The law is replete with references to words of art such as "good faith," "reasonable prudence," and "fundamental fairness." These terms suggest a host of behavioral maxims with varying degrees of relevance to the chairperson. Principally, it behooves the chairperson to avoid acting precipitously in decision making. Whenever possible, allow time for the necessary information gathering before acting on a problem. Rather than rely upon a single account or hearsay, seek confirmation and corroboration of facts and circumstances surrounding an event. Consider the possible consequences of any course of action and always evaluate possible alternatives which may accomplish the same or similar results with less risk of harm. Document your efforts to resolve problems, always articulating the basis for your authority to act and relating your action to the valid objectives or statement of purposes adopted by the institution.

Another homily that rings true is the admonition to act with honesty and candor. Nothing is more damaging to a chair's defense in a legal action than evidence of duplicious behavior, deceit, or misrepresentation in the role of chairperson. Such a proof will frequently give rise to a presumption that the chair acted with a malicious intent to injure, creating potential for individual liability and the award of punitive damages against the chairperson. The chairperson who adopts a Machiavellian mode of operation may find that chicanery, coupled with political scheming and half-truths, will result in retribution that reaches deep into the individual's pocketbook.

Although it is important to avoid the allegation of malice, a level of candor which admits that an institutional duty has been breached is not appropriate. Just as a physician would never say "oops" in the operating room, never admit liability in your effort to be "fair" to all concerned. Liability can be decided by the court as an ultimate question relating facts to law. Being sorry an injurious situation occurs is perfectly permissible, but admitting responsibility for the injury is unwise. Send a card of condolence, but do not confess guilt.

A chairperson should always keep in mind that courts are first and foremost the guardians of process. A number of substantive legal questions have been addressed in this chapter, but it is the procedural defect in an institution's policy that most often creates the basis for litigation. In this regard, the role of chairperson is particularly critical. Courts will often abstain from hearing a case if the aggrieved party has failed to utilize the institution's procedures for redressing an alleged wrong. Courts will intervene when the chairperson has failed to follow appropriate procedural standards or has created a potential injury for which there is no institutional appeal.

In most institutions, the department chairperson is uniquely situated to resolve procedural problems and reduce the likelihood of litigation. By encouraging the adoption of procedures that provide notice, impartial hearing, and timely administrative appeal, the chair can facilitate institutional arrangements that provide for self-regulation and mitigate the potential effects of arbitrary action. In a conscientious and earnest effort to inform others of and comply with the institution's procedural standards, the chair demonstrates good faith and fair dealing.

Neither Solomon nor Moses, the chair is recognized by courts of law as the institutional agent who must ensure compliance with administrative procedures, defend the academic standards of the department, and act in a multitude of ways to realize the valid educational objectives of the institution. Few judicial decisions have ever held the chairperson individually accountable for errors committed in a genuine effort to realize any of these purposes. In most cases, courts have granted a presumption of reasonableness and substantial discretion to the chair in order to ensure a measure of autonomy and authority consistent with effective and efficient management. The chair who recognizes those limited constraints imposed by courts is most likely to continue to exercise the authority so essential to his or her role.

Questions

1. List all the documents that have been published by your institution which contain commitments to students and faculty and which could be considered contractual in nature and perhaps legally

binding. Examples: Catalogs, bulletins, faculty handbooks, schedules, program and recruitment brochures.

2. Obtain copies of the documents you have listed and try to identify portions that imply legal obligations on your part as a department chairperson at your institution.

3. As chairperson of your department, what situations might arise where you could be charged with behaving in an arbitrary and capricious manner? If you have witnessed actions of chairpersons that might be deemed arbitrary and capricious, please describe these actions.

4. In your own academic department, what special areas of possible liability exist for which you need to take special precautions? (For example, hazardous experiments in laboratories, field trips, and so forth.)

5. Each institution has its own policies for providing or not providing legal assistance in instances of litigation. What are the policies of your institution with regard to providing legal counsel or economic assistance to chairpersons? In what areas will your institution come to your aid or defense in a lawsuit, and in what areas may it refuse to assist you? If you do not know the answers to these questions, you should consult appropriate officials at your institution.

Notes

1. Paulsen v. Golden State University, 156 Cal. Rptr. 190 (Cal. Ct. App. 1979).

2. Shuffer v. Trustees of California State Univ., 136 Cal. Rptr. 527 (Cal. Ct. App. 1977).

3. Maitland v. Wayne State Univ., 257 N.W. 2d 195 (Mich. Ct. App. 1977).

4. Watson v. Univ. of South Alabama College of Medicine, 463 F. Supp. 720 (S. D. Ala. 1979).

5. Hines v. Rinker, 667 F.2d 699 (8th Cir. 1981).

6. Behrend v. State, 379 N.E. 2d 617 (Ohio Ct. App. 1977).

7. Olsson v. Bd. of Higher Education, 426 N.Y.S. 2d 248 (N.Y. 1980).

8. *See* Craft v. Board of Trustees of the Univ. of Illinois, 516 F. Supp. 1317 (E.D. Ill. 1981)

9. Sawyer v. Mercer, 594 S.W. 2d 696 (Tenn. 1980).

10. Daum v. New England College, 422 A.2d 1035 (N.H. 1980).

11. 408 U.S. 593 (1972).

12. *Id.* at 599.

13. Davis v. Oregon State Univ., 591 F.2d 493 (9th Cir. 1978) and Haimowitz v. Univ. of Nevada, 579 F.2d 526 (9th Cir. 1978).

14. 408 U.S. 564 (1972).

15. *Id.* at 573.

16. 643 F.2d 870 (1st Cir. 1981).

17. Swain v. Bd. of Trustees, 466 F. Supp. 120 (N.D. Ohio 1979).

18. Jacobs v. College of William and Mary, 495 F. Supp. 183 (E.D. Va. 1980).

19. Nzomo v. Vermont State Colleges, 385 A. 2d 1099 (Vt. 1978).

20. 98 S. Ct. 948 (1978).

21. Aubuchon v. Olsen, 467 F. Supp. 568 (E.D. Mo. 1979)

22. Ross v. Pennsylvania State University, 445 F. Supp. 147 (M.D. Pa. 1978).

23. Tedeschi v. Wagner College, 427 N.Y.S. 2d 760 (N.Y. 1980).

24. Evans v. West Virginia Bd. of Regents, 271 S.E. 2d 778 (W. Va. 1980).

25. Goldberg v. Bd. of Regents of the Univ. of Colorado, 603 P.28 974 (Colo. Ct. App. 1979).

26. Goss v. San Jacinto Junior College, 588 F.2d 96 (5th Cir. 1979).

27. Lindsey v. Board of Regents, 607 F.2d 672 (5th Cir. 1979).

28. Cooper v. Ross, 472 F. Supp. 802 (E.D. 1979).

29. Eichman v. Indiana State Univ. 597 F.2d 1104 (7th Cir. 1979).

30. Berry v. Battey, 666 F.2nd 1183 (8th Cir. 1981)

31. *See* Stone v. Board of Regents, 620 F.2d 526 (5th Cir. 1980).

32. Hillis v. Stephen F. Austin State Univ., 665 F.2d 547 (5th Cir. 1982).

33. Adamian v. Lombardi, 608 F.2d 1224 (9th Cir. 1979).

34. 408 U.S. 169 (1972).

35. See, for example, 42 U.S.C. § 2000e (Title VII), 29 U.S.C. § 794 (Rehabilitation Act of 1973), 29 U.S.C. § 623 (Age Discrimination in Employment), 29 U.S.C. § 206(d) (Equal Pay Act).

36. 438 U.S. 265 (1978).

37. 442 U.S. 397 (1979).

38. Doe v. New York Univ., 666 F.2d 761 (2nd Cir. 1981).

39. 42 U.S.C. § 2000e.

40. 42 U.S.C. § 1681.

41. 604 F. 2d 106 (1st Cir. 1979), *cert. denied*, 444 U.S. 1045 (1980).

42. Bd. of Trustees of Keene State College v. Sweeney, 439 U.S. 24 (1978).

43. Kunda v. Muhlenberg College, 621 F. 2d 532 (3rd Cir. 1980).

44. Hill v. Nettleton, 455 F. Supp. 514 (D. Colo. 1978).

45. *See* Stukuls v. State, 366 N. E. 2d 829 (N.Y. 1977).

46. Dauterman v. State-Record Co., 154 S.E. 2d 919 (S.C. 1967).

47. Scarpelli v. Jones, 626 P. 2d 785 (Kan. 1981).

48. Stukuls v. State, 366 N.E. 2d 829 (N.Y. 1977).

49. Scarpelli v. Jones, 626 P. 2d 785 (Kan. 1981).

50. Stukuls v. State, 366 N.E. 2d 829 (N.Y. 1977).

51. *See* Joyner v. Albert Merrill School, 411 N.Y.S. 2d 988 (N.Y. Civ. Ct. 1978).

52. Dizick v. Umpqua Comm'n College, 577 P.2d 534 (Or. Ct. App. 1978).

References

ALEXANDER, S. KERN, AND SOLOMON, ERWIN. *College and University Law* (2nd edition). Charlottesville, Virginia: The Michie Company (1979).

EDWARDS, HARRY T., AND NORDIN, VIRGINIA DAVIS. *Higher Education and the Law* (with Cumulative Supplement). Cambridge, Mass.: Harvard Institute for Educational Management (1979).

HOLLANDER, PATRICIA A. *Legal Handbook for Educators.* Boulder, Colo.: Westview Press (1978).

KAPLAN, W. A. *The Law of Higher Education.* San Francisco, Calif.: Jossey-Bass Publishers (1978 and 1981 Supplement).

YOUNG, D. PARKER (ed.). *The Yearbook of Higher Education Law.* Topeka, Kansas: National Organization on Legal Problems of Education (1980, 1981 editions).

13

Department Accomplishments and Aspirations: Setting Goals and Developing Action Plans

The chairperson is frequently asked to describe the department's activities and accomplishments as well as its aspirations. Such requests can come from the central administration of the institution, from foundations and agencies that allocate grants and contracts, from accrediting associations, and even from other departments. The task of reporting department activities with clarity and precision can be irksome, but it can pay handsome dividends if done well. Although no one wants to spend valuable time describing what seems to be obvious and well known, the chairperson should remember that accomplishments taken for granted within a department are not necessarily noted or publicized elsewhere. The allocation of resources may be based on reports or documents that reflect the chairperson's skill in articulating the importance of the department's accomplishments and aspirations. Also, academic departments are being asked to justify their own existence with increasing frequency. Those who dispense funds for higher education usually try to give them to departments or programs that evidence a sense of direction and purpose and that show the greatest potential for achievement. Many potentially valuable activities have never been begun because the chairperson lacked motivation or was unable to report adequately the department's activities and goals. This chapter will focus on ways in which the past activities and the future direction of a department may be described.

Reporting and Evaluating Department Accomplishments

A chairperson is usually required to prepare and submit a report of the past year's activities to the dean or the central administration of the institution. A department that maintains adequate records of activities and files these in an orderly manner can compile its reports much more efficiently than a department that must send its members scurrying about once a year to find information that might have been amassed routinely and easily. An honest and well-written annual report can help a department determine its strengths and weaknesses and may suggest measures for improvement. Furthermore, when a department has an updated report of its accomplishments, it can more easily state its desires and aspirations. Answers to the questions below are useful in evaluating a department, developing a good annual report, and creating a data base for planning future activities.

Information about Students

- How many students are majoring in the department's field?
- How many students are enrolled in each course?
- How many degrees in the department's field have been conferred?
- How many students have received scholarships, fellowships, assistantships, grants, and gifts?
- How many students have won honors?
- How many new majors have been accepted for the coming year?
- How many minority students have been recruited, trained, and graduated?
- How are the students performing in terms of grade point average and national tests? How does student performance compare with that of past years?
- What theses, dissertations, or research reports have been completed?
- What percentage of the total number of lower-division, upper-division, and graduate students in the university is majoring in this field? Is the percentage increasing, decreasing, or remaining relatively stable? What accounts for the change or stability?
- What evidence indicates that students are receiving the courses and information necessary for the next stage of their academic or employment careers? How many and what percentage of graduating seniors in the department were admitted to graduate school? To what graduate schools were they admitted? How many and what percentage of graduates were employed in jobs for which they have been trained?

- What other schools and colleges within the university are sending students to this department? Are other departments asking for service courses? Has a systematic needs survey been conducted? What are the past, present, and anticipated student demands for courses in this department? What are the past, present, and anticipated job market needs for graduates of department programs?

Information about Degree Programs, Course Offerings, and Curriculum

- What courses were offered at each level during each term of the year and how many students were enrolled in each course?
- How many full-time equivalent students were generated by the department at each level?
- Have course syllabi been updated?
- Have courses been changed by using other media or more individual modes of instruction?
- Have new courses been added? How do these courses contribute to the program?
- Do the courses in the program meet the present and anticipated needs of the students and the job market?
- Has the program been reviewed? If so, by whom? A university committee? A state agency? Has the program been reviewed for accreditation?

Information about Faculty Members and Their Achievements

- How many full-time faculty members are in the department?
- Have new faculty members been added to the department?
- How many faculty members are on leave or sabbatical?
- Have any faculty members resigned?
- Have any faculty members been dismissed? Have any contracts not been renewed?
- Do any faculty members have reduced workloads?
- How many faculty members are temporary or part-time? Is the number of part-time or temporary faculty members increasing?
- Which faculty members have received professional honors or teaching awards?
- Have any faculty members received grants and contracts for research, development, or training?
- What is the record of publications by faculty members?
- Have any faculty members received awards for research or publication?

- What service activities have faculty members performed? For the school or institution? For professional associations? For the community?

Information about Equipment, Facilities and Supplies

- Are resources adequate to meet demands?
- Do any programs not have adequate resources? Are additional resources needed?
- Has new or special equipment been acquired for the department?

Information about Department Governance and Administration

- How is the department structured? What are the roles of department committees? To what extent do students participate in department affairs?
- Have any new policies been implemented for the department's operation?
- How is travel money allocated within the department?
- Is the level of faculty morale satisfactory?
- What other important activities or actions should be mentioned?

Aside from the official information that is required by the central administration and the dean, each department must determine for itself what data it wishes to collect and maintain on a regular basis. Answers to the questions above illustrate the kinds of statements that appear in annual reports, though requirements for these statements differ from one institution to another. Departments can obtain much information from the university's institutional research office, which collects and stores much of this data.

Most chairpersons see the advantages of using the previous year's annual report as a guide when preparing a report for the current year. This procedure has the positive aspect of ensuring that the most important continuing commitments and activities are given proper attention. The activities of most departments have an organic continuity, and it is not surprising that annual reports repeat a large volume of information from the year before. Since the annual report summarizes and reviews the department's history for a given year, it can be used to compare the year's accomplishments with those of previous years, thereby giving some indication of the state of the department. The report can show whether the department is growing or shrinking, flourishing or floundering, but the comparison will be based only on the standard of what the department has done in the past.

A department may designate a particular year as a normative standard—for example, the year of the greatest number of undergraduate enrollments; the year of the highest graduate enrollments; the year of the highest number of degrees conferred; or the year of some significant achievement in research, publications, or grants awarded. The department can then compare its current activities with those of the normative year.

Alternatively, the chairperson might want to know how the department measures up to other departments. A department can be compared with departments representing the same discipline at other universities in the region or in the nation. The department may also be compared with other departments within the same institution or with a set of department standards derived by a professional or accrediting association.

When a department wishes to compare itself with departments of the same discipline at other institutions, nationally top-ranked departments are often used as the basis for comparison. First, the department might look at characteristics that are easily measurable, such as the number of faculty members, the number of students, admissions standards, funding per student, and so forth. One frequently cited standard of comparison is the student-faculty ratio, the assumption being that the smaller the ratio, the more contact a student will have with faculty members, resulting in education of higher quality. Another way of comparing accomplishments with those of other departments of the same discipline at other institutions is to count the number of times a particular author is cited in the professional literature. By noting the department affiliation of the most frequently cited scholars, the chairperson can gauge with moderate assurance the ranking of his or her own department in the areas of research, scholarship, and publication.

A crucial but questionable assumption underlying judgments based on this procedure is that the future creative activities of the faculty will be like those of the past. Furthermore, whereas this form of comparison is based on objective, quantifiable evidence, it is limited by focusing on research, which is only one of the three major functions of institutions of higher education. The national ranking of graduate programs also reflects this focus, but in a much broader way. Unfortunately, graduate school rankings are often based on judgments that are extremely subjective and that may at times be woefully out of date. Nevertheless, in the "professional status sweepstakes" some department chairpersons commonly make sweeping assertions based on these kinds of data. Chairpersons and faculty members have to guard against believing that their past productivity indicates something about the present; to confirm this assumption, they must examine the department's current activities.

Sometimes departments are grouped with others at the same institution. Usually a group includes departments from related or cognate disciplines, such as those in the social sciences. Since there are no uniform or national standards for grouping cognate departments, some interesting problems can result. For example, a history department, because of its concern with literary exposition, might find itself grouped with a humanities or language and literature group, or the same department, if it emphasizes historical data analysis, might be grouped with the traditional social science departments. Psychology departments have been grouped with the social sciences when social-psychological relations were most important, with the biological sciences when the emphasis was on animal studies and experiments, and occasionally with the health sciences area when a clinical program was preeminent. Some departments may find that they are being compared with other departments in their college or university with whom they feel they have very little in common. Most of these groupings are for administrative convenience in monitoring and controlling budgets and expenditures and analyzing cost data. The chairperson who is required to respond to comparisons of this kind needs as much knowledge as possible about the other departments in the group in order to defend the interests of his or her department.

A department may be part of a discipline that, through its professional association, has developed a set of normative standards by which a department can evaluate itself. Some professional associations conduct evaluations using such standards when preparing to credential degree programs. These standards frequently specify such details as the percentage of the faculty that should possess the doctorate and the minimum number of faculty members needed to set up and maintain a bachelor's degree program. The existence of normative standards usually indicates a high degree of professional consensus on the most valued characteristics in that discipline, the activities considered appropriate within it, and the quality of education and accomplishments expected of students enrolling in and graduating from programs within it. Departments that aspire to meet minimum standards within the discipline tend to look to the professional association's guidelines; departments that are interested in meeting or exceeding the accomplishments of the top-ranked departments in the discipline tend to compare themselves with those departments.

Most forms of comparison mentioned above have a growth bias built into them; that is, they incorporate an assumption that progress toward some desirable end or level of achievement is demonstrable by continued growth and expansion. In today's world the potential for growth appears to be limited; the growth rate has slowed and, in many cases, is in decline. Many departments aspire to maintain their level of accomplishments despite declining resources, but such aspirations are difficult to achieve.

Describing Department Aspirations

An interesting question sometimes raised in academic circles concerns comparing the department not with other departments but with its own ideas of what it ought to be doing. How do the department's activities measure up to the purposes and aspirations of the university and the department? A department cannot compare deeds with aspirations unless it knows to what it aspires. Aspirations can be formally stated in writing or can exist only in the minds of the chairperson and the faculty. A written statement of purpose has certain advantages in maintaining stability and continuity as the department changes. Formulating such a statement also helps department members articulate their feelings about their proper roles and functions in the framework of the college or the institution. Ordinarily, such a statement is called a *mission statement*.

The term *mission statement* may seem a mildly absurd way to categorize an expression of department aspirations; for some persons the word *mission* has quasi-military or religious connotations. Nevertheless, those who control the purse strings, especially administrators and granting agencies, look for and expect to find mission statements in the proposals and requests they read and review. Stroking the hand that feeds you is hardly an intellectual justification for a mission statement, but the case can be argued on other grounds—for example, the need for a broad, covering statement of fundamental purpose. A hallmark of any intelligent activity, especially intellectual activity, is that the participants know what they are about. It is not unreasonable to expect a department to have a sense of what it is doing and where it is going. The mission statement serves as the foundation on which the department builds and justifies the grounds for its existence within the university. A department should forthrightly state its professional aspirations before making final commitments for an academic year. Then if it truly wants to take responsibility for shaping its professional destiny, it will, at the end of the academic year, compare its achievements with earlier aspirations.

Mission statements typically contain both abstract and concrete elements, which may range from the grandiose to the specific. They often contain ideological components representing widely held beliefs about the value of a college education, and they include societal as well as professional aspirations. The idealistic components of the mission statement have strong roots in American culture and continue to be affirmed, despite the odds against their being achieved. The mission statement is often based on two assumptions: that progress is an incremental movement toward some high aim and that the aim will not actually be achieved.

Many departments write their own mission statements, but not all do. Mission statements can be prepared by planning officials, external consultants, legislative committees, administrators, and, of course, faculty committees. Many mission statements have a formal aura about them; they often appear in master plan documents, budget request documents, long-range plans, and development grant applications. Mission statements often contain information and data that serve as guides for making appropriate decisions about a department's commitments. Often the statement about the department that appears in the university catalog stands as a mission statement. The chairperson, in conjunction with a faculty committee, should conduct an annual review of the mission statement and bring it up to date, if necessary. Systematic redefinition of the department's mission is appropriate at certain times—for example, after the departure of senior faculty members, when curricular changes are called for, and when resources become so scarce that the department's historic mission cannot be achieved. Listed below are some central characteristics of a good mission statement. Each characteristic is followed by an excerpt from a college or university catalog, but none of the excerpts is a complete mission statement in itself.

- A mission statement clearly identifies the department's overall purpose.

  The mission of the department is to train professionals who are capable of doing research in the methodology of biostatistics and to apply their statistical and quantitative knowledge to the solution of problems encountered in the community health field. [A biostatistics department]

- A mission statement describes the scope and character of the teaching, research, and service activities of the department. It identifies the persons or groups that the department serves, tells how it serves them, and describes the results of the service.

  ... to provide undergraduate instruction in physics for physics majors and to prepare elementary and secondary preservice teachers to meet state certification requirements. [A physics department]

  ... research is focused primarily on the pulmonary and cardiovascular system and the effects of environmental agents on human and animal health. [A physiology department]

... meets the needs of commercial fishermen in the southeast by providing extension services. [A fisheries department]

- A mission statement indicates the general direction in which the department is moving and furnishes a frame of reference from which department goals may be derived.

... teaches administrators and research workers to understand how to take advantage of modern computers in their work. [A computer science department]

- A mission statement should describe any resources or activities that distinguish the department from others and should emphasize any unique qualities the department may have.

... offers programs in bilingual-bicultural education, with special emphasis in Greek and Hispanic studies. [A foreign language department]

Chairpersons should beware of mission statements that are too broad and thus fail to show how the department differs from other departments. Other mission statements are too narrow and describe activities in too much detail. Following are two examples of complete mission statements based on actual statements found in university catalogs. The first is from a behavioral science department in a school of public health:

The Department of Behavioral Sciences is concerned with the application of social science theory, methodology, and empirical findings to the study of health and illness. The department serves as a resource to the School by providing the basis for systematic consideration and study of the social and cultural aspects of health problems and theories from the disciplines of sociology, anthropology, social psychology, and political science. Departmental students are prepared primarily for careers in research and teaching. The central focus of the department is in major areas of medical sociology and anthropology, including: individual motivation in health behavior; sociocultural factors in disease; health organizations and professions; comparative healing systems; and comparative sociopolitical contexts of public health.

The next mission statement is from an English department in an urban university:

The Department of English primarily serves the individual undergraduate student, the academic community, and society in general. The department seeks to develop the students' reading comprehension and writing skills in order to help insure maximum realization of their potential. The faculty hopes to develop understanding of the humanistic heritage and at the same time to stimulate the students' imagination and sense of joy in life by familiarizing them with British and American literature and with other literatures which have contributed to the culture. Courses are designed to foster creativity, and the department offers specific courses for students with identified creative gifts. The department attempts to teach the fundamentals of research; to stimulate the use of scholarly methods and attitudes throughout its programs; and to encourage the individual scholarship of its members. Through the discharge of the responsibilities described above, the Department of English strives to prepare students for such professions as teaching, law, and medicine, and for an individually enriched and socially productive life.

These examples are not perfect. A mission statement that meets the criteria already discussed is difficult to write. Nevertheless, each statement attempts to describe the particular department in a way that shows its special characteristics. The first of the two statements is more precise and specific than the other, perhaps because of the nature of the discipline.

Departments should have statements of purpose for the reasons already described. Many departments that have such statements prefer to call them *goals* rather than *missions*. What they are called is relatively unimportant compared with the substance of the statements. This chapter suggests a progression of specificity of aims, using the terms *mission, goal,* and *objective* to delineate increasing specificity. Nevertheless, there are numerous nomenclatures for the different levels of specificity and the ways in which they may be elaborated. One purpose of this chapter is to discuss and clarify this conceptualization. The vocabulary used here should not necessarily be considered superior to others; it is simply one that is widely used.

Having discussed mission, we can move on to the next higher level of specificity—goals. A goal has a specified or implied end, whereas missions are continuous. This is not to say that all goal statements must indicate the period of time within which they must be achieved. Goals may be short-term or long-term, but they must be realizable sooner or later; the department ought to be able to tell when a goal has been accomplished. To predict when some goals will be reached is sometimes difficult. In such instances, intermediate goals may be set in order to help develop plans for achieving the goals.

In addition to specifying a certain end, goal statements have other characteristics: they represent a logical extension of the mission statement; they are oriented toward specific results; they are explicit; and they are supported by a series of objectives. A *goal*, therefore, is a statement of intention to achieve a specified result that is compatible with the mission or purpose of the department and institution. It is the end toward which one or more activities are aimed. An *objective* is a statement of intention to achieve a specified result, which, when achieved, will contribute to the realization of the goal.

These definitions are best understood as stipulations. *Mission* and *goal* can be interchanged without doing violence to the language, and indeed some persons interchange these terms while others interchange the terms *goals* and *objectives*. So goals as well as mission represent the department's aspirations. Goals are simply more specific and action-oriented expressions of the results that the department hopes to achieve. Some departments feel that goals must be expressed in behavioral terms; that is to say, the goal should contain a specific time frame and indicators of achievement so that at the end of the specified time the department can easily assess whether the goal has been achieved. Other departments do not insist on such a high degree of quantification is goal statements. Certainly some areas of endeavor are more amenable to behaviorally stated goals than others.

Can a department develop goals that are not immediately related to its academic or educational mission? If academic goals are to be realized, the department must pay attention to its resources and plan to use them effectively. In many cases, departments need to set goals that deal with the acquisition and management of resources. A distinction may therefore be made between what are sometimes called *primary goals* and *support goals*. Primary goals are directly related to educational mission—i.e., the familiar triad of teaching, research, and service. Support goals are advocated not for themselves but for establishing conditions or situations whereby the primary goals can be achieved. Support goals within the department are concerned with the staff, students, physical facilities, department planning and management, record keeping and information gathering, and procurement of funding or support. For example, the goal of formulating department goals is a support goal that should lead to improvements in teaching, research, and service.

Following are examples of primary and support goals:

To identify entering freshmen with deficiencies in reading and writing skills and to improve those basic skills. [Primary goal, English department]

To produce graduates who will be eligible for admission to medical school. [Primary teaching goal, biology department]

To maintain the department's level of publications in scholarly journals held during the past three-year period. [Primary research goal, any department]

To provide advice and assistance to teacher education centers throughout the state. [Primary service goal, education department]

To establish an internship program for seniors in law enforcement. [Primary goal, criminology department]

To involve faculty in a faculty development program. [Support goal, any department]

To establish a system of department record keeping consistent with university policy. [Support goal, any department]

To obtain additional laboratory equipment. [Support goal, any science department]

Why should a department have goals? At a time when accountability is repeatedly used as a warning and a threat, department members should not only have a statement of their purpose but should be able to point to a set of goals that they expect to achieve. They should be able to express the professional aspirations of the department in ways that will allow those aspirations to be compared with actual accomplishments. The chairperson of a department that has stated its goals clearly and realistically and that has indeed achieved its goals within a certain period of time can make a good case for a fair slice of the economic pie that the dean keeps in the cupboard. Aside from the practical advantage of being able to say, "We said we would accomplish these things, and we have done so," goal setting serves another, more theoretical, purpose: it helps academicians not only know their purposes but also clarify their ideas about how those purposes can be fulfilled.

As mentioned earlier, goals must be realistic and attainable. The chairperson should try to avoid ill-conceived or badly stated goals. Following is a list of reasons that many goals cannot be realized or are flawed in other ways:

- Goals may be too specific, allowing for too little flexibility to take advantage of unforeseen opportunities or to deviate from a narrow path that may become blocked.
- Goals may be too broad or abstract, to the extent that the faculty cannot agree on what constitutes achievement.
- Goals may be too simple and trivial, to the point that even when attained they have little professional or political significance.
- Goals may be too grandiose to be attained given the existing faculty, student body, or resources.
- Goals may be too optimistic given the time or administrative support available.
- Goals may be overambitious in relation to the attitudes of the administration, the public, or the legislature.
- Goals may be too pessimistic or underambitious and may not reflect adequately the abilities and aspirations of the faculty.
- Goals may be contradictory and conflicting. When goals contributed by individual faculty members are not reviewed for consistency or realism by the chairperson or a faculty committee, the resulting set of goals may be contradictory.
- Goals may lack sufficient support from the faculty. If a chairperson develops a set of goals without faculty input and consensus, the goals may not be taken seriously or may be resisted or opposed.

The process whereby a department arrives at its goals is intimately related to the quality of the goals produced. An academic department is made up of persons who are likely to vary considerably in age, personality, style, and ability. Despite the stereotype of "the professor," anyone with academic experience knows that department members are rarely peas in a pod. Whereas it might be easier to get consistent and coherent department goals from a group of like-minded persons, the diversity of the faculty is probably a healthy thing, for a diverse faculty will have complementary skills. The problem the chairperson faces is how to derive a set of compatible expectations from persons whose styles and abilities differ. An unsatisfactory solution to the problem is to construct a department mold or procrustean bed that all members must fit. Such an approach is bound to stifle talent, creativity, and individuality.

Team building is a term much used in industrial management. Such language may rub academicians the wrong way, but the idea behind it is sound. The team metaphor may be applied to a university department; individuals with diverse strengths and talents may share a group of common expectations and aspirations, especially when those expectations enhance the careers of the individuals who make up the department. Although each faculty member rightly possesses individual goals, a department should be able to arrive at a set of expectations that are compatible and shared. Persons who have played on a team or in an orchestra know that it is possible to develop a solidarity of purpose that is very satisfying. A department that can come to agreement on goals can also develop esprit de corps and a sense of mutual support and interdependence. A chairperson can contribute to the well-being of the department by bringing its members together at appropriate times to review and clarify the aspirations they share for the department.

How can the chairperson encourage the department to develop its goals? No matter how appropriate the goals may be for a given department, they cannot be easily implemented without the support of the majority of the faculty. The chairperson, of course, should have some ideas concerning the direction the department might take, and he or she should present those ideas tactfully to avoid having them rejected out of hand. The chairperson's leadership style will influence the way the department arrives at its goals. Some alternative approaches to goal setting are listed below.

- The chairperson can prepare statements of department goals and objectives and circulate them to the faculty to stimulate discussion and input.
- The department chairperson can ask a faculty committee to discuss and recommend appropriate goals and objectives for formal review by the entire department faculty.

- The department can form a composite of the individual goals of the department faculty and make this composite the basic department statement of goals and objectives.
- The department can survey similar departments that have already established legitimate goals and objectives.
- The department can employ a consultant or a representative from an accrediting agency to review the department's strengths and support appropriate goals and objectives.

Whichever approach to goal setting is followed, the goals that the faculty ultimately adopts must be ranked. Thus, the faculty assigns priorities to its goals. This step is critical because it provides a guide for others who might attempt to evaluate the department. A priority list is also important when the faculty wants to reward members who make significant contributions toward achieving high-priority department goals. The department priority rankings of goals could be weighted and included in the annual faculty evaluation.

The department next needs to consider what must be accomplished in order to approach its goals. Activities and outcomes necessary to move toward a given goal should be specified. A statement that indicates an outcome and stipulates the activity leading to it can be called an *objective*. To speak of objectives is to speak of the concrete, the observable, the knowable. Although missions and some goals may be ambiguous and imprecise, objectives generally specify some observable product or result.

Objectives are, of course, closely related to the goals from which they are derived. For this reason, an objective taken out of context may be indistinguishable from a goal statement. Though some objectives in other contexts might constitute goals, objectives generally are more concerned with short-term effects than are goals and usually specify a time by which the result will be accomplished. Well-stated objectives have these characteristics:

- They are consistent with the goals from which they are derived.
- They are oriented toward specific outcomes.
- They identify activities by which the outcome or result is to be achieved.
- They are measurable in some way.
- They suggest an expected qualitative or quantitative change or accomplishment.
- They stipulate a time by which the result will be achieved.

As an example, let us reconsider the goal of identifying the freshmen whose English skills were deficient and improving those skills (see page 283). According to our criteria, the objectives derived from this goal should specify steps that must be taken to identify the freshmen and the measure of achievement or improvement that would be considered satisfactory by a certain time. Two objectives for this goal might be (1) administering and scoring Test ABC for all freshmen by October 30 and (2) raising the average score of deficient freshmen on Test ABC to the national norm of 540 by May 30.

Objectives that focus exclusively on results are often called *outcome statements.* The second objective could be converted to an outcome statement by rewording it in the following manner: "By May 30, 87 percent of all freshmen will score at least 540 on Test ABC."

Some faculty members resist stating objectives in quantitative terms because the numbers and percentages that are so often a part of those statements appear to be arbitrary. In some cases, such objections are justified. Why specify 87 percent instead of 83 percent or 90 percent or any other percent, for that matter? There may well be no reason for designating 87 percent, except that on the basis of past experience it seems to be an attainable percentage. Good judgment and common sense are needed when stating measurable outcomes.

Outcome statements contrast with *activity statements*, which typically describe what the students, faculty and staff members, and others *do.* Activity statements that are not linked to outcomes do not translate into good statements of objectives. Nevertheless, activity statements are frequently used as objectives, because the activities of educational processes are more readily observable than the outcomes. To observe a faculty member teaching and to specify what, where, and for how long he teaches is easy; to measure the long-term effects of that teaching is not so easy. When educational objectives are stated primarily as activities, too little emphasis is placed on educational outcomes. Although clearly specifying educational outcomes is an extremely difficult task, and in some disciplines may be well nigh impossible, faculty discussion of desired outcomes might be beneficial for all. The faculty should be able to distinguish between activities and outcomes and, wherever possible, should link outcomes with activities when formulating department objectives.

One further refinement of the planning sequence—mission, goals, and objectives—should be mentioned. In implementing an objective, list discrete tasks that must be accomplished. Developing a timetable for the completion of each task is sometimes useful. The term *milestone* is used to designate a task and the time by which it will be finished. Most granting agencies require that proposals for the funding of projects include a timetable with the designated milestones. A task that includes an activity, an outcome, and a timetable is a sort of mini-objective that is completed on the way to implementing the larger objective. In the same way, the completion of an objective contributes to the attainment of a goal. Objectives, then, can sometimes be seen as intermediate goals. For example, if one of a department's goals is to increase a specific research activity, an intermediate goal might be to obtain a grant for that activity. In another department, obtaining a grant might be considered an objective, a task, or even a goal. Whether a statement of department aims or intentions is called a task, an objective, or a goal does not matter as much as whether those statements can be expressed in a logical, orderly, and precise manner.

Developing Action Plans

The hierarchy of missions, goals, objectives, and tasks has been covered in some detail, but we have not discussed the process by which a department selects appropriate means for reaching goals. The careful consideration of how goals and objectives may best be reached is called *action planning*.

A hypothetical instance of action planning can be built around the previously mentioned example of the English department in an urban university. One department goal, which was related to its mission statement, was "to identify entering freshmen with deficiencies in reading and writing skills and to improve those basic skills." This goal, one of many recommended by a faculty committee appointed by the chairperson, was formulated in response to the faculty's general feeling that many incoming students were failing because they could not handle the material assigned. Some essay examinations did not contain a single sentence that was grammatically correct.

Since there was general agreement that freshman reading and writing skills needed improvement, a committee was appointed to develop an action plan for implementing the goal. The committee first prepared a clear statement of the department's status as it related to the goal. The department had a well-qualified, hard-working faculty that had no special training in remedial work. Some older faculty members were shocked at the idea that a university should concern itself with ill-prepared students and felt that the problem could be solved by raising admissions standards. Other faculty members were actively interested in working closely with students whose skills needed improvement.

The committee then prepared a list of alternative strategies and tried to specify for each strategy objectives and tasks that might help attain the goal. In this instance, three possible means to the same end were discussed. The first alternative was a set of objectives and tasks that focused on establishing a reading laboratory, with equipment acquired through external funding. The second alternative involved using prepackaged, pretested materials from the university's resource center. The third strategy suggested using undergraduates in a program of intensive tutoring. The committee leaned toward the idea of a reading laboratory but abandoned that notion when the department failed in its initial attempts to get a laboratory funded. The second strategy, using prepackaged materials, was chosen because it seemed a better way of doing things given the available data.   A minority of the faculty members preferred the tutoring plan, but they could not convince their colleagues that it was feasible.

The next step in preparing the action plan was to describe in detail the objectives and tasks that, using prepackaged materials, would help reach the goal and to specify a means of evaluating whether the action plan had been successful. The project would be considered successful if one-third of the participants brought their skills up to the average level of entering freshmen based on national norms. The goal suggested two objectives: (1) to administer and score a test for all freshmen and (2) to take them through a program that would improve their performance.

With the help of colleagues in the education department, the faculty of the English department selected a standardized test, specified a plan for administering and scoring it, and drafted letters explaining the program to the incoming freshmen. The second objective was also broken down into discrete activities and thoroughly described. The department decided to hire two graduate students to supervise the distribution and use of the prepackaged remedial materials. The students also were to monitor the progress of the freshmen students in the program and keep records. At the end of two quarters, the students would be re-tested. Those whose reading skills had improved would transfer to freshman English. Those who did not improve to the specified point would continue in the program. Thirty percent of the students who participated in the program made significant gains and entered the freshman course. In this case, the program proved moderately successful.

This case has been presented to give an idea of what action planning is like. The steps of action planning can be briefly summarized as follows:

1. Start with a clear statement of a desired goal.
2. Describe the department's status as it relates to the goal—i.e., show in a quantifiable way the relationship between where the department is now and where it wants to be.
3. List alternative courses of action that might be a means to achieving the goal or objective.
4. Analyze each alternative course of action, listing the tasks required and attempting to anticipate the consequences. Specify a means of evaluating the success of the action plans.
5. Rank the courses of action in preferred order of implementation.

6. Begin to implement the top-ranked course of action. Be prepared to shift to the next-highest ranked course of action if serious problems arise.

Some administrators use a simple technique to evaluate suggested courses of action for achieving a desired goal. Each course of action is rated in terms of (1) potential for achieving the goal, (2) cost, and (3) feasibility. The rating scale can be a simple one, such as "high," "medium," or "low."

Figure 13.1 shows a table that a chairperson developed to help him choose among alternative courses of action.

Another hypothetical case may be helpful in pointing out the relationships among the statement of mission or purpose, the annual report, goals, objectives, tasks, and action plans. The department, a small physics department, provides the following statement for the college catalogue:

> The mission of the department is to provide undergraduate instruction in physics for physics majors and for elementary and secondary preservice teachers, and to fulfill some of the general education needs of the university in the physical sciences. In addition, the department shall contribute to new knowledge in physics and physics education and shall serve local and regional needs in this area through programs for in-service teachers.

The department's annual report shows that it has six faculty members, adequate office space, good facilities for instruction, and an annual budget of around $200,000. The department's assets include well-equipped teaching laboratories, two young faculty members who are especially enthusiastic and recognized as excellent teachers, and other faculty members who have good theoretical capabilities in the field of physics. The report recognizes that the department members generally lack expertise and proven performance in experimental physics.

State law requires that faculty members teach a minimum of twelve hours per week or the equivalent, and the state college system has set

FIGURE 13.1. Evaluation and selection of alternative courses of action

PROPOSED ACTIVITY OR ACTION	Potential for Achieving Goal	Cost	Feasibility
#1	High	Low	Medium
#2	High	High	Medium
#3	Low	Low	High

minimum class size at twelve students. No significant college growth is anticipated. The need for general education will remain constant. The number of physics majors is expected to remain the same—i.e., about forty students. The need for elementary and secondary teachers is expected to remain constant or rise slightly, in contrast to the decline in teachers needed in other areas. In addition, there is a continuing need to upgrade the training of general science and physics teachers in the large regional school system.

Although this statement of the department's status is minimal, it will serve the purposes of this example. A greatly expanded information base would be essential for effective department planning and goal setting; for example, data about enrollment levels, number of majors, number of course offerings, faculty assignment patterns, and patterns of financial expenditures should be recorded over a period of several years. The resulting department "fact book" would be useful for planning and goal setting, preparing annual reports, writing grant proposals, justifying budget requests, and simplifying many of the department chairperson's other tasks.

At the urging of the chairperson, the physics department developed the following goals: (1) to increase the current level of faculty research and publications; (2) to train elementary education majors in physical science topics that are part of the public school curriculum; (3) to plan and implement a summer workshop for high school teachers; and (4) to improve the writing skills of undergraduate physics majors. Following are the goals with their objectives and tasks:

Goal 1: To increase the current level of faculty research and publications

Objective 1: Increase the amount of faculty time assigned to research

Task: Increase each faculty member's research assignment by 5 percent per year, to a level of at least 35 percent per faculty member

Task: To compensate for increased research assignments, increase class size to reduce the number of classes to be taught

Objective 2: Seek and acquire funding for research projects from external sources

Task: Conduct a proposal writing seminar in fall quarter

Task: Supply clerical and technical assistance for proposal writing

Task: Write grant proposals to potential donors

Objective 3: Publish six articles in refereed journals over the next two years

Task: Establish a biweekly research seminar for faculty members to discuss ideas and projects

Task: Discuss and, if feasible, implement a reward structure for publications

> *Task:* Provide clerical and technical assistance for research projects

Goal 2: To train elementary education majors in physical science topics that are part of the public school curriculum

> *Objective 1:* Revise curriculum of general physics course to suit needs of education majors
>
> *Task:* Meet with science supervisors in public school system to outline topics emphasized in curriculum —October 1
>
> *Task:* Alter course curriculum to encompass desired change—December 1
>
> *Objective 2:* Teach and evaluate revised course
>
> *Task:* Teach revised course—February 1–June 15
>
> *Task:* Administer and score department evaluation forms—June 15–20

Goal 3: To plan and implement a summer workshop for high school teachers

> *Objective 1:* Prepare list of desired subjects for high school teachers
>
> *Task:* Appoint committee to study National Science Foundation recommendations—September 15
>
> *Task:* Meet with school board and curriculum supervisor to establish needs—October 15
>
> *Objective 2:* Plan and publicize new program
>
> *Task:* Develop curriculum and select faculty—November 15
>
> *Task:* Advertise workshop in educational journals and newspapers—December onward
>
> *Objective 3:* Conduct and evaluate summer workshop
>
> *Task:* Teach workshop as planned—July 1–July 26
>
> *Task:* Prepare and administer questionnaire to evaluate program—July 25
>
> *Task:* Prepare and administer follow-up questionnaire—December 1

Goal 4: To improve the writing skills of undergraduate physics majors

> *Objective 1:* Plan writing seminar for fall quarter
>
> *Task:* Contact English department and establish interdepartment committee—January 1
>
> *Task:* Develop course in technical writing—March 15
>
> *Objective 2:* Teach and evaluate writing seminar
>
> *Task:* Announce course offering for majors, encourage students to register—September of next year
>
> *Task:* Read and evaluate students' efforts

Although the goals, objectives, and tasks are presented here in outline form, the outlines themselves are the result of action planning. After the physics department established its four goals, the faculty met to plan how these goals could best be implemented. Each goal became

TASKS	TIMETABLE	ESTIMATED COST
1. Review experience of other institutions using a computerized system	Sept. 1– Oct. 1	$600 (faculty time and travel)
2. Develop baseline data of test scores of students taking the course by the conventional method	Sept. 1– June 1	$500 (faculty time, student assistant time, data analysis)
3. Write programs needed to implement the system	Sept. 1– Jan. 1	$6500 (faculty time, programmer time, computer charges)
4. Test programs	Jan. 1– Mar. 1	$2500 (faculty time, computer time)
5. Evaluate achievement of students in computer-assisted programs	Mar. 1– Sept. 1	$500 (faculty time, data analysis)

FIGURE 13.2.   List of tasks, timetable, and estimated cost

the focus of an action plan that encompassed the steps described earlier. The objectives and tasks were formulated after the department members considered a variety of possible ways of achieving the goals. For example, when discussing the revision of the course for education majors, the faculty members spent a great deal of time and effort considering the possibility of converting the course to self-paced instruction using the computer. The action plan called for a series of tasks (see figure 13.2).

According to the calculations presented in figure 13.2, the cost of implementing the program would have been more than $10,000. The results of the first task, however, revealed that computer-assisted instruction worked better with students who were already highly motivated than with students who had limited mathematical and scientific interests and skills. The goal of a computer-assisted course was abandoned before much money was spent. The experience of other institutions was sufficient to convince the chairperson and the faculty that the contemplated innovation was not likely to succeed. Instead, the department decided to identify what subjects the schools wanted their prospective teachers to know. Then the chairperson assigned the department's most dynamic teacher to the course. The course requirements were tailored to the needs and abilities of nonmajors, and the evaluation showed its popularity. Some faculty members, however, thought that the new course was not quite rigorous enough, and the debate about its merits continues.

The idea to computerize the course, which was subsequently abandoned, actually came from the action planning that was undertaken while the first goal—to increase the level of research and number of publications—was being considered. Here the department was reacting to the fact that a member's application for promotion was rejected on the grounds of insufficient publications. The goal of increased publications was a result of the department's unease over the college's increasingly rigorous promotion and tenure policy. While the faculty was trying to conceive of ways to get more time to do research, the switch to computer-assisted instruction was suggested. Teaching through the computer would save faculty teaching time, which could be spent in research. Translating the idea of computerized teaching to a goal and an action plan, which included a description of how the objective was to be accomplished, led to the rejection of the idea. Implementing the idea would have required a significant amount of computer programming, storage of large amounts of information and test items, purchase of additional terminals for student use, and payment of staff to monitor the terminals for many hours every day. Evidence of the increased costs did not lead to the immediate abandonment of the tentative objective, though it did dampen some of the early enthusiasm. Proceeding with the action plan described above, however, the chairperson and department got enough information to warrant abandoning the plan.

To be able to distinguish between ideas and goals is useful. Computer-assisted instruction seemed to be—indeed, was—a good idea. When translated into a goal, with objectives and an action plan, the idea's flaws became more and more apparent. The university has been the repository of innumerable ideas that have devoured time and money for years. Usually no one has bothered to identify the goals, the objectives, or results associated with the idea. No one has identified the measurable and desired results that the idea is supposed to produce, and no time scale for accomplishing results has been established. That the idea itself endures is not surprising, for there is no way to assess progress or lack of progress of an idea. If progams are to be effective, however, they need to develop measurable goals and objectives that are oriented toward results.

Not every goal or objective can always be attained, but when a legitimate goal is not met, an active and strong department needs to review its activities and procedures seriously. The weak department is one that does not learn from mistakes and repeats useless routines year after year.

In this chapter, we have discussed ways in which the department can report its activities and pursue a rational course in attempting to chart its future. The need for a sense of purpose, the relationship of goals to the overall purpose, and the formulation of objectives that have measurable or observable outcomes have been detailed. Planning has been discussed here mainly in the language of behavioral objectives.

Although many academicians are put off by the language of behavioral objectives and its industrial counterpart—management by objectives—others are quite taken with these concepts. Some education planners seem to think that simply stating objectives in behavioral terms with clear specification of outcomes is all that is needed to clear up confusion in the university. Even if a department can state its objectives with clarity and precision, it still must be able to assess the quality of those objectives. Whether a department's objectives are good depends on much more than the form in which those aims are stated. This chapter has suggested ways in which some clarity in the statement of purposes and goals may be attained, but their qualitative assessment depends on the good judgment and insight of the chairperson and the department. A chairperson can help unify the faculty members by involving them in developing department missions and goals.

Department members who have been successful in obtaining grants from external sources know that to specify their plans using the terminology *mission, goals,* and *objectives* is useful and convincing. Stating the department's planned activities in ways similar to those described in this chapter can be a valuable tool for obtaining resources at a time of increasing competition for available resources. The chairperson must decide how much precision and quantification can sensibly be used in reporting and planning the department's activities. Effective leadership includes the ability to foresee the consequences of one's actions. Planning a department's activities intelligently implies that the chairperson should have a good idea of what will happen to the department if the plans are carried out.

Questions and Exercises

1. List, according to the following categories, some of your department's more important accomplishments during the past year:
   - teaching, including curriculum development, new programs, and innovative methods
   - research and publications of individual faculty members
   - service to the university, region, and nation
   - important decisions related to department policies concerning faculty, students, and staff; curriculum; committee structures; governance; expenditure of travel funds; and so forth
2. List, according to the categories given above, your aspirations for your department for the coming year. Formulate goal statements based on these aspirations.
3. Select a specific, genuine goal that your department wishes to

implement in the near future. Develop as comprehensive an action plan as you can, including objectives, tasks, and a time frame. Try to use the nomenclature suggested in the chapter.

References

CARNEGIE COMMISSION ON HIGHER EDUCATION. *Governance of Higher Education: Six Priority Problems.* New York: McGraw-Hill, 1973.

THE CARNEGIE FOUNDATION FOR THE ADVANCEMENT OF TEACHING. *Missions of the College Curriculum: A Contemporary Review with Suggestions.* San Francisco: Jossey-Bass, 1977.

FULLER, BRUCE. "A Framework for Academic Planning." *Journal of Higher Education*, January-February 1976, pp. 65–77.

GROSS, EDWARD. "University Organizations: A Study of Goals." In *Academic Governance*, edited by J. Victor Baldridge. Berkeley: McCutchan, 1976.

GROSS, EDWARD, AND GRAMBSCH, PAUL V. *University Goals and Academic Power: A Study in Conflict and Cooperation.* Washington, D.C.: American Council on Education, 1968.

MAGER, ROBERT F. *Goal Analysis.* Belmont, Calif.: Fearon- Pitman, 1972.

MIGATOKI, GLENN K., AND BYERS, MAUREEN L. "Module 1: Identifying and Organizing Academic Unit Functions." *Academic Unit Planning and Management.* Technical Report No. 75. Boulder, Colo.: The National Center for Higher Education Management Systems, 1976.

MURPHY, PATRICK E. "The Promises and Pitfalls of Marketing Research in Higher Education." *Liberal Education*, Spring 1980, pp. 102–15.

PERROW, CHARLES. "The Analysis of Goals in Complex Organizations." In *Readings on Modern Organizations*, edited by Amitai Etzioni. Englewood Cliffs, N.J.: Prentice-Hall, 1969.

PETERSON, RICHARD E. *College Goals and the Challenge of Effectiveness.* Institutional Research Program for Higher Education. Princeton, N.J.: Educational Testing Service, 1971.

SCHUTTENBERG. ERNEST M.; MCARDALE, RICHARD J.; AND THOMAS, WARREN S. "Goal Setting in Educational Organizations: A Systems Perspective." *Peabody Journal of Education*, July 1979, pp. 272–78.

———. *Toward Institutional Goal-Consciousness.* Princeton, N.J.: Educational Testing Service, 1971.

TRIVETT, DAVID A. *Goals for Higher Education: Definitions and Directions.* ERIC/Higher Education Research Report no. 6. Washington, D.C.: American Association for Higher Education, 1973.

14

The Budget Cycle: Preparing Department Budget Requests and Persuading the Dean

Obtaining appropriate university resources for the department is one of the chairperson's more sensitive responsibilities. Since the majority of the faculty tends to believe that departments are underfunded, ability to compete successfully for institutional funds is often seen as an important indicator of a chairperson's leadership quality. This perception appears to prevail even in departments that receive extensive external support from grants and contracts.

The budgetary procedures used by different institutions vary considerably. Many chairpersons, especially those who have been appointed only recently, may not be well informed about the budget process within their universities. Further, some tend to assume, often incorrectly, that the dean possesses extensive knowledge about their departments. Frequently, what may be an obvious problem to a chairperson is not so obvious to a dean whose academic home is in another department. Unless they have been briefed, deans are often unaware of department developments. For this reason, budget requests should include complete, updated information. Generally, the dean operates within a value system; consequently, the request should indicate how the requested resources will help meet college and institution priorities.

The purpose of this chapter, therefore, is to help chairpersons formulate department budget requests and prepare effective presentations about the department during review sessions with the dean. Formal budget requests may not be required of all departments. Nevertheless, the chairperson must be able to communicate department needs effectively when the opportunity presents itself.

The process of preparing a department budget is easier if the chairperson understands the broader aspects of budgeting within the academic context. This global view includes an appreciation of the budget review process within and outside the university, budget cycles, alternative budgeting systems, and the language of budgeting.

The Global View

Chairpersons who are responsible for preparing or supervising the preparation of budget requests should have a general understanding of the budget process at all levels and of the sequence of events preceding appropriation for the institution as a whole. Such awareness will not necessarily lead to an increase in department allocation. It will, however, provide an understanding of those political and economic realities that affect the budgetary process; it will also facilitate communication with a concerned faculty.

Many institutions begin preparing a budget request for the coming year's operation as much as a year in advance, and the chairperson must be able to communicate anticipated needs. The individual budgets may be reviewed at each level of the hierarchy, with each department chairperson meeting with the dean, each dean with the academic vice-president, and then all the top administrators meeting with the president. The institution's board of trustees may approve the final budget request, and, in the case of a public institution, the request is submitted to the appropriate state agencies.

Private Institutions

In the case of private colleges and universities, budget requests are reviewed and analyzed within the institution, and approval by boards of trustees is the final action necessary before internal distribution of funds. In formulating budget requests, chairpersons in private colleges and universities should be mindful of the institution's general financial health. They should be aware of the status of the endowment fund and the recent pattern of gifts and bequests. Since tuition payments constitute a sizeable portion of the income of many private schools, chairpersons should be able to anticipate the effects of increased tuition on department enrollments. At many private institutions, faculty members are expected to participate actively in a variety of fund-raising activities, in addition to generating contracts and grants.

Public Institutions

Budget requests from public institutions, even if approved by boards of trustees, are subject to external review and analyses before being acted on by the legislature. The depth and complexity of the external analyses depend on the type of governance under which the institution operates. For example, the University of Michigan, because it is not a member of a university system, will transmit its institutional budget requests directly to the governor's state budget agency and to offices of appropriate legislative staff. On the other hand, Florida State University, because it is one of several members of a state university system under a single governing board, must transmit its institutional budget request to the central staff of the Florida university system for review and analysis. The central staff will examine budget requests from each institution in the system and submit a recommendation to the offices of the governor's state budget agency and to the appropriate legislative staff.

In other types of state systems, individual institutional requests may not be forwarded to external agencies; rather, an aggregated system request may be submitted to the funding agencies. In this type of system, the institution's top officials meet together with the system staff throughout the budget development process and before the aggregation of all institutional requests. The system staff interprets the state budget guidelines and prepares the combined budget request, which is submitted to the system coordinating or governing board for approval. It is then transmitted to the governor's state budget agency and the legislative budget staff, which often meets with institutional representatives and the system staff to ensure that the budget request meets the needs of both the executive and legislative branches of government.

Thus, the institutions in the system may be listed separately in the system request and appropriations act, or they may be aggregated by program or some other classification system without institutional identification. Because many state legislatures have developed their own priorities for higher education, the institutional or system budget requests may be submitted to the legislative staff when the request is sent to a governor's budget agency. In almost all states, however, the governor's state budget request to the legislature is still treated as the official budget proposal.

At the state level, the possibility for increased appropriations depends on the level of economic activity and the taxes collected. Through the process of estimating tax revenues, state officials estimate the amount of "new" money that will become available. Legislatures almost always test budget requests against these estimates and against legislative priorities. Department chairpersons can obtain a ballpark estimate of "new" money for higher education by noting the priority given to education and relating it to the estimated percent increase in state tax revenues or moneys available for appropriation, an increase that is usually well publicized.

Within a bicameral state legislature, each chamber reviews budget requests and emphasizes its own individually determined state priorities. For this reason, the "super bowl" of the legislative appropriations process is the conference committee, created jointly by the two chambers to work out their differences. Because of the complexity and magnitude of the state programs, many important funding details are listed only in work papers or exist in "understandings" among state officials, legislators, and their staffs. Usually only a few items are of sufficient priority to be listed separately in the appropriations documents. Because the house of representatives, the senate, and the state budget agency each has only one or two persons functioning as higher education budget analysts, more unwritten rules and understandings about higher education budgets and appropriations may exist than are ever listed in the published appropriations act; there often is not sufficient time to spell out all details. Sometimes, as is the case in Florida, a "letter of intent" follows the appropriations act and gives supplemental instructions regarding the use of appropriated funds.

In recent years a few states have returned to biennial budgets in the hope that reducing the number of budget cycles will stimulate better planning and program analysis preceding preparation of the budget request. Double-digit inflation and rising energy costs, however, can also require supplemental appropriations in the second year. Furthermore, when legislators meet annually, they are tempted to "redo" portions of the budget in the second year. Nevertheless, the published two-year appropriation can provide some sense of continuity and confidence for department chairpersons, since actions in the second year of the biennium tend to involve supplemental funding.

In formulating department budgets, chairpersons in public institutions that are part of state systems should be aware of the process whereby a system budget request is formulated. They should know what the main issues at their institution are and what the system's priorities are. They should stay as informed as possible about the status of the request from start to appropriation. Knowledge of the schedule of activities at the legislative and system levels may help chairpersons plan functions at the department level. This type of information, as general as it may be, helps chairpersons put their department's priorities in a wider perspective and set their expectations at realistic levels. Department chairpersons in public institutions that are not part of university or college systems should be especially sensitive to legislative schedules and actions, which are transmitted directly to the institutions rather than through the central staff of a system.

The chairperson, then, should take a more global view of the budget process and learn as much as possible about financial conditions and priorities at all levels. If the legislature uses a formula to appropriate funds, the chairperson should know what the components of the formula are. In the case of an institution that is a part of a system, the chairperson should be aware of the system's technique for distributing funds among the institutions; he or she should be especially familiar with the procedures used to derive the resources that concern academic areas.

The Budget Cycle

Each budget cycle begins with the preparation of a *budget request.* A series of decisions are then made at various levels, taking into account the budget request and the funds available. These decisions lead to the development of an *operating budget,* which is an expenditure plan covering the period, usually a single year, for which funds are made available. At the end of each year a *financial statement* is prepared, showing the financial status at the start of the year, the activities during the year, and the financial condition at the end of the year. Finally, an *audit* is performed to verify that established rules and regulations have been followed. Budget cycles may overlap at some institutions—for example, a university could be preparing a budget request for a coming year at the same time it is preparing an operating budget for the current year. Chairpersons should be aware of budget cycles, since they affect insitutional decision-making processes.

Preparation of a Budget Request. This activity is usually begun well in advance of the time period for which resources are being requested—for example, the budget request for fiscal year 1983–84 may have to be prepared during late 1981 or early 1982. In the case of public institutions, the date for submitting a budget request depends on the dates of legislative sessions. The Florida legislature, for example, meets annually during April and May and considers the governor's spending plan, which was presented in late February; thus, the institutional budget request must be prepared during the summer of the previous year and submitted in October of that year. Because of recently adopted biennial budgeting, the budget request submitted in October 1980 covered the years 1981–83.

Universities take different approaches to the preparation of budget requests. For example, in the case of some private and public institutions, the department request may be the first step in a continuous planning process that eventually results in the allocation of an operating budget. At the University of West Virginia, department budget requests are submitted and priorities established at the college level, and college requests are then arranged in priorities at the institutional level. During the allocation process, these institutional priorities serve as the basis for distributing resources. At many public institutions, especially those funded through an enrollment formula, department requests may serve as the basis for distributing resources among departments within a college.

Thus, in the first approach, department requests are used in a continuous process to describe the institution's needs. In the second case, department needs are not aggregated and the distribution of resources to the institution and sometimes even to the school or college may depend on some other variable, such as enrollment. A third approach, which combines the two methods and which is becoming more widespread, is to distribute resources by expenditure categories to implement defined institutional priorities.

Regardless of the approach to generating an institutional budget request, chairpersons should involve themselves in the process as much as possible. The process provides one of the few opportunities for the department to describe its past successes and future objectives. Generally, the more that is known and understood about the complex activities of an academic department, the greater the possibility that positive decisions will be made. At the same time, however, chairpersons should be careful to keep their expectations at a reasonable level. Departments often request an amount that would be sufficient to accommodate all their needs. The funds to meet such requests are rarely available, however, and the chairperson should be prepared to receive fewer resources than were sought.

Allocation and Control of the Operating Budget. Allocation and control of a current year's budget occur after the state legislature has appropriated the funds, the college or university has received its allocation, and department operating budgets have been authorized. Chairpersons and deans exercise budget control by signing approval for proposed expenditures. They may find that, although their annual budget has been approved, the funds are not made available all at one time. This situation occurs in states that operate on a funds release schedule other than an annual one—for example, the state of Florida releases funds on a quarterly basis. If the state is on an accrual accounting basis, the accounting at the end of the fiscal year includes all obligations made during the year, and funds are "certified forward" to the next fiscal year to cover these obligations. This type of year-end activity normally occurs in states where unspent or unobligated funds "revert" to the state. Not all states operate this way, however.

Budget Close-out. The budget for the academic year is closed out in the last month of that fiscal year, at which time there is usually an end-of-the-year rush to complete authorized transactions and to prepare final annual reports. In states where state funds revert, chairpersons must be aware that any allocated funds not spent or encumbered during the allocation year will be lost to the department.

Expenditure Audit. The record of expenditures is generally audited by internal auditors during the current year or thereafter. Expenditures may also be audited by external auditors, who conduct audits of the institution for its board of trustees or for the state. Colleges or universities with large federal grants and contracts may have auditors present from different federal departments much of the year. Some foundations conduct audits simultaneously with reviews of programs they fund.

In any current budget year, all or most of these activities may be occurring at the same time, although they may be grouped variously and performed by special offices or service departments. For example, at the beginning of a new fiscal year, an institutional budget office may be allocating funds to departments, authorizing the payroll office to increase the salaries and benefits of persons receiving pay raises, compiling cost data for the budget request for the subsequent year, estimating the current and future revenues from student tuition and fees, helping close out last year's budget, and beginning planning for the future. Budget responsibilities may be centralized or decentralized within the institution. In the decentralized model, the activities may be distributed so that the planning office is concerned with the budget request, the controller's office with the implementation of current-year decisions, and the academic vice-president's budget office with all budget-related activities pertaining to academic areas.

The chairperson, aware of the complicated activities of the budget cycle, should maintain accurate records of expenditures, even though such records may also be kept in administrative offices. He or she should plan department expenditures wisely and systematically to avoid last-minute scurrying about to purchase supplies and services before the budget close-out.

Since the budget requested for a given year is usually prepared one or two years in advance, the department needs to know what activities it intends to pursue in the next year or two in order to request appropriate funds. Plans for the department's general future are linked to budget planning. The timetable and deadline dates established for completing the various stages in budget preparations are often used by chairpersons as a basis for scheduling academic planning sessions. Some chairpersons feel that planning is a wasted effort unless additional funds are expected to be made available. Such persons are not sensitive to the possibility that a department may be required to change or modify some of its academic activities to accommodate new societal needs or that at times such changes will have to be made without additional funding.

Academic planning is necessary whether anticipated funds for the coming year are more than, less than, or the same as the amounts allocated in the previous year. Departments can plan alternative courses of action to meet whatever situations occur, such as implementing new, unfunded projects in the event that unanticipated money should become available. Just as budget preparation is continuous, so should academic planning be continuous. Regular assessment of current positions and identification of key activities to be pursued will keep the department from straying too far from its missions and goals. Ideally, the planning process should take alternate possibilities into account. In reality, the tendency is to get the resources first and make the plans afterwards, especially in the case of annual appropriations.

Budgeting Systems

Institutions of higher learning use a variety of budgeting systems. When preparing budget requests, departments should follow the instructions distributed by the appropriate office of the institution. Specifically, the chairperson should be familiar with the budgeting approach used by his or her dean. Administrators who review budget requests may not attach sufficient importance to items that are not presented in a familiar format. The following summary of commonly used budget systems is presented here to expand the chairperson's language of budgeting.

Incremental Budgeting. The system of incremental budgeting usually uses last year's expenditures as a base; it estimates and justifies an increase, or increment, above the base. This system does not require an extensive analysis or review of goals. It is widely used in colleges and universities, mainly, no doubt, because it is easily comprehensible.

Usually, each category within a budget—such as faculty salaries, expenses, travel, and so on—is increased by some percentage or flat amount of dollars. The guidelines for preparing the budget request may identify the maximum percentage increases that will be considered. When the economy becomes unpredictable and tax revenues uncertain, the budget guidelines for public colleges and universities may direct each institution to prepare and submit several different budget requests, one with perhaps a 5 percent decrease, another with no increase, and still another with a 5 percent increase. The guidelines from a state budget agency may include such specific instructions, even when an institution uses a different budgeting system. The budget request selected for approval will depend on the actual amount of state funds that will become available for higher education.

One major advantage of the incremental system is that the base is already agreed upon; further agreement is needed only on the amount of the increment. Moreover, the incremental system does not preclude the review of programs during the decision process, nor does it preclude subsequent resource adjustments to the base. Not inherent in this system, however, is a complete examination of program objectives and outcomes during each cycle.

Zero-base Budgeting System (ZBBS). This system assumes that a department's objectives should determine its budget and that an assessment should be made of how well objectives are reached. Zero-base budgeting starts from the premise that each time a new budget is prepared, it must demonstrate that it includes the best combination of costs and benefits for achieving each goal or the effective operation of each program. Sometimes, even the alternatives that were considered and rejected have to be specified. The base of the incremental system discussed earlier is not taken for granted in the zero-base system. In the ZBBS only demonstrable needs are to be funded. The ZBBS involves the use of "decision packages" (programs described at various funding levels) and the ranking of these "packages."

When the zero-base system is attempted annually, administrators often take the documents prepared for the previous year, reread them, and add the information provided and the funds requested. Such practice leads the system away from its emphasis on objectives, nullifies the rationale for zero-base budgeting, and leads toward a reintroduction of an incremental system. An academic department's objectives do not vary significantly from year to year, however; consequently, the complete review suggested by the ZBBS may itself be questioned on the grounds of cost efficiency. The exercise of evaluating achievement of objectives at different funding levels becomes too uncertain, and generally organizations using ZBBS arrive at set percentages to be used.

The major problem with using zero-base budgeting in academic departments is the nature of faculty costs. Faculty salaries, which are a major portion of department budgets, remain constant or increase with the longevity of faculty members, regardless of changes in department, college, or university objectives.

Line-Item Budgeting. Most institutions use organizational units and expenditure categories, rather than defined programs and activities, as the basis for budget planning. An organizational unit is an academic department, center, institute, school, or college. Expenditures include such categories as salaries, expenses, equipment, and so forth. Salaries and expenses to be budgeted for an academic department, for example, would include the cost of programs in the department, such as instruction, academic support, and advising. This itemizing is called *line-item budgeting.* By adding the budgets of all organizational units in the institution, the total institutional budget can be determined.

Planning, Programming, and Budgeting System (PPBS). This system uses "programs" rather than organizational units as a basis for budget planning. A *program* is defined as a collection of related activities and services that together constitute the achievement of the goal. Theoretically, PPBS involves identifying objectives, listing alternative courses of action (showing cost benefit), choosing one alternative, and, finally, implementing the alternative through funding. Generally, funding (or at least the request) is related to workload measures for each activity.

In higher education, reaching a consensus on what constitutes a program is difficult. Following are examples of what some instructional programs include. If a stated goal is to provide instruction to all students in an institution, the program of instruction might consist of all courses offered by the institution. If the goal is to provide undergraduate instruction to all students in an institution, the program would include all undergraduate courses offered at the institution. The difficulty in defining *program* is so great that the term remains undefined in several state statutes governing higher education.

The National Center for Higher Education Management Systems (NCHEMS), a federally supported research agency, has developed a sophisticated budgeting model that defines a program of instruction as a discipline major or any collection of courses designed to satisfy curricular requirements for a degree or certificate.* This concept recognizes that each department makes only a partial contribution to the education of a degree-seeking student. The modern computer, with the aid of computer technology, can divide the cost for each student among all the departments in an institution, a calculation based on the level of student enrollment. The total cost for producing a degree in a given major can be estimated by adding the costs of the educational services provided to a student in that major by all contributing departments over a four-year period.

In addition to different types of programs of instruction, some institutions using PPBS have designated "academic support" and "student services" as separate institutional programs. Each program includes all the related activities and services that together contribute to the achievement of its respective goal. "Academic advising," including all activities related to this function, is sometimes designated as an institutional program in its own right and sometimes as a separate component of a larger program, such as "instruction," "academic support," or "student services." Occasionally, academic advising activities are

*Procedures for Determining Historical Full Costs: The Costing Component of NCHEMS Information Exchange Procedures, Technical Report no. 65, 2nd ed. (Boulder, Colo.: 1977), p. 16.

decentralized—i.e., an advisor may be placed in each department—in which case they become an integral part of a program of instruction.

Basically, PPBS incorporates the idea of the zero-base system that an organization's goals and objectives should determine its budget; in addition, however, it includes a long-range planning component. PPBS is strongly influenced by the rationale and techniques of systems analysis and represents an attempt to bridge the gap between planning and budgeting. PPBS also involves attaching cost estimates to the multiyear planning goals and objectives after the most efficient and effective means for achieving the programs' objectives have been identified. The selection and number of component activities contained in a program depend on the scope of the stated goal and the preferences of the person who is developing the system.

A budget plan that assigns moneys to organizational units usually focuses on resources as input to the instruction process rather than on output and goals, whereas a program budget plan that assigns moneys to defined programs provides the means to relate program activities to output and goals. Institutions using organizational structure for budget planning find managing and accounting for resources easier than do institutions that use program classification based on activities.

The statements of goals and objectives for several years and the resources required to achieve them become extremely tenuous during periods of rising costs and double-digit inflation. The need to revise five-year projections during each annual budget preparation, for example, may lead to incremental adjustments of the kind mentioned in connection with zero-base budgeting. In colleges and universities, long-range projections are subject to extensive revisions, partly because the turnover rate for chairpersons is high and because program priorities within departments change as frequently. Whenever new administrators, regardless of level, search for ways to implement fresh ideas within the department, school, or college, the probability is high that older goals and objectives will be changed. Rather than trying to follow a fully developed comprehensive plan to bring about change, most administrators adopt a strategy of shifting budgeted funds gradually from one set of programs to another. Some of the analytical techniques developed within the PPBS approach, however, have value in department planning. For example, the planning for a new program will be much improved if objectives, alternatives, workload measures, and resource requirements are estimated before the program is implemented.

Individual departments should not attempt to implement a PPB system solely for the purpose of facilitating data compilation for the budget request, especially if the dean or administrator is not familiar with or sympathetic to the system. PPBS, properly implemented, provides a great deal of detail and clarity, but the hard work of developing a system may be wasted if the department's priorities clash with the institution's priorities. In some institutions, experience has shown that when departments attempted five-year plans, much effort was devoted to projecting needs for adding new specialty courses in the face of declining enrollments. This kind of expanded need may be inserted in any budget request, regardless of the budgeting system in use. A department has a much greater chance of being successful in its requests, however, if it fully, accurately, and realistically justifies its needs, regardless of the budgetary system used.

Formula Budgeting

Formula budgeting uses formulas as a basis for preparing budget requests and for determining allocations. One purpose of formula budgeting is to provide equitable funding for all competing units, such as institutions in a state system or academic departments within an institution. The uniform application of formulas to colleges and universities in a state system tends to reduce conflict among presidents and, when applied uniformly within an institution, helps reduce conflict among deans, provided, of course, that the formulas have been agreed on and accepted by all concerned. Various formulas can be used for education budgets. Zero-base formulas, for example, derive resources based on estimated full-time equivalent (FTE) enrollment and the agreed-on cost per student. Some formulas, on the other hand, may address only increases or decreases to the existing base.

One formula, for example, involves multiplying the projected number of FTE students by the cost per FTE student. When applied to an institution across the board, regardless of discipline or student level, the formula can provide an estimate of the total cost for operating all academic programs in the university. The formula can also be applied separately to departments and programs, as well as to graduate and undergraduate students within programs. For example, estimates of operational costs can be calculated for lower-division students in biology, upper-division students in psychology, graduate students in chemistry, and so forth. The sum of the separate costs for each category will be the total operational cost for all academic programs in the institution. Before the formula can be used, however, a determination must be made of what constitutes a FTE student in each of the above categories, how many FTE students are expected to enroll in each category, and the cost per FTE student. (A more detailed definition of *full-time equivalent* appears later in this chapter.)

Another formula for developing budget requests involves multiplying the estimated number of needed faculty positions by the average faculty salary. This formula, when applied to an institution as a whole, will provide an estimate of the total faculty salary cost for the university. Before the number of needed faculty positions can be estimated, however, a determination must be made, for budgetary purposes, of what constitutes a faculty workload.

Several state university systems have, for a number of years, used workload formulas to determine the number of positions needed. "Normative" workload factors were estimated originally from turn-of-the-century teaching load data. For example, a faculty member who taught one 3-credit-hour course with 25 students in the class would generate 75 student credit hours (3 × 25). If the instructor taught four such courses during a term, the total number of student credit hours generated that term would be 300 credit hours (4 × 75). The workload factor for this instructor, therefore, would be 300.

The number of student credit hours generated by a course may vary, depending on its assigned number of credits and the number of students enrolled in it. At many institutions, as late as World War II, faculty members were expected to teach four courses each semester. For budgetary purposes, the average faculty workload per semester was described not in terms of the total number of courses taught, but in terms of the total number of student credit hours generated. Originally, workload factors were calculated only for the different levels of enrollment without consideration of discipline. Because many lower-division classes are taught by lecture and generally have larger enrollments than advanced classes, the average number of student credit hours generated by an instructor teaching the lower-division courses was expected to be larger. Figure 14.1 illustrates this type of approach.

The number of faculty positions needed at each level is estimated by dividing the faculty workload factor assigned to a level into the total anticipated number of student credit hours to be generated by the institution at that level. The total number of faculty positions needed by the institution can be estimated by totaling the faculty positions needed at all levels. Multiplying that total by an average faculty salary, regardless

FIGURE 14.1 "Normative" workload factors, by educational status of students.

EDUCATIONAL STATUS	"NORMATIVE" WORKLOAD FACTOR (EQUIVALENT OF ONE FACULTY POSITION)
Freshman or Sophomore	400 student credit hours
Junior or Senior	300 student credit hours
Beginning Graduate	200 student credit hours
Advanced Graduate	100 student credit hours

of rank or discipline, results in an estimate of the institution's total cost for faculty salaries. By constructing ratios between faculty positions and support or administrative positions, the number of support positions can also be estimated—for example, ten faculty positions might generate one support position. Thus a budget request can be built for all authorized and needed positions covering all functions within an institution.

The workload factors described above represent averages that do not differentiate disciplines. In reality, workload factors vary in size from one discipline to another because of the nature of the discipline. The number of students in music and art classes is much smaller than that in social science classes, thus making the workload factors in music and art smaller than that in the social sciences. The availability of the large computer makes possible the calculation, using documented or anticipated student enrollment, of workload factors for each discipline or department and for each enrollment level within each department. When data about disciplines from several previous years are averaged, more realistic workload measures can be derived. Table 14.1 contains a standard list of specific and broad discipline areas often used by institutions in reporting data to the federal government. Illustrated in the table are the workload factors in the State University System of Florida for 1976, adjusted according to those disciplines and the enrollment levels within each.

Thus far, we have discussed ways in which formulas can be used in the preparation of budget requests. Rarely is the same formula used both to prepare a budget request for an institution and to allocate resources within the institution. Most formulas in use are zero-based and have no variable that accounts for college or institutional priorities. Therefore, more faculty positions may be assigned to some programs than would be generated according to formula. On the other hand, this excess must be balanced by assigning fewer positions than are earned to certain programs with high student-credit-hour productivity. Thus, even though the formula for a budget request may be based on the number of FTE students generated by each department, each administrative level in a university may follow a completely different system for allocating funds to units at the next lower level. Chairpersons would do well to familiarize themselves with the formulas, priorities, and procedures used in both the requesting process and the allocation process.

Despite their usefulness, student-weighted funding formulas are creating problems for many colleges and universities today. The formulas are disliked because they usually rely on averages and because they reward high enrollments in the absence of other considerations. Moreover, in times of declining enrollments, the amount of

T A B L E 14.1 **Adjusted Base-Year Productivity (Workload) Factors, State University System of Florida, 1976–77**

DISCIPLINES	LEVELS			
	Lower	*Upper*	*Graduate*	*Dissertation/ Thesis (Combined)*
Agriculture & Natural Resources	420.00	240.00	108.00	60.00
Architecture & Environmental Design	300.00	240.00	120.00	45.00
Area Studies	240.00	240.00	84.00	60.00
Biological Sciences	360.00	240.00	132.00	45.00
Business & Management	480.00	360.00	192.00	60.00
Communications	360.00	240.00	168.00	60.00
Computer & Information Sciences	420.00	360.00	216.00	45.00
Education	360.00	380.00	228.00	75.00
Engineering	360.00	240.00	120.00	45.00
Fine & Applied Arts	180.00	120.00	84.00	75.00
Foreign Languages	240.00	180.00	84.00	75.00
Health Professions	360.00	180.00	108.00	45.00
Home Economics	300.00	300.00	180.00	60.00
Law	0.0	0.0	480.00	60.00
Letters	240.00	300.00	168.00	75.00
Library Science	540.00	300.00	228.00	60.00
Mathematics	420.00	360.00	96.00	45.00
Military Science	0.0	0.0	0.0	60.00
Physical Sciences	420.00	240.00	168.00	45.00
Psychology	540.00	360.00	204.00	45.00
Public Affairs & Services	540.00	300.00	168.00	60.00
Social Sciences	540.00	360.00	192.00	60.00
Technology	300.00	180.00	0.0	60.00
Interdisciplinary Studies	300.00	240.00	144.00	60.00
Continuing Education	0.0	0.0	0.0	0.0

SOURCE: "Derivation of Productivity Levels (Student Credit Hours) by Discipline and Course Level," Interinstitutional PPB Committee for Appropriation and Allocation of Academic Positions, Florida Board of Regents, September 20, 1976.

NOTE: Each factor represents the number of student credit hours that will generate one FTE faculty position at the different levels in each of the listed disciplines per term.

funds generated by the formula may not be sufficient to continue some academic programs of an institution. Such insufficiency results because most formulas are linear and do not consider that departments have fixed costs—i.e., a class of nineteen students may cost as much as a class of twenty-one students. In addition, formulas do not take into account the difference in costs due to faculty seniority, rank, and labor market rates. Thus, some formulas fail to provide the equity that was the very rationale for their initial application.

Most funding formulas are based on a cost analysis of some kind in which data are stated in terms of cost per FTE student. The availability of the electronic computer makes it possible to process the large volume of data needed to conduct cost studies. In *A Study of Cost Analysis in Higher Education,* the American Council on Education reports that none of the existing costing systems was useful to institutional administrators in improving or managing higher education. Nevertheless, many state-required formulas continue to rely on these cost data.

Formulas that use averaged data derived from several institutions in a system generally tend to reward the teaching institutions at the expense of the research universities. Some states, like North Carolina, have different funding systems for different kinds of institutions. State budgeting systems that vary according to the mission, role, and scope of each institution in a system are now gaining much attention. Should such a system emerge formally, it would quite likely be applied to the departments within a college or university. The congruence of a department's goals and objectives with those of its parent institution would then become much more important for internal funding purposes.

The Language of Budgeting

The budgeting process is often perceived as mysterious and esoteric. Some persons find it dry and boring, and those who find it fascinating frequently choose some facet of it as a vocation. To the layperson, the jargon used by finance experts seems to be incomprehensible except to a chosen few, and those who understand it are thought to be "important." In actuality, the budget process is part of planning and is frequently less precise than it may appear. Although we may not demystify the entire process by explaining some of its intricacies, this discussion will help chairpersons become familiar with the more common terms related to budgeting. Let us review some of these terms.

1. *FTE* is a commonly used abbreviation that stands for "full-time equivalent" and refers variously to students, faculty, and staff. This concept is often used in formula-base budgeting.
   a. *FTE student.* Let us assume that a full course load for a typical undergraduate has been designated as 15 credits per term. For budgeting purposes, therefore, one undergraduate student enrolled for 15 credits of course work is considered to be one FTE student. Similarly, three students enrolled for 5 credits

each, or a total of 15 credits, are considered to be one FTE. The number of credit hours designated as equaling one FTE may change according to the level of the courses or the level of the student. At many institutions, one full-time equivalent graduate student is 12 credit hours.

b. *FTE faculty and staff.* A faculty or staff member may be appointed on a full- or part-time basis for an academic or calendar year, depending on the institution's policy. Faculty members on full-time appointments are generally expected to devote 100 percent of their professional time and effort to the job to which they are appointed. What constitutes 100 percent of time and effort of a faculty member's professional life has not been clearly defined, however. Those institutions and departments who need a definition must stipulate their own.

For salary purposes, a faculty member who receives 100 percent of a salary for a designated period of time is considered one FTE faculty member for that time period. Some faculty members are appointed to two or more departments or offices simultaneously, and their salaries come from different budgets. For example, a person may receive 75 percent of his or her salary from a department and 25 percent from the dean's office. The fraction of the total salary that comes from each budget also indicates that fraction of FTE faculty assigned to each department or office. Similarly, a person who receives 25 percent of his or her salary from a contract or grant is considered to be 25 percent FTE "on the grant" and 75 percent FTE "in the department."

A faculty member whose full salary comes from a department budget and who is considered one FTE faculty member, as far as that department is concerned, is usually assigned a variety of activities, each of which is expressed as a percentage of full-time effort. For example, a faculty member's teaching effort may be assigned 50 percent of a FTE; research, 30 percent; and service, 20 percent. An institution may determine the total number of FTE faculty involved in research by adding all the individual percentage FTEs assigned to research and thereby estimate the total salary costs of the institution's research effort. Similarly, the total number of FTE faculty involved in the teaching of undergraduate lower-division courses can be estimated by adding all the individual percentage FTEs assigned to teaching lower-division courses.

A faculty member whose formal appointment is 25 percent FTE in the dean's office and 75 percent FTE in a department may devote 50 percent of his or her department effort to teaching and 50 percent to research. In this case the total teaching assignment of FTE is 37.5 percent (50 percent × 75 percent). Similarly, the total research assignment of FTE is 37.5 percent. Many urban colleges and universities employ a considerable number of part-time faculty members, each of whom is appointed to a fraction of one FTE position and is paid accordingly. If an institution hires three part-time faculty members, appointing one to a 0.5 FTE position, another to a 0.6 FTE position, and the third to a 0.3 FTE position, the three will constitute 1.4 FTE positions (0.5 + 0.6 + 0.3). Despite the many ways of calculating FTEs and their percentages, however, one faculty member can never be counted as more than one FTE, regardless of how hard or how many hours he or she works.

The FTE concept is also applied to nonacademic staff. In the case of staff, however, the percentage of FTE is based on the relationship between the number of assigned hours of work during a given period and the number of hours that constitutes a full workload for that period.

2. *SCH*, another common abbreviation, usually refers to "student credit hours." One student taking a 4-credit-hour course per term generates 4 student credit hours. Fifteen students enrolled in a 3-credit-hour course per term generate 45 student credit hours (3 × 15). SCH may also refer to "student *contact* hours," the number of clock hours spent in contact with faculty members. One contact hour in a lecture class per week per term is usually equivalent to 1 credit hour. In the case of laboratory classes, however, 3 contact hours per week per term will often equal only 1 credit hour.

3. *Expenditure categories.* Resources may be allocated to institutions and departments in expenditure categories. The purpose of allocating funds in categories is to exercise control over how the money is spent. In many states and institutions, transfer of moneys from one category to another is not permitted or is permitted under restricted circumstances, such as a 5 percent limitation on transfers. Categories may vary from state to state, but the most common ones are listed and defined below.

a. *Salaries*—Includes the funds required to pay salaries of persons in permanent or regular positions.

b. *Benefits*—Includes funds for additional commitments made to employees, such as retirement, social security matching funds, health insurance, and so forth.

c. *Temporary personnel*—Includes funds for temporary help, such as student assistants and peak load supplemental employees.

d. *Graduate assistantships and fellowships*—Includes funds for teaching and research assistantships and fellowships.

e. *Expenses*—Includes funds for supplies, travel, telephones, postage, equipment lease, rent, and so forth.

f. *Equipment*—Includes funds for equipment, such as typewriters, duplicating machines, laboratory equipment, furniture, and so forth, which become the property of the institution. Sometimes equipment that costs less than a designated amount may be purchased with funds from the expense category.

g. *Capital funds*—Includes funds for construction of new buildings. In some states, funds from this category may be used to pay for building renovations.

h. *Lump sum*—Institutional funds are sometimes allocated in "lump sums"—i.e., the funding agency does not constrain institutional expenditures by category. In such cases, the institution makes its own decisions on the percentage of funds to be spent on salaries, supplies, equipment, and so forth. Institutions with this flexibility may provide the same flexibility to individual departments.

4. *Sources of institutional support.* Institutions usually get their funds from a variety of sources. Some of these funds are for general institutional support, while others may be directed toward specific purposes. The most common sources are listed below.

a. *State funds* are obtained from the general revenue of the state and usually make up the major source of a public institution's operational funds.

b. *Incidental funds* come from student tuition payments, library fines, application fees, and so forth. Sometimes contract and grant overhead funds are included in this category as well.

c. *Contract and grant funds* are obtained from foundations and government agencies for the purpose of financing specific projects and research activities.

d. *Auxiliary funds* come from revenue generated by institutional auxiliary activities, such as bookstores, housing, health center, duplicating services, and so forth. These operations are designed or mandated to be self-sufficient. Generally, normal operating funds from the university may not be used to support them. Profits generated by an auxiliary activity may be used for institutional purposes such as scholarships.

e. *Agency funds* are funds that the institution holds and disburses on behalf of an agency. A university service fraternity, for example, is in this category.

f. *Activity fee funds* are collected as supplements to tuition and are used to support such activities as student clubs, intercollegiate athletics, and other student-related activities. Although often included within agency funds, they may be handled separately. How these funds are controlled and regulated varies from institution to institution, but there seems to be a trend toward student involvement in activity fee control.

g. *Investment earnings* are generated by investing funds from the above categories if their immediate expenditure is not required. The investment earnings are generally used as discretionary funds by the institution. Sometimes state statutes prohibit public institutions from investing state funds.

h. *Other discretionary funds* may be obtained from the profits of concessions and vending machines and are generally retained by the institution for discretionary purposes.

i. *Scholarship and loan funds* may come from government or private sources. Included, usually, are funds to support the federal College Work-Study program.

j. *Foundation funds* include gifts and donations; generally these are not administered by the university but by a university or college foundation that is incorporated as a separate entity. *Restricted funds* are those given for a special purpose, such as for a particular school, college, or activity; *unrestricted funds* are those that have not been specifically designated. Usually, the foundation board decides how to use them.

k. *Athletic funds* are the revenues from the intercollegiate sports program. Usually, these funds are also external to the institution and are controlled by an athletic board.

Allocations within the Institution

When an institution is informed of its level of resources for a given budget period, it begins the process of internal distribution. Before moneys are disbursed, however, the institution sets aside the dollars needed to pay for continuing commitments and expenses. These cuts are generally determined by an office in the central administration, such as the budget office or controller's office.

The total cost of the faculty and staff is one of the first determinations that must be made. The related question of how to deal with unfilled positions is answered in various ways by different institutions. In some cases, unfilled positions are treated as if they belong to the departments where the vacancies occurred, while in other cases all positions are reclaimed by the central administration, which reallocates them to the same or different departments on the basis of demonstrated need.

Regardless of the differences among position control policies, the computation of total institutional personnel costs is the first step in the allocation process. Next, the central administration must decide how much to take "off the top" to fund mandated expenditures. Money must be reserved for liability insurance, workmen's compensation, and continually increasing utility payments. Third, some funds are reserved in order to cover revenue shortfalls or unanticipated expenses. Fluctuating enrollments do not allow dependable projections of income from tuition, and in times of unstable enrollments the funds to be reserved may have to be increased.

After the necessary funds for the purposes described above have been reserved, the remainder of the budget, usually called "operating funds," is distributed to the vice-presidents, often on the advice of a university budget committee. Each vice-president, in turn, must distribute the funds to the units in his or her division. The vice-president for academic affairs allocates money to the academic deans, who subsequently make disbursements to the departments.

Early Commitments and Interim Requests

Appropriation schedules for state legislatures are often out of phase with institutional deadline dates for making and implementing planned distribution decisions. Some state universities never know for sure what their fiscal-year budgets will be until after the fiscal year has already started. Because of the number of administrative levels involved in making budgetary decisions, departments are usually the last to be informed about what resources they will have for the new budget year. For a part of the year, therefore, most chairpersons will be uncertain about resources and must make tentative decisions without exact budget information.

Even under biennial budget conditions, when the legislature appropriates funds for two years at a time, there is still bound to be a period of uncertainty while departments wait for distribution decisions to be made within the institution. This uncertainty increases the difficulty of administering a department under any sort of plan or set of priorities. For example, a chairperson cannot wait until late August to learn whether a new faculty position has been allocated; March is about the latest time to begin recruiting a new faculty member for the fall term. Similarly, the chairperson of a department with a graduate program, to avoid losing prospective graduate students because of uncertainty about available support, needs to know by February what to expect for the next year in terms of allocations for assistantships and fellowships. The chairperson should be informed as early as possible whether requests for new positions will be approved, whether he or she will be authorized to recruit for positions that will be vacated because of resignations or retirement, and what the level of support for graduate students will be. A strategy used by many chairpersons is to prepare and submit an interim request to their deans and academic vice-presidents asking them to make certain commitments in advance of the normal allocation cycle. Chairpersons may also seek early commitments for summer school operation.

The *interim request* is a procedure whereby the academic vice-president or dean, prompted by sound arguments from the chairperson, makes commitments in advance of the actual receipt of funds. Important results of early commitment may include a rise in faculty morale, improved planning for summer courses, and recruitment of good faculty members. The major effect, however, is the well-being of the department chairperson, whose uncertainty level is reduced because planning for the summer and fall quarters can proceed in a timely and appropriate manner. Everyone concerned should understand the potential for problems and the risks involved in making decisions based on early commitments, for it is possible that the anticipated funds may not become available. The chairperson must then be ready for the consequences and be prepared with contingency plans.

Although early commitments could be made quite easily in the early 1970s, when continuous enrollment increases generally assured the dean of additional resources, times have changed. Relatively stable enrollments, allocations increasingly earmarked for special purposes, and special constraints for the use of resources have caused uncertainties for the deans and vice-presidents nearly equal to those that chairpersons face.

The chairperson's ability to recognize the new uncertainties, communicate that understanding to the dean, and demonstrate willingness to share the risk with the dean can result in optimal resource planning and allocations if the dean and academic vice-president are able and willing to make early commitments. As in all high-risk situations, the chairperson must plan for and be able to deal with unanticipated consequences. In any event, when critical situations arise, the dean should be informed of the negative effect of any delay in decisions. A successful chairperson is likely to be one who is aggressive and tenacious in pursuit of a decision from a dean.

Comprehensive Fiscal-Year Requests

In times of decreasing enrollments and diminishing resources, the system of distributing funds to departments and programs according to enrollment may no longer serve the institution's best interests. This distribution process may have worked well in the late sixties and early seventies, when enrollments were continually expanding and institutions were generously supported by legislatures and patrons. When scarce resources are divided among departments according to their relative enrollments, however, some programs with high priority within the institution or the college may not receive sufficient funds to maintain or achieve quality. Although enrollment cannot be ignored when allocating funds, many institutions are beginning to place more emphasis on demonstrated relative need within the context of structured priorities. Consequently, clear and effective documentation justifying programs and purposes for which funds are being requested must accompany each budget request.

Academic departments compete for funds not only with each other, but also with other administrative units within the university. In the central administration the vice-president for academic affairs represents academic departments, just as the vice-presidents for administration and student affairs represent departments and units in their respective divisions. In making the budget case for academic programs, the academic vice-president uses the aggregation of documentation prepared by department chairpersons and deans. Unless the academic vice-president has sufficient and useful information at hand, he or she may be placed in an inferior negotiating position when participating with the other vice-presidents in the initial process of resource distribution. Chairpersons required to prepare comprehensive department budget requests, therefore, must give serious attention to the task of providing strong supporting documentation.

Before and during the process of preparing a budget request, the chairperson should reflect on how best to present the department's needs and what information would be most pertinent and persuasive. He or she should also make a realistic appraisal of the funds expected to be allocated to the institution for the coming year. During budget preparation time, and perhaps at other times as well, the chairperson should keep informed of legislative actions and of amounts previously allocated to higher education in general and, specifically, to his or her university for each of the last several years. If the university's allocation or expected allocation compares favorably with the previous year's allocation, there is a reasonable chance that a department's request for funds to cover basic needs, program changes, and improvements will be granted.

If the university's allocation does not compare favorably with the previous year's allocation, the chances for success in obtaining major increases are slim. Such circumstances are discouraging to the entire academic community, especially to chairpersons of departments whose programs command high enrollment and high visibility. These chairpersons feel that, without adequate funding, their departments will be unable to maintain their academic status and reputation for quality. In such instances, some chairpersons may propose that funds within the college or university be reallocated and that their departments be given additional funds, even at the expense of other departments. In theory, reallocation of resources to accommodate shifts in enrollment and changes in program priorities should be possible; in practice, major reallocations seldom occur.

The allocation patterns within universities reveal that few moneys are available for immediate reassignment. Usually, approximately 70 percent of university funds are expended for salaries; the filled positions supported by those salaries are really not suseptible to reallocation because they are held by specialized and often tenured professionals. Approximately another 10 percent of university funds is reserved for items that the university cannot control, such as utilities, leaving 20 percent to be used for operating needs. Realistically, however, only a small portion of the 20 percent is available for redistribution. Even departments whose programs have low enrollment and low priority require a minimum level of support. Any reduction in their budget could result in their demise.

One indicator of a university's ability to fund new or expanded department activities can be derived by comparing the overall increase in the university budget from one year to the next with the increase in average salaries over the same period. If the overall institutional increase is at least 2 percent greater than the salary increase, the university is in a relatively good position to meet department requests for additional operating funds. This type of situation exists, for example, when the institutional allocation has been increased by 10 percent over last year and the increase in average salaries is only 8 percent. On the other hand, if the overall institutional increase is less than the average salary increase, the university is hardly in a position to consider even minor requests for additional funds. Such would be the case with an institution whose overall allocation is 5 percent above last year's but whose increase in average salary is 8 percent. Obtaining information regarding the university's current allocation and how it relates to the previous year's allocation may take some effort. Occasionally, local newspapers will carry the information; or a call to the dean or to the budget office may produce results. Knowledge of the university's situation will help the chairperson maintain realistic expectations and see the final allocations in proper perspective.

Budget-Planning Strategies

In preparing a comprehensive budget for a department, the chairperson should construct a schedule of critical events for which plans must be developed and budget needs identified. The following list of questions may serve as a guide for making such a schedule.

- What is the probable retirement date of each faculty and staff member?

- When will any faculty members be eligible for tenure evaluation? For an "up-or-out" review?
- Which faculty members will become eligible for sabbaticals in the next five years? Which are likely to apply for them?
- Which faculty members are likely to obtain external support and seek release time from teaching and other regular assignments in the next several years?
- Which faculty members will develop sufficient visibility to be recruited by another institution during the next five years?
- Which faculty members are likely to leave voluntarily within the next few years?
- Which faculty members are changing their career emphases from professorial to administrative roles?
- Which college or university administrators whose academic home is in this department are likely to return in the next several years?
- Given current enrollment trends and reasonably reliable forecasts of jobs for graduates and so forth, what is the probability for change in the number of student credit hours generated over the next several years?
- Is it possible, given the available data, that the department will have a surplus of faculty members in the next five years? A shortage?
- If program changes are planned for the next few years, are these likely to cause increases or decreases in enrollments?
- When is the next department self-study due? When is the next professional reaccreditation scheduled?
- Is the number of students who graduate likely to change? Will the department initiate new degree programs at existing levels? At different levels?
- Will competition with other educational institutions prove detrimental? If so, when?

Flexibility in Transferring Funds from One Expenditure Category to Another

Chairpersons should be familiar with the degree of flexibility permitted the department in transferring funds from one expenditure category to another. Such flexibility—or lack thereof—will influence the presentation of a budget request. For example, the chairperson of a department that has a justifiable need for additional instructional personnel wishes to ask for funds to meet this need. He or she can ask for salary funds, which can be used to fill permanent positions, or for temporary employment funds, which can be used to hire part-time instructors. The chairperson would prefer to add permanent positions, because once allocated they tend to remain in the department. The request for funds, however, may not be approved in time for the department to recruit adequately for new faculty positions by the fall term. If the salary line dollars can be easily converted to temporary employment funds, the funds for the new positions can be used to hire adjunct instructors. If this flexibility is not permitted, the positions will have to remain unfilled during the long recruitment period and there will be a delay in meeting instructional needs. The chairperson, if he or she knows the degree of flexibility allowed, can then decide whether to request funds for permanent positions or for temporary positions. In the latter instance, the dean should be informed of the need for additional faculty lines in the subsequent year.

Similarly, if the department is permitted to transfer money from the expense category to the equipment category, the chairperson is sometimes able to make more efficient use of moneys available. For example, a department that is paying annual leasing fees from its expense category for a duplicating machine may find buying the machine cheaper in the long run, thereby precluding the yearly outlay of expense moneys. Purchases of equipment, however, must be paid for out of the equipment expenditure category. If the department's equipment expense fund is low, the only way the purchase can be made is by transferring funds from the expense category, provided that such a transfer is permitted. By knowing in advance how much flexibility for transfer exists, the chairperson will know the best strategy for obtaining the equipment in question.

Unanticipated Availability of Reserve Funds

As mentioned previously, universities often keep reserves to offset possible shortfalls in incidental income. When and if a university establishes that the funds kept in reserve are not needed, these funds may be distributed to departments. Most often these reserves are held for the equipment category; thus, additional equipment needs can be accommodated late in the year. The chairperson should be aware of the department's unmet needs so that he or she may respond quickly to inquiries by the dean when unused reserve funds become available. Since the turnaround time for expending the reserves may be short, the chairperson with available information stands to gain the most.

The Department's Role in Meeting Institutional Commitments

All departments should have a firm idea of the institutional purposes and goals they are expected to meet. Further, the chairperson should be aware that the type and condition of the department determine the nature of the budget request to be submitted to the dean. The department chairperson should be able to associate his or her budget request with department, college, and institutional goals and identify those strengths that specifically fit in with the institution's priorities. Different departments meet different institutional needs and commitments. Following are examples of five types of departments whose activities include performing specific functions needed to meet the institution's commitments.

1. *Departments that exist solely because of the university's commitment to an academic discipline.* Examples are classics and humanities departments, which generally do not attract large numbers of students or generate large amounts of contract and grant moneys. These departments often have stable enrollments and do not rank high in the institution's priorities for resource allocations. Nevertheless, they have traditionally been identified as indispensible components of the liberal arts, and their contribution to the university is felt to be important. In documenting their budget requests, such departments should stress the quality of their programs, since their enrollment figures may not be impressive.

2. *Departments that offer large numbers of service courses.* Many English and mathematics departments belong in this category. The budget requests of these departments should use official enrollment figures as a basis for demonstrating the need for personnel and instructional support funds. Even though these departments might also have good graduate programs, their requests should emphasize service to other departments and relate needs to anticipated enrollment increases.

3. *Departments that are heavily involved in community needs.* Examples are education departments with a large number of in-service teacher training activities. (Note that these types of activities are not associated with enrollments.) Budget requests from such departments should emphasize past achievements and ask for funds to expand or improve their programs.

4. *Departments that are able to obtain outside contracts and grants to support expanding research programs.* Departments of natural and physical sciences frequently belong in this category. Budget requests should show how the outside funding augments internal allocations, as well as the extent to which the benefits derived outweigh any overhead or matching funds that the institution must provide as a condition for obtaining the contract or grant.

5. *Departments that are closely tied to professions.* Schools of law, nursing, and social work are examples. Budget requests of these departments or schools should clearly state societal and professional demands and pressures to maintain quality programs. The requests should also emphasize the added instructional costs necessary to ac-

commodate changing certification requirements, professional regulations, and so forth.

The preceding list has been compiled to show that all department budget requests should not be developed according to the same strategy.

A further consideration is the department's perception of itself. A department that already has or is striving for a national reputation will want to emphasize its gains or losses during the current year and note the effect its national exposure has had on the university. Federal and state grant awards, prestigious publications, and improvement in student quality are developments that should be included as background in the budget request. If the department perceives itself as regionally oriented and has no serious intention of competing in the national arena, it should present information that shows its local influence. If the department is basically a service department, the budget request should include information about current faculty loads, as well as a statement of the positive effect that additional resources would have on generating credit hours.

We have discussed alternative strategies that a chairperson might use when preparing a budget. Deans, however, have their own personal styles and react in different ways to various requests. Moreover, some have their own ideas about the nature of department goals. Because the priorities that the dean has in mind are not always apparent, the chairperson should not try to outguess him or her but rather present department needs in a straightforward manner. The chairperson must maintain credibility with the dean. Overstatements and inaccuracies in budget requests may rapidly erode the chairperson's credibility. Annual budget requests that contain well-developed, accurate documentation and that reinforce department objectives and priorities will have a cumulative beneficial effect over the years in shaping the dean's perception of the department.

Preparing a Budget Request

The comprehensive budget request should include relevant background information to update the dean's knowledge about the department. The information used should be "official" information, so that precious discussion time is not wasted in disagreements over facts and figures. University fact books, published financial reports, and information that has been widely distributed should serve, as much as possible, as the sources of the data presented. Each institution has an office of institutional research, which is responsible for providing accurate information to external agencies. Therefore, if published information is unavailable, that office should be consulted for data or for verification of the accuracy of unpublished data.

Several indicators of the department's workload and its relative standing within the university should be compiled and kept current. These indicators include department trends and comparative data. A recommended way of showing *department trends* is to compile the following types of data for each of the last three years and to project figures for the next year:

1. number of credit hours produced by the department
2. number of students majoring in the department's discipline
3. number of service courses offered
4. average class size of service courses
5. number of faculty members and percent distribution of faculty effort in instruction, research, public service, and other areas
6. number of teaching and research graduate assistants
7. number of nonacademic staff persons, such as secretaries and technicians
8. effect of federal and state funds

The presentation of *comparative data* should show rates of change, ratios, or statistical averages:

1. percent change in credit hours for the department compared with percent change for the university
2. faculty-student ratios compared with those of similar departments
3. average faculty instruction loads compared with those of similar departments
4. faculty-support staff ratios compared with those of similar departments

Drafting the Request

The budget request should review, as concisely as possible, the various programs within the department, stressing the program's age, its relative academic and professional standing, and its strengths and weaknesses. The presentation should be clear, logical, and brief.

The request should include a summary of how the department is organized. Faculty members' names should be associated with department functions wherever possible. Faculty members who have served on recognized university-wide committees should also be mentioned, as well as those who are active in state and national professional groups.

After providing the background information, the chairperson should present the department's precise needs for the coming year. This section of the budget request should incorporate appropriate strategies, such as those discussed earlier. Once the background information has been clearly presented, then programs and indications of desired activities may subsequently be referred to by title.

The favorable effect of funding the proposed budget request should be described, along with the negative effect of not funding the requested improvements. If partial funding can provide some reasonable progress toward the stated goal, this information should also be stated, accompanied by a phased schedule for obtaining the remainder of the resources needed in future budget years.

A table should be provided to serve as a summary that communicates the essence of the budget request. It will further serve as a visual aid in budget discussions with the dean. The dean will become more familiar with the department and its requests if the chairperson frequently refers to the data table during budget discussions.

Budget-Related Discussions with the Dean

Much is to be gained and nothing lost by frequent discussions with the dean concerning the resources needed and the problems faced by the department. Chairpersons tend to review developments only at annual budget meetings, but they should take the initiative to call the dean's attention to problems as they occur. Conferences with the dean should be requested during the year, and matters to be discussed at these conferences should be well documented and should clearly indicate a continuous pursuit of department goals. The chairperson should provide the dean—in advance of any meeting, if possible—with facts and figures, estimates of the budget's effect, and the statement of needs. Oral presentations and face-to-face discussions should amplify, further explain, or emphasize the points set forth in the written documentation. This procedure allows for improved communication and better understanding of the request; it also helps bring about optimal results at allocation time. Consistency is necessary in describing department needs. In essence, the chairperson may help shape a dean's behavior by fostering a more rational approach and increasing the quantity and quality of the dean's response.

If the chairperson has some question about the results of a meeting with a dean, he or she should prepare a memorandum that sets down the details of the discussion, including points of agreement, action to be taken, and dates for future decisions. When shared with the dean and the department faculty, the memorandum may serve as a basis for department planning during the upcoming fiscal year.

Well-documented budget requests presented in a logically organized format will provide deans with information that may be helpful in the rational allocation of funds. The approaches described here may not always result in an improved resource allocation. They should, however, build credibility for the department. Further, they may help clarify the dean's perceptions of the department and his or her expectations about its future achievements.

Setting explicit goals—no matter how desirable for an institution, school, or department—is a difficult process, for goals are not usually formulated until the amount of available resources has been established. This process is a reversal of the rational planning model and results from increasing economic contraints placed on education. A chairperson should understand the major commitments that, in effect, are the implied goals of the school, college, and institution. Then he or she can better target the available funds for appropriate areas, programs, and components. The budget request presentation described above can elicit responses from the dean that should help the chairperson better understand the dean's philosophy. Furthermore, this presentation should improve the dean's understanding of the department.

Questions and Exercises

1. a. Is your department expected to prepare and submit a budget request, formal or informal, describing resource needs?
   b. If not, how are the resource needs of your department made known to the administration? Who makes the request for you?
   c. If yes, how detailed a budget request are you expected to prepare?
2. a. Within the administrative hierarchy of your institution, how many levels must review the budget request submitted by or for your department?
   b. What external reviews, outside of your institution, are conducted? Who conducts them?
3. Speculate on the special political, social, and economic factors that might, in the next two to five years, have an effect on the funding for your department.
4. At your institution, who decides the institutional priorities? Who decides the department priorities? Who decides how many resources your department will receive?
5. How successful were you in obtaining resources for the department last year?
6. a. What calendar must your department and institution follow in preparing a budget request? What is the rationale for using this calendar?

    b. What specific deadline dates must be met by your department in preparing a budget request? How do these deadlines fit in with the other activities that must be conducted in the department?

7. What is the primary role of your department in helping the institution meet its commitments? Is the primary role to conduct research, train graduate students, train undergraduate majors, teach courses, provide community service, or provide professional training? Does it have some other role not listed?

8. a. List, in decreasing order of priority, your department's five to ten most important resource needs—such as personnel, equipment, space, supplies, services, and so forth—during the next three years.

    b. In requesting funds for each of the needs listed, what strategies would be most effective in persuading your dean or academic vice-president to provide the necessary funds?

9. Estimate the likelihood that all the needs listed will be funded.

10. Which needs have the greatest likelihood of being funded? Which have the least? List the needs in decreasing order of likelihood of being funded.

11. Would your chances for obtaining funds be increased if you included in your budget request some mention of how the department's role helps the institution meet its commitments?

12. Review the various types of departments described for budgeting purposes on pages 303 and 304 in this chapter.

    a. What type or types does your department represent?

    b. Are there any defining characteristics which should be added to the departmental taxonomy to adequately accommodate your department? If so, what are they?

    c. Do you disagree with the taxonomy? Suggest a better interpretation.

13. One of the most difficult tasks in developing the budget is to ensure that the data and the words are related and consistent. Another difficulty is preparation and presentation of tight arguments which are logical, complete, and supported by data or information. Such arguments are crucial if enrollment increases are not anticipated. Consider the following statements and determine if the justification each one presents is adequate. If you were the dean, which of the following justifications would you consider seriously? Why? Which would you not consider seriously? Why?

    a. Our faculty-to-student ratio is too high at 22. Indiana State's ratio is 15.

    b. Unless one additional position is provided we shall not be able to meet the demand for accounting courses. The demand is such that we need two more basic classes and one more intermediate class. The resulting credit hours, at current productivities, will generate two postions for the university.

c. We absolutely must have more secretarial positions. The School of Education has 12 positions more than we do.

d. We must have more expense money for travel and telephones.

e. We recognize that the appropriation to the university is not sufficient to fund inflation, but if additional travel funds were available we would be able to enhance our prospects for additional grant support. Currently, I have two faculty members in Washington, and they report that we have been awarded continuation of our big training grant.

f. We need more laboratory equipment!

g. We would like $7,200 to purchase a Xerox duplicating machine. This will release $3,600 of expense funds which are currently being used for the lease payment.

h. Extraordinary salary increases are requested for: Dr. Smith, who was elected president of the national association for next year and should help enhance our national reputation; Dr. Jones, who received the university's teaching award; and Dr. Doe, who chaired the undergraduate policy council, had a full teaching schedule, and brought in a $150,000 grant which is supporting 10 graduate students.

i. The salaries in the school of business are too low. We may lose some faculty next year.

j. Additional resources requested for next year include three new faculty, two secretaries, and one computer programmer.

References

ADAMS, CARL R.; HANKINS, RUSSELL L.; AND SCHROEDER, ROGER G. *Literature of Cost and Cost Analysis in Higher Education.* A Study of Cost Analysis in Higher Education, vol. 1. Washington, D.C.: American Council on Education, 1978.

BUDIG, GENE A., ed. *Dollars and Sense: Budgeting for Today's Campus.* Chicago: College and University Business Press, McGraw-Hill, 1972.

CARTER, E. EUGENE. *College Financial Management.* Lexington, Mass.: Lexington Books, 1980.

CARUTHERS, J. KENT, AND ORWIG, MELVIN. *Budgeting in Higher Education.* AAHE-ERIC/Higher Education Research Report No. 3. Washington, D.C.: American Association for Higher Education, 1979.

COGAN, ROBERT. "The Design of Budgeting Processes for State-Funded Higher Education Organizations." *The Journal of Higher Education,* September-October 1980, p. 556.

Colleges and Money: A Faculty Guide to Academic Economics. New Rochelle, N.Y.: Change Magazine Press, 1976.

Confronting the New Depression in Higher Education. Washington, D.C.: Academy for Educational Development, 1973.

GREEN, JOHN L. *Budgeting in Higher Education.* Athens, Ga.: The University of Georgia Press, 1972.

HALSTEAD, D. KENT. *Statewide Planning in Higher Education.* Washington, D.C.: Government Printing Office, 1974.

JELLEMA, WILLIAM W., ed. *Efficient College Management.* San Francisco: Jossey-Bass, 1972.

KALUDIS, GEORGE, ed. *Strategies for Budgeting.* New Directions for Higher Education, no. 2. San Francisco: Jossey-Bass, 1973.

MICEK, SIDNEY S. (ed.). *Integrating Academic Planning and Budgeting in a Rapidly Changing Environment: Process and Technical Issues.* Boulder, Colo.: National Center for Higher Education Management Systems, 1980.

MILLETT, JOHN. *Resource Reallocation in Research Universities.* Washington, D.C.: Academy for Educational Development, 1973.

NATIONAL ASSOCIATION OF COLLEGE AND UNIVERSITY BUSINESS OFFICERS. *College and University Business Administration.* Washington, D.C.: NACUBO, 1975.

Procedures for Determining Historical Full Costs: The Costing Component of NCHEMS Information Exchange Procedures. Technical Report No. 65, 2nd ed. Boulder, Colo.: National Center for Higher Education Management Systems, 1977.

15

Assigning and Reporting Faculty Activities

Department chairpersons differ greatly in the way they perceive their roles and responsibilities in assigning activities to faculty members. Some believe that the professional nature of university teaching and research forbids the formal assignment of faculty duties. Others hold that a chairperson is a manager of resources, especially human resources, and that he or she is responsible for the department's success or failure in helping achieve the university's mission and goals. The latter view clearly requires that the chairperson take an active role in assigning faculty duties. In recent years, legislative demands for accountability and union demands for explicitness in faculty-administration relationships have strengthened the view that the chairperson must play a role in assigning faculty activities.

The trend is for chairpersons to assume *more* rather than less authority and responsibility in faculty assignment. The State University System of Florida, for example, has for several years required a formal assignment of faculty activities; it even requires a periodic audit of such assignments. Further, the collective bargaining agreement between the United Faculty of Florida and the Florida Board of Regents specifically requires faculty assignments. Many other public and private colleges and universities have similar kinds of requirements.

Finally, college and university budget models may be based on minimum or average workload data of this kind; some multicampus university systems also have such standards. In some states the legislatures have passed laws establishing minimum workloads for faculty, such as 12 student contact hours per term for university faculty and 15 for junior college faculty. Some departments wrongly implement this policy by treating the established minimum workload as if it were a maximum workload. A chairperson may not believe in the worthiness of such laws, but where they exist, legislators expect faculty activities to reflect the laws' intent. Compliance with the law, however, does not mean that the university should use the 12-hour law as the framework within which all assignments are made. Assignments should be based on the department's goals, objectives, priorities, and policies, including the needs of the faculty and students. In implementing these goals and policies, every effort must be made not to violate the 12-hour law, should one exist.

Benefits and Purposes of Explicit Assignments

The chairperson has extensive responsibilities for assigning faculty duties, and this task is directly related to faculty evaluation. Most college and university administrators now understand that evaluations should be based on the performance of specifically assigned activities. They realize that individual faculty members and the groups who represent them wish to ensure that faculty members are not denied promotion, tenure, or salary adjustments because of failure to perform tasks they were never explicitly assigned in the first place.

Explicit assignments serve other important purposes in addition to evaluation. The development of equitable workloads among the department faculty almost demands a record of the particular assignments made to each faculty member. Systems for equalizing workloads are sometimes included in department policies. On the other hand, some faculty members believe that workload equity is a matter that they themselves must determine, rather than some absolute institutional standard of equivalency that they must follow. Such policy statements as those passed by the American Association of University Professors recommending numbers of teaching credit hours on the basis of the number of new and old preparations have been helpful guidelines in this matter. By making formal, explicit assignments, however, the chairperson is able to adhere to the department's policy, implement its goals and objectives, and maintain data to explain his or her good judgment in managing human resources.

Similarly, as students' needs are assessed and changes required, the chairperson can modify faculty assignments, thereby shifting faculty effort to cover these needs. If some subject areas are not covered or developed, the department can undertake some long-range planning so that it can do more than just fill the gap at the last minute. An analysis of the extent to which explicit assignments are completed may show the need for new faculty resources or professional career and development counseling.

Policies governing formal assignment of faculty duties generally include statements such as the following:

Faculty members should be assigned duties and activities in writing. These assignments must be clearly stated, and those receiving them should acknowledge them as understood.

The department chairperson, by virtue of his or her responsibility for attaining department goals and objectives, is the person who should make faculty assignments.

Effective faculty assignments require clear statements of department goals, objectives, and workload policies. The proper functioning of the department depends on the chairperson's maintaining adequate records and consulting extensively with faculty members before and after the assignments are completed.

Preparation of Assignments

What are the essential requirements of an assignment of duties? How detailed must the assignment be? How often should an assignment be made?

The department chairperson who tries to understand the many conflicting requirements for faculty assignments can reach several conclusions. A chairperson may conclude that the best procedure is to make assignments as brief and as general as possible. In this way maximum flexibility may be preserved, thereby ensuring that all bases are covered, no matter what needs may come up during the year. Unfortunately, assignments that are brief and general are usually vague and subject to broad interpretation by the faculty member as well as the chairperson. Vagueness can make it impossible to determine whether the assignment has been completed successfully. In the event of a faculty grievance over tenure or promotion, the chairperson may be hard-pressed to substantiate any judgments made if he or she can present no clear evidence of duty assignment and performance criteria.

A chairperson who has faced only one grievance resulting from an assignment that is too vague or general is usually convinced that highly detailed assignments are necessary and justified. Even so, endless arguments may ensue, depending on how the assignment is worded, about the degree to which the various assignments were completed. In some cases, faculty members may demand tenure, promotion, or salary increases, claiming they have completed all the detailed assignments given them and then submitting evidence to support their claims. A problem may also surface if a faculty member refuses to complete a task that needs to be done but that was not listed as part of the agreed-upon detailed assignment made earlier in the year.

The two problems described above might have been avoided if the assignments had been precise. An assignment must be general enough to provide some flexibility for both the chairperson and faculty member, and it must be detailed enough so that both understand what performance is expected and what will serve as a basis for evaluation.

Chairpersons should be particularly alert to the information about assignments contained in the various documents that must be acknowledged by each faculty member. Some institutions notify faculty members of their next period of employment by means of a salary letter; it may contain general language indicating, for example, that for the fiscal year the person will be paid a specific sum for teaching, research, service, and other such functions as assigned. A person may be appointed for only part of a year or as a part-time employee during a school year; the assignment for a part-time faculty member may be more specific than for the full-time faculty member, e.g., the teaching assignment may consist of one specific course.

As the formal employment relationship between faculty members and the institution evolves, however, the salary letter often becomes merely a notification of salary award, whereas the contract document becomes the actual instrument of notification of employment and salary level. The contract document may contain a variety of other information, including a detailed statement of requirements in legal terminology. The assignment in the contract still may be given in functional terms—i.e., teaching, research, and service—but it may also list specific tasks—e.g., teaching one graduate course off-campus. In preparing a contract, the dean's office may solicit information from the chairperson about any special assignment terms to be entered in faculty contracts. At the same time, a chairperson should check with the dean's office to make sure that a faculty member is not assigned activities that are not likely to be required or performed—for example, a faculty member who has been assigned teaching as a full-time workload should not be assigned any research or service activities.

A chairperson might be required to solicit from each faculty member a projected work plan for an entire academic year. This plan might be the basis for the annual contract and the assignment of workloads each term. Note that institutions operating on the quarter calendar sometimes attempt to spread the annual department workload as evenly as possible over the four quarters. In such instances, full-time faculty members may have an opportunity to work during the summer quarter in lieu of another quarter. This type of arrangement, if approved by the chairperson, would be indicated in the work plan. Because plans of this kind are developed in early spring for the subsequent academic year, they are subject to change. Regular consultation with each faculty member should enable the chairperson to anticipate any changes and to make the necessary adjustments to the plan.

The chairperson usually is not required to agree to faculty members' requests concerning workloads; nevertheless, the assignment of a faculty member's workload or schedule should not be arbitrary or capricious. Consultation is a standard of collegiality; to impose a work assignment on academic professionals may be a denial of their expertise. In emergencies, of course, faculty members must be assigned certain tasks to ensure coverage.

In some universities, the annual projected work plan for each faculty member may be converted to an official document, and as such it will often include the details for each term of the contract year. The plan is not always implemented as originally prepared, however. The chairperson may change an assignment before it is fulfilled; the faculty member may undertake one or more activities not included in the assignment; or the faculty member may not perform an assigned activity. The alert chairperson will discover the existing discrepancies during periodic consultation each term and take appropriate corrective action. A consultation before a term begins, specifically to confirm and adjust the assignment as needed, should reveal the changes a faculty member is planning or anticipating. Such preterm conferences also inform the faculty member of possible changes that the chairperson may request to meet changing conditions in the department.

The chairperson should adjust the assignment planning or workload projection records to reflect the activities actually performed. Similarly, he or she should obtain explanations from faculty members as to why certain assigned activities have not been performed, especially when nonperformance represents a breach of agreement or a failure to support important goals, objectives, and priorities of the department. It is equally important that faculty members be commended, in writing, for tasks well done, new activities successfully undertaken, and so on. The chairperson should communicate to the dean and other appropriate university officials any extraordinary achievements by faculty members.

Equitable Assignments

A chairperson must be concerned not only with each faculty member but also with the department's total functioning and how its workload can be distributed equitably among all the faculty. He or she must not only keep in mind the needs of individual faculty members but must also assess the effect that a person's assignment may have on the other faculty members in the department. If, for example, a faculty member is assigned to teach a course for the first time and is given some released time from other teaching responsibilities for course development, who will assume the other teaching responsibilities of that faculty member?

When assignments are shifted among the faculty members to distribute the workload equitably, the chairperson may have a difficult time trying to find the proper combination of activities for each person. The chairperson will have to assess each faculty member's skills and competencies to make sure the workload is spread equally among those who can best perform it. In some departments, the faculty may decide to assign priority factors for various activities. Some activities have

FIGURE 15.1. Point system in which points are assigned for specific tasks included in faculty assignments

ACTIVITY	POINTS
Teaching	
COURSE TEACHING	
One lecture course	8 points
One seminar course	5 points
One lab course	3 points for first 25 students; 1 point for each additional 25 students
ONE-ON-ONE SUPERVISION*	
Director of master's thesis	4 points
Member of master's committee	1 point
Director of doctoral dissertation	6 points
Member of doctoral committee	2 points
Directed individual study, supervised research, or supervised internship	1 point per student; maximum 4 points per term; maximum 2 points per student
*Research***	
Sponsored research project:	
Under $10,000	4 points
Over $10,000	10 points
Other activities	
Member of department or university committees	The number of points allowed for each activity is determined by the
Chairperson of department or university committee	chairperson based on the time and effort involved and the importance
Administrative assignments within the department	of the work to the department.

*The maximum number of points allowed for all one-on-one supervision during any academic year is 30. Points for the first four classifications listed in this section are given on completion of the graduate degree.
**The maximum number of points allowed for sponsored research during any academic year is 40.

higher priority than others, depending on the effort required and the comparative importance of the activity as perceived by the department. The priority factors expressed as points are used in calculations that result in the assignment of equitable workloads to the faculty.

Very few departments find a priority system either necessary or desirable, but some have used it successfully. Figure 15.1 shows a system used by one large, research-oriented social science department in a major university in allocating points for specific activities.

The department that used this system listed all its activities, regardless of who carried them out, and allocated to each activity the number of points designated. The sum of all the points was divided by the number of department faculty members to determine the average point load. The workload for this particular department amounted to 1056 points. Since the department contained sixteen faculty members, the average, or equitable, load was 66 points per academic year. Figure 15.2 shows three examples of faculty workloads and point allocations.

This point system was not used for evaluation purposes but only to help equalize the assignments given to individual faculty members. Any point system is cumbersome, and the result may not be much different from the result obtained by means of another system. Faculty members with heavy teaching loads continue to be assigned heavy teaching loads, and productive researchers are allowed reduced

FIGURE 15.2.   Sample of workloads and point allocations

	POINTS
Faculty Member A	
Six lecture courses (8 points each)	48
One-on-one supervision	19
No grants	0
No committees	0
Total	67
Faculty Member B	
Three lecture courses (8 points each)	24
One lab (3 points each)	3
One-on-one supervision	22
Two grants (10 points each)	20
Total	69
Faculty Member C	
Four lecture courses (8 points each)	32
One lab (3 points each)	3
One graduate seminar	5
One-on-one supervision	13
Committee assignment	5
One grant	10
Total	68

teaching loads. Some faculty members, however, feel more secure with a point system of this nature. Quite often, a faculty member will challenge the point values that the chairperson has allocated to certain activities.

Equitable faculty workloads can be accomplished in two ways: (1) by assigning workloads that are equitable term by term; or (2) by assigning workloads that are equitable when averaged over the academic or fiscal year. Averaging workloads over an academic year allows the chairperson to assign heavier teaching loads during terms when enrollment is unusually high and lighter teaching loads during terms when enrollment is usually lower. Moreover, faculty members may be willing to undertake an extra heavy load one term in order to have a light load the following term, during which they will have more time to concentrate on their own professional interests.

The first step in preparing teaching schedule assignments for a given term is to review the teaching schedules of previous years for the same term. This information—together with information from the faculty and an awareness of personnel changes, curriculum changes, changing student interests, and so forth—can serve as the basis for developing teaching schedules for the current term.

In assigning teaching activities, the chairperson should ask the following questions about each faculty member's assignment:

- Has this faculty member taught this particular course before? Does he or she have more than one new course to teach?
- How many new preparations does this faculty member have? Will special assistance be needed for labs, computer usage, and so forth?
- Do these courses require any special activities, e.g., field trips, demonstrations, and so forth?
- How much evaluation of student work will be required?
- What is the mix of level of courses? The size of the estimated enrollment?
- How many thesis and dissertation projects is each faculty member directing? On how many committees is each serving? How many students is each counseling?
- How many undergraduates are being advised by each faculty member? What other undergraduate activities is each supervising or sponsoring?

Clearly, the chairperson must be flexible in assigning percentages of effort for each faculty activity. He or she should move away from rigid formulas and toward individual judgments about the workloads assigned to each faculty member. The examples given in figure 15.3 indicate that a wide range of assignments may be equivalent and, hence, equitable. Note that two faculty assignments can appear quite disparate and yet be considered functionally equivalent. The explanation following each example presents the factors used by an academic vice-president of a major university to determine that the percentages assigned each category of activities were in agreement.

FIGURE 15.3.   Sample of equitable faculty assignments

		FACULTY MEMBER A	FACULTY MEMBER B
Example 1			
Teaching	67%	2 classes (8 hours)	4 classes (16 hours)
Research	20%	Research Grant	Research grant
Service	13%	1 committee	3 committees
	100%		
EXPLANATION OF EXAMPLE 1			
Teaching		*Graduate classes; 2 in-depth preparations*	*Same course; no additional preparation*
Research		*Self-explanatory*	*Self-explanatory*
Service		*University committee*	*Routine department committees*
Example 2			
Teaching	75%	3 classes (12 hours)	3 classes (9 hours)
Research	20%	No funded research grant	Research grant
Service	5%	2 committees	1 committee
	100%		
EXPLANATION OF EXAMPLE 2			
Teaching		*2 sections of same class*	*3 different classes*
Research		*In process of preparing a grant for funding*	*Funded grant*
Service		*Routine department committee*	*College committee*
Example 3			
Teaching	67%	5 classes (20 hours)	3 classes (15 hours)
Research	18%	No research project	No research project
Service	10%	No definite service activity	1 committee
Advisement	5%	Advisement	Advisement
	100%		
EXPLANATION OF EXAMPLE 3			
Teaching		*Undergraduate sections of same class; 4 activity classes; 1 lecture class*	*3 large classes (different course taught each term requiring preparation and work outside of class)*
Research		*Needs to develop some research and creativity pursuits*	*Needs to develop some research and creativity pursuits*
Service		*Chairperson will make a definite curriculum assignment prior to the beginning of the term*	*Department work*
Advisement		*Assigned students*	*Assigned students*

The number of credit hours of teaching, generally, is not a good measure of workload. For example, a 16-credit-hour load that consists of teaching the same course to four different undergraduate classes of twenty students each might be a light load for an experienced faculty member who has taught that course many times before. In contrast, an 8-credit-hour load that consists of teaching two entirely different courses to two different classes of forty students each might be a heavy load for a new, inexperienced faculty member who has never taught either course before, especially if the two courses required more themes and reports from the students than did the first faculty member's course. The chairperson should not hesitate to assign the same courses to two faculty members, giving one a 50 percent teaching assignment and the other an 80 percent assignment if the faculty members' relative experience and qualifications warrant the difference in assignment and would result in a similar "real" workload for each faculty member. To be more consistent, the chairperson may wish to assign the faculty member with less experience to 80 percent of full time for teaching a course that includes time for course development. Clearly, department needs and course workloads—not some requirement for a report— should determine the most efficient and effective use of faculty resources.

The equitable assignment of faculty duties systematically allows the chairperson to formulate and implement plans for attaining department goals while assisting faculty members in reaching some of their personal goals. This harmonizing, after all, is one of the purposes of assigning activities. The chairperson's success in this activity may well determine his or her effectiveness as an academic administrator and leader, since personnel assignment activities and decisions constitute a major function of the chairperson's role. Chairpersons who are inadequate personnel managers could become liabilities to their departments. Some chairpersons find personnel decisions so disturbing and distasteful that they resign. On the other hand, chairpersons who are interested in these kinds of problems and learn to cope with them may find rewarding careers in university administration.

Performance Criteria for Functional Assignments

For the busy chairperson, the task of assigning faculty activities commonly becomes a chore that must be done hurriedly. All too often the task is performed by making a simple list of the things the faculty member will probably be doing in the next few months. An even more unfortunate situation occurs when the faculty member is allowed to complete the assignment form without consulting the chairperson. In neither case has a real assignment been made, and the chairperson is forfeiting an opportunity to manage valuable human resources for the improvement of the department. Yet making periodic term assignments can sometimes be a distasteful waste of time. Assignment schedules that consist of a simple listing of the same set of duties each term are basically useless.

How can assignments be transformed into useful aids to the chairperson's already difficult task of resource management? A few suggestions about activities for each performance area should provide an indication of the essentials of a good assignment and should stimulate further thinking about the subject. The key is to think of each assignment in terms of how a chairperson should evaluate success in completing the assignment, i.e., what criteria should govern each assignment in each area?

Teaching Assignments

The assumption that teaching assignments should consist only of a list of courses to be taught is invalid. About the only thing that can be evaluated with such an assignment is whether or not the courses have been taught! More important, the performance of such an assignment must certainly be evaluated as "average." What could be the basis for an above- or below-average performance when everyone completes the assigned courses?

At the very least, a teaching assignment should rest on a clear understanding that the *quality* of the teaching will be evaluated. Further, a clear statement, preferably in writing, should be provided as to the types of evidence, such as student evaluations or peer review, that will be used in making the evaluation. It is the chairperson's responsibility to ensure that clearly stated criteria for evaluation are established by the department and are understood by all the department members.

Teaching assignments can be made with a degree of sophistication. The success of a teaching assignment should probably be measured in terms of what students learn, either in absolute terms or in relative terms (such as student growth). But have you, as the chairperson or as a department member, defined what is expected of a student who completes a given course? If so, and if the learning outcomes are stated in measurable terms, successful course instruction will be measurable in terms of student learning. Of course, many faculty members will object to this method of measuring teaching success, citing inaccuracy of tests, differences in student ability or motivation, and a variety of other arguments. Admittedly, precise measurement of effective outcomes, such as attitude changes, does lag behind precise measurement of cognitive outcomes. Nevertheless, student learning is the primary goal of teaching and can be taken as one measure of successful teaching.

Other activities that might be included in the teaching assignment are developing courses; revising syllabi; updating laboratory experiments; converting courses to computer-assisted instruction; training, monitoring, and evaluating graduate teaching assistants; and other related activities. To avoid misunderstandings, the department faculty should agree that these teaching assignments are appropriate.

Research and Creative Activity Assignments

Research and creative activities seem to play an increasing role in the assignment process and, in many departments, are necessary conditions for promotion and tenure. Again, the necessity of specific assignments and the insistence on clearly stated criteria for evaluation are essential. Probably everyone can think of faculty members who have been talking research for years but have yet to produce a successful grant proposal, research report, publishable paper, or anything else that might be considered a significant contribution. These "wheel spinners" could write books of excuses and reasons for their failure to finish various projects—if only they had a little more time!

If research or creative actvity is to be included as part of a faculty assignment and if it is to be evaluated at a specific time, the faculty member should be able to provide a documented plan of action with some sort of time schedule for completing various parts of the research activity. The action plan might include such information as the title of the project; whether a library review of the literature is required; when the project will be completed; whether a proposal for outside funding is planned and when it will be completed; whether laboratory equipment must be acquired and assembled and how much of the laboratory effort can be completed this term; and what efforts at data collection and processing are required. If the faculty member is writing an article for publication, he or she should note whether a rough draft can be completed this term. If a graduate student is scheduled to complete a thesis, note what must be done to assure that he or she will be able to complete the research.

If the faculty member cannot provide a detailed action plan, perhaps the research should *not* be assigned! If the plan can be stated clearly, the assignment should indicate that the research effort will be formally evaluated in the future. Failure to accomplish set goals means that the assignment has not been completed, and this failure should be reflected in an evaluation. Of course, the faculty member may have good reasons for failing to complete an assignment. The chairperson has the responsibility for ascertaining and assessing the validity of these reasons, converting this information to appropriate evaluation judgments, and adjusting the assignments for the next term accordingly.

The term *failure* may be considered unduly harsh when assignments are being evaluated; perhaps *noncompletion* would be less grating. Regardless of the term used to describe this unfortunate situation, the chairperson must make sure that failure is not rewarded or allowed to slip by without appropriate reaction.

Service Assignments

Service is an assignment activity that may include a range of activities, such as attending local service club meetings or serving as a member of campus or interinstitutional committees. For example, a faculty member may be assigned to develop and deliver off-campus presentations designed to alert the public to services offered by the university, gain support for an on-campus program, or attract students to the campus.

Again, the chairperson should think seriously about the real purpose of making such assignments and how their success can be evaluated. If a faculty member is assigned to a university committee, is regular attendance at meetings expected? Is regular attendance considered "outstanding" or just "average" performance of this assignment? Should the department chairperson ask the head of this committee to provide an evaluation of the faculty member's performance? If the faculty member was assigned to contact local high schools and explain new department programs, is the mere making of the contacts sufficient for successful completion of the assignment? Or does success require that a larger percentage of students in the schools contacted attend the university? Just why is this assignment being made? Will it really benefit the department, college, or institution?

Another kind of service assignment is holding office in a state or national professional society. Most chairpersons will insist that such activties bring "honor" to the home university. No doubt they do, but the effect is difficult, if not impossible, to measure. Fortunately, a chairperson is seldom called on to explain such benefits to taxpayers or legislators. Although service assignments can be made considerably more specific than most currently are, it is difficult to assign these types of activities in a way that makes objective evaluation possible. On the other hand, membership in professional societies has traditionally been considered a part of the academic life, and holding office in those societies has traditionally been deemed worthwhile. Some public institutions now require a written report from faculty members about the benefits—academic and other—of attending regional and national conferences.

Reporting of Faculty Activities

The discussion so far has focused essentially on the distribution of the department workload. The formalization of these assignments has come about because of such developments as collective bargaining, increased disagreement with tenure and promotion decisions, and, in some cases, state statutes.

The reporting of faculty activities, however, is a result of the quest for increased accountability. Specifically, any university that accepts federal or state contract and grant funds must be able to provide proof that the contracted amount of effort has indeed been expended on the contracted activity. Payroll certifications that would satisfy accountability requirements are often deemed too cumbersome; therefore, a quarterly or semester report on activity is generally substituted. Universities that have recently been audited by federal agencies have been told that the effort of the support personnel, as well as the effort of the faculty, must be certified. In the absence of clear federal guidelines, universities have developed their own reporting systems. Many of these systems not only satisfy federal agencies but also provide chairpersons and deans with pertinent information and allow cost studies to estimate costs more closely. Thus, many colleges and universities have developed detailed categories of activities, coupled with standard definitions, in order accurately to record data about faculty workload. The amount of detail reported on these activity forms seems to be increasing; the forms all focus on standardized reporting techniques and rely on computer processing for handling the increasing volume of data.

Recommendations for the data elements and counting procedures, as well as for the activities to be reported, can be found in relevant technical reports of the National Center for Higher Education Management Systems and in circulars. Following is a list of broad categories adopted by one state:

A. General academic instruction
   1. Lower-division instruction
   2. Upper-division instruction
   3. Graduate instruction
   4. Thesis supervision
   5. Dissertation supervision
   6. Department research

      7. Academic advisement
      8. Other instructional activities
  B. Community education
  C. Preparatory and adult basic education
  D. Institutes and research centers
  E. Individual or project research
  F. Patient services
  G. Community services
  H. Cooperative extension services
  I. Academic administration—management
  J. Academic administration—governance
  K. Curriculum development
  L. Academic personnel development

The data recorded for each category are the percentages of effort a faculty member has spent on each activity. When compiled, the data are circulated through the organizational hierarchy to state budget, legislative and federal officers. Academicians almost always view these reports negatively, seeing them as yet more bureaucratic encroachments on their lives.

The requirements for reporting faculty activities can have a significant effect on a department, however, and the chairperson should be sure that the reports accurately reflect not only the assignment but also the actual work accomplished. Accurate and complete reporting is essential for a number of reasons. First, the reported activities must not violate previous contractual agreements with a federal agency. For example, a faculty member who, for a given term, has contracted to spend 100 percent of full time on a research project funded by a federal agency cannot teach a course or otherwise share in the department workload during that term. If he or she does teach a course and therefore does not provide 100 percent of full time to the research project, the university may be required to repay a portion of the funds secured. Thus the chairperson must be familiar with faculty commitments when making assignments and reviewing reports of actual activities.

Second, many universities, under state legislative directive, annually conduct a cost study across all disciplines. These cost studies use information about faculty workload data as primary data. Cost-study reports, now being published across the nation, show instructional costs and cost per credit hour by discipline for each university. Since information about faculty workload may be the primary data for these calculations, the assignments made by the department chairperson can significantly affect the cost results in his or her discipline. The cost study could become the basis for legislative funding in future years and thus takes on major significance.

Third, faculty activity reports are used internally by institutions for various studies of costs and faculty workloads, and, sometimes, for collective bargaining purposes. Again, the accuracy of these data may have some effect on the department in terms of the allocation of financial resources and faculty positions and in possible grievance actions.

FTE Assignments

Faculty activity assignments are generally reported as fractions of a full-time equivalent (FTE) faculty position. The chairperson usually specifies the fraction of a full-time workload (1.00) for each assigned set of activities for each faculty member. For reporting purposes, each assignment is specified in terms of a decimal fraction of an FTE position, e.g., 0.50, or as a percentage (50 percent) of an FTE workload; the total of the fractional assignments must not exceed 1.00 FTE.

Many chairpersons, however, have difficulty accepting this concept because *full time* cannot easily be defined in terms of hours per week. Some chairpersons insist that their faculty members work sixty hours per week and should, therefore, be assigned more FTE, perhaps 1.50 FTE. An exception to the 1.00 limit may occur when a faculty member is assigned a full load, whatever that happens to be, and then is also assigned some overload activities, such as teaching in a division of continuing education. On the other hand, part-time faculty members are always assigned some fraction of an FTE, e.g., 0.50 FTE. Thus, what constitutes an overload, or a workload greater than 1.00 FTE, is determined by circumstances and by policies of institutional offices and divisons other than the department.

Although some chairpersons would argue to the contrary, full-load assignment cannot exceed 1.00 FTE for full-time faculty members, regardless of the number of credit hours taught, the total hours worked per week, or the "extra" activities that the faculty member may plan to do during the term. Previous examples (figure 12.3) have shown that functionally equivalent percentages of an FTE for two faculty members may not necessarily reveal the great differences in their patterns of activities. Furthermore, the same activity for two persons, each teaching a section of the same course, may result in significantly different FTE percentages. Accurate assignment of FTE fractions for each faculty member's activities depends greatly on the chairperson's understanding and experience in reviewing assignment reports and in questioning faculty members about their actual efforts with different assignments. Consulting with an experienced chairperson and with the technical staff processing these data can also be helpful.

In colleges or universities where minimum workload standards are important policy matters, chairpersons must be extra cautious not to use the minimum standard as the definition of a 1.00 FTE or as a basis for assigning fractions of FTEs to faculty activities. As repeatedly stated, the standard is a minimum, not a maximum, and usually refers only to the minimum number of class contact hours expected of a faculty member. This minimum number of class contact hours, be it 12 or 15, may constitute whatever percentage of an FTE workload is deemed appropriate by the chairperson and the department. A faculty member complies with the law or policy by satisfying the minimum contact hour requirement, but the law or policy does not tie the required minimum number of contact hours to any particular percentage of FTE workload assignment.

Chairpersons who misinterpret the minimum workload policy and make assignments on the basis that 12 class contact hours is a maximum load and thus represents 1.00 FTE often complain that no time is left for teaching, research, or service. This misunderstanding creates problems at those universities where every faculty member has been instructed by contract to perform some research and service in addition to teaching. Moreover, a faculty member who is teaching more than 12 contact hours may or may not be overloaded. As indicated in the section dealing with equitable assignments, a 20-contact-hour load may not be heavy at all, while an 8-hour load for a new faculty member may be a weighty 50-hour-a-week job. In sum, the workload standards should not be a basis for making assignments per se but should be implemented by ensuring that the faculty members perform their assigned activities and that the total department effort complies with the workload policy.

Sometimes workload policies may be satisfied by the compliance of a complete academic unit, such as a department or college, rather than by the compliance of each person in the unit. In such cases, workloads are averaged for each unit; that is, all instruction hours are totaled for a given unit and divided by the aggregate FTE faculty. A related problem concerns the interpretation of the differences between workload standards expressed as contact hours and as credit hours. For example, 3 contact hours in a lecture class per week per term are considered 3 hours of credit, but 3 hours of laboratory class per week per term may be considered only 1 hour of credit. Lecturing for one hour supposedly requires more effort on the instructor's part than supervising a laboratory class for one hour. The concept of the contact hour is also used to measure counseling and advising time with students. In any event, the chairperson should know precisely what is required for each particular FTE reporting category.

Faculty activity is generally reported in terms of percentage of effort. For example, a faculty member might report 75 percent of his or her effort in instruction and 25 percent in research, regardless of whether the total effort constitutes a 1.00 FTE appointment or any fraction thereof. To reiterate, assigning a specific portion of a 100 percent effort to each of the categories of teaching, research, and service is a distributive measure. Federal authorities no longer recognize the concept of "donated time." A faculty member cannot, within a given term, expend 100 percent of his or her effort within a research project and also "donate" the time required to teach a course.

In addition, the concept of "loans and borrows" is no longer accepted by federal authorities. Thus, a faculty member paid 100 percent from a contract during a given term cannot teach a course that term and be released from teaching during a following term to work on the contracted activity. If federal auditors observe this type of arrangement, they will recommend that the university repay the federal agency for the portion of time the faculty member did not expend on contracted activities during the term of the contract and will ignore the effort of the following term.

"Donated time" and "loans and borrows" are just two concepts that chairpersons must fully understand. A knowledge of external commitments is extremely important in making assignments and reviewing activity reports.

A General Assignment Strategy for Chairpersons

Clearly the chairperson's task of making faculty assignments is complex. It requires an understanding of many rules and regulations; it depends on a clear understanding of department goals and objectives; and it requires a significant number of judgmental decisions. A convenient and useful strategy by which to establish term assignments is outlined below. This strategy assumes that the chairperson already has department goals, objectives, and priorities clearly in mind; that the faculty have consented to these; and that the chairperson is fully aware of the department members' interests, strengths, and experiences. The strategy comprises eight major steps.

1. Establish the instructional, research, and service workload that the department as a whole can be expected to accomplish during the term. Questions to be answered include these: What total FTE can be assigned? (That is, how many full-time equivalent faculty members, including graduate assistants and faculty adjuncts, are available to accomplish the department's work?) What relative effort among the categories of instruction, research, and service would best serve department interests and contribute to department goals?

2. Identify the courses to be taught during the term and the courses

that are optional. Consult with faculty members, students, and other department chairpersons to assess the needs and demands here.

3. Determine the special requirements that have been imposed on faculty members for the term. Ask the faculty for this and other pertinent data. Which faculty members will have released time on research grants? What institution, college, or department committee assignments have already been committed for the term? (Note: If you as chairperson find these "external" commitments heavy, remember that you have control over most of them! If you do not, it is time to get your data together and have a long talk with the dean!)

4. List, for each faculty member, adjunct, and graduate assistant available to your department, the activities to which you tentatively expect each person to be assigned, without reference to time or fraction of FTE for each activity. Your choices of assignment should reflect both the department's needs and each faculty member's professional development (tenure, promotion, research, and so forth). The total listing for all faculty members should include each area and activity identified in items 2 and 3 above.

5. Determine how much effort, preferably in terms of fractions of FTE, you expect the faculty member to devote to each activity listed; double-check this with the faculty members as needed. If you use fractions of FTE, remember that the total FTE must equal exactly 1.00. If you use hours, the total hours assigned are not too important since, for reporting purposes, hourly assignments for each activity will ultimately be converted to the appropriate fraction of the total hours assigned (i.e., to a fraction of a 1.00 FTE). However, be aware that a 20-hour teaching load, if otherwise equivalent, may be 0.50 FTE for the 40-hour-a-week person but only 0.36 FTE for the 55-hour-a-week person. If hours are to be taken seriously, some standard hourly effort rates may have to be developed to ensure that persons doing equivalent work share the same workload report fractions. For these and other reasons, the standard fractional FTE (plus or minus x percent) for particular activities may be the best understood and simplified measure of assigned (and reported) effort.

The crucial issue is whether or not the final assignment is realistic in terms of what a faculty member can be expected to accomplish and perform well. In making the FTE assignment, the chairperson's judgment on such matters as faculty experience and department needs in teaching, research, and service activities is extremely important.

6. Assess the reasonableness of each faculty assignment both in terms of the activities assigned and the time or fractional FTE allowed for the activity. If inequities exist, adjustments among the faculty or in the total effort assigned may be necessary, but note that some equity adjustments may be moved to another term.

7. Identify evaluative criteria that you will use to assess each assignment being made; these activities typically are faculty activities but may include expected outcomes. Be as quantitiative as possible. Both you and the faculty member must share an understanding of how the level of success in completing the assignment will be determined.

8. Discuss each assignment with the appropriate faculty member. Consultation may be required by a collective bargaining agreement or state laws. A consultation may reveal new information or become a negotiation session, making further assignment changes necessary. The final assignment decisions, however, should remain in the hands of the chairperson.

These steps provide a reasonable and sound strategy for assigning faculty duties. The chairperson will want to involve the faculty in as many of the steps as possible but particularly in steps 1 and 2, where the department's goals, objectives, and priorities are established and form the basis for the planned quarterly activities. In addition, the chairperson should consult with each faculty member after the start of a term to make sure all is going as planned.

Questions

1. What ways are there to define "work load" other than one of the following:
   a. total hours per week (including all activities)
   b. total (100%) professional effort (including all activities)
   c. total credits of courses taught
2. Discuss the pros and cons of each way listed in question 1.
3. How can institutional expectations of faculty be incorporated into a departmental definition of a work load?
4. Should a departmental definition of faculty workload be considered a minimum or maximum expectation for evaluation purposes. Give reasons for your answer.
5. a. What are the advantages of keeping on file a written list of institutional assignments or expectations for each faculty member?
   b. What are the disadvantages of too much detail in the written list?
6. a. In determining a proper workload for an individual faculty member, should more time for class preparation be allowed to a faculty person who is teaching a course for the first time than to a faculty member who has taught the course before. Give reasons for *not* allowing it.
   b. Should time for research be included in a faculty member's con-

tracted workload? Give reasons and circumstances for a "yes" answer. Give reasons and circumstances for a "no" answer.

7. In your department, what is considered a maximum teaching load? Is it a certain number of courses or course credits taught per term, a certain number of contact hours per week, or something else?

8. If a person is assigned a maximum teaching load in your department, does this teaching constitute a full-time workload? If it constitutes less than a full-time workload, what other assignments do you give to make a full-time workload?

9. Is the teaching load of your department divided equitably among the faculty members, or do some members have larger teaching loads than others? Do faculty members who have the same size teaching loads receive the same percentage of FTE for teaching? In your department, what constitutes the workload of one FTE faculty member?

10. Have you ever reduced a faculty member's teaching load in order to assign him or her to other activities? Please explain.

11. In making assignments, do you follow any special procedures to ensure that the assignments are equitable? For example, do you assign a faculty member a specific number of points for each activity, and is he or she considered to have a full workload when the sum of all the earned points reaches a predetermined number? Or do you have some other method for ensuring equitable assignments among your faculty? Please explain.

12. Have any of the teaching, research, or service assignments to your faculty members ever been tailored to help them develop a special competency or overcome a weakness?

References

ADAMS, WALTER. "Faculty Load." *Improving College and University Teaching*, Autumn 1976, pp. 215–18.

BARE, ALAN C. "The Study of Academic Department Performance." *Research in Higher Education*, 1980, 12(1), 3–22.

BOSSENMAIER, MONICA. "Faculty Perceptions of Academic Advising." *Nursing Outlook*, March 1978, pp. 191–94.

BROWN, STEPHANIE. "Approaching Faculty Productivity as a Mechanism for Retrenchment." *New Directions for Institutional Research*, Winter 1979, pp. 45–54.

CRESWELL, JOHN W. "Faculty Acceptance of a Workload Survey in One Major University." *Research in Higher Education*, May 1978, pp. 205–26.

DYER, JAMES S., AND MULVEY, JOHN M. "Computerized Scheduling and Planning." *New Directions for Institutional Research*, Spring 1977, pp. 67–86.

FAWCETT, JACQUELINE. "Integrating Research into the Faculty Workload." *Nursing Outlook*, April 1979, pp. 259–62.

FEASLEY, CHARLES E. "Faculty Workload Formulas in Competency-Based Programs." *Education Technology*, November 1978, pp. 30–32.

HARPER, RONALD L. "Faculty Activity Analysis." *New Directions for Institutional Research*, Spring 1978, pp. 73–81.

MARCH, HERBERT W., AND DILLON, KRISTINE E. "Academic Productivity and Faculty Supplemental Income." *Journal of Higher Education*, 1980, *51*, 546–55.

McLAUGHLIN, GERALD W., MONTGOMERY, JAMES R., GRAVELY, ARCHER R., AND MAHAN, BEATRICE T. "Factors in Teacher Assignments: Measuring Workload by Effort." *Research in Higher Education*, 1981, 14(1), 3–17.

NELSON, THOMAS MORGAN. "Instructor Judgments of Classroom Assignments in Teaching Psychology." *Higher Education*, February 1978, pp. 83–86.

SOMMERS, ALEXIS N. "University Productivity." *Educational Record*, Winter 1977, pp. 251–56.

SWOFFORD, RONALD. "Faculty Accountability Workload and Evaluation: A Synthesis." *Community College Frontiers*, Spring 1978, pp. 51–53.

WALKER, JOHN E. "Research First, Teaching a Distant Second." *Journal of Thought*, January 1979, pp. 11–14.

16

Managing Curriculum and Human Resources: Full and Part-Time Faculty

In these times of budgetary restrictions, declining enrollments, and fiscal instability, the need to stretch department resources to obtain maximum benefits becomes increasingly important. The chairperson must be aware of the resources available to the department and the various ways they may be managed. Although no blueprint for successful management exists that can be uniformly applied to all departments, some common allocation problems can be addressed, and the following discussion suggests various approaches to solving these problems.

Two important resources that the chairperson must manage are time and people. One way of maximizing the use of time is to manage the curriculum efficiently. A well-managed curriculum can free valuable time for faculty members to pursue creative and scholarly interests. The faculty, students, and staff constitute the department's human resources. These human resources must be carefully nurtured and cared for if the department is to achieve its goals.

Management of Curriculum and Time

By efficiently managing its curriculum, a department can often effect savings in faculty time and instructional materials without compromising the quality of instruction or causing undue inconvenience to students. Conversely, if little or no planning time is devoted to the curriculum, the department may overextend its faculty, compromise its goals, and create morale problems that may be difficult to resolve. In other words, without planning, the teaching program may become inefficient, costly, and obsolete.

Departments must take the time to look at their offerings objectively. For example, the information about the department contained in the university catalog may be incorrect or out of date; some courses listed may no longer be offered, and the content of others may have been altered. The chairperson should ensure that the department's course offerings are appropriately and accurately described. Courses also must be related to the task of providing a coherent and sequential program of studies within the discipline and should not be offered only to satisfy the desires of individual faculty members.

Scheduling classes and assigning rooms are important activities that are sometimes carried out without consideration either of department goals or of data derived from a systematic analysis of needs. Sometimes scheduling duties are carried out by a staff assistant without adequate faculty guidance. Clearly, curriculum management is an important task that should be supervised by the chairperson, who should analyze past experience, examine complaints, and review suggestions for improvement. In effect, he or she should develop and implement reliable and relevant procedures for dealing with the curriculum. The task of curriculum management consists of making such decisions as which new courses will be offered, who should teach particular courses, and which courses might be canceled. All these responsibilities are part of the task of managing instructional resources.

One method of monitoring the curriculum is through a department curriculum committee. In many departments, such a committee may already exist, though it usually has only the responsibility for evaluating proposals for new courses. The committee's task, however, could be expanded to include many other aspects of curriculum management. Following are some suggested responsibilities for an active curriculum committee in the areas of approval of new courses, elimination of existing ones, course schedule and sequence, and curriculum review and analysis.

Approval of New Courses

Before approving any new course, the committee must take into account certain consequences. First, the committee should ask whether the new course will add to the content or perspective of the subject matter of the current offerings or whether it will substantially duplicate another course offered by this department or another.

A second consideration is the possible effect of the new course on other courses in the department. Will it draw enrollment away from department courses currently offered, or will it generate additional enrollment? If it generates new enrollment, will the enrollment in other university departments be affected? Is the course to be a core, elective, or service course? Will it primarily serve majors, nonmajors, undergraduates, or graduate students?

A third consideration is the effect of the new course on faculty members' teaching assignments. Will some department members have to assume an additional workload, or will a course currently offered be canceled so that its instructor can be assigned to teach the new course?

Finally, the committee should consider the effect of the new course on current physical or financial resources. Will the new course require materials and physical facilities that are not available to the department? Will the new course require an internal reallocation of funds or the acquisition of new funds?

When considering a new course proposal, then, the committee should analyze it in terms of, first, its educational contribution, e.g., course content, methodology, and prerequisites; second, its effect on enrollment, e.g., shifting enrollment and additional enrollment; third, its effect on workload, e.g., effect on current faculty and courses; fourth, budgetary limitations, e.g., faculty positions and the cost of new materials; and fifth, availability of space, e.g., laboratories, classrooms, and special requirements including library acquisitions and services. The committee should also examine the place of the new course within the current sequence of courses and its probable effect on the student. For students, the proliferation of courses may not only allow but even encourage early specialization. In some disciplines, specialization may narrow the opportunity to obtain a well-rounded higher education, but in other disciplines specialization may be desirable.

The department, when considering a course proposal, may need to revise its curricular goals. Such goals and objectives often include specifying the kinds of knowledge a student should obtain while majoring in the department's discipline, the competencies that the student should be able to demonstrate successfully, and perhaps even the kinds of problems the student should be able to solve. Such information may be necessary for courses currently offered as well as for proposed courses to show how the courses relate to the department's curricular goals.

The decision to approve a new course should be based on careful consideration of the information obtained during the review of the proposal. Often, a committee will not consider the effect of a new course on department enrollment. Frequently, adding a new course only disperses students majoring in the field among a greater number of courses offered by the same department. In such a case, the average class size would be reduced and the faculty workload would be increased, but the total department enrollment would remain unchanged. The effect of a new course on department enrollment, while not the major factor in deciding whether to approve the course, remains an important consideration.

Elimination of Courses

Eliminating obsolete courses allows more efficient use of available resources and reduces the amount of misleading information appearing in catalogs and counseling manuals. Some researchers have even suggested that a course be dropped when a new course is added. Such a mechanical approach, however, may be indicative of unimaginative planning or desperation caused by declining resources.

A periodic review of enrollment in all courses is a systematic way for the curriculum committee to begin the task of designating courses to be eliminated. The ability to conduct an enrollment review depends in large part on the records kept by the department staff or on the availability of these types of data from the college or university institutional research office.

Such a review opens up at least three alternatives for the committee. First, a course that generates a minimum number of students might be retained if it were determined to be beneficial to the students enrolled in it. Enrollment could be enhanced, perhaps, by changing the meeting time or by offering the course less frequently. Second, the review could result in a course being eliminated because the committee determined that the content was no longer of interest or that another course was meeting student needs and drawing enrollment away. Third, the reviewing committee could recommend that course content, methodology, or emphasis be changed to revitalize the course. These decisions, when made well in advance of registration, enable the chairperson to allocate instructional resources wisely. Courses that continue to be offered but that are ignored by students should undergo stringent scrutiny.

The course offerings should be revised as little as possible during the registration process. Some departments allow university policies about minimum class size to determine which courses are to be dropped. The obvious drawback of this approach is that the reassignment of faculty members whose courses have been dropped is not determined by careful review of curricular or other department needs. Such inadequate curriculum planning and management usually results in ad hoc assignments, last-minute switching of instruction obligations, and "default" research or public service assignments. In addition, the department loses the opportunity to support student needs.

Some departments announce more courses than will eventually be taught and wait to see which courses actually attract the most students and which attract the fewest. Courses with few students are then dropped. The difference between this approach and the "no planning" approach is that in this case an alternative assignment has already been worked out should enrollment be insufficient to justify the course.

Course Schedule and Sequence

When developing a schedule of classes, the department must consider the needs of students, the availability of appropriate classroom space, and the time preferred by students and faculty members. A review of past experiences and careful scheduling of core and elective or service courses may lead to an improvement in class schedules and faculty workloads. The schedule also must take into account special characteristics of the department's students; for example, if a large number of the students are working full time, scheduling morning classes makes little sense.

The department would be wise to review its courses annually. Information such as the number of approved courses, the number and frequency of courses actually offered, the enrollment gathered, and the number of students who dropped each course affords the department an opportunity to exercise control over its course offerings. Perhaps examining records of students majoring in the field as to courses taken, sequence, and so forth may help determine whether the recommended sequence is being followed.

Following are four examples of hypothetical situations that would require in-depth analysis. In each case, the academic year is based on the quarter calendar.

1. Course A was offered all four terms and had the following enrollment: fifteen students during fall quarter; eighteen during winter quarter; fourteen during spring quarter; and seventeen during summer quarter. A review of student course sequences may indicate that no disruption would occur if the courses were offered only in the winter and summer terms. (The assumption here is that faculty resources would be available in the summer.) Furthermore, because the course is required for students majoring in the field, the total annual enrollment may not be substantially reduced. Thus, by offering the course only twice a year, the department has decreased its instruction workload without substantially decreasing enrollment.

2. Course B has been taught during three terms, and each term its enrollment has been low. Examination of the situation reveals that the course has always been offered in the late afternoon. If increased enroll-

ment is desired, the course might be moved to "prime time," e.g., late mornings at residential universities, or evenings at universities with a large number of part-time students.

3. A department has 127 approved courses, but only eighty-seven of them were offered last year and eighty-three were offered the year before. Twenty-five of the approved courses had not been offered in either of the last two years, while two of the offered courses (four sections each) accounted for 75 percent of the department's total enrollment. This situation suggests that a curriculum review, including a close examination of the department's curricular goals, is in order.

4. During the past few years the enrollment in an upper-level undergraduate course has consisted mostly of graduate students. Perhaps this course should be offered as a graduate course.

Curriculum Review and Analysis

The importance of periodically reviewing courses before adding, eliminating, expanding, or revising them cannot be overstated. The periodic review should encompass enrollment data, revised course syllabi, statements of course objectives and student objectives, and any other special or relevant information about the courses.

Another form of curriculum analysis can be conducted using data showing department interrelationships. A given department may list all its courses and indicate the number of students majoring in other fields who are enrolled in each course. Knowing the extent to which other departments provide students for each course may be the basis for adjusting course content or method of presentation. Table 16.1 shows how such information can be arranged in a matrix. By collecting this type of data from other departments, a given department may also discover what courses are serving its own majors. Therefore, the effect of referring students to courses outside the department can be estimated. A department that offers service courses to students majoring in other fields can estimate the effect of curricular decisions by these other departments.

Almost all universities that have computerized student data files have the capability to construct such a matrix, which is usually called "the induced course load matrix." Chairpersons should contact their institutional research offices for help in obtaining the data.

Data and Information Requirements

Institutional research offices amass a large body of data, often for purposes of program evaluation. If the chairperson feels that such information would be useful, even if no formal review is scheduled, he or

TABLE 16.1 Sample of an Induced Course Load Matrix: Student Credit Hours Generated Fall Term 1977, by Program Major and by Department, San Luis State College, Domingo, Florida

Departments	PROGRAM MAJORS, LOWER LEVEL										Total Student Credit Hours by Department
	Undeclared	Arts; Humanities	Biological Science	Science; Math	Social Sciences	Agriculture	Business	Health Sciences	Food Science Technology	Ornamental Horticulture	
Business	803	185		44	527	33	2514	38	35		4,179
English and Foreign Language Literature	261	1287	139	405	1206	314	784	442	146		4,984
Fine Arts	276	1153	14	84	230	8	149	63	20		1,997
Life Sciences	184	472	227	93	1174	1067	273	1492	53		5,035
Physical Sciences	249	786	198	1608	805	505	923	847	161		6,082
Social Behavioral Sciences	228	841	118	189	2116	99	595	331	104		4,621
Vocational Tech.	203	12	7	31	8	22	3	756	1927	870	3,839
Total Student Credit Hours by Major	2204	4736	703	2454	6066	2048	5241	3969	2446	870	30,737

Note: 15 student credit hours generate 1 FTE student

she should contact the office of institutional research and request the information. The chairperson should understand that the data received are only as good as the data submitted to the centralized information sources. If there is a discrepancy between the data provided by the office and the chairperson's own knowledge, the chairperson should determine the reasons for the discrepancy and attempt to correct the data.

An improved curriculum, then, helps the students and the department alike. A system of curriculum management may be a departure from the common practice of allowing individual faculty members to determine the courses they want to teach. But a planned approach may be preferable to a situation where courses are frequently cancelled at the last minute, contracts must be revised, and students are unable to progress systematically through their programs of study. Planning is not synonymous with inflexibility, nor need it cause a decline in academic quality. By the same token, proliferation of courses is not synonymous with improvement in academic quality. By assigning time to a faculty member to revise a course or two, the chairperson may be making a short-term investment leading to increased student satisfaction and reduced faculty workload.

Management of Human Resources

As enrollments stabilize or decrease and enrollment-based funding drops, the number of constraints on the institution will increase at all levels. Effective use of human resources will become essential but can be accomplished only if the chairperson is fully aware of the department's workload and can project assignments over the whole academic year. In general, he or she needs to know the department's workload, understand the faculty members' professional and personal concerns, and then be able to interpret and communicate department needs while negotiating assignments with the faculty and staff. Clearly stated department goals and reliable historical data about all department resources will allow the chairperson to justify assignments in terms of the department's objectives. The ability to estimate requirements for an entire year, rather than treating each term as a unique entity, will help stimulate acceptance of heavier workloads during some terms.

Faculty

Very few departments have enough faculty members to do everything that needs to be done for the university, the community, and other constituents. A department chairperson may need to juggle academic assignments to ensure that sufficient effort is expended on instructional activities to cover student demands while at the same time providing appropriate research and service time for the faculty. Careful planning of teaching assignments is required to allow time for research and service, particularly for younger faculty members, who must make reasonable progress toward promotion and tenure. Typical complications arise when established faculty members accept outside contractual obligations and have to find substitute teachers for the classroom. In addition, faculty members going on sabbatical may leave gaps in the teaching program and require replacement. As suggested in the preceding section, curriculum planning and management can provide a degree of flexibility. In any event, the chairperson must be able to show the faculty that each department member is treated fairly.

An equitable distribution of the department workload may be achieved by several methods. Some chairpersons make all assignments, while others depend on a committee process. A recommended technique is participatory planning. This method is not always the most efficient planning tool, since it requires extensive communication among faculty members.

Several arguments can be made in favor of the participatory planning model, however. An open discussion among faculty members who are familiar with the courses they teach can facilitate decisions about the sequence of courses, the frequency with which they are offered, the level of performance that can be expected of students following the sequence, and so on. The faculty can devise equitable procedures for assigning introductory courses as well as those courses with unusual workload requirements. Workload policy governing the balancing of large and small courses with new and old preparations can be most readily developed through participatory planning. Moreover, peer pressure tends to reinforce policies developed in an open manner.

The chairperson sometimes has the difficult task of determining whether particular faculty members are competent to teach certain courses. In a period of expanding resources and enrollment, a department may have added specialists and specialized courses. When these specialists leave, their specialized courses, having become a part of a subcurriculum, remain.

The chairperson must then choose among several possibilities: convincing another faculty member to step in temporarily; reassigning the course to another faculty member and allowing course development time; recruiting a part-time teacher; replacing the course with one that is already being offered either within or outside the department; or, with the approval of the faculty or students, dropping the course. Other considerations may include the graduate faculty status of the proposed substitute instructor or even a strong expression of preference by the dean or academic vice-president for one of the alternatives. In any event, the chairperson needs to know about the faculty members' specialty training, their current specialty interests, their reputations for teaching effectiveness, and other characteristics that are relevant to the assignment process.

If the chairperson decides to retain the course offering, he or she will usually have to persuade the most able candidate from among the faculty to accept this new responsibility. The chairperson must proceed cautiously, however, so as not to give a "proprietary deed" for the course to the substitute teacher until and unless the other faculty members concur. "Ownership" can be a prime motivating force for the teacher to develop and enhance a course. On the other hand, a faculty member who regularly teaches the same courses, year after year, may become bored with them and become ineffective in the classroom.

The middle ground between ownership and boredom can be attained through a system of rotation. Even the specialized courses in many departments can be taught by more than one professor. Every faculty member might be required to be prepared at least to take responsibility for additional required or specialized courses. These arrangements can be worked out cooperatively, with the approval of the chairperson, after vitae and teaching records of each faculty member have been reviewed. The chairperson's genuine concern for faculty development will be tested in such cases. Finding the right opportunities for growth and improvement for each faculty member is a challenging task.

The problem of reassigning and revitalizing courses also occurs when enrollment in two related courses declines so markedly that they have to be combined to meet minimum enrollment standards. Prior "ownership," expertise in the subject matter, and rank and seniority in the department may complicate efforts at reassignment. The new activities required of faculty members who will have smaller teaching loads is a topic that ought to be discussed before or during the time that courses are being combined, not afterwards. A clear statement of department goals, as well as an inventory of research and service activities for each faculty member, would be helpful to those involved in reassigning courses.

Declining budgets and an increase in faculty grievances may well lead to a squeeze on human resources, which will, in turn, retard a department's progress toward achieving its teaching and research goals. In such situations the department's mood and productivity may depend more heavily on the manner with which faculty workload assignments are handled than on the assignments themselves. Perhaps greater involvement by the department faculty would be helpful. In essence, by using open planning to make teaching assignments, the chairperson can help change the faculty's perception of administrative capriciousness and promote unity of purpose within the department.

This method, even though the results may not be ideal, may be perceived as more fair and, therefore, more palatable.

Understandably, the participatory process can create numerous problems for the chairperson. Moreover, there may be insufficient time to implement the process. Sometimes a chairperson will not know until July what the department's allocation will be for the upcoming academic year, which begins in August or September. Yet faculty assignments for a given calendar year must be made much earlier than July. One solution to this dilemma is to implement the planning process in the preceding February or March. At the least, information from the faculty can be obtained and feelings aired. An estimate of instructional resources with alternative assignments can be made, and the result can be fine-tuned in the fall.

Essentially, planning with 90 percent of the information available is superior to no planning at all. Also, decisions that are generally understood and that are accepted by the majority of the faculty are more easily implemented. An open planning process that relates operational necessities to department goals is one technique for achieving important objectives. Furthermore, a process by which all faculty members can identify their contributions and feel productive will tend to minimize friction within the department.

Most descriptions of the planning process give the impression that it is a smooth, well-oiled operation, when in actuality it is usually a fitful and uneven affair. Planning consists of the working out of tensions among various opinions and ideas, and often occurs as a result of pulling and pushing by various factions within the department. Integrating differing opinions into a working and realistic plan requires a great deal of effort.

Part-Time Faculty

Part-time faculty are not a new phenomenon in higher education, but their numbers are now quite large. In the fall of 1980, for example, Florida's 28 community colleges employed almost 9,000 part-time faculty as compared to half that number of full-time faculty. The growth of part-timers in American community colleges began in the 1960s with an 80 percent increase during the 1970s. This contrasted dramatically with only an 11 percent gain in full-time faculty. Even the four-year institutions in this period had a 38 percent increase in part-time faculty, with only a 9 percent increase in full-time staff. In general, full-time faculty continue to outnumber part-time persons because four-year institutions employ mostly full-time staff and do not count graduate teaching assistants as part-timers. Clearly, part-time instructors are here in large and probably increasing numbers. For purposes of the following discussion, the terms part-time faculty and instructors are used interchangeably.

Some institutions find that part-time faculty members provide flexibility, since they can be hired as needed to meet changing student course and program enrollments and because their salaries are generally lower than those of their full-time counterparts. Also they may bring vitality and new ideas to programs suffering from static faculties and declining enrollments. Part-time faculty members are often used to staff new and experimental programs to test the student market before an institution makes any firm commitments. Part-timers have proven so useful that some institutions are converting certain of their full-time positions into a greater number of part-time positions.

A 1980 study of part-time faculty by a select committee of Florida community college presidents identified the following eight key advantages in the employment of this group:

1. The cost is less.
2. The commitments of the college are fewer.
3. They generally have a positive attitude.
4. They are usually up to date in their fields.
5. They are an excellent source of recruitment for full-time positions when openings occur.
6. They may understand the part-time students and their problems better than their full-time counterparts.
7. They are rarely unionized.
8. They provide a vital link with the local community from which they are drawn.

There are also problems associated with employing part-time faculty. Those most often mentioned include:

1. Part-time faculty members often feel exploited with respect to salary.
2. There is a lack of program continuity when a large share of the faculty is part-time.
3. They are often not available for student advising or counseling during regular office hours or before class which in some cases also imposes heavier than normal counseling responsibilities on full-time faculty.
4. They are suspected of devoting insufficient time and effort to their course preparations.
5. They do not contribute to the out-of-class tasks of the faculty, such as committee work, curriculum development, etcetera.
6. Full-time faculty members, when outnumbered by the part-time group, often fear that departmental program governance could be taken over by the part-timers.
7. The cleavages and frictions between full and part-time faculty

members may be more disruptive to the program than the existence of a completely full-time though obsolescent faculty.
The successful utilization of part-time faculty members requires a substantial understanding of their characteristics and special needs. A
large survey of part-time instructors undertaken by the Tuckmans* in
1980 reveals some interesting facts about the makeup of this group. Following is a slightly modified and expanded version of the classification
and description of the seven categories of part-timers contained in the
Tuckman report.

1. *Full-mooners* are persons who, in addition to their part-time jobs,
hold full-time positions elsewhere of at least 35 hours per week for 18
weeks of the year. This group, comprising 27.6 percent of the sample,
includes many full-time faculty members at nearby universities and
community colleges, as well as local business and professional persons.
A good example of a full-mooner is a certified public accountant who is
recruited to teach introductory accounting courses.

2. *Students* are persons employed in departments other than those
in which they are seeking degrees. These part-timers, 21.2 percent of
the sample, are often graduate students from near or distant colleges or
universities. Some are still doing course work while others are writing
their dissertations. It should be noted that graduate teaching assistants
within their own departments are usually not reported as part-time instructors by the universities for whom they work. If they were counted,
the numbers reported would be quite different.

3. *Hopeful full-timers* are persons holding part-time positions
because they are unable to find full-time employment and comprise
16.6 percent of the sample. These fully qualified persons are becoming
a national concern because they represent a generation of scholars who
are unemployed due to the lack of academic jobs. They hope that their
part-time positions will develop into full-time employment.

4. *Part-mooners* are persons who simultaneously hold two or more
part-time jobs of less than 35 hours per week for more than one week.
They comprise 13.6 percent of the sample and like the hopeful full-
timers often seek full-time employment. Members of groups 3 and 4 are
the so-called itinerant or gypsy scholars of the 1980s.

5. *Homeworkers* are persons who do not want full-time employment because they are taking care of a relative or child at home and
comprise 6.4 percent of the sample. These individuals are often unemployed spouses who possess a variety of graduate credentials and experiences. Along with the full-mooners they provide a stable cadre of part-
time instructors.

*Tuckman, Howard P., and Tuckman, Barbara H. "Who Are the Part-timers and What Are
Colleges Doing for Them?" *Current Issues in Higher Education*, No. 4, 1981, pp. 4 and 5.

6. *Semi-retired* are persons who seek activities to fill time made available by retirement and make up only 2.8 percent of the sample. These individuals who often possess considerable talent and ability may also contribute to the stable core of part-timers. They may need the extra income to compensate for inflation and rising taxes which have reduced their fixed retirement income. In rural areas, the home-workers and semi-retired can be the main sources of part-timers.

7. *Part-unknowners* comprise the remaining 11.8 percent of the sample. They give a variety of reasons for becoming part-time which do not fall into any of the other categories.

Traditionally, part-time faculty members have been used to meet unexpected needs for additional instructional staff when full-time instructors become ill, are given sabbaticals, or receive unexpected leaves of absence. They have been the typical source for teaching courses offered at night, weekends, and in the summer, and for courses taught off-campus through extension and continuing education programs. Part-time faculty most often teach one or more courses with no other responsibilities assigned. They are usually paid less than the salary rate of full-time faculty members because they have not been required to advise students, participate in the governance system, and so on. Most writers point out that to require such participation will lead to increased costs.

The enrollment of the typical younger student is decreasing in many colleges and universities. These diminished numbers are being partially compensated for by increased enrollments of older students in evening, weekend, and off-campus programs. Since these programs are often taught by part-time instructors, it is clearly in an institution's best interests to insure that part-time faculty members are of a quality sufficient to meet the instructional goals of the institution. If part-time instructors are either unhappy with their conditions of employment or inadequately skilled to do a satisfactory job of teaching, the resulting student dissatisfaction could affect enrollments. At the same time, questions about the rights and privileges of part-time faculty have been raised in collective bargaining negotiations and in lawsuits in state and federal courts. Consequently, some institutions have begun to think seriously about establishing separate personnel policies for part-time faculty members.

Institutions that have concerns about the present or future use of part-time faculty need to develop clear policies about the expected duties and responsibilities of these individuals. Does the department wish part-time faculty members to be involved in departmental affairs beyond the single task of teaching courses? Should they participate in curriculum development, departmental governance, committee work, and student advisement? What provisions will be made to ensure that part-time faculty are providing quality instruction to their students?

Few part-time instructors are willing to assume additional responsibilities without expecting additional compensation. Moreover, the involvement of part-timers in issues of governance and curriculum could alter the direction and character of the department. It therefore behooves a department to consider carefully the extent to which it wishes to employ part-time faculty for the many different types of services which they may be capable of providing. These questions are not intended to either encourage or discourage the use of part-time faculty for noninstructional tasks but rather to illuminate the implications and possible concerns that may arise when extensive use is made of part-timers. Whatever is decided and agreed upon should be included in a written policy statement which clarifies what the institution expects of them and what they can expect from the institution in terms of length of appointment, remuneration, and assigned duties. It is also important that the part-timer not be given any false expectations concerning the probability of future employment, either part- or full-time. Some of the topics and issues which have arisen in selecting and utilizing part-time faculty are discussed in the following paragraphs.

Recruitment and Selection.   Part-timers currently available to an institution are often able to recommend acquaintances who may be qualified and interested in a particular part-time teaching assignment. Department chairpersons can telephone or write their counterparts in nearby institutions. Community college division chairpersons can make contacts at the better high schools in order to identify the most experienced teachers, including outstanding substitute teachers. Affirmative action officers and professional women's network coordinators can also be contacted. If need be, a classified advertisement can be placed in nearby city and college newspapers.

To aid in selection of candidates, a job description could be written listing, for example, all of the desired qualifications and expected duties, as well as the pay range and whatever benefits might be available. If the position is not tenure earning or not renewable, the written description should so indicate. If feasible, the chairperson should involve full-time faculty in the selection decision. In an emergency, the chairperson may not have the opportunity to check credentials until after a selection decision is made, but such emergency hiring without checking credentials should be kept at an absolute minimum. Since at present there exists a large supply of unemployed persons with graduate degrees, there is no reason why a part-time person should not be as qualified as a full-time instructor in the same department.

Salary.   There are several bases for determining the salary to be paid a part-timer. The most common is to pay a flat rate for a course. Sometimes a part-timer is paid at the same rate that a new full-timer receives for teaching the same course. Occasionally, hourly rates are used. At some institutions the rate of pay will depend on the size of the class, with more pay for enrollments above a minimum number, such as 35. The purpose is to provide a modest incentive to the instructor to teach the "oversize" class. Another factor often considered in salary determination is the formal educational and professional experience of a part-timer. One with more formal educational or recognized professional experience, such as a certified public accountant, might command more than the minimum amount per course.

Perhaps the most important factor to be considered here is the relation between the typical amount per course paid to part-timers and the overload payments available to regular faculty. Whereas the difference between computed hourly rates for part- and full-time faculty members can be justified on the basis of responsibilities that full-time faculty have in addition to teaching, the argument does not hold for differences between the pay which part-timers receive and the overload pay which a full-time faculty member receives for teaching the same course. At institutions where financial difficulties preclude annual salary increases, an offer of overload pay at the part-timers' rate may be used as an economic incentive to regular faculty. Incidentally, once these pay differences are determined, it could be the institution's policy that full-timers be given the option of overload pay before the part-timers are sought and hired. A by-product of such a policy could be a rise in faculty morale.

A number of other pay issues raise concerns about basic fairness to part-timers. Part-timers new to an institution may be required to attend orientation sessions. Whether they should be remunerated for this attendance depends upon local policy, but if the services of a particular person are valued, a modest payment can be a good incentive. Other issues focus on the matter of compensation for time spent in course preparation. What if a course does not fill with the minimum number of students? If the institutional policy is firm that the course should be terminated after the first meeting when a minimum is not met, then it seems only fair to compensate the part-timer for some course preparation effort and for the time spent meeting the first class. A policy of this kind shifts the responsibility for marketing and forecasting anticipated revenues to the administration and away from the part-timer. Of course, if a college or university does not want to guarantee a minimum compensation in the event that the class is canceled for lack of enough students, then the minimum enrollment for earning compensation must be stated forthrightly in the employment offer and contract which the part-timer receives.

Fringe Benefits.   The area of fringe benefits is important for the part-time faculty because about 70 percent of them are not employed elsewhere in places where they qualify for such benefits. A 1980 study published by the American Association of University Professors indicates that as many as 60 percent of the part-time faculty with Ph.D.s who work more than half- but not full-time receive a wide variety of fringe benefits. Fewer of those Ph.D.s working less than half-time receive the same benefits. Health insurance, often perceived as the most important benefit, is extended to about 85 percent of part-timers who work more than half-time, and to about 60 percent of those employed for less than half-time. Health insurance as part of the total compensation package is also the benefit for which part-timers have the greatest need because so few of them have another job. Many group insurance carriers are willing to discuss special programs for part-timers.

Expectations.   As mentioned earlier the formal expectations of the part-timer's duties should be stated clearly in a written document. A genuine meeting of the minds is desirable before a formal contract is drafted. One of the ways to begin the effort of clearly stating expectations is to include them in a formal memorandum to the part-timer who is being offered employment. The prospective part-timer then can respond by asking for desired clarifications or modifications. This somewhat formal procedure can help ensure clear and complete communications before the new term is at hand.

The items to be included in the memorandum should cover the title of the course and related details, the position title, pay and benefits offered, the course cancellation policy, the extent of duties beyond teaching the course and whether pay will be provided for other than nonteaching duties. In addition, the memorandum should include information about required texts or tests, and the rights and restrictions relating to tenure, renewal, and consideration for full-time employment. It is important that office hours, if any, be stated explicitly, and that office space be assigned for this activity. Details about other rules and regulations that may apply to the part-timer in addition to those appearing in the memorandum and contract should be stated. If a part-time person is covered under a collective bargaining agreement, this should be explained. The prospective part-timer should be invited to examine the college catalog, bargaining contract, faculty constitution, and so on.

Vested Interests.   One of the more difficult issues concerning the employment of part-time faculty members is whether they may acquire a vested or property interest in their part-time jobs. This is, of course, a legal question, but at the present time it is without clear definition. Some community college administrators are sufficiently concerned that they do not permit the same person to be employed part-time for more than two years continuously. This very cautious and conservative attitude could prevent retention of very able part-time instructors. The other end of the spectrum is to treat part-timers the same as full-time faculty, but on a prorated basis. To date hardly any institutions follow the latter pattern. Currently a number of statements have been drafted for inclusion in contracts which explain the limits of an institution's responsibilities to a part-timer. For example, some contracts clearly state that successful teaching does not guarantee that the part-timer will necessarily be considered again for another part-time job. Similarly, if it is institutional policy that part-timers are ineligible for tenure, this is stated explicitly in the contract. In some states a part-time person who works more than half-time for several years and is paid at a prorated full-time faculty salary may qualify for tenure.

These issues also have impact on policy decisions providing for increases in compensation or addition in benefits after a part-timer has worked successfully two or three years. The concern here is that these rewards may be perceived as resulting from seniority rights, and imply an entitlement to continuing employment in the part-time position. If these rewards were based only on the results of systematic evaluations and specific evidence of meritorious performance, perhaps a disclaimer could be inserted stating that length of time in continuous service on a part-time job is not sufficient to qualify a part-timer for those rewards.

In sum, the employment contract should state both what is intended and not intended when a person is hired as a part-timer. Furthermore, part-timers who work more than 50 percent on a regular basis may acquire a vested interest in their jobs that may require the institution to treat them like full-time faculty. Obviously, legal counsel should be sought before a firm policy is set. Clearly, a department chairperson would benefit from advance planning if part-timers are to be used.

Management of Part-Time Faculty.   It is very difficult to supervise part-time faculty members in the same ways as full-time faculty members. Institutions may have to provide "night" deans, secretaries, and support personnel to help part-timers perform their assigned responsibilities effectively. The remoteness of part-timers from mainstream activities makes it necessary that they too be evaluated, counseled about their performance during the term, and given suggestions for improvement. These activities allow the institution to exercise a degree of quality control over their part-time teachers. Below are some frequently made recommendations for improving the performance and morale of part-timers.

Support Services.   Part-timers who work in the week day during regular hours can usually obtain support services with proper advance notice to typists, librarians, media specialists, etcetera. But those who work in the evenings and on weekends have greater difficulty. One solution is to have some secretaries and librarians work flexible hours, and provide the part-time faculty and their students with the adjusted schedules. Most clerical support services need to be available only through the first half hour or hour after a class begins in the evening. Arrangements for support services on weekends require a specific cost-benefit or feasibility analysis to ensure that the institution does not commit unavailable resources.

Institutional Information for Part-Timers. One of the best ways to confront the many concerns which can divide full- and part-time faculty is to involve a committee of full-time faculty, working with department heads and deans in drafting a handbook of policy information for part-timers. Policies for part-timers should be based on principles of equity. Where full- and part-timers face similar tasks and are equipped with similar qualifications, they should be governed by the same policies; where full- and part-timers have different tasks and responsibilities, they should be treated differently.

The institution's community can be informed about the part-time faculty in a variety of ways. The part-timers can be listed in the annual catalog, or a separate publication containing information about full- and part-time faculty could be distributed. Frequently, a yearbook format is used, with photographs and biographical sketches including degrees earned and special expertise. If the full- and part-timers are listed together under their department, division, or discipline, then both day and night students would be informed about their entire faculty.

Performance Evaluation and Professional Development. Given the direction of the courts in expanding the due process rights of part-time faculty, it would be wise for department heads and deans to arrange for a performance evaluation of each part-timer at least once a year. Evaluation is also desirable as a quality assurance policy, and should be implemented whenever a significant number of part-time persons is employed in an academic year. Such a number might be five persons or 50 percent of the number of full-time faculty, whichever is larger.

Part-time faculty may not resist performance evaluation as much as full-time faculty. The evaluation of part-timers will usually be based primarily on their teaching effectiveness, and the same techniques used for evaluating teaching performance of full-time faculty may apply unless they are specifically assigned and compensated for additional duties. Many, if not most, part-timers have had no teaching experience, nor have they been instructed in testing and measurement procedures. The results of performance evaluation can be used to determine which areas of subject matter or technique need improvement. Then, opportunities should be provided so that the part-timers who desire to be reemployed can learn ways to improve their teaching. Such opportunities might include seminars on instructional methods and grading procedures.

Dealing with Part-Timers' Concerns. Part-timers are often isolated from ongoing discussion and explanations of institutional policies and procedures, especially when they teach at nights or on weekends.

Therefore, they stand a good chance of misperceiving, misunderstanding, or simply not being aware of new or changed directives and requirements about which other faculty members have been informed. Some of these changes may appear arbitrary or capricious to an uninformed part-timer. A way to avoid conflict may be the periodic scheduling, perhaps once a semester, of a conference to explain institutional policy and procedure. Part-timers have expressed concerns about a number of issues in which they feel the need for more involvement, information, or equitable treatment. Following is a list of some of these concerns:

1. the right to participate in selecting textbooks, making up exams, and structuring courses
2. criteria for evaluation of performance
3. criteria for continued employment in the part-time position
4. information on who represents their interests in the department, college, or university when working conditions are being discussed
5. information about their rights to negotiate, grieve about, or appeal salary offerings, especially when their salaries for subsequent terms reflect no increase for inflation or no relationship to the increments of full-time faculty
6. information on how to receive consideration when full-time openings occur
7. assurances that exercise of rights to academic freedom will not result in nonrenewal.

Whether part-timers are entitled to use the grievance procedures which may have been established for full-time faculty depends on institutional policy. Providing access to existing grievance procedures may provide the isolated part-timers with confidence in their institution, and assurance that a reliable means is available for processing their concerns.

Enhancing Prestige. It is useful to enhance the prestige of part-time faculty. This may be accomplished in many ways, including holding an official orientation especially for them, displaying pictures of both full- and part-time faculty in the same brochures and welcoming their attendance at fall and spring faculty meetings. Also, they might be sent personal invitations to attend receptions or social affairs hosted by the president, dean, or board of trustees. A chairperson can do much good by shepherding and introducing part-time faculty at annual or term presidential receptions. If the chairperson can recruit full-time faculty to assist in the shepherding and introducing, then so much the better. The good feelings and benefits from social activities often provide the beginning of trust which, when honored on all sides, provides the absolutely best means by which to solve problems and build a viable institution.

Support Staff and Graduate Assistants

Clerical, administrative, and professional employees, known as support personnel, are invaluable to the chairperson in carrying out the department's functions. Since staff members are often the first persons whom a visitor to the department encounters, the chairperson should insist that courtesy be shown to everyone, especially students, whether in person or on the telephone.

The effectiveness of staff members, of course, is determined by the quality of their training. New secretaries and staff assistants are often assigned duties and responsibilities for which they have had little or no previous experiences. Many new employees are at a disadvantage because they do not know how to operate within the university network. One way to solve the problem is to arrange a meeting between the new staff member and his or her counterpart in another department and to allow the experienced employee to discuss duties and responsibilities with the newcomer. A new secretary must learn not only what to do and how to do it, but also whom to ask for help—for example, whom to call when a payroll error occurs or whom to contact when a purchase order needs special handling. This type of information is not usually found in procedural manuals, but it is nonetheless important. Time can be saved and department efficiency improved if the department staff knows the informal "people" network within the university.

Further, the chairperson should encourage the department staff to meet the staff of the dean's office as well as the staff of administrative offices with which they have frequent contact. Even though the university system abounds with rules and regulations, having good interpersonal relations and knowledge of who can expedite matters will help get the job done more easily.

Although competent clerical staff members frequently perform their duties with little direct supervision, at times they must be closely supervised, and registration is one of these times. The chairperson should see that the staff has the necessary information, that student flow has been considered, and that the appropriate persons are available during the registration process. The chairperson should also communicate clearly to all staff members precisely what is expected of them. Staff members should be included in department activities such as picnics and social events, for inclusion in such events stimulates loyalty and understanding.

The chairperson should try to keep abreast of personnel rules and regulations, especially those that govern recruiting, promotion, appointment, advancement, and termination. In times past, a chairperson who was authorized to hire a secretary simply went out and hired one. This approach is no longer possible. A bewildering variety of rules and regulations governs the process of announcing vacancies, interviewing candidates, meeting equal opportunity criteria, and choosing which candidate to hire. Failure to follow established procedures can result in a lot of problems, not the least of which might be legal action. Furthermore, the chairperson should not make promises of advancement unless he or she intends to keep them.

Regulations regarding personnel may vary from one institution to another. Therefore, the chairperson would be wise to consult with the appropriate institutional personnel officer for guidance.

New chairpersons may not be aware of the fact that terminating the employment of a secretary or other member of the support staff is no simple matter. In addition to causing great trauma, termination involves a host of established procedures that must be scrupulously followed to meet the requirements of due process. Some chairpersons may find it easier to tolerate a secretary's inefficiency or ineptitude than to go through the complicated process of termination. Occasionally, a department has been forced to retain an unwanted employee because of its failure to follow the rules. Consequently, the chairperson should be very selective when hiring.

Our discussion should not be taken to mean that the dismissal of employees whose performance is unsatisfactory is impossible. The task is indeed a difficult and onerous one, but knowing and following the rules makes it achievable. Here again the chairperson should consult with the institution's personnel officer even before discussing the contemplated action with the employee.

Departments that employ graduate assistants for instruction and research support must treat the students fairly and humanely. The chairperson should make sure that the process of awarding assistantships is rational and orderly and that the period of time for which the assistantship is offered is unambiguous. Awards should be made as early as possible, but without undue haste. The students' qualifications should be reviewed carefully, and assignments should be within the capabilities of the assignee. Student workloads should not be too disparate, since student morale can suffer if some students feel that they are being required to work much harder than others. Low student morale can affect the mood of the whole department.

Students

Students are one of higher education's most important resources. Without them there would be no universities and no departments. Most institutions of higher learning depend on funds that are linked to the number of students enrolled. Those departments that experience sharp decreases in enrollment are understandably concerned about losing faculty positions and other resources. To ensure their ability to survive, some departments feel compelled to recruit large numbers of students to make up for the decreases. In so doing, they admit a greater number of marginally qualified students than they ordinarily would have.

The ideal situation, of course, is when a department attracts enough students of good quality to ensure adequate funding. How can a chairperson encourage good students to enroll and simultaneously foster programs that stimulate student interest and participation?

Students are attracted to institutions, programs, and departments that offer them the most in terms of quality of instruction, financial support, and other less tangible benefits. On the undergraduate level, students who are shopping for a major field of study are likely to be impressed with programs that spend time and effort making the introductory courses lively and interesting. The chairperson should, therefore, encourage the most outstanding, dynamic instructors to teach the lower-level courses. In addition, graduate teaching assistants who are given charge of sections should be carefully supervised. Students appreciate lectures that are well organized and well developed and grading policies that are fair rather than punitive. Unfortunately, many faculty members have never spent time thinking about teaching methods. They ought to be persuaded to do so.

The department should also encourage the creation of student advisory committees and help them find faculty sponsors. The chairperson should regularly meet with groups of students to obtain student reactions to department services and policies. A student committee might even be commissioned to assess student opinion about the department, the faculty, and course offerings.

The chairperson should also be alert to student complaints about poor teaching and inappropriate behavior of faculty members and be prepared to investigate recurring complaints. Often a prompt discussion with the faculty member may be in order. Occasionally, the chairperson may have to consult with the dean or academic officer about serious allegations.

Inquiries from current and prospective students should be answered promptly and courteously. In general, someone should be in the office at all times both to respond to student questions and to make needed referrals. Similarly, replies to correspondence, especially about admissions, should be made within two or three days, at most. The chairperson should periodically emphasize to the faculty and staff the importance of prompt responses. Faculty members should be urged to contact personally those applicants who seem to be well qualified. A caring attitude will impress potential students and can influence their choice of a university.

Another activity that may benefit the department is recommending students for honors, grants, awards, fellowships, and so forth. Individual faculty members, as well as committees, should be encouraged to name students who deserve recognition or rewards for their achievements. Recognition of student accomplishments is a sign that the department cares about its students; furthermore, publicity about outstanding students enhances the department's reputation.

Departments should also try to keep in contact with their graduates. Alumni are sometimes willing to make contributions to fellowship funds and library collections and can also help graduates obtain employment. Maintaining contact with alumni may allow a department to conduct follow-up surveys, which can be useful in times of self-study.

The chairperson may be called on to help students with problems encountered elsewhere in the college or university. The department staff can help develop a useful informal network of "problem solvers" throughout the university. Students who have encountered problems can be plugged into the network.

Occasionally, a chairperson must deal with students who exhibit aggressive, destructive, or violent behavior. Neither threats against faculty members nor threats of suicide should be taken lightly. The chairperson should be aware, before a crisis arises, of campus security procedures as well as the availability of medical services and psychological services. Many departments have developed, with the help of students, codes of student conduct. Other departments have used students to help resolve problems of cheating and vandalism.

Chairpersons should be aware of institutional policies and procedures concerning student misconduct and be prepared to use student advisory committees to manage student problems. Of course, chairpersons should also be cognizant of federal rules concerning privacy for student records.

Some Typical Problem-Solving Situations

Following are four examples of problems that chairpersons have encountered when trying to decide how best to allocate department resources. Most discussions or problem-solving techniques contain essentially the same elements: alternative solutions to the difficulty and some method of evaluating or ranking the alternatives.

Example #1

The chairperson of a geology department is faced with increasing demand for more frequent offerings of some of the more specialized petrology courses. He draws up a list of alternative solutions to the problem and evaluates each alternative using three criteria: (1) its potential for solving the problem; (2) its cost; and (3) its feasibility. These criteria are admittedly a bit fuzzy, but they have a certain logic. They allow the chairperson to determine what the chances are that the proposed solution, if implemented, will actually solve the problem; how much the proposed solution will cost; and what the chance is that it can be implemented. The chairperson considers five alternatives.

1. One possibility is to hire additional faculty members to meet the increased demand. More instructors would certainly solve the problem, but the cost would be high and the chances of getting new lines approved by the dean are not good.

2. A second alternative is to reduce the number of courses offered by the department and shift faculty members to the petrology courses. This approach would solve the immediate problem at practically no cost, but the faculty members whose courses would be dropped would surely object and the sequence of course requirements in other specialties would be disturbed. Therefore, the likelihood that this alternative could be implemented is only fair.

3. A third suggestion is to hire additional graduate teaching assistants to help teach the petrology courses. Unfortunately, the courses are too specialized to be taught by graduate assistants. Graduate students, however, might be used to teach other courses, especially basic courses, thereby freeing faculty members to teach petrology. In this case, the potential for solving the problem is somewhat higher. Although the cost of employing additional graduate students would not be as prohibitive as hiring additional faculty members, obtaining funds for this purpose would not be easy.

4. A fourth alternative is to increase the use of instructional technology. Although programmed instruction is a viable technique, the faculty feels uncomfortable with it. It has the potential for partially solving the problem, but the effort involved in gearing up to use it would be fairly expensive, and the probability that the faculty could be motivated to develop such a system is not high.

5. A final alternative is to reduce the number of sections by increasing the number of students per section. With fewer sections to teach, the instructors would have time to devote to teaching petrology courses. The costs here would be negligible, and the proposed plan would be relatively easy to implement.

The chairperson draws up a list of these five alternatives. He then ranks each criterion on a three-point scale: "high," "medium," and "low" (see figure 16.1). Examination of the list reveals that the fifth alternative combines high potential and high feasibility with low cost. The chairperson, therefore, does select this alternative.

	POTENTIAL FOR SOLUTIONS	COST	FEASIBILITY
1. Additional faculty positions	High	High	Low
2. Reduction in course offerings	High	Low	Medium
3. Increase in graduate assistants	Low	Medium	Medium
4. Increased use of instruction technology	Medium	Medium	Medium
5. Reduction in sections per course	High	Low	High

FIGURE 16.1. Ranking of alternatives to accommodate course demand.

In many instances, however, the choice is not so easy. Two or more alternatives may be equally attractive. Approaching a problem in the manner suggested above can help eliminate some suggested solutions quickly and allow the department to concentrate its energies on deciding among the most feasible alternatives. Some chairpersons do not feel compelled to put all the alternatives in writing, preferring to debate the issue mentally. Whether the chairperson writes down the alternatives or not, the decision process is basically the same. The chairperson could also organize a group of faculty members to handle the task of listing alternatives and making rational choices.

Example #2

Our second example of a resource allocation problem is much like the first, although more complicated. A department of interior design experiences a steady enrollment increase in a department subspecialty, nonresidential (industrial and institutional) space analysis and design. The courses in the subspecialty are taught by Faculty Member S and Faculty Member J and their graduate assistants. The two professors are nationally recognized as experts in the field. Conscientious and productive, they are trying to implement a design internship program that requires much travel and supervision. While capable of doing research, they have published nothing in the last two years because their teaching duties have been so time-consuming.

To allow themselves more time for research, Faculty Member S and Faculty Member J request that additional faculty members be assigned to help teach the nonresidential design courses. The chairperson, recognizing that productive research is indispensable to the faculty members' careers and the department's reputation, wants to do everything possible to provide the faculty members with research time.

A review of the course enrollments in the subspecialty shows that the two faculty members are, indeed, carrying heavy instruction loads (see figure 16.2). All the courses, with the exception of IDE 4220L, are 5-credit-hour lecture courses. The exception is a 3-credit-hour laboratory class that requires supervision. The institution is on a quarter calendar, and every course is taught every term. The faculty members' failure to carry out their research interests is understandable, for each course was offered four times a year.

The chairperson, when considering possible solutions, realizes that other department members will be unwilling to teach the nonresidential courses because they are not primarily interested in that aspect of interior design. Hiring new faculty members, on the other hand, is not at all feasible given the budgetary constraints at that time.

The chairperson then asks himself whether the classes could be offered less frequently without a decline in enrollment and whether the classes could be increased in size without a decline in quality. Discussions with faculty members and students indicate that the lecture courses could be taught just as effectively even if they were much larger and that they could be offered every second term without depriving students of the opportunity to complete their required courses within a normal time frame. The laboratory course would have to be taught each term because the number of student work stations is limited; no more than twenty students per term can be accommodated.

Example #3

The first two examples present allocation problems that involve creating additional time for faculty members to conduct research or to teach new courses. The third example deals with the opposite type of situation. Because of circumstances beyond the department's control, certain of its activities have been reduced, leaving the faculty members with considerable time that is not fully occupied. The challenge is to create activities to replace those that have been curtailed.

The department of modern languages in a large urban university suffers a drastic decrease in enrollment when the undergraduate curriculum committee of the college of arts and sciences votes to abolish the foreign language requirement for the baccalaureate degree. Although the university is not absolutely devoted to funding departments on the basis of student credit hours taught, the situation in the modern languages department is very serious. The department is demoralized, the funding for graduate students is reduced dramatically, and even schol-

	Fall		Winter		Spring		Summer	
Course	Enroll-ment	Faculty Member	Enroll-ment	Faculty Member	Enroll-ment	Faculty Member	Enroll-ment	Faculty Member
IDE 4200	15	S	16	S	15	S	14	S
IDE 4220L	19	S	19	S	18	S	16	S
IDE 4240	23	S	25	S	29	S	20	S
IDE 4300	30	S	35	S	38	S	25	S
IDE 5943	28	J	26	J	20	J	22	J
IDE 5943r	12	J	14	J	18	J	16	J

FIGURE 16.2. Instructional load, courses in nonresidential design subspecialty, department of interior design.

arly senior professors who do little undergraduate teaching seem to be affected.

The chairperson reviews the situation in her mind. From the outset, she realizes that the least desirable solution to the problem would be to dismiss nontenured faculty members and to abolish certain programs, but she also realizes that this possibility might become a reality in the absence of other viable solutions. Aware that the university will not reinstate the language requirement, she nevertheless decides to make contact with several other departments to emphasize the value of foreign languages at the undergraduate level. She considers several ideas, but before deciding on a course of action, she needs answers to the following questions:

- How many areas and programs would continue to encourage their undergraduates to take language courses as electives for cultural or practical reasons?
- Would it be profitable for the department to reschedule and restructure its undergraduate teaching to accommodate the university's urban environment?
- Might rescheduling some courses to the late afternoon or evening attract a new student clientele? If offered to the adult community as part of a continuing education program, would such courses find acceptance?
- How many secondary school foreign language teachers might be interested in attending in-service courses designed especially for them?
- Would the department faculty cooperate with other departments to develop interdisciplinary programs of a cultural nature?
- Could special foreign language courses be designed to serve business needs? Foreign manufacturers need instruction manuals translated into colloquial English. Similarly, American manufacturing companies with a large export market need staff to translate instruction, repair, and service manuals from English into foreign languages.
- Could special training be provided for persons who want to develop competencies in translating such manuals?

Some of these ideas are good ones; some are not. The chairperson must try to assess the potential benefit and the feasibility of each alternative. Perhaps all the alternatives taken together may not be able to reestablish lost enrollment. The department's survival at its present size may well depend on its importance to the university's overall mission. If that is the case, a written report justifying the retention of the current faculty members may become necessary. The chairperson should anticipate the possible need for such a document and involve the faculty in preparing it even before a request is received from the dean or vice-president.

Example #4

In our fourth example, the chairperson of the department of urban and regional studies in a medium-sized university receives a memo from his dean, who has just returned from a conference in Washington. The dean has learned that a certain federal agency is about to initiate a new program for funding university projects in community development. In the memo, he suggests that the department consider submitting a proposal for a grant to fund a three-year project at $100,000 per year. In a subsequent telephone call, the dean again raises the subject of the desirability of the department's pursuing a federal grant in community development as described in his memo.

Before making any commitment, however, the chairperson wants to satisfy himself that a project funded by this particular federal agency would benefit the department; that faculty endorsement and support could be obtained; that certain department members have the competency to write a persuasive proposal; that sufficient department resources could be made available to those writing the proposal; and that the department would be able to carry out the proposed project successfully should it be approved.

Let us review the questions that go through the chairperson's mind: Can a project be developed that meets the goals of both the agency and the department? How will the project benefit the department and its faculty members? If the project does not contribute to the department's goals or the faculty's benefit, it should not be pursued.

Let us assume that in this case the chairperson has positive feelings about the dean's suggestion and believes that the project would be a good one for the department. His feelings are buttressed by several sound reasons: some faculty members have the necessary competencies; the project would give visibility to the department and the university; the project would provide hard data for valuable publications by faculty members; and, last but not least, funds would be available for graduate assistantships and salaries for summer faculty members.

The next step is to determine the best way to get faculty support. The chairperson remembers full well the circumstances when he tried to obtain support for an idea by presenting it for the first time to the whole faculty during one of its meetings. To overcome the department's initial negative reaction took several months of difficult lobbying. He later learned from a friend who was a seasoned administrator that a group will usually have a negative reaction to any idea that is presented for the first time to the group as a whole. Therefore, he decides to discuss the idea individually with some department members, especially those who are faculty leaders. If they cannot see the advantages to the department and their support is not forthcoming, the idea should be dropped, at least for the time being.

Once the support of key faculty members is obtained, the chairperson must think about the best time for placing the matter on the agendum of a full department meeting. At the meeting, all faculty members will have an opportunity to express themselves, and those colleagues with whom he has spoken earlier can be counted on to support the idea and emphasize its potential advantages to the department.

After satisfying himself and his faculty that the department should prepare a proposal, the chairperson must make decisions about who should write the proposal and what resources can be made available for the effort. He reviews in his mind all the department members and their respective workloads. The faculty consists of three full professors (including the chairperson), four associate professors, and three assistant professors. Among the faculty members are experts in the areas of transportation planning, housing and community development, health planning, and environmental planning.

Two faculty members, Smith and Jones, are recognized experts in community development and are especially suited to the task. The chairperson wonders whether the task of writing the proposal could be added to the existing assignment of either or both professors, whether a workload must be reduced in order to make time available, and who will assume the excused duties in the event a person's workload is reduced.

The chairperson now examines the existing workloads of Smith and Jones in terms of the number of courses each teaches, the number of students in each course, the time required for preparation of lectures, research involvement, committee assignments, and so forth. He finds that the workloads of both professors are approximately equal.

Smith indicates that he is willing to be the principal writer if he is given a reduced workload. When he is asked what part of his assignment he would prefer to relinquish, however, Smith produces a list of his reasons for not giving anything up. He volunteers some personal time for the assignment. Jones is also willing to write the proposal, but he is not very enthusiastic about it because much of his personal time is taken up with outside consulting activities and he depends on the income the consulting produces. In order for Jones to write the proposal, he would have to curtail his consultations.

The chairperson assigns Smith to be the writer and suggests that for the coming term Smith either cancel one undergraduate course or turn it over to a well-qualified graduate student to teach under Smith's supervision. In either case, the time saved would not be enough to carry out the entire task, so Smith will have to devote some of his personal time to the activity. Smith agrees to accept the responsibility for writing the proposal and selects one of his best graduate students to teach the undergraduate course.

The chairperson also considers the costs of writing the proposal in terms of staff time and department money. The secretarial staff consists of two full-time secretaries and a half-time typist. The chairperson must decide whether the staff can provide the necessary help to the proposal writer. If not, can expense dollars be used to hire a temporary typist for the final draft? What would have to be cut from the expense budget in order to hire the typist? Expense dollars usually pay for items such as travel, duplicating, telephone, and office supplies. A reduction in any of these categories could involve some changes in department operation. For example, what would be the effects of cuts in travel money? How would the faculty react if travel money that had already been committed could not be delivered? Might the dean be willing to provide either money or secretarial time for so worthy a project?

Finally, the chairperson ponders the personal costs of pursuing and administering the grant. How much time will he have to spend supervising the preparation of the proposal? How much time will be spent supervising the activities of faculty members who will be involved in implementing the project? The chairperson must consider the effects of any ambitious undertaking on himself as well as the department as a whole.

When resources are shifted to accommodate an added activity, the department equilibrium becomes upset. Some faculty members may feel that they are being asked to sacrifice too much for an undertaking that does not seem to benefit them personally, and the chairperson must be prepared to soothe them.

Whenever a department considers taking on some significant, previously unanticipated activity, all the variables of department operation must be carefully examined. Important decisions should be made on the basis of available data. Some of the data is to be found in department records, and some may be obtained from the office of institutional research. Chairpersons should learn about the kinds of data that are available in a college or university office of institutional research, how to obtain such data, and how to use it to the department's advantage.

Questions and Exercises

1. Think of a problem involving the management of time, curriculum, and human resources that your department or some other department has encountered during the past two or three years and that was resolved satisfactorily. Make a list of the steps taken to resolve the problem. What circumstances led up to the problem? What alternative courses of action could have been taken?

2. Think of a problem involving time, curriculum, and human resources that is currently being encountered in your department or some other department and that is as yet unresolved. List the steps that can be taken to resolve the problem using the procedures described in the chapter. What circumstances led up to it? What alternative courses of action might be taken? Which course of action seems to be best?

References

BESS, JAMES L. "Classroom and Management Decisions Using Student Data: Designing an Information System." *Journal of Higher Education*, May-June 1979, pp. 256–279.

BLACKBURN, ROBERT, ET AL. *Changing Practices in Undergraduate Education.* Berkeley: Carnegie Council on Policy Studies in Higher Education, 1976.

BOWEN, HOWARD R., AND DOUGLAS, G. K. *Efficiency in Liberal Education: A Study of Comparative Instructional Costs and Different Ways of Organizing Teacher Learning in a Liberal Arts College.* New York: McGraw-Hill, 1971.

BYARS, LLOYD L, AND RUE, LESLIE W. *Personnel Management: Concepts and Applications.* New York: Holt, 1980.

THE CARNEGIE FOUNDATION FOR THE ADVANCEMENT OF TEACHING. *Missions of the College Curriculum: A Contemporary Review with Suggestions.* San Francisco: Jossey-Bass, 1977.

DRESSEL, PAUL L. *College and University Curriculum.* Berkeley: McCutchan, 1971.

———. *Handbook of Academic Evaluation: Assessing Instructional Effectiveness, Student Progress, and Professional Performance for Decision Making in Higher Education.* San Francisco: Jossey-Bass, 1976.

FRYER, THOMAS W., JR. "Designing New Personnel Policies: The Permanent Part-time Faculty member." *College and University Personnel Association*, Spring 1977, pp. 14–21.

GREENLAW, PAUL S., AND BIGGS, WILLIAM D. *Modern Personnel Management.* New York: Holt, 1980.

MAYHEW, LEWIS B. "Curricular Reform and Faculty Well-Being." *Educational Record*, January 1963, pp. 53—61.

――――. "Curriculum Construction and Planning." *Handbook of College and University Administration*, edited by A. S. Knowles. 2 vols. New York: McGraw-Hill, 1970.

SPRUNGER, BENJAMIN E., AND BERGQUIST, WILLIAM H. *Handbook for College Administration*. Washington, D.C.: Council for the Advancement of Small Colleges, 1980.

TUCKMAN, HOWARD P., AND BARBARA H. "Who Are the Part-Timers and What Are Colleges Doing for Them?" *Current Issues in Higher Education*, No. 4, 1981.

TUCKMAN, HOWARD P., AND VOGLER, WILLIAM D. "The 'Part' in Part-Time Wages." *AAUP Bulletin*, May 1978, pp. 70–77.

17

Faculty Views about Management and the Joys of Being a Chairperson

The term *management*, when used in connection with the operation of a college or university, tends to create uneasiness among some faculty members. They view management as a process primarily associated with business organizations and reject the idea that the same management process is appropriate for institutions of higher education. Consequently, faculty members react negatively to terminology used by management specialists and are skeptical of programs designed to enhance the management skills of their department chairpersons.

Although the term *management* can be defined in many ways, most definitions reflect the concern for accomplishing organizational goals and objectives by working with and through individuals and groups. In attempting to achieve organizational goals, the manager must perform such functions as planning, organizing, motivating, and controlling.

The principles and processes of management, according to many writers, are applicable to all types of organizations, including educational institutions. The concern for accomplishing goals and objectives is just as important for colleges and universities as for hospitals, government agencies, and industrial corporations. Moreover, the same management functions are performed in colleges and universities as in other organizations, but the individuals or groups of individuals who perform these activities in educational institutions are not generally called managers.

Regardless of whether or not they are called managers, however, the persons responsible for carrying out the basic functions of management must have a complete understanding of management functions as well as certain interpersonal skills. Business executives, government agency heads, and department chairpersons all require the same interpersonal skills if their organizations are to be managed effectively.

Many chairpersons have difficulty perceiving themselves as managers or administrators. Some prefer to think of themselves as facilitators, even though they perform functions that come under the heading of management. Their preference for the term *facilitator* may be a response to department members' negative attitude toward the term *manager*. Also, the use of *manager* implies a supervisor-subordinate relationship. Even though department chairpersons are expected to provide their faculty members with some "guidance" (a euphemism for *supervision*, perhaps?), faculty members consider themselves colleagues and peers of the chairperson, not subordinates.

Some writers classify academic department chairpersons as "middle management" in educational institutions. Although this classification may be correct from the standpoint of an organizational chart, the reaction of chairpersons to this classification ranges from amusement to irritation. After all, chairpersons are faculty members who have been chosen to assume the additional responsibility of providing leadership for their colleagues. How dare anyone call them "middle managers"!

Since most chairpersons retain their faculty status and continue to perform faculty duties even while serving as chairperson, they are able to reflect the concerns of their fellow faculty members about the management process. Faculty members fear that close supervision might stifle their creativity, that management by objectives might eliminate the flexibility they feel professional academicians need. Being required to provide a detailed statement of their objectives for the next one or two years is a new experience for most faculty members. They are concerned about the consequences of not being able to meet all their stated objectives. They fear that they will no longer be able to add new objectives or drop old ones in the middle of the year, as they have been able to do in the past. They worry that the quantitative types of performance evaluation used in industry to measure "output" will not adequately evaluate the quality of performance in the areas of teaching and research and that, hence, a faculty member's value to the department might not be properly recognized and rewarded.

The truth of the matter is that the principles and processes of management can be adapted for use in academic departments in a manner that is nonthreatening to the faculty. In adapting these principles, the chairperson must take into account the concerns and sensitivities of the faculty members in his or her department and assure them that most of their concerns are unwarranted.

Despite their claims to the contrary, most chairpersons receive enough satisfaction from being chairpersons to want to continue in the position for as long as possible. One young chairperson of a sociology department stated, only somewhat facetiously, that the only thing worse than being chairperson of the sociology department is not being chairperson of the sociology department. Despite complaints about paperwork and other so-called unpleasant duties, 90 percent of chairpersons serving three-year terms said that they would seriously consider serving an additional term if invited to do so.* For some reason, faculty members expect the chairperson to suffer while carrying out his or her duties and they tend to get suspicious or anxious when the chairperson appears to be enjoying the job. Chairpersons, who were once faculty members themselves, are aware of those feelings, and play along by complaining of the rigors of the role. When chairpersons meet together socially, outside the hearing of their faculty members, they sometimes admit to each other that there are indeed joys in being a chairperson. What are the areas that are most satisfying to them? There is status and prestige to be had in the position, even though it is sometimes greater in the community at large than it is within the institution. Even when the chairperson receives no additional material benefits for undertaking the responsibilities of office, there may be considerable psychic rewards. For example, there is the personal satisfaction derived from helping others with their professional development and from helping to guide and build an effective academic program. There is the challenge of leadership, which many people find invigorating. They find rewards in guiding the guiders of students, shaping curricula, defending the interests of the department, and interacting with other academic leaders, including deans and vice-presidents. Many have come to feel that their ability to motivate others to greatness perhaps exceeds their ability to motivate themselves. Some of these chairpersons want to enhance their administrative effectiveness by developing whatever additional skills are necessary to implement the management processes. Some chairpersons see the acquisiton of such skills as a prerequisite for further advancement in academic administration.

Many books written about management are organized around a series of management processes. Each process is defined and described in some detail without reference to any particular level of management or type of organization. Examples are given of situations in which the process can be used to help resolve a problem. Readers of these books are expected to select the processes that are pertinent to their organizations and to adapt them to their own situations. Although such books may be useful to many different types of managers or would-be managers, they are rarely used by department chairpersons who are looking for solutions to their problems.

*Survey conducted in 1977 by Allan Tucker, unpublished.

The present book is organized around selected major problems, issues, and concerns that confront most departments. The problems are described in some detail and several suggestions are offered that might help resolve a problem. These suggestions are not identified as management processes, although that is what they are. Descriptions of management processes, therefore, are included in the book but only as they apply to selected department problems.

The text avoids much of the management terminology and nomenclature that intimidate the academic community. It emphasizes, however, the value of applying sound management procedures to all administrative levels in colleges and universities. The book is directed specifically to chairpersons' concerns about the use of the management process in seeking solutions to department problems.

Index